Getting God's Ear

GETTING GOD'S EAR

*Women, Islam, and Healing
in Saudi Arabia and the Gulf*

Eleanor Abdella Doumato

COLUMBIA UNIVERSITY PRESS

NEW YORK

A portion of the introduction, "Making Connections: Knowledge, Rituals, and Healing," appeared in the journal *Islam and Christian-Muslim Relations* 9(3)(1998) as "Receiving the Promised Blessing: Missionary Reflections on Ishmael's (Mostly Female) Descendants."

Photographs reproduced from Arabian Mission archive collection and directly from *Neglected Arabia* by Russell Gasero, Archivist, Gardner A. Sage Library, New Brunswick Theological Seminary. Used by permission.

COLUMBIA UNIVERSITY PRESS
Publishers Since 1893
New York   Chichester, West Sussex

Library of Congress Cataloging-in-Publication Data
Doumato, Eleanor Abdella.
    Getting God's ear : women, Islam, and healing in Saudi Arabia and the Gulf / Eleanor Abdella Doumato.
        p.   cm.
    Includes bibliographical references (p. 285) and index.
    ISBN 0-231-11666-7 (cloth). — ISBN 0-231-11667-5 (paper)
        1. Women—Saudi Arabia—Social conditions—20th century.
2. Women—Religious life—Saudi Arabia—History—20th century.
3. Women healers—Saudi Arabia—History—20th century. 4. Women—Legal status, laws, etc.—Saudi Arabia—History—20th century.
5. Wahhābīyah—Saudi Arabia—History—20th century. I. Title.
HQ1730.D68   1999
305.42'09538—dc21   99-35113

Casebound editions of Columbia University Press books are printed on permanent and durable acid-free paper.
Printed in the United States of America
c 10 9 8 7 6 5 4 3 2 1
p 10 9 8 7 6 5 4 3

To my father, Ernest Abdella
and to the memory of my mother, Sophie Rosen Abdella

CONTENTS

Contents

ACKNOWLEDGMENTS

Getting God's Ear has been a nineteen-year work in progress, in the sense that I have been exploring issues of women and society in Arabia and the Gulf since 1979, when I first went to Saudi Arabia with my family to live. During the years in Saudi Arabia, many friends and colleagues shared with me their insight and knowledge and provided critical introductions. Since I began writing this book, others have read various drafts of my work, offered encouragement and criticism, and inspired me in ways they could not have known. To all these friends and colleagues my gratitude is due.

My thanks go especially to Gaby and Maria Matta, Hisham Mosely, Chet Richards, Jo-Anne Hart, Elaine Combs-Schilling, Rt. Rev. Fr. Abdulahad Doumato, Victoria Doumato, John Esposito, Susan Slyomovics, and Abubaker Bagader. I am grateful to Gwenn Okruhlik for her insightful comments on the manuscript, and to Elizabeth Fernea not only for reading the manuscript in full but also for being so unfailingly generous in her encouragement and friendship over the years. My thanks also go to Professor Charles Issawi for graciously extending a handshake in 1985, without which there would have been no Ph.D.; to Professor Richard Bulliet for his willingness to take me on as an unknown returning student and for telling me that there was such a thing as an Arabian Mission; to Charles Gosselink for allowing me to see his father's collected letters; and to Russell Gasero of the New Brunswick Seminary for his guidance in using the seminary's archives and for his help obtaining photographs.

I would also like to thank the Pembroke Center for Teaching and Research on Women at Brown University, where I spent a year as an affiliate; the American Council of Learned Societies, for a travel grant; and the Watson Institute for International Studies at Brown University for providing me with an academic berth during the writing of the manuscript.

It is not enough simply to say thank you to my father, Ernest Abdella, for sticking with me during my graduate school years in the early 1970s when I should have held a job.

The people most deserving of my thanks are my husband, Gabriel Doumato, and our three children, Alex, Madeline, and Jennifer, who spent their earliest years sharing our adventure in Arabia.

Throughout the text the reader will observe variations in the spelling of Arabic names and places occurring in quotations. Najd, for example, is also spelled Nejd; Jouf is also Al Jouf, or Al Jauf, or Al Jawf; Anayza Bedouin may be Anaza or Anaiza Bedouin, Bedawy, or Bedawin. Kuwait is also Kuweit, or Al Kuwait, or Al Kuwayt; Ibn Sa'ud is also Ibn Saoud or Saud; and the definite article may be elided with its noun or not, as in Kitab at-Tawhid or al-Tawhid, Al Rashid or Ar-Rashid. I have retained the original spelling in all direct quotations in order to preserve the integrity of the material, but elsewhere in the text I have used standard English spellings where possible. For the comfort of the general reader, I have avoided diacritical marks and have used the apostrophe for both the 'ayn and the hamza.

The word "Wahhabi" may be troublesome to some readers. The correct term for believers in the movement to which it refers is "Muwahhidun," usually translated as "Unitarians": those who believe in the oneness of God. That translation would clearly be a source of confusion for the general reader, however, as "Unitarian" has quite another meaning to English speakers. "Wahhabi" is derived from the name of the founder of the movement, Muhammad ibn Abd al-Wahhab, and was used by the movement's detractors during the revival period of the early twentieth century, as well as during the movement's rise in the late eighteenth and early nineteenth centuries. Today, however, as the movement's theological perspective has become established well beyond the borders of Saudi Arabia, it has become the general term in use in Western languages, where it has lost much of its pejorative connotations. For this reason, and for lack of an alternative, I have chosen to use it throughout.

Getting God's Ear

Prologue

Getting God's Ear is about women, religion, and healing practices in the Arabian Gulf region and in Najd, the central region of the Arabian Peninsula, during the first half of the twentieth century. It is about women's access to religious knowledge and to sacred space in a male-centered environment that marginalizes women's access to both, and about ways women strive for agency and sacralize their own space in an effort to experience community and to heal and be healed; it is about women's ways of getting God to hear them.

This book, however, began as something else: it began as an inquiry into the persistence of women's separation in contemporary Saudi Arabia. It began as a curiosity about what seemed to me to be a preoccupation on the part of the Saudi government with controlling the things women do and about what seemed to me to be a complacency, if not complicity, on the part of women in incorporating these controls into their daily lives. I was curious about why women's behavior was so much more restricted in Saudi Arabia than in any other place in the Middle East where I had lived or traveled, whether Iran, Syria, Lebanon, or Egypt.

In my attempt to find answers to these questions, I began to look at the culture of Wahhabi Islam that is peculiar to Saudi Arabia's politically dominant region, Najd, where for almost two and a half centuries this conservation interpretation of Islam has been nurtured and its rules of behavior promoted through public policy. I began to explore the possibility that

Wahhabi Islam may have over time laid a foundation for the uniquely narrow public space available to women today and contributed to a culture that undergirds the persistence of women's separation. However, how I got from the question of women in contemporary Saudi Arabia to *Getting God's Ear* and a historical view of religious knowledge, rituals, and healing, not just in the Wahhabi Najd but also in the Sunni and Shi'a towns of the Gulf, takes some explaining.

Saudi Arabia's Contest Over Culture: Women as Person or Cultural Icon?

I first arrived in the kingdom with my husband and two small children in 1979 and stayed for five years. I had the good fortune to have arrived just in time, because 1979 marked the tail end of Saudi Arabia's brief flirtation with social liberalism and the beginning of the end of the oil price boom that had fueled the country's development explosion. It was the events of that year that were to bring society careening head on, face to face with itself, with the result that Saudi society turned inward and for the next few years all but closed its doors to foreigners living in the kingdom.

In November 1979 a former theology student led an attempt to seize the Grand Mosque in Mecca. The leader of the attempt, Juhaiman ibn Muhammad ibn Saif Al Utaiba, was a former seminary student and protégé of Abd al-Aziz bin Baz (died 1999), Saudi Arabia's most influential religious scholar. In a series of pamphlets distributed the previous year, Juhaiman had called for an end to Western influence in the kingdom, to television, gambling, Western-style universities, conspicuous and extravagant spending, particularly on the part of the royal family, and the presence of all foreigners.[1]

Across the kingdom, nowhere were these Western influences more obvious or perceived as more odious than in women's place in society. During the year preceding the mosque siege, women had been a subject of continuous public discussion. Newspaper and magazine articles written by both men and women, by laypersons and by ulama, debated whether women should be allowed to drive, where women should be allowed to work, and what type of education was appropriate for girls. Exposés examined the vulnerability of women in marriage—they could be divorced without even knowing about it and lose custody of their children—and discussed the emotional stress caused by polygyny. Responses pointed out the positive aspects of the system that gave preference to men: the family, it was argued,

2

provides a safety net for everyone, and a woman always has her father or brother to take care of her; cowives are helpmates to each other and keep each other company; multiple wives provide a moral guarantee against illicit sex.

Some complained in the press about the legal requirement that a woman be accompanied by a male relative in order to board an airplane, and others replied that Islam calls for women's protection and insisted that women be chaperoned for their own safety. Newspaper cartoons pointed out the abuse of child marriages, and religious scholars and physicians debated abortion and birth control. Debated too was the necessity of wearing the face veil: Was it a religious requirement or merely a tradition and thus dispensable? If only a tradition, was it still necessary to preserve women's femininity? Perhaps, some suggested, veiling should be recognized as the physical impediment to clear vision that it was and be discarded.

While public discussion about the role of women was going on, the public visibility of women was in fact increasing dramatically. For the first time there were thousands of women, primarily daughters of illiterate mothers, who were high school and university graduates, the beneficiaries of an educational system that had been inaugurated less than twenty years before. Local newspapers publicized the work of women's charitable societies, established in commodious headquarters with meeting rooms, classrooms, and dining halls, and provided weekly calendars of events for women's organizations, both Saudi and international. The nightly television news featured women newsreaders, barefaced, the hair wrapped in a chiffon scarf tied in a fashionable knot at the side of the head.

Women owned and invested in businesses and bought and sold property, their names appearing in newspaper listings of real estate transfers. Saudi women physicians and nurses of foreign nationalities worked in hospitals and private clinics where men were sometimes their patients and their employees. They were employed as social workers, administrators, and journalists who sometimes published under their own names. At the same time, women were achieving unprecedented success in secondary schools, graduating in higher proportions and after fewer years of schooling than were boys and achieving similar success at the university level, where by the early 1980s there were more women graduates in the humanities than there were men. The spirit of the times was optimistic: whatever the immediate obstacles to professional opportunities, some thought, these would surely be overcome with time: "I know there are no jobs for women in engineering now," a student studying engineering abroad told me, "but this is what I want to do, and who knows? We are changing. Who can say that in five years women won't be able to work in every profession?"

Ambivalence

But the ambivalence of society toward these changes was everywhere apparent: the new King Sa'ud University in Riyadh, then in the planning stage, was to be built to accommodate 25,000 students, men only. The women's branch of the university, then housed in a compound of crumbly, whitewashed buildings filled with bare-bones furniture, would inherit the old men's campus, where the library shared by the two campuses was housed. Girls' schools were surrounded by extra-high walls, with backup screens behind the entry gates so that when the gates were opened the interior courtyards would remain invisible from the street. Boys' schools, on the other hand, stood on open land. In the girls' schools, there was no physical education at all (although there was a permanently drained swimming pool at the women's branch of the university), while boys could be seen playing soccer in every schoolyard. University women could study most of the same subjects studied by their male counterparts but not those subjects that might lead to their mixing with men. The girls' secondary school curriculum was similar to that of the boys but remained under the tutelage of the Department of Religious Guidance rather than under the Ministry of Education, which administered the boys' schools. The point was to ensure that schools did not deviate from the official purpose of educating girls: to make them better wives and mothers and prepare them to be teachers or nurses, occupations "that suit their nature."[2]

Newly inaugurated bus service opened with fanfare as the answer to the transportation needs of women, who are not allowed to drive, but after the buses had been in service for a few weeks, women were assigned seats at the rear and required to enter and depart from the back so that they would not be seen or stared at by male passengers seated at the front. Local newspapers carried stories about women's organizational activities, but no photographs of Saudi women were printed, even in papers carrying pictures of Saudi men and foreign women. When Lady Diana Spencer, newly engaged to the Prince of Wales, wore a low-neck dress that caused a sensation in the European papers, her photo in the *International Herald Tribune* appeared on Saudi newsstands smeared with black Magic Marker from the neck down. In a Riyadh supermarket, anonymous head shots displayed on the wall of an automated portrait booth showed two rows of faces: one of men and the other of women with a swath of black ink neatly drawn across the eyes.

Every foray of women into newly acquired pubic space had to be disguised as something it was not, as something absolutely compatible with traditional values. This meant pretending that whatever they were doing, women would not be seen by unrelated men and that they were doing things that were merely an extension of their natural roles. Women could be factory owners and investors in small businesses, but by working through hired male managers they could avoid mixing with unrelated men (these managers, it seemed to me, were being treated conceptually as sexually neuter, just as were hired male drivers and male house cleaners and tea servers). Women could work in hospitals, where in theory they would treat only women patients, when in fact women physicians and nurses treated all patients alike.

Women could be active in charitable societies—one program being carried out in 1982 employed university students to knock on doors in poor neighborhoods to offer advice on household hygiene to disadvantaged women—and supposedly avoid coming into contact with unrelated men. Yet I used to attend Arabic classes at the al-Nahda Society in Riyadh, where I, along with women who entered the society grounds fully veiled, would talk with the male Sudanese serving staff as though there were no moral barriers between men and women. Saudi Arabia had then a labor law protecting women employees that would be on the wish list of the most liberal feminist agenda—long paid maternity leaves, job security, and time off during the work day to nurse infants—but opportunities for the employment of women were severely limited by the legal stipulation that sex segregation be a prerequisite for women to work outside the home.

Women Caught in the Anomalies of Change

No segment of society, it seemed to me, was untouched by the underlying incompatibility between the absolute ideal of women's separation and dependency on men and the new opportunities and destinations suddenly available. My intimate circle of Saudi friends was made up of women I had met at a French language class the first year I was in the kingdom. Some of these were people who traveled abroad often and could afford not to work. A few, but not all, had hired drivers to take them wherever they wanted to go and servants to take care of the cooking and shopping and childcare. We were all mostly in our thirties, with young children. These are people who came to my home, as I went to theirs, but I do not want to identify them by their full names in print because to do so would be perceived as an invasion of privacy, regardless of what I said. I never once met any of these women's husbands, in spite of our weekly gatherings in each other's homes, but in the women-only context in which I knew them, to me, some of them seemed to have it all: close families, children, educations, affluence, and, above all else, self-confidence that they could display in two or three languages.

There were, however, limits to the extent of this self-confidence, and limits to our intimacy, that became clear to me after I was indiscreet enough to ask questions I should have known to avoid. The first year I had gone to Saudi Arabia, the granddaughter of Prince Muhammad, brother of the then ruler, King Khalid, had been executed at the behest of her grandfather for the crime of disobedience, having chosen to marry without permission. At a morning coffee in the home of one of my French-class friends, Nawal, I wanted to talk about it. The room was crowded, humming with soft conversation. "Did you hear about the princess who was killed?" I asked a little too loudly, speaking to no one in particular. Suddenly, there was silence. I knew it was from both embarrassment and anger, and I was instantly struck by my stupidity in having raised the question where I did.

Nawal filled the empty space in as gentle a way as she could muster: "Perhaps," she answered softly, "she did something she wasn't supposed to." The moment passed, and the humming picked up again, but a few minutes later another guest met my eyes and let me have it: "If she had been properly punished," the woman's voice practically hissed, "she would have been put in a hole in the ground up to her neck and stoned to death." I sensed immediately that these were theatrics. The speaker was Rima, a striking Lebanese woman who was then coping with a philandering husband and was short on patience. Criticism had been implicit in my question, and no one wanted to hear it from an outsider. The execution had been as remote from the personal experience of everyone else in the room as it was from mine, but my bringing it up was a reminder of a latent threat, an emblem of women's lingering vulnerability even after all the education, the close family, and even the successful career. Rima was just letting me know that she resented being questioned about things she couldn't condone but didn't want to criticize, at least not in front of me, things that she was furthermore powerless to change.

Whatever day-to-day restrictions governed the things women did, some of my friends' lives were virtually untouched by them because money gave them insulation—but not completely. My friend Hayat, for example, was a divorced mother of five and a businesswoman fluent in three languages. As the only member of her family actually residing in the kingdom, it fell to her to oversee the development of a shopping mall in Riyadh owned by her father's trading company, as well as to supervise the maintenance of an oasis date farm on the outskirts of the city. She was, in every sense, a competent, autonomous, working adult—except for the time she received a call from her father in London, asking her to come immediately to be with her mother, who had fallen ill and was in the hospital. Hayat threw some clothes into a suitcase and had her driver take her to the airport right away, but she was turned away at the check-in counter and not allowed to board the plane. She did not have a letter from her male guardian granting her permission to leave the country.

Because Hayat was divorced and her father was in London, her guardian would have been her sixteen-year-old son. "Can you imagine!" she said, relating this experience later. "I was so angry. I was so humiliated. I had to miss my flight, drive out to the school, get my son, and bring him back to the airport so he could give his permission for me—his mother—to get on the airplane."

My friend Gaby Matta, an engineer who had brought his family to Riyadh from Beirut at the start of the Lebanese civil war, had an insight to share with me about everything that piqued my curiosity in Saudi Arabia, including why Hayat could not get on that airplane. The guardian rule that prevents a woman from traveling alone or checking into a hotel alone is simply an extension of the customary practice that a respectable woman does not leave her neighborhood unless accompanied by a male guardian (her *mahram*), who could be a little boy, a servant, or a husband. It's a rule, Gaby explained, that got fixed into law when the state started to expand and move in on areas that were once the prerogative of the head of the family.

Only two decades earlier, certainly within Hayat's lifetime, the onus of having to be chaperoned would have been less poignantly felt, because there were few cars or roads and fewer places to go, not to mention little money for travel abroad or even to other cities in the kingdom. But by 1982 air travel had become commonplace, families were mobile and living all over the kingdom and abroad, and the flexibility of social custom had hardened into inflexible government policies that deny driver's licenses to women and empower airline clerks to say no to women wishing to travel alone.

In Riyadh I found that even women who never left their houses, who were barely literate, who never saw the suq and were in no position to take advantage of new opportunities for work or travel, were touched by the incompatibility between their lives as secluded women and the opportunities and destinations then available. I learned about the vulnerability of secluded women through my friend Nuf, who was then twenty-three and the second wife of a man who, with his brothers, owned a chain of sporting goods stores. Her home was a third-floor apartment in a building she shared with her husband's first wife (he visits me every day, she would say). The three-story building was surrounded by a wall but situated within a larger walled compound of five houses, one for each of the four brothers and their wives (they had two apiece) and one where the brothers would take their meals and receive their guests. I was at Nuf's only once, for the wedding reception of her cowife's daughter. Otherwise, I always met Nuf on Fridays at her mother's house, the only place, she always told me with some pride, that she ever went outside her own home.

Nuf had been born in a village too soon to have gone to public school—the first schools for girls only started in 1960 in the larger towns—but she had gone to a *kuttab*, a Qur'an memorization school, for some months when she was a child and had learned to identify letters, a skill she showed off to me by sounding out the name of the tailor on the label of my *'abayah*. Nuf's eleven younger sisters and brothers were then in school or would soon be, and they were becoming part of a world that Nuf would never be able to enter. One Friday morning when I was visiting a lively argument broke out. Nuf's mother and five younger sisters and I were seated around the breakfast cloth spread across the floor. Two of the girls, then in seventh and eighth grade, were teasing each other about what they would be when they grew up. One wanted to be an airline hostess. The laughter and yelling went back and forth, one talking of the fun of traveling all over, and the other asking why would she want to wait on other people like a servant.

Nuf listened and laughed along with the rest, especially when their mother interrupted with, "Well, you want to be a hostess? Get up and get the coffee!" but at the same time, she had been an outsider to their conversation. Unless some radical change occurred in her husband's thinking, Nuf would never even see an airplane. She would always be sitting at home waiting for his visit, even after her own children grew old enough to go to school. School had become a dividing line that would cut through families and generations. The door that had opened for some was a door closing others out, and Nuf's struggle to share some part of her sisters' new life was visibly painful.

The Problem of Physical Space

Modernization had come too suddenly. Like a person dressed in ill-fitting clothes, the whole society seemed to squirm in the discomfort of new phys-

ical spaces and new things to do that could not be reconciled with sex segregation and the dependency of women on men that it entails. Take my gynecologist's office, for example. When pregnant with my third child I went
to a woman gynecologist in Riyadh whose receptionist was a man. He had
to be a man, the doctor explained to me. It would be awkward for a Saudi
woman to be a receptionist with patients being delivered to the clinic by
their husbands or hired drivers. Besides, she went on, the patients were used
to having men speak for them. While I waited my turn in the women's waiting room—the men waited in the adjacent reception area—I and everyone
else were privy to the intimate details of each woman's medical history: the
receptionist, who, as a man, could not go into the women's waiting room,
took the information the only way he could, by shouting at her, and she back
at him, through the wall.

In 1980 the German firm of Phillipe Holzman was completing a low-rise
housing complex for soldiers of the Saudi National Guard and their families.
Located on the old Airport Road, which was then becoming the main commercial thoroughfare in Riyadh, the housing had been designed with a communal swimming pool and every modest amenity: each apartment had a living and dining room, kitchen, bath, and bedrooms and was delivered to its
occupants fully furnished in Danish modern. These apartments represented,
in every sense, the perfect starter homes for young American or European
families. The people who occupied these apartments, however, were former
Bedouin or Bedouin villagers, and what they needed was divided living
space that duplicated village housing, homes with separate entryways for
men and women and separate living areas with private space for women so
that when outsiders entered the home they didn't intrude. Above all, they
needed homes that could be accessed without an elevator, so that women
would not have to risk being thrust into a confined space alone with a
stranger every time they wanted to come home or go out.

"When I go to make repairs, I ring the bell, and suddenly there are shouts
and scurrying and doors slamming," my cousin Fu'ad Shemmo told us. Fu'ad
was employed by Sojex, a company with a maintenance contract for the National Guard housing. "I have to let them know in advance when I am coming, but then I still have to wait a long time until someone opens the door.
The women are hiding anywhere they can get out of sight . . . in the closet,
or in the bathroom even."

Once, he told us, he arrived by appointment and was met at the door by
a man with a key in his hand. "The family are in the kitchen," the man said.
"The door is locked, and I have the key." Then, holding the key so Fu'ad was

sure to see it, he added, "I'm on my way to work, but you can feel comfortable and work here all morning without disturbance." The man left, taking his key with him. For the next three hours, as Fu'ad installed electrical outlets throughout the apartment, voices of small children and their mother could be heard from within the kitchen, a room—Fu'ad noted—with no access to a bathroom or telephone.

Extraterritorialized Space

New kinds of spaces also meant the loss of old familiar space. Neighborhoods were disappearing, as families moved into new development areas funded by government subsidies. High-rise hotels went up where there had been only desert scrub, while goatherding families still camped on the surrounding ground. I was living in a single-family home in the newly developed Olaya district on a street that dead-ended in the desert. There were exactly two other houses on our street when we moved in, but we returned from a three-week holiday with our children to find our house in the shadow of the rising skeletons of three "rush-housing" apartment towers. (Ten years later, when the Gulf War erupted, we saw these towers on the news: still without permanent occupants, they had become a temporary home for refugees from Kuwait.) Across the city, elegant restaurants opened in hotels, and fast-food places became ubiquitous where no restaurants at all had existed before. Public schools, clinics, sports clubs, charitable societies, and hospitals were creating destinations that to many were previously unknown.

The old suq was being replaced, piece by piece, by shopping strips and supermarkets. Shopping malls structurally resemble the covered shops of the old suq, but they don't replicate it. The old suq was a place with boundaries. It was a labyrinth of alleyways lined with stalls arranged according to the type of merchandise sold. The old suq was a place where women shopped in the fabric and clothiers' areas but did not cross over to the alley of the vegetable sellers or a little beyond to the butchers. In the old suq only men shopped for food. In the old suq grizzled men with little staffs, the *mutawwa'in*, patrolmen of the Society for the Promotion of Virtue and Prevention of Vice (*Hai'at al-amr bi al-ma'ruf wa al-nahia 'an al-munkar*), walked about looking for any woman whose face might be uncovered or whose 'abayah might be a little short. The mutawwa'in kept moral order: when the muezzin sounded the call to prayer, they made certain that the shutters of the stalls slammed shut and tried to hustle the men off to the mosque. When the shutters went down, the women went home. Situated on the lap of the main mosque and central town square, the boundaries in the suq were marked by time as well as space.

But where were the boundaries in the supermarket or the mall? These were foreign places that invited foreign behavior. These were places I came to think of as uncharted territory. The new shopping areas had foreign names and sold foreign goods that were unfamiliar: purple peppers from Holland, frozen whole rabbit and frogs' legs from France, and cheeses and beef from England. The only barrier to imported foods was the Saudi government equivalent of the U.S. Food and Drug Administration that screened out food stuffs that were not *hallal* (permissible according to Islamic law), such as pork, alcohol, and shellfish. In those days virtually nothing produced in Saudi Arabia, except for fresh vegetables, was sold in those shops, unless it was something manufactured by a foreign company doing business in the kingdom. Fresh milk, for example, was first available in Riyadh in 1980, produced by a Danish company that established a dairy farm in al-Kharj.

The malls and supermarkets were staffed by Europeans and Asians who didn't speak Arabic, and many of the customers, like me, were foreigners. They were places where women took their children for an outing, where young Saudi couples went out for an evening of shopping together. In the old suq one would never have seen a man and a woman shopping together; in fact nowhere outside the home could one see a man and a woman together, let alone walking hand in hand. The new markets were uncharted territory, inviting experimentation. So what were the rules?

All these new spaces had to be commandeered in an attempt to make them into familiar space, to redraw the boundaries, to reaffirm the lines between men and women. As soon as the new markets opened, efforts were made to restore the old boundary lines. The call to prayer was piped over a loudspeaker, and a prayer space demarcated off to one side. The mutawwa'in arrived, delivered in city police vehicles to roam the aisles of canned corn and tomato paste, checking once again on women's clothing but now emboldened with a new power: the ability to attach the passport or identity card not of an offending woman but of her husband and to invite him to report to committee headquarters to answer for his wife's behavior. In spite of these powers of enforcement, however, the old boundaries could not be resurrected. From the malls to the schools to the vast interface with technology and education, from people's habits to people's ways of thinking, Riyadh had become—to use an expression of my husband, Gabe—extraterritorialized space, culturally extraterritorialized. The new Riyadh was being shaped, concrete block by concrete block, into foreign space, space that was desired and desirable and that invited Saudis to step inside.

Resistance and Reaction

During that brief period during the late 1970s, encouraged by a government committed to economic development, a political and intellectual elite had been attempting to reinvent traditional values and in the process had begun testing society at its edges, pushing at the margins and retreating only tactically where they met resistance. Resistance was indeed smoldering, even among many who were in a position to benefit from the economic changes taking place, and the focus of resistance could be heard echoing in the rubric of "upholding Islam," "traditions," and "family values." Resistance coalesced around the yearning to set boundaries around Western influence—symbolized most poignantly and felt most personally in the changing roles of women—so that when Juhaiman called for an end to that influence, he tapped into a deep reservoir of discomfort across Saudi society.

The government's immediate response (after beheading Juhaiman and sixty-two of his followers) was to mollify those feelings of discomfort by putting renewed energy into restrictions on foreigners and on women. For example, the Society for the Promotion of Virtue and Prevention of Vice, an agency funded by the government, issued "Guidelines to Our Brothers in Humanity about Proper Dress and Behavior in Saudi Arabia," asking women to cover their hair, arms, and legs and for men not to jog on the street bare-chested and in shorts.[3] I received my copy, as did two thousand other members of the International Women's Club, a group whose activities became, with good reason, a primary target of the morals police. The club was the epitome of Western cultural hegemony, and its activities were as visible as its members: in a country where the unveiled face of a Saudi woman on the street was unusual, foreign women were arriving in packs at the Intercontinental Hotel, where lectures, fairs, and business meetings took place, where women organized themselves into craft, sports, fitness, and gardening groups, groups that toured together, planned art shows, and, worse, even attempted to organize social evenings for dinner and dancing with husbands.

Westerners organized in groups magnify themselves and the cultural differences they project. Organizing in groups to achieve a common purpose—which is illegal without a permit in Saudi Arabia—is itself associated with the cultural habits of Europeans and Americans. The bigger problem, however, was what those groups were doing, for many of their activities were not at that time pursued openly by Saudis and were indeed offensive: the mixed-sex use of swimming pools and mixed-sex evening classes for adults at the British Community School, for example, not to mention jogging on public streets in shorts, country dancing for couples, and *The Rocky Horror Picture Show* performed live onstage (public dramatic presentations of any kind, even movies, are not allowed), and women's exercises performed outdoors, though in private walled compounds.

The new restrictions sought to draw a tangible line between "them" and "us," between foreigners and Saudis and between Muslims and everybody else. The Interior Ministry told the International Women's Club—which has long since been disbanded—not to accept memberships from Saudi women. Other organizations where Western and Saudi women met were actually disbanded, which brought an immediate end to the French language program at the French Cultural Institute where I had met the circle of Saudi mothers who became my companions over the years I lived in Riyadh. Non-Saudi Muslim children were removed from the French, American, and British schools by order of the Ministry of Education, and all of us with children in these schools had to submit documentation proving religious affiliation to show that our own children were not Muslim.

At the same time, a new round of restrictions to lower the public visibility of women was inaugurated. The morals police rigorously routed out women working as secretaries in offices, and for a week my husband and I shared our two-room hotel suite with a Lebanese couple in hiding because the morals police in Dammam had caught the wife working in her husband's office and had confiscated both their passports. The morals police also looked for unmarried couples eating in restaurants or riding in cars and for improperly dressed women. New rules extended the arm of the morals police into government-owned housing compounds for foreigners; recreational areas such as pools, playgrounds, and community clubhouses were to have separate hours for men and for families. New penalties were decreed for foreigners who obtained work permits illegally.[4] Scholarships enabling Saudi women to pursue graduate study abroad were curtailed, along with commercial licenses for women who failed to prove they had hired male managers to run their businesses, and a *fatwa* was issued, but not implemented, saying that a woman must be physically accompanied by a male guardian—as opposed to just having a letter from him—in order to travel.[5] Both abortion and the sale of birth control devices continued to be banned, along with the right for women to drive cars or check into hotels alone.

Women newsreaders disappeared from the television screen, along with the lively ongoing newspaper debate about women's role in society. In its place we heard for a period of time only rhetoric about woman as the repository of traditional values: The ideal woman is a wife and mother; she is the woman who raises the new generation of Muslims, wears the veil, guards her modesty, obeys her husband, remembers her prayers, and expresses her opinions through her brothers, her father, or her husband. She is the woman who takes care of her family, and, because the family is at the heart of Muslim society, she performs the most noble task that society can ask of anyone. In one lecture broadcast on television, the *shaikh* who was speaking admonished Saudi women not to be like foreign women but to think of themselves as precious jewels, covered and protected, not seen by just anybody on the street.

Along with the lowered profile of women came an attempt to erase expressions of Western culture in public places. Western music was banned from shops, and Western names for shops—in those days most of the new stores had English and French names such as Green House Supermarket, Panda, and Euromarche—were to be translated into Arabic. Dressing rooms in clothing stores had to be locked up (they were viewed as potential places of assignation), and mannequins, dolls, and women patrons entering tailor shops were banned. For most Sunni Muslims representation of the human form is inappropriate only in places of worship, but to the government-employed shaikhs of Saudi Arabia, even clothing mannequins and dolls are offensive. It was considered indecent for women to patronize tailor shops because of the physical contact required to fit clothing.

The morals police had a point about tailor shops. Once, and only once, I took a piece of fabric to a tailor shop, which like nearly all tailoring shops in Riyadh was run by Pakistanis. The tailor approached me as if to take my measurements but grabbed my breast and stuck his other hand between my legs instead. Whether the man was motivated by deprivation or perversion was not a point of interest to me at the time, but I did wonder why, since it was clearly a problem for women to patronize male-run tailoring shops, no women-only shops were allowed. How did women get their clothing made?

It seemed to me that keeping men and women separated by removing women from every public place possible was being given precedence over women's access to goods and services. This included access even to places intended for women only. In 1980, at a time when women-only beauty shops were being closed down in Riyadh (again, as potential places of assignation), I flew to Al Khobar, the oil company town in the Eastern Province, to spend the day with a friend, Suhair al-Edris, who was then director of community services at ARAMCO. Suhair had agreed to introduce me to acquaintances of hers who were working or were in business and to share her experiences as a professional woman encountering the new tide of religious conservatism.

That year the Eastern Province had been the recipient of the Ayatollah Khomeini's zeal to export Iran's Islamic revolution. The Saudi government, wanting to discourage any nascent Shi'a nationalism and insulate itself from accusations of being soft on un-Islamic behavior, had given the Society for the Promotion of Virtue and Prevention of Vice a huge increase in its budget. Furthermore, Suhair said, the society was hiring enthusiastic young men who were graduates of the Imam Muhammad ibn Sa'ud University as mutawwa'in. These mutawwa'in had carried out some dramatic raids in the Eastern Province, each one aimed at keeping women out of the public and away from men. They had closed down a beauty salon called Venus, for example, even though it had a valid commercial license. Suhair was a friend of the owner. She said that while there were customers inside (wet hair being cut and wax treatments in progress), the mutawwa'in had stormed in, told everyone to get out, and put a lock on the door. The lock was still there a year later, in 1981, when, Suhair told me, the mutawwa'in, *ghutrahs* (head cloth worn by a man) draped dramatically across the lower half of their faces, had raided the Carlton Hotel in Dammam while a band was playing and men and women were dining together. They escorted the members of the band off the stage and prevented everyone from leaving. After a lecture on morality, they collected the identity papers of the Saudi nationals present, and then everyone—sufficiently terrorized, Suhair commented—was sent home.

Suhair's personal encounter with the newly energized mutawwa'in occurred when her sister Samia's clerical training program was invaded. "Invade" was the only word to describe the event, she told me, expressing the rage her sister felt at the time. Samia had been director of the program, which was designed to prepare high-school-aged girls—most of whom were children of ARAMCO employees—for office work with the oil company. The mutawwa'in had turned up in four-wheel drives and begun asking the drivers parked in cars outside the training program building who they were and who they were waiting for. It turned out the drivers were neighbors or relatives of the girls in the training program, but not their fathers or brothers. The morality police then marched right into the building, Suhair said, ordered the students to give their names and fathers' phone numbers, and then called the fathers to come and take their daughters home. From the viewpoint of the mutawwa'in, Suhair told me, the school was trying to funnel young women into what would be an immoral situation: they would be working in offices, and men might be there; they might even have a man as a boss. ARAMCO decided that to challenge the morality committee for the sake of "Saudi-izing" the workforce wasn't worth the potential problems. The training program ended, and Samia was out of a job.

As the wave of cultural affirmation rose during the years after the mosque siege, plans surfaced to uncover new places where women could be employed in ways that would not offend Saudi Arabia's version of Islamic morality. One experiment was women-only banking, and women's banks opened with great publicity, touted as an example of how an Islamic society could respond to everyone's needs and still maintain its sex-segregation values. I went to the three that opened first in Riyadh—the Saudi-American Bank, the National Commercial Bank, and the privately held Al-Rajhi Company for Money Changing and Commerce—and talked with employees. Al-Rajhi was then just servicing money transfers and interest-free deposits, but the other two banks were heavily engaged in public relations work to attract women customers, in the hopes more women would apply for commercial loans. A year after the banks first opened, I was told, the commercial loan business was disappointingly small. All that really happened is that money was being shifted from one side of the bank to the other, and women customers were using the banks mostly to transfer funds to children living abroad.

The government, after taking credit for allowing the women's banks to open, was not being helpful, the manager of the National Commercial Bank told me. Even when a customer was approved for a business loan, she said, the government consistently denied visas for foreign workers hired to staff women-owned businesses. "We don't know what the government really wants," she said. "Like just now," she added. "We approved a loan for a women-only tailor shop, but we can't get the visas to bring in women from the Philippines to do the work." Then she told me about her invitation to speak at the girls' college in Riyadh to explain the bank's services to them: she had arrived wearing a business suit, and the guard at the gate would not let her in because she was not wearing an 'abayah.

At that point, I felt, the state was paying a lot of lip service about accommodating what newly educated women were saying they wanted. At the same time, it seemed to me that it was offering crumbs of appeasement, confident that all sorts of people—from government bureaucrats to high school principals to mutawwa'in to the lowliest guards at the schoolhouse gates—could be counted on to express their disapproval.

Running into *Fitna*:
How I Learned that Personal Morality Is a Communal Affair

The Saudi national preoccupation with things women do could not remain simply an unresolved curiosity for me because the events of those years affected my life very personally, from the moment I began my stay in the kingdom. For the first two months of 1979, my husband, Gabe, and I, along with our children, Alex, then aged three, and Madeline, just a year and a half, lived in a newly built residential hotel while we searched for a permanent home. Our suite consisted of two comfortably furnished rooms, one a bedroom and the other a combination living room and kitchen. Each room had a single bank of windows that overlooked the back wall of a neighboring apartment house. This, along with the green-carpeted hallway that led from our rooms to the stairwell, was the space available to me for feeding, dressing, and bedding down our children, for playing with them, and for passing the day.

The hotel had a swimming pool, and it was important to me. At that time Riyadh had virtually no public recreation facilities and none that were appropriate for small children. There were no public libraries, or parks, or even—in 1979—shopping malls where women with small children could go comfortably. I could not take the children for walks: women—even veiled women—did not go for walks on public streets. A woman on the street, I found, was conspicuous by her presence, regardless of how she was dressed. Infant strollers could not be pushed safely: either there were no sidewalks, or the sidewalk would come to an end, forcing me into the street, or, at that time, with the new city still under construction, those sidewalks that did exist in residential areas were littered with leftover bits of building rubble such as bricks, bathroom tiles, and the occasional abandoned cement mixer.

Each day during those two months, I had a choice: either the pool or the two rooms upstairs facing the wall. The pool, fortunately, turned out to be a gathering place for the handful of expatriate mothers with small children whose husbands worked in the nearby King Abd al-Aziz Hospital. At home in the United States a day by a swimming pool would not have been my first choice, but in Riyadh it meant companionship for me and for the children and something to stave off monotony. The pool was completely invisible from the street: the area was enclosed on three sides by a twenty-foot wall of stucco-faced concrete and on the fourth side by the elevation of the hotel building. Being attached to a residential hotel the pool was theoretically accessible to the public, but because the hotel was occupied by Europeans and Americans staying in Riyadh on short contracts, it functioned as a little cultural island.

One afternoon, shortly after we arrived, the children and I were at the pool with other mothers and young children, when a shower of small stones fell around the pool area, striking one of the women. I looked up to see a man leaning against the scaffolding of a building under construction beyond the back wall. He was staring down at us in silence. He said nothing, and we forgot about him.

The next day, however, a sign appeared at the entrance to the pool area. It read, "Men Only." Women and by default their children, were no longer permitted. I confronted the hotel manager, my little son, Alex, standing at my side in his bathing shorts with his orange plastic floaties slipped over his arms, and my Madeline in her diaper straddling my hip. Why were we no longer permitted in the pool? I angrily asked him. Beyond the glass doors I could see single men, American and Canadian, making themselves comfortable on chaise longues. The manager—a young Lebanese—was very embarrassed and apologetic but firm: he had been visited by a morals policeman, a mutawwa', who said that he had received a complaint that there were women sitting around the pool "naked," distracting workmen at the building site next door. "The mutawwa' told me," the manager explained, "that if any of the workmen are hurt because they are distracted by the women, I will be held responsible, because I let women sit naked right under their noses." He said it was too risky for him to let me or any other woman into the pool area at all.

I couldn't absorb the logic of what he had said. Why was I expected to be responsible for what a workman on a scaffold might feel or not feel, for what he might decide to do or not do? If this man was offended by my wearing a bathing suit, why didn't he look some other way? Shouldn't he be responsible for his own actions? Why were we, as women, expected to guarantee the behavior of some stranger? Why did his right not to see me take precedence over my right, and my children's right, to swim?

It was by then May in Saudi Arabia, and the daytime temperatures easily reached 110 degrees Fahrenheit. Being trapped in a small apartment with little children was claustrophobic. As mothers responsible for children we had few options, but whatever recreation there was belonged to men only. I felt very bitter. How did this fit with the nobility of motherhood? I wondered. Where could families enjoy recreation together as families? What are family values, anyway?

I was not a novice at navigating the social waters in conservative areas of the Middle East. I had, after all, spent two years living as a young single women in Iran as a Peace Corps volunteer, in a city called Mashhad that was then, ten years before the Islamic revolution, an exceptionally conservative area and the site of the shrine of the Shiite imam Reza. I knew full well the conservative morality that demanded modest dress for women. I knew that it was unacceptable for women be alone on the streets—not to mention living alone outside a family—as I was doing in Iran, and I had learned through bitter experience that extreme discretion in personal behavior was necessary to remain respectable. As women Peace Corps workers living alone, my colleagues and I were so out of the realm of propriety in Mashhad that one high school principal suggested we must be criminals who had been sent to these out-of-the-way places as punishment. Why else would we be there, without protection? What kind of families could we come from that our fathers would let us live alone so far away from home?

In Iran I had learned the consequences of bending moral rules. Occasionally when I walked the three blocks from my home to the university where I taught I was hit by pebbles thrown by a child or slapped by a passerby. Whatever I wore to be modest—a long trench coat and scarf, for example—made no difference. The assaults were not against me as a foreigner but against me as an unchadored woman walking alone on a public street. When an Iranian secretary from the university walked home with me, wearing, like me, a coat and scarf, a motorcyclist slowed up behind us, slapped my companion on the cheek, and drove off. She said not a word. We walked on, each of us pretending that nothing had happened, but I knew that the only reason she had been hit and not I was that she had been walking on the edge of the unpaved roadway and the cyclist could get to her more easily than to me.

In Iran I learned that clothing signified definitively whether or not one was respectable. A woman in public without a chador was *lokht* (naked), as I heard shouted at me. The morality was inconvenient but very straightforward: if you didn't wear a chador, you were open to insult, and it was your own fault. Saudi Arabia was different. Saudi Arabia defined decorum as not being on the streets at all, as a total obliteration of the woman's face and body, as the obliteration of her public identity, and this raised the stakes in a way unknown in Iran even when the Islamic Republic began enforcing chadorlike clothing for women during the height of revolutionary fervor. For a woman, decorum in Saudi Arabia was not a matter of personal responsibility with personal consequences but a debt owed to society to preserve public order, and responsibility for women's proper behavior therefore lay with the state. Getting this logic into my head was the most important lesson I learned. Once I got it straight, what the mutawwa' had said to our hotel manager made perfect sense: In 1979 I had never heard the word *fitna*, but I knew the concept behind it. I knew that the moral order of society is a burden that belongs to women because women represent temptation. Covering the body is not just an act of personal modesty, it is an obligation owed to the whole community, an obligation women in specific owe to men in general. It was *my* obligation.

The pool incident was a moment of awakening. Now I understood how things worked. But understanding didn't make me like it, and I didn't understand why a society made up of well-traveled, educated men and women wasn't turning its back on the morals police and the moral order they were trying to enforce, or why a government so committed to development financed and supported the morals police and their operations.

Why Were Women Complacent, if not Complicit?

In the aftermath of the mosque siege and the stream of government-imposed regulations on women's behavior, I was struck repeatedly by the dearth of resistance on the part of the women I knew. Some of my acquaintances in fact began to buy into the rhetoric of family values and even began wearing Saudi-style veiling that completely concealed the face rather than the token veiling they had used before. Some young women were adding black gloves to the outfit of obliteration; one teenager studying at the Teachers' College who used to visit me in my home told me how she wanted to wear *hijab* (Islamic covering) when she went to Geneva for the summer: "If I really believe women are supposed to wear hijab," she asked me as if wanting my approval, "I should wear it all the time, right?"

To some degree it seemed to me that this behavior represented a practical choice: with women now emblazoned on the flag of the nation's culture, wearing hijab was an opportunity to appear patriotic, to display one's commitment to what were being touted as "Saudi values," and no one wanted to jeopardize a husband's financial connections by flouting behavior standards being promoted in the political culture. But emotional reasons also explained why women were being drawn into the nationwide resurgence of traditional values. One, it seemed to me, was that government-imposed regulations on women represented a cultural anchor. Rules meant to enforce a certain kind of behavior validated that behavior. They were an affirmation of who people were at a time when the state was encroaching on individual prerogatives and the inundation with things American was turning cultural pride into cultural confusion.

Rules that upheld women's modesty and dependency on men also represented support for the integrity of the family. Measures such as limiting the sale of contraceptive devices; maintaining the Shari'ah (Islamic law) as the only basis for marriage, divorce, and child custody; requiring that a Saudi man seek official permission to marry a foreign woman; issuing identity cards to males only; and limiting the types of employment to which women were entitled were ways of ensuring continuity in religious values and family traditions, even as the physical environment was being unrecognizably transformed. These policies spoke especially to the empowerment of men, but I thought they also worked to shore up families being pulled apart as young couples became economically independent and moved out of their parents' homes or got state jobs and moved to different towns altogether. They responded to feelings of alienation between illiterate parents and college-educated children who had little to say to one another; to the blurring of social boundaries and the utter loss of familiar space. I remember well my landlord coming over to check on his house a few months before we were to leave Saudi Arabia for good. He told me how he looked forward to the day he and his wife could afford to move into the house themselves (they were still living with his parents). "This living-together business," he said, "is the source of all our trouble."

Then there was the practical side of rules controlling women. Rules also provided a refuge from uncertainty: If women stayed in school too long, would they be considered undesirable for marriage? If they worked, could they really take care of their children at the same time? Did they want to work at all, and if they did, would they choose to work in mixed-sex situations that could be perceived by others as compromising?

What Changes Has Time Brought?

Almost twenty years have passed since I first went to Saudi Arabia with my husband and children. When I returned to Riyadh in 1996, I found a city that was physically larger and more modern than it was in 1983 when I was last there yet culturally more insular. Its streets were clean, with wide, lushly planted boulevards, and there were numerous shopping malls, a system of medical care that is the most extensive in the Middle East, a new university, and a fortresslike diplomatic quarter with island gardens in the streets, their plantings so mature as to convey an impression of having been established long ago.

A whole generation of young Saudis has come of age since the years I lived in Riyadh, a generation that never experienced the revolution of physical space that changed a dusty town into the sprawling city of possibly four million that it is today. Today, with a majority of the population under the age of fifteen, illiterate women will soon be in the minority. The number of women students in Saudi Arabia's colleges and universities doubled in the ten years between 1983 and 1993[6] and will double again by the year 2000.

Many of these women want to work. In fact many of them need to work both to support themselves and to continue the involvement in the wider community outside the home that they experienced as students. Yet while over the years the number of women in the workforce has increased substantially, in pace with the increase in population, the percentage of Saudi women in the workforce remains almost the same.[7] The reason is that there has been no softening in the institutionalized valuation of women's separation. This remains the case in spite of the consistently higher achievement of women over men in secondary and higher education, in spite of women university graduates flooding into the job market by the tens of thousands, and in spite of an economy vastly overburdened with foreign workers whose positions could be filled by Saudi women.

The value placed on keeping women separate has if anything been reaffirmed with the renewed empowerment of the morals police force, whose members are younger, better educated, more numerous, and more ubiquitous than before. The public-sector areas where women can work are still confined primarily to medicine, education, and social services. In other professional occupations and in private enterprise, the logistics of public sex segregation remain a challenge that is met with varying degrees of success: now there are shopping malls that cater exclusively to women and so can be staffed by women, and in 1997 one hotel announced it had permission to train women to market banqueting facilities to other women.

Government policies sustain the barriers of sex separation that not only limit women in the workforce but in any endeavor that requires independent agency. Women still are not supposed to travel without permission of their mahram, for example, and neither may they access state benefits as individuals or seek government office. Women's not being able to drive ensures their continued dependence on men: a 1990 demonstration in Riyadh for women's right to obtain a driver's license ended with the temporary loss of employment, public humiliation, and confiscation of the passports of the women demonstrators.[8] The censure of the demonstrators was broad-based, coming from women university students as well as from the morals police (who posted broadsides calling the women demonstrators "harlots"), the Interior Ministry, and the head of the Council of Senior Ulama, who issued a fatwa declaring that "women should not be allowed to drive motor vehicles, as the Shari'ah instructs that things that degrade or harm the dignity of women must be prevented."[9]

The limitations on women's right to obtain commercial licenses have become more onerous: previously, commercial licenses were issued to women on the condition that they show they had hired male managers; now, such licenses are not to be issued at all if the type of business requires contact with foreign workers or government agencies. What kind of business would require no contact with a government agency?

In spite of the massive influx of women into the educational system, the international dialogue of women's rights is passing Saudi Arabia by. When the United Nations Fourth World Conference on Women met in Beijing in 1995, one of the only countries in the world without an official delegation was Saudi Arabia. The country's Council of Senior Ulama condemned the aims of the conference, which called for equality between the sexes, but would not have approved sending women to any conference where men would be attending as well. Saudi women did not appear at the NGO (nongovernmental organization) Forum either, even though women from every other Middle Eastern country attended as NGO representatives.

In my view, the culture of female separation persists in Saudi Arabia to a degree unmatched in the Arab world and indeed in the wider Muslim world until the rise of the Taliban in Afghanistan in the 1990s. The question that I found perplexing in 1979 is as valid now as it was then: why does the separation of women from men continue to have such appeal, and why does it persist? The boundaries around women have not only not diminished but appear to have been reaffirmed. What more telling paradigm could there be than the opening of a women's mall? Some will say a woman's mall can be seen as an emblem of progress because it opens up an area of retail employment previously closed to respectable Saudi women. Twenty years ago, after all, morals police specifically looked out for women working in shops—and apprehended them—even if they worked in the back where they wouldn't be seen. And I remember the Pakistani tailor with the groping hands and appreciate the advantages of separation. Women doing for other women is liberating. It is dignity.

But at the same time, a shopping mall that caters exclusively to women and whose employees are exclusively women is a statement that no matter how impractical economically, sex segregation is here to stay. A women's mall shuts down a space for sex integration that has always existed between the shopkeeper and the customer and, more important, not only validates segregation values but further institutionalizes them in a way that has no historical precedent. Women's suqs in the past and present centuries were places where women sellers gathered but where men as well as women shopped. The women's suq I knew in the Riyadh of 1980 was a cluster of marginal businesses located in an out-of-the-way alley behind the butchers' suq, and the sellers were impoverished women at the bottom of the informal market, squatting on cloths under makeshift awnings because as women they there excluded from the stalls in the regular market. But even there, unlike in the new women's mall, there was the opportunity for men and women to mix because the women's suq was open to everyone.

I wonder whether the woman's mall will one day be to an integrated mall what the women's suq was to the main suq. Certainly, nearly anywhere one looks across the globe, separate facilities usually mean unequal facilities. A case in point is King Sa'ud University, where the new campus is for men, while women's facilities are scattered at various locations around the city. A current medical student tells me that her classes in medicine are taught directly by male professors, just as the men's classes are in all subjects, but in the social sciences and humanities, she says, women students communicate with male professors through telephone and television hookup. The main library is located conveniently for men on the main campus. Women, on the other hand, have a very small library in another part of town and may use the main library—if they can get to it—only during certain specified hours on certain specified days. The men's and women's mosque at one of the public hospitals I visited in 1996 showed the same disparity: the women's mosque (located opposite a women's bathroom with a sign that admitted "Muslim ladies only") looked like an afterthought. It was a sparse, white-walled, high-ceilinged room with a *qibla* (the niche in the wall indicating the direction of Mecca) and carpets laid randomly over sections of the floor, some folded over because they were too long for the space. It was a pared-down version of the men's mosque down the hall, a room with molded archways, accented with honey-colored wood paneling and handsomely fitted with wall-to-wall carpets.

Separation values are also being reaffirmed with a new proposal for a separate women's industrial zone, because the logistics of keeping the sexes separated in an industrial setting render the employment of women in factories unworkable. Will women owners of these factories have access to government ministries to lobby for the interest of their businesses? Will they experience complications or shutdowns when male expertise is required on the factory floor or male brawn on the loading dock? Will sex segregation make women-only industry noncompetitive, or will women's industry become, out of practical necessity, as in the hospitals, another venue for sex integration in the workplace?

Today it would be unfair to suggest that women are complicit or even complacent about the rules that restrict their lives. The whole society—far from being monolithic—is polarized on the issue of women's segregation. As one young woman from Riyadh, a hospital lab technician who once appeared as a newsreader on Saudi television, put it, "For every person who thinks like me and is willing to take chances, there are two who want everything to stay the same." In other words, at the same time that development has produced a cultural revolution in the thinking of one part of society, it has also created a cultural chasm down society's middle.

Repression of dissent makes it impossible to gauge on which side the weight of public sentiment falls. If some women appear to buy into the prevailing ideology, this could be because there is a price to be paid for not buying into it. The lesson of the driving demonstration that took place in November 1990 was to keep silent. Wherever I went in Riyadh—and I was there for the purpose of speaking to women's groups—I met women who whispered to me that they had been in jail, or had been fired from their jobs, or wanted to tell me what was happening but would have to wait to speak to me alone.

The Persistence of Tradition:
State Agendas, the Development Explosion, or Tribalism?

The state is certainly responsible for the suppression of women activists, along with the suppression of all kinds of liberal activism. The state is also responsible for turning customs guiding women's behavior into enforceable rules. The rules are in place because they have a political purpose: they create the appearance of the monarchy's willingness to secure continuity in everyday life; they are a way to tap into the reservoir of emotional discomfort engendered by development and to turn it to the state's advantage. Not only do the rules help the Sa'ud family garner popularity, but they reaffirm the legitimacy of a monarchy that quite literally advertises itself as Islamic, with the Qur'an as constitution. Rules about women focus loyalty on the self-proclaimed Islamic monarchy because the rules are defined as emanating from Islamic standards of behavior. Religious identity is furthermore the single cohesive ideology holding the Kingdom of Saudi Arabia together, and it is one that rationalizes the ruling family's hold on power over areas of the peninsula that have no affiliation with the Saudi family and in fact only antipathy toward them.

But why should the Saudi state choose to invest Islamic meaning in women's behavior more than in the behavior of men? Today men no longer answer to a daily role call in the mosque when once attendance was required; money is openly deposited in banks where interest, forbidden in the Qur'an, is drawn; tobacco, a once-forbidden substance, is smoked openly; and music and dancing, also once forbidden, are enjoyed by everyone. What everyday behavior is there left that can be enforced? Alcohol, drugs, and the behavior of women. Women's behavior is enforced and turned into a symbol of cultural authenticity not only because it can be but because enforcement is welcomed, with the effect that women's public invisibility has come to act as a visible symbol of the monarch's piety.[10]

Dissenting opinions about women's separation and dependency are therefore a political problem for the state that needs to be silenced. But it would be a circular argument to suggest that segregation persists in Saudi Arabia today because the ruling powers suppress dissent. Silencing opposition to the enforced dependency of women would serve no political purpose unless the ruling powers believed that these policies bought the allegiance of important constituencies who want to lock in the dependency that women's segregation guarantees. In other words, the state is a facilitator of women's separation but not the source of its persistent appeal.

Some argue that the reason for the persistence of women's separation in Saudi Arabia is obviously the shortness of its exposure to the West. "What can you expect?" the argument goes. "Saudi Arabia had no colonial experience. Najd in particular was almost completely isolated until the introduction of oil revenue at midcentury. It hasn't had enough time." But this argument presupposes that colonialism was the necessary pivot that moved society toward feminist activism or that it is only through years of being exposed to examples from the West and Western education that women's rights in less developed countries are promoted. Neither of these is true.[11] In many of the Gulf towns, furthermore, where women play a far more public role in society, the presence of British colonials was too limited to have had much of a social impact. If time were the determining factor, then we would be seeing movement toward liberalization after a whole generation of Saudi children had come through the schools and into adulthood, not the reverse.

Another explanation lies in the tribal character of the Arabian family. Lila Abu-Lughod describes how in tribal societies family honor is dependent on women's acting with modesty and deference to men.[12] Tribal groups moreover are exclusivist. They avoid marriage with people who have no tribal affiliation, and tribal groups that consider themselves aristocratic (*qabila*) avoid marriage with people belonging to low-status tribal groups in order to preserve their prestige. The point of controlling women through sex segregation and other mechanisms such as the mahram rule is to make sure women do not make compromising alliances that would humble the family or defy the authority of male relatives who are above them in the family hierarchy.

Because tribal groups are politically dominant in Saudi Arabia and tribal culture is an important referent for Saudi society, the idea of tribal honor certainly plays some role in the continuing appeal of sex segregation and rules controlling women. The tribal explanation goes just so far, however. Today, even for tribal people, money has created its own kind of aristocracy, taking something of the edge off the appeal of blood purity in forming marriage attachments. Women's education and employment has also undercut the ability of male relatives to assert the authority over women they might have exerted in the past. Moreover, Saudi Arabia's population is not all tribal; in fact probably the majority are not. There are just too many other kinds of people who today have Saudi citizenship: descendants of migrant workers from India, Africa, and the gulf region; indigenous blacks; low-status and nontribal Bedouin groups; descendants of slaves and descendants of foreigners who came for the pilgrimage and stayed; indigenous inhabitants of the Abha district, who are of Yemeni origin; the immigrant agricultural workers of the Hasa oasis in the Eastern Province; and twentieth-century immigrants from other Arab countries.

The tribal theory also begins to falter as an explanation of the continued separation of men and women when one looks at Kuwait and Bahrain, two states politically dominated by related tribal groups where sex segregation is not practiced to the degree it is in Saudi Arabia. In both states women drive.

Even with the religious revivalism that swept the Gulf in the late 1980s and the voluntary adoption of Islamic dress by young women, the covering of the face is the odd exception, not the rule. In Kuwait, even though women cannot vote in national elections, they vote and run for office in local elections and hold positions in the ministries. And in Kuwait the university is sex integrated, and even an attempt by the tribal-Islamist–dominated National Assembly to bring segregation to university education failed.

Looking for an Answer in History

So where was I to look for an explanation? I could see that I would have to look for historical precedent. What was the one thing, I asked myself, that distinguished Saudi Arabia from its neighbors? The only answer is the Wahhabi revivalist movement that has for two centuries dominated Najd, the home of the ruling dynasty, and has shaped government social policies in all the rest of the peninsula that came under Saudi rule in the twentieth century. What I searched for was an understanding of the historical unfolding of Wahhabi beliefs in social practice. I looked to see if there were any way in which Wahhabi beliefs, propagated and enforced by state powers, could have helped to undergird and shape a uniquely durable culture of women's dependency and separation.

This was not an easy task, because there is little, if anything, in Wahhabi theological texts that explicitly refers to women as opposed to men, except in the case of distinctions between the sexes that apply to the Sunni tradition generally. Wahhabi theology in fact is drawn out of the bedrock of Sunni tradition. Instead of focusing on theology, then, I looked at social practice. My method was to work backward: I searched for comparisons between what we could know about daily practices of women in Najd with practices of women in the Sunni and Shi'a Gulf towns that are geographically and culturally close to Najd but are not Wahhabi. It was only after discovering a rich body of information about women's ritual activities and healing practices in Kuwait and Bahrain, activities I knew from my own experience were unknown or little practiced in Riyadh, that I went back to Wahhabi texts. By looking at the central tenets of Wahhabi theology, the emphasis on religious learning, correct prayer, and its very explicit ritual prohibitions, I could see that the movement—while not overtly targeting women—specifically affected the things women do in a way that it did not affect men and their activities. It was only then that I could see the connection between access to knowledge and correct ritual practice, between correct ritual practice and the act of healing, between all kinds of ritual practices and group cohesion. Exploring these connections and the impact that different religious traditions have had on them eventually led me to write this book.

This book, then, is not about the question that originally drove my research; as the epilogue shows, I found in Wahhabism one part of a larger matrix that helps to clarify the tenacity of cultural constraints on women in contemporary Saudi society.

Making Connections

Knowledge, Rituals, and Healing

This is a book about women, religion, and healing practices in Najd and the Gulf region during the first half of the twentieth century, about ways women structure their spiritual lives in opposition to male-defined orthodoxy, and about the influence of Wahhabi Islam in shaping a different experience for those who lived under Wahhabi dominion. This period of time begins with the happy coincidence of the reappearance of the Wahhabi movement and its missionaries in the Arabian peninsula and the arrival in the Gulf of missionaries from the Reformed Church in America. At the other end, this period closes with 1950 and the opening of a new era, when the effects of foreign penetration, population mobility, and westernization that oil wealth was to produce began to alter the social landscape. Because the correspondence the Arabian Mission produced over half a century is an unrivaled source of information on society in the Gulf during this period, this book is also, inevitably, about the American missionaries whose writings form its informational core and whose voices inform our understanding of Arabian women's experience. In this introduction, therefore, I include a discussion about the mission and the nature of the literature the missionaries produced, as well as a commentary on the use of travel writing for the writing of history.

What is the connection between women, religion, and healing? What is Wahhabi Islam, and what does it have to do particularly with women? Acts of worship and acts of healing, along with attitudes about who should do it and how, are linked together by the thread of religious knowledge. These connections are dependent on ideas about the meaning of knowledge prevalent in the Gulf region and central Arabia at the opening of the twentieth century, and so this is where I begin.

Knowing, Knowing God, and Getting God's Ear

At the turn of the twentieth century, in towns along the Arabian Gulf shore and in Najd, the central province of what is now the Kingdom of Saudi Arabia, knowledge of religion was the very definition of knowledge. Religious knowledge was knowledge of the physical universe, including the physical state of humankind, with all its pain, deformities, and diseases. The physical world was furthermore full of the inscrutable, which ought not to be challenged because the world—in the present, past, and future—had been prearranged according to God's plan. At the same time, however, religious knowledge incorporated mechanisms to intercede in God's plan. The Arabian Gulf vision of the world would have been at home in the eighteenth-century England of Alexander Pope: the apparent chaos and injustice of this world was but illusion, for God imposed an invisible order on things for His own purpose, and because all things come from God, whatever happens, however painful, must be reconciled with some ultimate good.

The presence of God, mediated through God's holy book and the legacy of His messenger, was pervasive in human interactions as well. "Mohammedanism," wrote Paul Harrison, a medical missionary with the Reformed Church in America's Arabian Mission, "is founded upon an underlying philosophy of the universe, a great overwhelming conception of God. Built upon this there are a system of ethics and a theory of human destiny, an organization of the family and a complete social structure." Like most commentators on the region, then and now, Harrison talked about Arabs and Muslims categorically, as though they represented a distinct and homogeneous species of mankind: "Thus religion in the Mohammedan's mind is not simply a series of doctrines concerning the relations between God and man. Every human and social relationship is included, every governmental and industrial organization, every physical and intellectual activity. Religion in the Arab's mind is a complete system of life."[1]

Knowledge of religion was therefore also knowledge of law, and law meant the laws of God; it meant knowledge of correct behavior to assure harmony in the community of believers on earth and admission into paradise in the hereafter. Religious knowledge, just as in England until the late nineteenth century, was the most socially prestigious kind of knowledge. Even for the well-educated, philosophy, medicine, and science remained largely undifferentiated from religion, and so religious knowledge was also the sine qua non for accreditation as a medical practitioner, teacher, judge, or ritual specialist and even for recognition as a competent fortune-teller, truth diviner, or amulet maker.

At the opening of the twentieth century, scholars in the Gulf region were not struggling to reconcile the truth of scripture with the truth of science as their contemporary European counterparts had been doing since the publication of Darwin's *Origin of Species*. In the town of Kuwait and in Manama, the capital of Bahrain, there was as yet barely an echo of the reformation well under way in Egypt that was reinterpreting Islamic law to meet the demands of a changing world. Similarly, the publication of Qasim Amin's *The Liberation of Women*, which took Cairo by storm in 1899, provoked no discernible response in the Gulf at all. During and after World War I, however, Egyptian newspapers, magazines, and even scientific journals flooded the Gulf towns, and Western technology made an impressive showing with steamships, automobiles, and munitions, as well as telephone lines, airplanes, electricity, desalinization plants, and medicine. Harrison wrote in 1924 that, "however imperfectly the Arab may understand the methods of science, its results are patent and obvious" (p. 265). While Najd remained unpenetrated, "in the coast cities along the Persian Gulf," he wrote, "the influence of the West has been very pervasive and powerful. As in many other parts of the Orient, there is not a department of life where its influence has not been felt" (p. 263).

Najd, unlike the Gulf, remained immune to the intellectual currents swirling to the west. In fact, during and after World War I, it was in the throes of an Islamic reformation of its own kind, not to reinterpret Islam to adapt to modern conditions but to reaffirm it. Najd was the seat of a militant resurgence of the Wahhabi movement that was being propagated along with Ibn Sa'ud's conquest of the Arabian peninsula between 1902 and 1926. This movement specifically rejected reformist thinking, refusing to accept any interpretation of correct Islamic practice that was not in conformity with the practice of the Prophet and his companions as interpreted by the scholars through the first three centuries after the Prophet's death. During the time of the revival, Nadji Wahhabism was being exported through missionary activity as far away as Kuwait, where the ruler was concerned enough about its influence to close the pulpit to Wahhabi preachers, and was backed up with political power in the province of Hasa and later in the town of Unaiza, where the reformed religion had been rebuffed in the previous century. The towns of Ha'il and Buraida in northern Najd needed no converting: they had remained Wahhabi since the movement first arose in the mid-eighteenth century.

The Wahhabi movement asserted the oneness of God, expressed in the renunciation of any sort of supplication to intermediaries between God and man (and woman, in particular) such as saints, angels, jinn, martyrs, or even the Prophet, as well as the renunciation of magic, fortune-telling, and truth divining. To the Wahhabis, all these acts are polytheism (*shirk*). Since the purpose of the Muslim community, the Wahhabis believed, was to fulfill God's laws according to the practices of the Prophet and his companions, knowledge of the Qur'an and Hadith was incumbent on each true Muslim so that the community as a whole could know what was right behavior and live their lives in conformity with it. As a matter of public policy, however, and also out of respect for their knowledge of Shari'ah, in practice it was the ulama (religious scholars) who assumed the role of arbiters of correct behavior.

The pursuit of religious knowledge, for women as well as for men, was not only basic to Ibn Abd al-Wahhab's vision of creating the pure Islamic community, it was also basic to being an educated human being anywhere in the Gulf region, whether one was Sunni or Shia. Religious knowledge was necessary for correct religious practice, and correct practice was at the core of communal life. For men, orthodox prayer in the mosque, especially the Friday prayer, signaled membership in the community of believers. Because God was the Creator and the ultimate determiner of all things, correct worship was the accredited way to exert influence on events otherwise beyond one's control.

Yet in this God-centered world women's access to religious knowledge was limited in comparison to that available to men. When it came to religious worship, women in Najd and the Gulf—unlike women in some other parts of the Muslim world, including the Hejaz—were outside the mosque or on its margins, outside the place where prayer is best performed, outside the place where men learn their religion. "Mosques are for *men* to pray in," Paul Harrison wrote. "Women are supposed to pray just as faithfully as the men, but they pray at home." "However," Harrison adds, "the Friday services are frequently listened to by numbers of women. They can be seen sitting closely veiled outside the sacred precincts" (p. 236). Whether in a Bedouin encampment, where the mosque is drawn in lines of stone on the ground, or in the congregational mosque of Riyadh during the great revival, or in the neighborhood mosques of the Gulf towns, women's place was outside the "sacred precincts," on the edge, at the back, or not there at all. Women prayed at home, often alone or often in disorder by orthodox standards. Women outside the mosque struggled to hear what was being said inside, trying to earn merit in the eyes of God, trying to get God's ear.

The meaning of women's exclusion from the "sacred precincts" and their limited access to religious learning is what this book is about. What kind of access to religious knowledge did women have? Did women have access to the professions for which religious knowledge was a prerequisite, and how were women's presumed natural roles as midwives and healers shaped by their access to knowledge? Were they able to worship in a manner that would grant them equal merit in the eyes of God, and were they able to replicate in their own way the communal worship in congregation that the community held to be the essence of Islam? More specifically, did Wahhabism make any difference to women's access? Did the Wahhabi insistence on all believers knowing God and His Prophet open doors to learning that were closed to women in the non-Wahhabi Gulf? Did the Wahhabi insistence on conformity in personal behavior and attendance at Friday congregational prayer provide for women, as for men, the stage on which to demonstrate admission into full membership in the community of believers?

Gender, Ritual, and Healing

If the answer to any of these questions were uniformly in the affirmative, Islam and societies in Islamic settings would be unique among world religious traditions. Every major world religion is permeated with hierarchic models for men and women,[2] and these models for sex difference have filtered through the societies that adhere to these religious traditions. As Rosemary Reuther has argued, "religion has been not only a contributing factor, [but] undoubtedly the single most important shaper and enforcer of the image and role of women in culture and society."[3] In every major religion, women are excluded from leadership roles in orthodox worship. Jesus appointed men as his apostles, and only men may be priests; women may not so much as set foot on the space around the alter of Christ in Eastern Orthodoxy; in the Judaic Mishna women were excluded from the centers of holiness and could not perform or even participate in the liturgy.[4]

In orthodox traditions, including that of Islam, wherever women are included as ritual participants or objects of veneration, their roles are established through their relationship to a man or defined by their sexuality, while the roles of men are not:[5] Mary is a virgin; the nun marries Christ; Fatima is Muhammad's daughter married to the imam Ali. Women become sanctified as martyrs by hiding their female sexuality and becoming—to use Susan Harvey's phrase—"honorary men."[6] In Orthodox Judaism, women, who have no formal liturgical role except for lighting Sabbath candles at home, become holy by purifying themselves after menstruation: by becoming holy to a man.

In all societies, wherever religion, philosophy, and science remain undifferentiated, the skills of the healing practitioner are derived from, or operate in conjunction with, religious knowledge and performance. Healing through ritual persists even in societies that recognize medical science as fully separated from religion, the Church of Christ, Scientist, being one example. Ritual can also be part of the treatment, as in the lighting of votive candles in orthodox churches, the weekly Episcopal women's prayer meeting, the ecstatic prayer of the Charismatic Christians, or the spirit possession dancing of the Zar.

In ritual healing everywhere women participate as both patients and healers. The woman healer may be respected for her skills and seen in a positive light by society at large as fulfilling an extension of her role as nurturer, say Hoch-Smith and Spring.[7] On the other hand, these same skills may be seen as something negative and potentially dangerous, and the healer viewed by society as the cause of illness or misfortune, that is, as a witch (p. 21). The negative perception of the woman healer is fueled by scripture in the three major monotheistic traditions, where witches are described as female and where women are associated with evil in general: their bodies are polluting to men and must be ritually cleansed before entering sacred precincts, or they are more lustful than men, devious, a temptation to men and the source of social chaos.

Women who act as healers, midwives, and witches consistently appear across religious traditions as society's nobodies: they are old, poor, widowed, Bedouin or peasant in urban society and black in a white society, and potential objects of fear even as they perform desired services. Michelle Zimbalist Rosaldo suggests that in many societies women who defy the ideals of male order will be seen as anomalous, abnormal, and hence threatening: what is out of order is the witch's, healer's, or midwife's unorderly relationship to male power. Authority is usually vested in men, she writes, but when women exercise informal power, as in the professional role of healer, this power becomes threatening to the perceived normal order of things.[8] Thus when age and its accompanying loss of fertility and presumed loss of sexual appetite/appeal undermine the rationale for controlling women, women achieve some degree of independence (the Qur'an is explicit about women's semiautonomy after menopause),[9] but independence can be perceived negatively and turned into a sign of danger. The independent woman as danger is axiomatic in fairy tale and fable: Snow White's beautiful stepmother becomes an old hag when she assumes her witch persona; the witch who eats children in Hansel and Gretel is a woman who lives alone; Cinderella's wicked stepmother becomes wicked when she is widowed and no longer under the control of Cinderella's father.

The notion of woman as anomaly, as it has been adapted by Jacob Neusner and applied to the Mishna, a second century A.D. code of rules for Jewish society,[10] has resonance for the place of women in every major religious tradition. In the Mishna, women are by definition an anomaly, he writes, in the sense that "masculinity was the normal form of humanity and femininity was deviation" (quoted on p. 195). Things are normal when women are subject to particular men, he says, but when they are not, as when they become betrothed, enter or leave a marital union, or are widowed, they become threatening and irregular. The only criterion of significance for women in the Mishna, Neusner says, is when they are sanctified by being made subject to men, and the essence of woman's abnormality, the reason she must be sanctified, says Neusner, is her sexuality. "Women" is the title of one of the six parts of the Mishna, and it is directed toward bringing "under control and into stasis all of the wild and unruly potentialities of sexuality, with their dreadful threat of uncontrolled shifts in personal status and material possession alike."[11]

Becoming part of a spiritual community may be a desired objective for women in religious traditions where women are excluded from leadership roles and marginalized in the public communal rituals of the orthodox tradition. This is particularly true in sex-segregated societies in which opportunities for women to engage in group activity outside the family are limited. This is where the ritual expert who caters to women's needs becomes important. "In many societies female physiological processes require that women come together for treatment, consultation, and education," write Hoch-Smith and Spring. "The job of the ritual expert is to control and channel this suffering; ritual experts create a 'community of sisters' by acting upon female physiology. The midwife, the medium, and the healer are the archetype of nurturance *in relation to* their patients. . . . Relationships built on the healer-patient tie and the ritual expert-to-novice tie crosscut ties based on kinship, friendship and residence." "Ritual" they write, "validates bonds between women."[12]

Hoch-Smith and Spring's observations could as well be applied to women visiting saints' shrines and participating in Zar possession rituals in Muslim societies. Elizabeth Fernea's films on shrine visitation and spirit possession in Morocco illustrate the sociability that takes place among women participating in either type of ritual. In both kinds of ritual, Fernea shows, women also experience connectedness through the spiritual communication that takes place among the supplicant, or possessed person, the medium, or *shaikhat az-Zar*, and the dead saint, or Zar spirit.[13] In Fatima Mernissi's analysis of visits to a saint's shrine in Morocco, she describes what she sees as psychological healing, empowerment, and a sense of community experienced by the women who visit these shrines. Shrine visitation, she suggests, can be critical to the mental health and well-being of otherwise powerless women by providing an opportunity to share common grievances ritually, to feel the blessing of the saint, and to come away with hope.[14]

For women in sex-segregated societies, especially for urban women, shrine visitation creates a sense of community that has few other venues outside the family. In the course of training and providing service, women who become ritual specialists also form close personal bonds with other women, creating an association "which crosscuts otherwise hierarchic social orders. . . . We suggest," say Hoch-Smith and Spring, "that such female communities provide an alternative, essential, and basic mode of human relatedness for the entire society."[15]

Wherever women are marginalized in the orthodox tradition and barred from the sacred precincts, their spiritual needs and their need for community are channeled into ritual performances they *can* do, and what they can do is often done in response to needs in their personal lives. The connection between participation in women-centered rituals and the conditions of women's personal lives has been well documented in many studies focusing on all three of the monotheistic traditions, as well as in animistic religions and possession cults.[16]

Susan Sered's observations on the ritual lives of elderly Kurdish Jewish women in Israel illustrate how women have developed ways to sacralize female experience by "domesticating" rituals adapted from the male-dominated orthodox tradition. Having no religious training or knowledge, excluded from the synagogue in Kurdistan, and relegated to the balcony of the synagogue in Israel, these women personalize rituals and symbols of the orthodox tradition and redirect them toward safeguarding the well-being of family members, living and dead. Women are supposed to say a formal prayer while lighting Sabbath candles, for example, but they can't because they don't know the prayer, and so instead they use the occasion to ask God in their own words for favors.[17] These Kurdish-Jewish women also travel to the tombs of saints, bringing gifts of candles, flowers, and fabrics in the hope of establishing a reciprocal relationship with a saint and to bargain for his or her intercession with God on their behalf (p. 21). In the Muslim tradition, asking God for a personal favor—or asking a saint to intercede with God on one's behalf—is central to *moulid* (commemoration of a saint) ceremonies, the Prophet's Birthday celebration, and visits to the tombs of Muslim saints that take place regularly in most parts of the Gulf region. In these rituals, women incorporate some of the language of the orthodox prayer tradition but turn the occasion into a ritual that satisfies personal needs and is performable according to the limits of their knowledge and access to sacred ground.

Spirit possession, like other heterodox rituals, is an appealing alternative wherever women are marginalized in the orthodox tradition. "The peripherality of women is . . . a general feature of all societies where men hold a secure monopoly on power positions and deny their partners effective jural rights," writes I. M. Lewis.[18] Spirit possession, he says, is a compensation for these women's exclusion and lack of authority in all other spheres of life. Lewis's deprivation theory goes a long way toward explaining the prominence of the Zar spirit possession societies among the social elite and the socially segregated in the Gulf region during the first quarter of the century. It also helps to explain the reappearance of the Zar among middle-aged women in Kuwait in recent years, among women who have been culturally and physically marooned as a result of rapid modernization. Mostly illiterate, moved out of intimate neighborhoods and into suburban developments, these are people who cannot take part in the cosmopolitan life of Kuwait and at the same time have been physically separated from adult children, who no longer share much in common with their parents.[19]

Lewis' deprivation theory can be applied not just to possession cults in Muslim settings but to any spiritual community that offers marginal members of society a clearly defined identity and a sense of community: Jehovah's Witnesses, for example, tend to be women who are economically disadvantaged, less educated, and single; similarly, fundamentalism within Catholicism has been shown to attract Catholics who are economically deprived, uneducated, socially marginal, and middle aged.[20] And in all major religious traditions, women's rituals are marginalized or devalued in relation to orthodoxy. Sometimes participants in these marginalized rituals are viewed with suspicion and at times even condemned. I. M. Lewis's observation that orthodoxy defines itself by defining what it is not helps to explain why this is so. Negating peripheral cults, observes Lewis, is a way that universal religions define and redefine orthodoxy. The catch, he says, is that "the price centrality pays to marginality for providing this service is, in effect, the ambiguous power it cedes to the latter."[21]

Women Under Wahhabism: A Crucial Difference

Here is the core of what I suspect constitutes a crucial difference in religious experience for women living under Wahhabi power, as opposed to those living in the Sunni or Shia societies of the Gulf: Wahhabi authority defined itself very specifically in opposition to saint worship, praying at graves, votive offerings, and Sufi *zikr* chanting and dancing, as well as fortune-telling, spell making, truth divining, and amulet wearing. In short, in asserting their own brand of orthodoxy, the Wahhabis denigrated techniques of personal and spiritual empowerment in contradiction to orthodox standards that were available to women and condemned communal rituals that appealed to women's needs.

This is not to say that women's rituals as such were targeted, because men engaged in these heterodox rituals too. Nor is it to say that Ibn Abd al-Wahhab singled out women as being prone to performing these rituals any more than they are singled out in authoritative Sunni Hadith. The difference lies in the fact that the rituals condemned were the only communal rituals available to women, and no alternatives were offered in compensation. Men, on the other hand, still had the mosque, and not only was the mosque under the Wahhabis the true center of community life, but prayer in the mosque became the emblem of the community living according to God's laws. In comparison to men's access to religious worship, women under the Wahhabis were to some degree—like the contemporary Zar adherents—physically marooned by the Wahhabis' narrow view of ritual space. And the problem for women went one step further: in asserting what is orthodox by negating what is not, "centrality" (correct worship of the One God in the Mosque) ascribes to "marginality" (saint worship, moulid, Ashura, and Zar) some "ambiguous power." What is ambiguous is anomalous, and what is anomalous is threatening, out of control, dangerous, and—when it comes to heterodox methods of healing, knowing, and hurting—often ascribed to women. As the following chapters show, religious texts attribute these characteristics specifically to women when they refer to the practice of these marginal rituals.

The Chapters

The following chapters look at the intersection beween religion and learning, worship, and the practice of medicine among Sunni and Shi'a of the Gulf region and among the Wahhabi of Najd, tracing the way these different versions of orthodoxy shaped different experiences for women.

Chapter 1, "Women and Religious Learning: Piety and a Matter of Propriety," explains the centrality of religious learning to knowledge and the pursuit of an education in societies of the Gulf and Arabian peninsula, showing the disparity between boys and girls in access to learning, in the social validation of learning, and in what each was expected to achieve by virtue of his or her education.

Chapter 2, "Prayer, the Mosque, and Ways Women Worship," discusses the limitations on women's access to the mosque and the alternative ritual practices available to them. A look at Wahhabi attitudes about modes of correct worship and their ritual practices shows that women were allowed into the mosque, unlike women in the Gulf, although their presence was not required, as was men's, and they were allowed to attend only on special occasions. On the other hand, Gulf women experienced a range of alternative rituals that were forbidden to women under the Wahhabis.

Chapter 3, "The Healing Power of Words: Ink, Spit, and Holy Speech," builds on the problem posed for women by limited access to religious knowledge and limited or no access to the mosque, showing how the educated woman healer applied orthodox healing techniques but could not do so according to the same standards acquired by accredited male healers and revealing how denial of access to the mosque made them dependent on men for the best medicines.

"Engaging Spirits: Prophylaxis, Witchcraft, Exorcisms, Trial by Ordeal, and Zar," chapter 4, looks at preventive medicine and healing techniques based on exorcising, appeasing, or communicating with spirits, techniques that were inherently in opposition to standard orthodox therapy. The chapter includes a discussion of techniques of fortune-telling and divining truth, skills based on the principle that there exist spirits whose purpose is to cause harm and the recognition of animism in inert objects whose prescient powers can be harnessed. The Zar is discussed as a healing fellowship available to women everywhere in the Gulf, western Arabia, and Egypt but not in regions dominated by the Wahhabis.

The next chapter, "When Words Fail: Surgeries, Smells, and Salt-packing," deals with the realm of healing not based on ritual but on practical curative techniques derived from observation and experience and from prescriptions in the Prophet's Hadith. This chapter considers how separate systems for dealing with illness can exist simultaneously and without contradiction and discusses techniques of cautery, herbs, concoctions, contagion and inoculation, surgery, and the most important healing practice of women, midwifery.

The final chapter, "Community, Gender, and the Spiritual Experience: Some Conclusions," brings together the threads of the gendered character of learning, ritual, and healing practices and discusses the different implications for women in the Wahhabi Najd. Wahhabism set the dominant mode of religious thought and practice for Najd. This mode of religious thought and practice denied legitimacy to ritual practices that invoke intercession, which are fundamental modes of women's worship. Denial of intercessionary modes of worship undermines women's ways of establishing community with other women. Wahhabism encouraged learning for women but did not promote the institutions for women whereby learning could take place to the same standard to which men were entitled. In spite of prayer in the mosque being placed at the center of community life, women's access to the mosque was never promoted as it was for men. The result was that not only was women's perceived competence as teachers and as healers undermined, as it also was in the Gulf, but most healing techniques available to women, along with opportunities for spiritual community, were actually condemned. In concrete terms, if the healing societies of the Zar, the groups that assemble for votive offerings, and the more subtle linkages formed among healer, apprentice, and patient or saint, medium, and supplicant were not absent in Najd, they were certainly pejorated and viewed with suspicion.

In my conclusions, I also bring together ideas about gender that are explicit in Wahhabi explanations of correct and incorrect rituals and implicit in daily practice. Taken together, I suggest, these ideas constitute a gender ideology that was emphasized during the first half of the century along with the spread of Wahhabi missionary activity and the conquests of Ibn Sa'ud. Furthermore, I connect the ritual prohibitions of the Wahhabis to the drawing of gendered boundaries in physical as well as conceptual space, which, I suggest, constitutes the historical underpinnings of the single most critical issue confronting Saudi women today. In an epilogue, I return to the question of the influence of the past on the present and discuss how these ideas about gender mesh with state-sponsored rules constraining women in the present day and also with gender ideologies articulated by contemporary shaikhs, and I take up the implications of these continuities for the future.

Sources: The Arabian Mission and Missionary Women's Writing

The most intimate look at the world of Arabian women of the Gulf and Najd in the era before the First World War—and probably up through the 1940s—comes through the documents of the Arabian Mission of the Reformed Church in America. The group was established in 1889 as a nondenominational mission dedicated to the task of doing "pioneer mission work in some Arabic speaking country, especially on behalf of Muslims and slaves." After a tour of Persian Gulf towns under British colonial influence, mission founders Samuel Zwemer and James Cantine selected the Gulf and Arabian Peninsula for two reasons. First, the British Empire was on the horizon to open the door for mission work in these territories, which otherwise would not have allowed the missionaries in; second, the founders—who evaluated the Gulf as a mission site long before Ibn Sa'ud revitalized Wahhabi Islam and began his conquest of the peninsula—determined that "in Arabia especially the Muslims are less bigoted, and are more readily influenced by and accessible to the truth of the Scriptures." The destination once decided, the call for missionaries and funds to support the mission decreed that "the field is ready. The work so long neglected is urgent. The descendants of Ishmael stand ready to receive the truth and the promised blessing."[22]

Thus armed with purpose, the Reverend James Cantine, who had only just graduated from the New Brunswick Seminary in New Jersey, arrived in Basra to establish the first missionary station. In 1893 a second station was established on Bahrain Island, followed by another in Musqat. In 1910 a fourth was opened in Kuwait, at a time when there was only one Western foreigner in the town, the British political resident.

Taking the "Battle" on Tour

The mission had its own original theme song, "The Arabian Mission Hymn," and the strategic objectives of the missionary enterprise were laid out in military terminology: The annual meeting of the mission was called "a council of war,"[23] and when one of the pioneer missionaries died he was eulogized as "the first member of the Arabian Mission to lay down the weapons of his earthly warfare."[24] To the missionaries, the ultimate goal of their labors was "the occupation of the interior from the coast as a base."[25] They would one day "occupy inland Arabia," which to them meant Najd, "the very citadel of Islam,"[26] and they could foresee a time when mission stations (the Wahhabis notwithstanding) would be established in Buraida, Hufuf, Riyadh, Ha'il, and ultimately even in Mecca and Medina. To this end, they set up a series of temporary outstations for the purpose of offering medical services and disseminating Bible literature, and they took tours of Hasa, rural areas of Oman, among Bedouin near Kuwait, and ultimately Riyadh. From these missionary tours, as well as from the permanent missionary stations, we have descriptive information about the major towns and villages in the interior and, along the Gulf, of Bedouin encampments and oasis villages.

In 1917, when the first medical tour to the capital of Najd was performed at the invitation of Ibn Sa'ud, Dr. Paul Harrison became one of the first writers in English, followed shortly by St. John Philby, to enter the city of Riyadh in the present century. After this first tour to Riyadh, which occurred while the Ikhwan movement was in full flower, the mission was invited to send a doctor annually. The mission viewed these invitations as a momentous opening, because at that time missionaries and foreign travelers alike agreed that no visitor entered Najd except on the personal invitation of the Sultan.[27] In 1933 the mission attained another first (also a first for travel writing in southern Najd), when Dr. Louis Dame was permitted to bring his wife with him on tour, as well as a woman doctor and Indian nurse. In spite of the recent date, the inclusion of women was a unique occasion, not just for the missionaries but for their Saudi hosts, for this marked the very first time that any Western woman had entered Riyadh.

Neglected Arabia *and Its Authors: a "Burning Love for Those in Darkness"*

The literary traces of the Arabian Mission are in the form of personal letters to family members, autobiographies, memoirs, business letters to mission headquarters, letters exchanged between missionaries in the field, short stories based on experiences, field reports, articles in magazines and journals, and unpublished descriptive materials from the personal collections of missionaries. Some of the unpublished writings are housed in the library of the New Brunswick Theological Seminary and others at the Hartford Seminary. There are in addition collections of correspondence in private possession, such as the correspondence of George Gosselink, missionary in Basra for approximately forty years. The most important source of missionary writings for the Gulf and Arabian Peninsula is a pamphlet series called *Neglected Arabia*, published from 1892 to 1962. Originally entitled *Field Reports of the Arabian Mission*, the name was changed to *Neglected Arabia* in 1901. In 1949 the name was again changed to *Arabia Calling*, and in 1962 publication ceased.

These pamphlets are an unparalleled source of information for writing about social history in the Gulf. The pamphlets must, however, be read with an awareness of the purpose and point of view of the missionary writers. The missionaries were committed to the belief that Christ's message was the salvation of mankind and that their labors in the dark land of the false prophet were a privilege bestowed on them by God. By 1909 twenty-nine missionaries had been sent to the Arabian field. Nine of them were doctors, and nine were clergymen; sixteen were men, and thirteen were women, and all were exceptionally well-educated for their time. Paul Harrison, for example, was a graduate of the Johns Hopkins School of Medicine, which was the first medical school in the United States to require a college degree for admission and a four-year program to graduate.[28]

Both men and women tended to be young people of high achievement who gave up promising careers and comfortable lives in exchange for an experience fraught with physical discomfort, humiliation, and meager tangible rewards. Malaria, typhus, tuberculosis, dirt, flies, heat, and head lice were constant companions to them and their young children. In fact, during the first two decades of the mission, one of the missionaries became a permanent invalid after surviving an attack of typhus, five others were dead, and two young children of Bahrain missionaries had died of dysentery. In later years, there were also a number of deaths in bizarre circumstances: in 1929 Dr. Henry Bilkert was shot to death by a party of Wahhabi Bedouin near Kuwait; in 1913 Dr. Sharon Thoms fell off a pole to his death while stringing telephone wire between Musqat and his new station in Mutrah; Dr. Paul Harrison's first wife, a mother of four small children, disappeared from the deck of a steamer in the Gulf as the family headed home to the United States for a holiday.

The hazards of missionary work were great in relation to the fruits of evangelism. In the words of a mission child raised in Basra, "My parents used to say there were more dead missionaries than live converts."[29] In the face of so much adversity, their perseverance in an enterprise that never made the slightest inroads toward the goals that originally inspired the mission is testament to the missionaries' commitment to the belief that the salvation of man was in Christ and that they were Christ's privileged agents.

In spite of the hazards of missionary work in the Gulf, young missionaries didn't view the choice they had made as one of sacrifice. Rather, it was an exciting, even exhilarating, opportunity to do God's bidding. Some missionaries even believed that they had been specially called. Cornelia Dalenberg, for example, dedicated her life to mission service after hearing a lecture on mission work in Arabia that was presented to nurses and medical students in Chicago. Of her experience listening to the missionary recruiter, Miss Dalenberg wrote, " 'This is no accident that I am here,' I thought to myself as I heard her words. I cannot describe the feeling that passed over me, but it stayed with me for the rest of my life. It was something like a fire—a constantly burning flame that ignited in my heart that night." "Do men and women receive a 'call' to enter mission work?" Miss Dalenberg wrote. "I cannot speak for others, but I know I did. It was impelling, unforgettable, and undeniable."[30]

For the majority of missionaries who arrived before 1940, joining the mission was a lifetime commitment. James Cantine, the founding missionary, remained with the mission in the field until 1927. Dr. Paul Harrison, who joined the mission directly after graduating from medical school and wrote profusely of his missionary experiences, stayed from 1909 until 1954. Dr. and Mrs. Louis Dame remained with the mission from 1919 until 1936. Unmarried missionaries married other unmarried missionaries, and in later years some of their children married the children of other missionaries and returned to join the mission of their parents. They were not in the Gulf for short-term adventure. In the words of Nurse Dalenberg, who joined the mission in Bahrain in 1921 and remained for forty years, "I see two qualities in the missionaries: burning love for those living in darkness, and also a commitment to mission service" (p. 230).

Commitment, Conviction, and Mutual Condescension

In the letters and reports sent back to the Mission Board, contradictory attitudes toward the people the missionaries had come to evangelize are manifest. Understanding, sympathy, generosity, and a willingness to seek out the positive and learn more are combined with an assurance, implicit in the purpose of their presence there and explicit in some of their writings, that the civilization in which they labored was vastly inferior to their own. During his first journey to Riyadh, Paul Harrison could observe that "the Moslem conception of God is one of the world conquering ideas of the world's history. It has proved strong enough to overcome the appetite for physical stimulants. Strong enough to abolish race prejudices in the hearts of men and make out of divergent and hostile races a single brotherhood of believers, but it is a significant fact that as Islam travels away from Arabia this fundamental conception of God becomes more and more diluted."[31] In his two books and countless articles in "Neglected Arabia," Harrison repeatedly extols the religion of Islam, in particular what he saw as its quintessential expression in Riyadh during the revival, to the extent that a reader might suspect that Harrison the missionary was himself on the verge of conversion.

> The visitor in Riadh finds himself in an atmosphere where the overwhelming conviction of God's omnipotence makes superstition impossible, where even tobacco is forbidden, where race prejudice has disappeared, where indeed not simply are certain specific rules obeyed with great fare, but where the whole present world has shriveled into insignificance in men's minds as compared with the tenets of their faith, and its interests. And this is not devotion to something that is dead and fixed and historical. It is seethingly alive. The tremendous movement for the Islamizing of the Bedouin tribes is only one indication of what lies underneath.

However, at the same time that Harrison could see so much good in Islam for the people of Arabia, he was constantly searching for its failings, and his faith in the goals of Christian evangelism never wavered: he yet looked forward to the time when a mission station would be opened in the heart of Arabia, "for there are few cities the occupation of which would seem so important to the Kingdom of Christ as Riadh" (p. 5).

The missionaries, as inheritors of the European colonial attitude toward the Middle East and "the Arabs," were also products of their time, and the quality of missionary observation was sometimes obscured by popular ideas about Arab society that had gained currency with the translation of *The Arabian Nights* and nineteenth-century European romantic paintings depicting scenes of Arab sensuality. So certain were Western visitors to the region that they possessed knowledge about "the Arab" that preconceptions continued to obscure observation even when direct experience was at hand. In 1918, after having lived and practiced medicine in Kuwait, Bahrain, and Musqat for nine years, Paul Harrison wrote a letter to a colleague in Kuwait, Edwin Calverley, saying, "I had ambitions at the beginning of the year, and I have still, to produce an article dealing with the Moslem attitude toward women, and to this end consumed about a quarter of 'The Arabian Nights' in its original tongue, as a sort of sidelight."[32] Harrison would read a medieval fantasy to help him understand the twentieth-century society in which he was living; what he subsequently produced is the following analysis of the sexual appetites of the oasis Arabs of Bahrain and the disposable Arab female that suggests he learned from his experiences exactly what he went looking to find:

> All animal appetites are strongly developed in the Arab, but
> nowhere has the development been so unbalanced and harmful as in
> the appetites and passions which are connected with sex. These ap-
> petites are perhaps as intensely developed in the Arab as in any race
> in the world. . . . The Arab knows three pleasures, perfumes to
> smell, food to eat and women to enjoy. . . . The customs that the
> Arab's appetite has created allow him four wives and as many con-
> cubines as he desires. He may divorce any wife at his pleasure and
> sell any concubine. Thus he may change partners at will and con-
> tract a new alliance at any time the fancy strikes him—whenever in
> fact he finds his first partners getting a trifle old or otherwise unat-
> tractive, quite commonly after they have borne children and have
> therefore less to offer in the way of sex gratification.[33]

Experiences in the clinic helped shape Dr. Harrison's opinion, for the most common ailment he was asked to treat was "inability," and he admits that he interpreted this as an indication of sexual appetite. Had he lived to see the introduction in 1998 of the impotency pill Viagra, which is in such high demand that urologists are dispensing the drug on preprinted prescription forms, he might have had a different interpretation. The introduction of the pill in the United States showed that "inability" is a common problem, but one that American men simply did not talk about, even to their doctors, until the promise of treatment outweighed their sense of shame at having the condition. When foreign doctors opened clinics in the Gulf in 1910, it was with the promise of better medicines. Should men of the Gulf who came to these clinics have been viewed as gluttons seeking an aid to sexual license, or, like American men in 1998, should they have been viewed as patients seeking treatment for a medical condition?

A Plea for Donations: May the Peace of a Christian Death Be Shared by
"Our Moslem Sisters"

Neglected Arabia and field reports sent back to the Mission Board reflect the position of the missionary writers vis-à-vis the audience to whom these materials were addressed. The annual field reports were essentially progress reports to an employer, and so the information contained in them presented the missionaries' activities in the best possible light. *Neglected Arabia* was published in pamphlet form to be distributed among member churches and other interested parties in order to awaken interest in the activities of the Arabian Mission for purposes of fund-raising. The authors needed to show success: they don't report botched operations; they do write of their successes selling Christian Bible "portions" through the Bible shops in mission station towns and in village outstations. The pamphlets were geared to prove the purposefulness of the missionary enterprise. By describing how desperately debased Arab life was, they could show how deeply Arabian people needed Christ's message and then make the plea for financial support that concludes so many articles in the pamphlets.

The plea for support was often incorporated into the articles by women missionaries, because Muslim women were the specially designated recipients of the missionaries' sympathies and it was missionary women who had access to them. The following, from an article entitled "A Christian and a Moslem Deathbed," is an example. In this article, a fictitious Christian deathbed scene is imagined and described by the writer, Mrs. Josephine Van Peursem. The dying women is at peace, surrounded by family, clean linen, and the words of the Lord. This scene is then juxtaposed with one in which a woman is dying of bubonic plague in Bahrain, alone in a shack outside the house. Her family are revolted by her condition and afraid to get too close to her, but they try to coax her from a distance to recite the Muslim testimony of faith before she dies. The missionaries arrive and bravely clean her bed ("cleanliness is next to Godliness") with no thought for their own safety, and they hear the dying woman speak:

> "There is no God but God, and Mohammed is his prophet," came
> from the dying lips. In her next breath she was cursing her lazy
> daughters and neglectful and unfaithful husband. All her life had
> been a life of misery. Cursing is more natural to the Moslem than
> singing to the Christian. And yet here was hope in her for a better
> beyond. She did not blame her false prophet for this loveless life.
> She blamed God.
>
> Then she received the message we were there to bring her, the
> beautiful message of Christ's love for her. She listened acquiescently
> to the words and the call of the Saviour—"Come unto me all ye
> that are weary and heavy laden, and I will give you rest."

. . . Reader, compare this experience with the one preceding, and thank God for Christian mothers. Go down on your knees and ask the Lord to guide you in doing your share that the peace and assurance of a Christian death may soon be shared by our Moslem sisters.[34]

Another article, published in 1919, discusses some of the effects of the First World War on the personal lives of women in Basra and concludes:

The Moslem woman's life is a troublous one, even in normal times. Judged from our standpoint, it is almost too troublous to bear. During my sixteen years in Arabia I have not been in a single Arab home where the relations between a man and his wife were such as a Christian woman could endure. The wife is always more or less of a slave to be beaten or divorced at will. All this she has to accept without questioning, however, for she is taught that "Allah has decreed it."
. . . In these days when the Christian world is sending on much prayer for those who are suffering because of the war, I hope our readers will not forget to pray for this little corner of the war area. We long for the Moslem women to learn that Christ can lift their burden of sorrow and care, and also their greater burden of sin.[35]

Respect and Emulation: The Missionary Woman's Angst

The biases explicit in missionary literature are shared by both men and women writers, but women writers had an additional reason to become the conveyers of the special bias that all missionaries reserved for the status of Muslim women. The reason can be traced to the feminization of the missionary enterprise in terms of both missionary personnel and the objects of their evangelism. It had become clear almost from the founding of the mission—conceived originally as a mission for men—that the strategy of learning Arabic and preaching was not going to work, especially since Zwemer and Cantine had had to hire Syrian Christians not only to teach them Arabic but to do the preaching for them, and that they would need to offer some sort of social work to attract potential converts.[36]

By the turn of the century, mission societies worldwide had adopted similar strategies for gaining access to potential converts, and social service had come to be viewed as a legitimate technique of evangelism. The women who were recruited into mission service therefore were to be professionally trained people who would introduce the Christian message to those who came in search of medical care or schooling. The professionalization of women's work for women in missions was happening worldwide. It was occurring not only as a response to needs in the field but also to the professionalization of the leadership of women's missionary societies in America, where by the late 1890s "educated motherhood" had become the prevailing cultural paradigm for ideal womanhood. The ideal woman was to be not only a moral and virtuous mother, but one who was also professionally trained in homemaking and child care and who was also competent and socially useful.[37]

The mission societies in the United States, like the missionaries abroad, also realized that women missionaries were an absolute essential if missions were ever to find success, for it was women who nurtured and molded children, and in many areas of missionary labor, such as China and the Muslim world, male missionaries had no access to women.[38] In the world of evangelical missions to the Muslims, the need for women missionaries with professional skills was recognized as urgent and special. At the Cairo Conference of 1906, a special appeal on behalf of Muslim womanhood was endorsed, in which it was stated that

> there is no hope of effectually remedying the spiritual, moral and physical ills which [Muslim women] suffer, except to take them the message of the Savior, and that there is no chance of their hearing, unless we give ourselves to the work. No one else will do it. That lays a heavy responsibility on all Christian women. . . . Each part of the women's work being already carried on needs to be widely extended. Trained and consecrated women doctors, trained and consecrated women teachers, groups of women workers in the villages, an army of those with love in their hearts to seek and save the lost [*sic*].[39]

The Arabian Mission recognized that if they could target the Muslim woman, they could target the heart of the Muslim home, and the mission was already hiring professional women to take up the challenge. In 1902 there had been ten members of the Arabian Mission, and the four women among them had come as wives of missionaries. By 1906 nine women had joined the Arabian Mission, and three of these held medical degrees. Of the twenty-eight missionaries in the field in 1910, nearly half were women, and of these five were single. By the following year, the mission had established stations in Musqat, Bahrain, Kuwait, Basra, and Amara, and four additional trained women physicians joined the mission. The growing proportion of women in the Arabian Mission reflected trends in the U.S. missionary movement, which was at its height between the years 1890 and 1920: in 1915 more than three million women were included on the membership rolls of some forty denominational female missionary societies, with over nine thousand missionaries in the field worldwide, at least half of them women.[40]

Whether the missionary professional was a physician, nurse, teacher, or evangelist, mission appointments required an additional period of study at one of the missionary training schools that proliferated in the United States. Schools such as the Hartford Seminary in Connecticut or the New Brunswick Seminary in New Jersey offered special programs designed to equip the missionary to harness the evangelizing opportunities afforded by their professional skills. That evangelism was a project dead at the starting line without the medical work was explicit on the mission side in the recruitment of doctors and nurses. The higher degree of respect afforded medical missionaries by Gulf people was also explicit in the offering of unsolicited monetary gifts and invitations to visit in high places. Hence the writings from the evangelical side of missionary work at times reflect the evangelist's gall at being shunted aside by the success of the new social service professionals: As Gerrit Van Peursem, a missionary charged with "evangelical work," protests, "every missionary in Arabia puts the Evangelistic first and foremost, that the ultimate aim is not the body, not the mind, but the soul of the Arab. No one will think that I speak disparagingly when I say that the other departments of our activity are not ends in themselves, but noble and admirable means to an end."[41]

The evangelical missionaries, both men and women, were kept busy with the daily business of the mission, which was prayer and Bible reading as the prelude to medical care. Patients would wait outside the Kuwait mission hospital each morning for the doors to open in order to receive a numbered ticket. After these had been distributed and the patients assembled inside, prayers would be read in two separate sections of the hospital grounds, one for men and one for women. Hospital in-patients received prayers and talks on religion as they convalesced. (Prayer and Bible reading also were the core curriculum at mission schools, where English as well as Arabic was taught along with hymn singing to melodies of Bach, Haydn, and Handel.)

While both men and women were assigned to educational or medical work, women missionaries had an additional responsibility. They engaged in systematic visiting, and in the Gulf it had a name, *zenana* work. They were to befriend women and cultivate relationships with them in order to introduce Christian dogma into Muslim households. In 1899 Amy Zwemer kept a diary of her visiting duties. "On Jan 1," she wrote, "four women called, talked with them about Christianity and played the little organ; on Jan. 5th, I visited the house of Sheikh so and so, had a good time reading and talking to the crowd of women about Christ."[42] In Bahrain in 1916 Minnie Dykstra conducted prayer meetings with musical accompaniment in her home that attracted both Sunni and Shia women. Other missionary women took their sewing to the homes of their neighbors, where they visited, and, as they reported in letters to the Mission Board, sang Christian hymns and offered prayers.

Underlying this form of mission work was the ideological residue of the notion of the ideal woman common in mid-nineteenth-century America, an ideal that emphasized the primacy of motherhood in women's lives. American Protestant womanhood, according to this view, found fulfillment in creating a wholesome Christian environment in the home.[43] By influencing her husband and children and by contributing to her church and community, the American woman could diffuse her nurturing and refinement throughout society. Taken abroad to heathen lands, the example of American Protestant womanhood in their daily lives could even instruct the whole world.[44] "Housework" as an integral part of missionary efforts was explained in a 1925 *History of the Arabian Mission*: "This is not mentioned in the reports as work, but gentle reader, it is! And then there is the missionary value of our Christian homes, which is just as great as of yore, for the relation of husband and wife according to Christian standards is still a topic of conversation fruitful of many helpful lessons."[45] Simply by entering the Muslim woman's home and inviting her to her own, the woman missionary could make a positive impression and change women's lives for the better. By virtue of their Christianity, measured in partnership relations with their husbands, clean linen, orderly households, educated children, and community service, they could in their daily lives provide a model worthy of the world's emulation.

This message comes through in some of the missionary women's writings, where every failing in the life of the Muslim woman had a counterpoint in the good fortune of Protestant women, the suggestion being that if only Muslim women would know Christ through the example of the missionary woman, she too could share in that good fortune. In 1916 Dr. Eleanor Calverley wrote the following fund-raising plea:. "American women, what have you been doing today? Think over the details of your happy and interesting life. . . . Remember how your family gathered around the breakfast table?" Then she reminds readers that the Muslim woman cannot sit with her husband at meals. "How proud you were of that blooming daughter as she came home from school and told you of her studies, her athletic achievements, her good times with boy and girl friends, her hopes and ambitions?" Then Dr. Calverley tells her readers how little Arab girls have no school and sit all day long drinking coffee and smoking cigarettes, dreaming only of a handsome young husband who will likely turn out to be a toothless old man. She concludes, "Christian women, thank God that you were not born to the lot of Moslem women! May our thankfulness not content itself with mere words of gratitude. You and I can bring to our Moslem sisters the abundant life which Christ brought to us."[46]

Instead of adulation, missionary women sometimes encountered scorn, and their writing at times reflect their angst at failing to gain recognition as people to be emulated and as competent professionals with special talents to offer Arab society. Occasionally these frustrations erupted in a hail of resentment, as the following example from the writings of Eleanor Calverley illustrates. "Another element in the Moslem religion, as it affects the women," she writes, "is the spirit of fanaticism or intolerance. When one has seen the curl of scorn on the lips of the Muhammedan woman, dirty and ignorant though she may be, as she listens to the Gospel preached by a Christian missionary, one begins to suspect the depths of hatred and conceit in the Moslem heart. That the Christian has education, skill, or a position demanding respect, has no weight with her. An infidel is an infidel and cursed for ever."[47]

In the Field and on the Home Front: Taking Setbacks Personally

Feelings of resentment at being rejected by Muslim women were exacerbated by policies established by the mission. Mission women had been hired as professionals to provide the essential lure that evangelism could not offer on its own, yet the mission treated them as second-string players. Mary Bruins Allison, a latecomer who joined in 1934 and stayed for forty years, felt that the mission devalued women's contribution. For a woman, she recalls with some bitterness in her memoir, marriage to a person outside the mission meant the end of her appointment by the board. A man who was a missionary, on the other hand, could not only marry outside and maintain his post, but his new spouse was automatically considered a member of the mission staff and received a salary, even if she were untrained and devoted her time exclusively to taking care of home and children. Men and women missionaries were also paid on a different scale, regardless of their professional capacity, so that as a doctor Allison received less than the evangelical missionary and less than other doctors at her station who were men.[48]

Missionary women in the early twentieth century had set a level of expectation for themselves—and a level of expectation had been set for them—that could not possibly be satisfied. By U.S. standards, missionary women had fulfilled the ideal of their generation. They were educated, they were activists, they had professional skills, and they were exemplary wives and mothers as well, and for this they expected recognition. They expected to be respected as professionally accomplished persons. They expected that the skills they possessed in delivering babies, for example, would be sought after, when in fact it was only after many years in the field that missionary women doctors were ever called to attend normal deliveries. They expected that the example they set by working cooperatively with their husbands would evoke respectful awe if not emulation, when in fact all it evoked was curiosity. They expected that teaching their children, especially the girls, and sending them off to boarding school and college would cause Muslim women to regret the early marriages and pregnancies of their own daughters, but instead Muslim women only wondered how they could send their children so far away.

American Protestant women had incorporated their womanhood into the missionary endeavor, but they were demanding recognition from a society that did not measure female accomplishment by the same standards. Furthermore, the recognition that missionary women believed their professional accomplishments had earned them was not only questioned in the mission field but was being subverted in the United States as well. Even as the women's suffrage movement was on the verge of success, by the close of the First World War women's voluntary societies, including the women's missionary societies, were dissolving. Even earlier, around 1910, the professionalization of medicine had brought about the closing of many substandard medical schools and schools of midwifery, while at the same time qualified medical schools were closing their doors to women entirely. As a result, the woman physician was coming to be viewed as the occupant of a lower order of the profession.[49] Thus when the woman missionary was experiencing rejection as a Christian missionary, that same rejection touched on her self-esteem as a doctor and as a woman.

Men had similar experiences in finding their work as doctors belittled while being insulted as unbelievers, but in the rare instances in which men expressed in writing their feelings about these experiences, they usually wrote of them with detachment and humor. Whereas women tended to internalize the rejection and see it as an attack on what they as Christian women and as professional women had to offer, men tended to separate the verbal insults from their personal selves as well as from their professional competence and to deflect them toward the fact of their Christianity. Unlike women, men as missionaries were not offering up their personal lives as models of emulation to be admired or disliked, and whatever insult or rejection they may have experienced in the course of their missionary work, their professional status as competent teachers or doctors remained untouched.

No Intimate Friendships but a Most Valuable Source for Historical Inquiry

Even with their ideological undercurrents, the writings of American missionaries, in particular missionary women, remain a most valuable source for historical inquiry. Gulf missionaries traveled and lived in places where very few Western women or men had gone before, including villages up and down the Arabian coast and into Najd. And in spite of the relatively recent dates of the Arabian Mission, its records provide some of the earliest material available on Arabian society in practice, especially for Najd. The information on the intimate world of Arabian women that missionary writings bring to light is unparalleled in the writings of foreign observers, and in some cases it is the only source available at all. We learn, for example, of ways in which women compensate for their exclusion from the mosque through religious rituals that are exclusively female and of the ways in which exclusion from the mosque could deprive women of the best medicines. We also learn about medical practice, diseases and cures, the celebration of religious holidays, the education of children, the managing of premarital pregnancies, folk remedies, techniques of birthing and the art of midwifery, female handicrafts and female employment, and we even find out how the Ethiopian cult of the Zar was integrated into the social lives of Gulf women.

As doctors and nurses, missionary writers had unique access to ordinary families and to the very intimate world of women that would have been impossible to other outsiders, male or female, and would not appear in any other type of historical material, whether court cases or commercial or government papers. While these writers had their biases, their experiences cannot be denied. If they thought that modesty and segregation practices were harmful to women, these views were understandable, for missionary doctors and nurses did in fact have to perform emergency surgery on women in their homes because the patients' husbands would not allow them to go to the hospital; they did in fact examine the bodies of victims of an alms-giving stampede who had suffocated when, unconscious, their face veils were doused with water and left in place for modesty's sake; Harrison did in fact remove a sixty-pound abdominal tumor from a woman that was paraded before town notables as evidence that she was ill, not pregnant, and therefore innocent of adultery.

The writings of the Arabian Mission allow us to see changes over time in a way that few other sources could. These writings represent a focused look at Arabian society in specific areas stretching over a seventy-year period. Not only do we see changes in Arabian society but changes in missionary perspectives as well, including changes in the nature of what the missionaries chose to write about. By 1930 the judgmental quality of missionary writing waned as the mission came to accept that being a witness for Christ's goodness was sufficient justification for its presence in the Gulf and the missionaries were no longer striving for the impossible goal of evangelism. A more secular America after that time fostered greater tolerance for diversity in religious persuasion, and the beginnings of oil money—not even considered in Harrison's day—and the development possibilities this money facilitated, placed the missionaries in the position of willing—but not necessarily needed—helpers in the medical and educational fields for which they had formerly been the sole source of competence.

It is not an accident that most missionary writings that discuss family or gender relations from any perspective are the writings of women. This is not simply because only women had access to the women's quarters of private homes. It also suggests that men did not have access to men's quarters or to the intimacy of men's circles. Indeed, taken on the whole, the writings suggest that neither men nor women of the mission had close personal relationships with the people they had come to proselytize. In the world where they had elected to spend their productive lifetimes, they were always outsiders. In fact, even in the women's writings, there is rarely a suggestion of the reciprocity implicit in equal relationships; missionary women visit Arab women as evangelists or as doctors but not as friends.

In all cases we find no intimacies, no deep personal friendships between missionaries and local people. The missionary writers are outsiders looking in. They describe what they see and what they know of their patients and of the people in whose homes they are guests. They describe the towns and villages, the Bedouin tents they visit, the methods of oasis farming, the construction of native boats that sail the Persian Gulf, how food is preserved and prepared aboard ship, who formed the crew, methods of navigation in the Gulf, and the condition of the pearling industry; they describe the handiwork and daily life of women, family life, marriage and divorce, the celebration of holidays, the religious lives of women, the education of children, diseases, and desert treks. As colorful and rich as these writings are, they reveal their authors as people belonging to a closed community in an alien land. Nevertheless, in the Arabian context, where men and women have left few if any literary traces of themselves and where but a few foreigners previous to the missionaries had any access to women at all, the importance of the access that missionary men and women had into the world of Arabian society cannot be overestimated.

Other Sources: Travel Writing and Ethnography

Discussion about Najd and about Bedouin in the Arabian peninsula for any time period before the mid-twentieth century is impossible without reliance on travel writing and ethnographies. Paul Harrison's journey to Riyadh in 1917 and St. John Philby's mission to the court of Abd al-Aziz in the same year marked the first opportunities for serious information gathering about Najd in the twentieth century.[50] Until then, European knowledge of the southern Najd equaled the sum of a handful of travelers' accounts, and northern Najd, having been visited by a few more travelers, was only slightly better known to Europeans and Americans. Most of these travelers had skirted the coast of the peninsula or seen the towns of the Hejaz or even visited Mecca in disguise. The government of India maintained agencies in the towns along the Gulf coast, which commercial and military personnel frequented, but until the latter part of the nineteenth century, the best-known view of central Arabia remained that seen from the border lands on the edge of the Syrian desert. Because of its geographic inaccessibility and continuous warfare, the interior of the peninsula remained largely unexplored by European writers until the middle of the nineteenth century, when a few travelers journeyed into Najd, but even then only perhaps two of these reached as far south as Riyadh.

These nineteenth-century travel writers were exposed to different geographical areas, traveled at different times, and experienced different political and economic conditions. In addition, most of the travelers to the Arabian peninsula came with a particular purpose, and this focused their attention on some directions but not on others. Furthermore, each was writing for a different audience. Below I discuss the travel writers whose works I most frequently cite in this book.

John Lewis Burckhardt

John Lewis Burckhardt, a Swiss educated in Leipzig, was a scholar and adventurer who traveled to the Middle East on a mission to search out the sources of the Niger under the auspices of the African Association of London. In order to learn Arabic, he first went to Aleppo in 1809 and remained there for two and a half years. While in Aleppo, he perfected his Arabic and read Arabic literature to the point that his proficiency and knowledge commanded respect,[51] and during this period he made trips to Lebanon, Palmyra, and the mountains by the Dead Sea and discovered Petra for Europe. From Aleppo, Burckhardt moved to Cairo, and after a brief venture up the Nile, he crossed the Red Sea to Jeddah. Always observing and writing, from Jeddah he went to Taif, Mecca, and Medina, which he was the first European to enter after Mehmet Ali expelled the Wahhabis from the Hejaz. It was timely for Burckhardt to be present for the demise of the Wahhabis in Hejaz because he had been present in Aleppo two years before when Wahhabi forces entered the Hauran, an achievement that represented the height of their expansion.

Burckhardt's journeys resulted in two books: his *Notes on the Bedouins and Wahabys*, which is in part a compendium of information on Bedouin life, particularly the northern Anayza, and in part a collection of materials for a history of the Wahhabis; and his *Travels in Arabia*, which is a detailed, meticulous account of everyday life, economy, and politics in the towns of the Hejaz. Burckhardt never embarked on his exploration of the sources of the Niger, for he died in Cairo in 1916, shortly after his books were finished.

Burckhardt's work on the Bedouin has been criticized because, in spite of the breadth of information contained in his *Notes*, he never stayed among them for an extended period of time. The information contained in *Notes* is instead the product of his conversations with Bedouin whom he met in the Damascus and Aleppo bazaars and with those he met and with whom he encamped during his excursions into the Hauran and the surrounding Syrian deserts.[52] By the time Burckhardt wrote *Notes*, however, he had been traveling in the area as a Muslim for more than six years. He was fluent in Arabic, and from his own continuing experiences he had the opportunity and knowledge to cross-check his information. Furthermore, with regard to the Anayza Bedouin, just because he talked with Bedouin primarily when they came into town as opposed to in their encampments does not mean he was getting secondhand information.

Georg Augustus Wallin

Georg Augustus Wallin was a classical scholar trained in oriental languages. A Swede born in Finland in 1811, he received a classical education in the Swedish university town of Helsingfors and in the course of his studies read French, Russian, English, and German in addition to Arabic and Persian. His dissertation, written in Latin, was entitled "On the Principal Differences Between Classical and Modern Arabic." After completing it, he studied at the Oriental Institute of the University of St. Petersburg under a Persian *mirza* (secretary) and a shaikh of the Al Azhar in Cairo.

His journey to Arabia in 1845 came about as the result of a travel grant for research in Egypt and Arabia chiefly for the purpose of the comparative study of Arabian dialects. Hoping to journey to Mecca, Yemen, and ultimately to southern Najd, Wallin first prepared himself for the journey by studying medicine in Europe for six months so that he could travel as a doctor and vaccinator. He then went to Cairo in order to perfect his fluency in colloquial Arabic and, because he planned to travel as a Muslim, studied Islamic law and theology and learned to intone the Qur'an.

Wallin made two separate journeys into Najd. In 1845 he traveled to Najd through Jouf and Ha'il, and in 1848 his route took him through Tabuk, Taima, Ha'il, and then into Iraq. Although he spent more time in the intimate company of Bedouin than had Burckhardt, Wallin recorded disappointingly little about them. In Arabia, his main interests turned from philology to the religion of the Wahhabis and the teaching in the mosques of Najd. Everywhere Wallin traveled, he sought information about Wahhabi proselytizing, praying practices, and mosque sermons and about where and how Wahhabi beliefs and prohibitions were put into practice and what constituted scholarly learning for the Wahhabis. He was also a careful observer of the ethnic configuration of oasis villages and of the processes by which Bedouin interacted and became one with settled people.

William Gifford Palgrave

William Gifford Palgrave was a graduate of Oxford and the son of Sir Francis Palgrave, the founder of the Public Records Office. In 1853 he converted to Catholicism and became a Jesuit priest, and at the time of his journey to Najd in 1862–63, he had been living and preaching with a Jesuit order in Bikfaya, Lebanon. His Arabic was fluent, as reports of his Jesuit preaching in Syria reveal, so he was able to travel as a native Syrian doctor. Palgrave's expedition to Arabia, which was to be a missionary journey to extend the light of the Roman Catholic faith, was financed by Napoleon III, as the expedition was also to research the possibilities of extending French commercial and strategic interests in the Gulf area.

Palgrave's itinerary took him from Maan across the Nufud to Ha'il, from whence he traveled to Riyadh. His book *Personal Narrative of a Year's Journey through Central and Eastern Arabia (1862–1863)* contains political and theological insights about the Wahhabis, especially in the court of Riyadh, as well as much descriptive information about the commerce, agriculture, and people, including the black population, foreigners, and women, of the towns of Najd.

A controversy over the authenticity of Palgrave's *Narrative* began as soon as he returned to England, when Rev. Percy Badger, a Protestant missionary, suggested that the visit had not actually taken place. The rancor underscoring this accusation was fueled by a suspicion that Palgrave had gone to Najd in order to spy for Napoleon III, something that was only proven recently.[53] St. John Philby became Palgrave's most severe critic, and the controversy over Palgrave's visit rang through the pages of the *Geographical Journal* through the 1930s, as succeeding travelers reported retracing Palgrave's steps in Hasa and judging for themselves whether particular geographical descriptions of Palgrave's were accurate. The controversy has probably been now laid to rest by Benjamin Braude, who argues persuasively that Palgrave did indeed make the journey to Najd on which his book is based.[54]

Lewis Pelly

Lewis Pelly followed Palgrave into Riyadh in 1865. He had been appointed British Resident in the Gulf in 1862, and his purpose in going to meet the Wahhabi shaikh Faisal Al Sa'ud was to determine why the French were trying to establish contacts with Najd and whether they were aiming for a French-dominated Arabia on Britain's route to India. He was also to gather geographical information on the interior of Arabia. The published record of his journey, *Report on a Journey to Riyadh in Central Arabia (1865)*, reveals that he was most successful in pursuing the latter objective. His journey was brief: a one-month round-trip from Kuwait to Riyadh. His dry account does

· include, however, some interesting commentary on the clothing, foods, crops, and commerce of Najd and Hasa, as well as on the flavor of the Wahhabi court and the personality of its ruler.

Charles Doughty

Charles Doughty's *Travels in Arabia Deserta* is the most important piece of Arabian travel literature written in the nineteenth century and possibly the greatest piece of travel literature ever written. Doughty went to Arabia in 1876, when he was already, at age thirty-three, a seasoned solitary traveler. After taking a degree in geology at Cambridge, in 1870 he had set out on what was to become ten years of wandering. Beginning in Holland, he went on to Italy, Sicily, Algeria, Spain, and Greece, and in 1874 he went to Palestine and Syria and then to Egypt and through the Sinai. When he reached Petra, he heard of a place called Maidan Salih where there were ancient writings on stone that no European had ever seen before. He decided to go there and take impressions of the writings.

His plan was to go first to Damascus in order to learn Arabic, and from there he would join the annual Hajj caravan to Mecca, leaving the caravan at Maidan Salih and rejoining it for the return journey to Damascus. Once at Maidan Salih, however, and having achieved his purpose, he determined not to return with the caravan. Instead, he gained an introduction to a local Bedouin shaikh and wandered off into the desert with him and his people. Eventually he left the Bedouin in the village of Taima and proceeded to Ha'il. From there he went to Khaibar, a village of blacks in Hejaz, where he was forced to stay for two months when a Turkish governor would not allow him to leave. When he returned to Ha'il he was made unwelcome by the emir's deputy, and he departed for Buraida, where he stayed only long enough to be assaulted and driven out as a Christian. In Unaiza, Doughty stayed for several weeks under the protection of the head of the ruling family, and from there he made his way with the butter caravan to Mecca, where he was to part ways with the caravan at the last halt before the holy city. Threatened with death at knife point for being a Christian, Doughty was saved by a slave who took him to the sharif of Mecca in Taif, who sent him to the English consul at Jeddah, and from there Doughty embarked for India. When he reached Bombay, almost two years had passed since his departure from Damascus.

Doughty was the first European traveler to spend an extended period of time among Bedouin, and wherever he went there appears to have been no limit to the subjects that interested him. He had begun his journey with no particular purpose except "to add something to the common fund of Western knowledge" and to explore his own inexhaustible interests, which included "the Story of the Earth, Her manifold living creatures, the human generations and Her ancient rocks."[55]

As a writer, Doughty thought of himself as "a disciple of the divine Muse of Spenser and Venerable Chaucer" (1:31), and he addressed himself to an educated audience that would appreciate the language he constructed to convey the sensitivities and the grandeur of his experiences in Arabia. "It is idle," he wrote, "to imagine, that any man not a well-taught lover of his tongue, can enter into the Garden of the Muses."[56]

The language in which *Arabia Deserta* is written makes the task of reading it from beginning to end a formidable one. Doughty's words are sometimes deliberately archaic, sometimes archaic words are juxtaposed with common language, and sometimes his words are even made-up. Often he uses inverted syntax, and his meanings are amplified by literary and biblical allusion. His language forces readers to consider each individual word, to read with the dictionary at their side, and to reread. One consequence of Doughty's use of language—besides, for Doughty, difficulty in finding a publisher—is that the book has not been read as widely as it deserves to be.[57] The book, however, contains a meticulously detailed index that Doughty himself compiled, and for this reason Doughty's work is at once one of the most often cited in scholarly writing about nineteenth-century Arabia and one of the least read.

Lady Anne Blunt

In 1878, Lady Anne Blunt and her husband, Wilfred, set out for Najd simply for pleasure, curious to see the Bedouin way of life and also, because they shared an interest in horses, to see for themselves the famous stud of Emir Rashid at Ha'il. Blunt was a diplomat, a member of England's landed gentry with no money, while Lady Anne was a granddaughter of Lord Byron and heiress to a comfortable fortune. Both spoke Arabic fluently.

The two were roughing it as they traveled across the Nufud as Europeans, without subterfuge and even without escort except for one employed helper. Their journey began in 1878 at Damascus, from whence they proceeded to Basra and Jauf, where Lady Anne learned about the education, veiling practices, and courtship customs of Najdi people, and, as she describes with a vividness only matched by Doughty, the slave ministers of the

Al Rashid rulers. At Ha'il, Lady Anne also had access to the harem of Emir Rashid, and brief though her encounter was, hers is one of the extremely few descriptions of the women's quarters of a Najdi home in the whole nineteenth century. She was the only Western woman to travel to northern Najd until Gertrude Bell's visit in 1913–14.[58]

Harold R. P. Dickson

Harold R. P. Dickson, the author of *The Arab of the Desert* and *Kuwait and Her Neighbors*, was born in Beirut in 1881, the son of Britain's consul-general in Jerusalem. He was educated at Oxford, served in the Connaught Rangers and then in the Indian Army, and was sent to Mesopotamia in 1914 because of his knowledge of Arabic. Dickson's books share some of the qualities of travel literature, as each is a compendium of anecdotes, experiences, and factual information, though gained not from a single journey but from a lifetime of work and living in the Gulf region. In 1915 he was transferred to the political department and under Sir Percy Cox assisted in the organization of a civil administration in southern Iraq. He then became assistant political officer in charge of the district of Suq al-Shuyukh on the Euphrates and was later appointed political officer at Nasiriyah, a territory that included the Muntafiq tribal confederation. After the war he was transferred to Bahrain as political agent, a post he held until 1920; then, in 1929, after a series of other appointments, he went to Kuwait as political agent during the Ikhwan rebellion and was thus personally involved with the principal actors of the rebellion and in its resolution. After retiring from the army in 1936, Dickson remained in Kuwait with his wife, Violet, for the rest of his life, employed as the local representative of the Kuwait Oil Company.

Dickson's views on the Bedouin Arabs tend occasionally toward the romantic, and this may be due in part to his having been wet-nursed by an Anayza woman of the Ruwala Bedouin. His views also tend toward the patronizing and are occasionally, for someone who claimed close friendships with Bedouin women, silly: "The Arab woman," he once wrote, "likes nothing more than to be pregnant." His associations with Bedouin people, however, had been equaled by few others in his time. Furthermore, sections of his books were written by his wife, who also spoke Arabic, or contain information gathered by her during her own experiences in the desert, and as a result Dickson's books offer details about the intimate lives of Bedouin women that have never yet been duplicated.

Henry St. John Philby

British explorer, ethnographer, historian, and Muslim convert Henry St. John Philby first crossed into the heartland of Arabia in 1917 on a mission to Riyadh on behalf of the British government. His meeting with Ibn Sa'ud that took place at that time was the beginning of a close personal association between the two men that was to last until Ibn Sa'ud's death in 1953.

Philby and his Arabian adventures are far too well known to be reviewed here, but it is important to note that no twentieth-century history of the peninsula could be complete without reference to his literary works. Between 1918 and his death in Beirut in 1960, Philby produced fifteen published books, eleven unpublished books, four official government reports, and at least fifty published articles.

The Narrative as a Source of History

Because I refer so extensively to narrative writing, including travel writing and ethnographies, in the following pages, I want to make a few general observations about the narrative as a source in the writing of history. The strength of narrative is in the breadth of information, particularly about the mundane and everyday, that it can capture and preserve. Unlike consular reports, treaty documents, or local political chronicles, the topics addressed in travel writing are limited only by the interests, observations, and chance timing of the writers and their positions relative to their subjects. The narrative, unlike other kinds of sources used in history writing, does not usually compartmentalize information. There are rarely any neatly contained units of information to which the reader may refer for information on a given subject. This in fact is the greatest strength of such writing, because the act of dividing information into neat categories requires excluding some of it. If something doesn't fit into one category or fits into numerous categories, where is it to go? If an author begins with fixed categories in mind, he or she may fail to record or even to perceive anomalous details.

Travel writing in particular involves the recording of observations as they occur, as well as reflections on those observations, images that jog the memory and impel writers to expand on earlier themes, alter opinions, point up contrasts with prior experiences, retell the story in light of each new place visited, and refocus their vision as they come to know their subject in each new context and from each new, perhaps altered, personal perspective. No predetermined boundaries define what is suitable to record, and this is what makes Philby's *Arabia of the Wahhabis*, Blunt's *Pilgrimage to Najd*, and Doughty's *Arabia Deserta*, for example, such vast stores of information. Like the correspondence, reports, and vignettes of everyday life in the mission pamphlets, travel writing must be read from beginning to end. Pieces of information have to be found, understood in context, and sorted, and this process may have to be repeated each time new subjects arise for consideration. In effect, readers must index and collate everything they find, for there is no other way to gather the desired information and to present it as fully as the writer understood and experienced it.

While the information contained in narrative writing is seductive in its wealth of information, it is mined with the potential for false readings. To grab one piece of information off a page in isolation may be to grab an elephant's tail and call it snake. In addition, the writers often speak in generalities that may really only apply to specifics; what is observed at one moment may not be true the next, or may not be true according to the observation of another writer, or may not be true at all: the Arab woman, one writer says, is quiet in her mourning, while another tells us that the shrieks and wails of women ring throughout a neighborhood when a death occurs; some say the Arab woman never leaves her house, while others report that they go out all the time, while yet another tells us that the Arab woman is so confined to her house that even when desperately ill she would rather die at home than disobey a husband who forbids her going out; disease is rare in Najd, except for smallpox, says a long-time visitor in Riyadh, while another agrees but says barely a man of the desert lives to fifty years, and missionary doctors, on the other hand, found that mortality was extremely high as a result of German measles, mumps, and chicken pox; epidemics of cholera, smallpox, and plague; and chronic dysentery, malaria, venereal disease, malnutrition, and tuberculosis.

The use of the narrative can also lead one to generalize from disasters, as the historian Barbara Tuchman has warned,[59] because it is the unusual that makes news and the unusual event that people think worthy of recording. When Tuchman's caveat is considered in the context of available narrative materials dealing with the Arabian peninsula, the opposite turns out to be the case. It is local histories that record the unusual because, like the most famous chronicle of Najd, *'Unwan al-Majd fi Ta'rih Najd*, of Uthman ibn Abdullah ibn Bishr, which follows the House of Sa'ud up to 1850–51, contemporary local histories are focused exclusively on the acts of rulers, tribal wars, villages taken, booty seized, and body counts. When personalities enter the picture, it is usually in the form of the biographical sketch and the subjects are nearly always men. By contrast, in all the narrative literature used in this book, sober recording of the mundane is the rule while disasters are the rarity. In the few descriptions of events of high drama that are recorded, there is furthermore no attempt to generalize from them, and they are virtually never referred to again in subsequent writings. I can think of but two examples (both of which I alluded to earlier), and these were told dispassionately: Paul Harrison tells us that he removed a sixty-pound cyst from the abdomen of a woman who was not living with her husband at the time and that the excised cyst was collected by the woman's father and paraded through the streets of Manama in order to restore the reputation of the family; the other report describes the death of a score of women caught in a stampede to receive alms, who, lying unconscious, died of suffocation when their veiled faces were doused with water to keep them in place.

Travel literature and ethnography represent what some may call an outsider's view. After the publication of Edward Said's *Orientalism* in 1978, outsider observations came to be viewed as the quintessential source of the orientalist perspective, a negative rendering of Eastern society and culture skewed by the prejudiced and uninformed eye of the Western observer, a person who cannot really understand the cultural context of what is being described but has the power to define and construct reality for the Western reading audience. The outsider is a transient, taking literary snapshots that communicate but a minute slice of the larger scenario, frozen at a single moment in time. The voice of authority, some suggest, the voice to be listened to, is the indigenous voice, the native who knows his or her own society from the inside. According to this point of view, outsider sources, and especially missionary sources, are lodged somewhere on the bottom rung of the hierarchy of credible sources for scholarly research.

If one subscribes to this dichotomous view of knowledge, then the validity of source material becomes dependent on the identity of the writer and not the credibility of what he or she is saying: Are we to embrace what is told to us when the speaker is indigenous and despise the same thing when it is told to us by the outsider? Do we assume that the former is sympathetic and so anything negative he or she reports must be true?

Whether the terms "insider" and "outsider" accurately designate boundaries of authority, and whether these boundaries are helpful to the historian, is open to question. Hafiz Wahba, for example, was an Egyptian by nationality, but he was also an adviser to Ibn Sa'ud in Riyadh for over a decade as well as his education minister. Is Wahba's vantage point on Najdi society that of an insider or an outsider? Is Harold Dickson an outsider because he was a British political officer educated in England, or an insider because he was born in Damascus and spent his childhood and most of his adult life in the Arab world, spoke Arabic fluently, and was sufficiently intimate with Bedouin of the Kuwait region to write the most exhaustive compendium on Bedouin life produced in the twentieth century?

The authenticity of what writers have to say seems to me more related to how they are situated in relation to their particular subjects than to their personal identities in relation to the places they have studied. Eleanor Calverley, for example, traveled to the Gulf as a physician with the Arabian Mission in 1909 and stayed for twenty-one years, yet on occasion when she writes about Muslim women in relation to their personal lives it is hard to imagine that she knew any. On the other hand, when she writes of women's medicine and medical problems—from domestic violence to the pernicious medical consequences of the Gulf midwife's practice of packing the vagina with salt after birth—she speaks with an authority that for the time when she wrote cannot be matched by any other source.

Ameen al-Rihani was a Lebanese American who spent only a few months in Najd, having returned to Riyadh with Ibn Sa'ud after the 1922 Uqair conference that fixed the borders between Kuwait and Saudi Arabia. Rihani's pen dripped with acid sarcasm when he wrote about what he took to be the totally gratuitous Najdi sense of superiority and the holier-than-thou attitude of the Riyadh ulama. On the other hand, he did go into the sultan's storerooms to observe and record the distribution of food, clothing, and cash to every male person who wandered into Riyadh and asked for subsidies. Not even Philby has left us such a detailed account of the rentier state in action before the discovery of oil.

Underlying the argument for preferring the insider to the outsider account is an implicit assumption that the insider approaches his subject if not with objectivity than at least with a sympathetic understanding that the outsider is presumably unlikely to possess. The weight of literature published by the late 1990s by Middle Eastern men and women writing about their own societies belies this presumption of sympathy, however. In fact the contrary appears often to be true, as indigenous writers may use the fact that they were born into a particular society as a passport to criticizing it. Much of the literature produced by men and women of the Gulf region not only has not painted an appealing image of Middle Eastern culture but has done much to bolster the credibility of earlier, negative narrative accounts by corroborating what they say. From narrations of honor killings, forced marriages, and *hadd* punishments to reports of derogatory speech by men about women in general, there is nothing in the narrative accounts from the first half of the century that has not been reaffirmed by indigenous authors writing about their own societies in the 1980s and 1990s.

I think it must now be obvious that everyone has a point of view that affects literary outcomes regardless of the scholarly credentials, sex, or position of the writer, and, as Lila Abu-Lughod puts it, "since every member of a society experiences life from a particular vantage point, it could be argued that a picture of society that claims generality is a fiction."[60] As a generalized category, the orientalist perspective may also be a fiction. Margaret Tidrick has shown in her work on nineteenth-century travelers to the Middle East that they all spoke in different voices and entered on their travels with distinct agendas and very different backgrounds, and their writings reflect these differences clearly. The same may be said for the members of the Arabian Mission who were, despite the commonality of their objective, different people, each carrying his or her own mental baggage and his or her own hopes, which changed over the length of time in service. Furthermore, each person's expectations were different from the start depending on whether he or she came to the Gulf in 1889, 1912, or 1940. In the end, if one wishes to produce social history for any time or place, one must recognize that the story being told is also a story about the informants whose observations and experience went into its making.

Women and Religious Learning

Piety and a Matter of Propriety

One of the means missionaries used to spread the Gospel was to circulate Bible literature in Arabic, and so they were particularly sensitive to the ability of women candidates for proselytism to read. Mission field reports were dotted with informal estimates of literacy rates and comments on who could read and who could not. Josephine Van Peursem estimated in 1911, for example, that among her limited acquaintances in Bahrain, about 3 percent could read the Qur'an.[1] Much later, in a reflective glance at the twenty years she had spent in Kuwait, Eleanor Calverley would write that "very few of the women of eastern Arabia have the ability to read."[2] Other commentators on the Gulf reiterated the missionaries' presumption of very widespread illiteracy in the Gulf and Arabian peninsula, and this presumption was echoed years later in a 1960 United Nations economic survey that reported a statistically impossible 100 percent illiteracy rate for women in Saudi Arabia.

Yet report after report from the missionaries themselves mentioning encounters with women who could read belies this presumption of vast illiteracy. In the Gulf and Arabian peninsula, there were schools, or classes, or private tutors available for the education of girls as well as boys even well before the advent of public education for girls in Saudi Arabia in 1960 and in Kuwait and Bahrain the late 1930s.

While "ignorant" is a term liberally applied to the population of the Gulf region, their "literacy"—the extent to which the population had the ability to read Arabic text—may not be the best guide for determining whether or not men and women were educated. What qualifies as "educated" is a relative judgment. In the Gulf and Arabian peninsula at the turn of the century, education meant religious learning: the objective was to know the Qur'an and parts of the Hadith, to know how to pray and how to follow the rules of behavior of the Muslim community, and this required memorization, not necessarily reading. Only at higher levels, when one studied commentaries on the Qur'an, law, Arabic grammar, medicine, and history, was the ability actually to read text taken as a qualitative advantage. Even then, standards for religious learning varied within regions and communities, depending on the religious environment and resources available. Any judgments about the education of women can only be meaningful in the context of the educational resources available in the community and women's access to those resources in comparison with men's.

Access to religious learning was influenced not only by sex difference but also by the effects of the Wahhabi movement in areas under Wahhabi rule. The evidence is overwhelming that the emphasis Muhammad ibn Abd al-Wahhab's movement placed on knowledge of Qur'an and the Prophet's Sunna—his customary behavior and opinions drawn from Hadith—brought about increased opportunities for obtaining religious learning. Theoretically, women had a share in these opportunities, and at least one scholar has even claimed that Wahhabism brought about an educational renaissance for women.[3] It should have, since the Wahhabis promoted religious learning as the only means for Muslims—men and women alike—to realize a return to pure Islam.[4] But how much do such statements tell us about what actually happened in the past? What did the Wahhabi religious revival mean in practice for education and for women's access to it? When compared with women's religious learning in the Gulf, did the Wahhabi movement bring about enhanced opportunities for women? Comparing education practices in the Gulf and in Najd shows that the Wahhabi movement did increase opportunities for women but that whatever was available to girls in Najd was still less than what was available to boys, and there is little to suggest that there was more opportunity than what was generally available to girls in the Gulf towns.

Religious Learning Among the Wahhabis

Fundamental to the practice of Wahhabi Islam since its inception has been to educate believers in the Qur'an and the Sunna so that they can live their lives according to God's laws. In "The Three Fundamentals, With Their Proofs," Muhammad ibn Abd al-Wahhab wrote: "Know—may God have mercy upon you—that it is incumbent upon us to know four principles. The first is knowledge, consisting of the recognition of God, of his prophet and of the religion of Islam, as supported by evidence from the Quran and Hadith. The second is acting according to this knowledge; the third is propagating this knowledge and the fourth is patience in the face of adversity to it."[5]

Religious knowledge is considered obligatory for both men and women,[6] and the "Three Fundamentals" specifically addresses the need for women as well as men to obtain this knowledge: "Know that God desires every Muslim man and woman [*muslim wa muslima*] to understand these three principles and to act according to them."[7] The "Three Fundamentals" have been widely circulated throughout the peninsula at least since the first conquest of Mecca in the early nineteenth century, when John Lewis Burckhardt obtained and translated a copy as the "Creed of the Wahhabis";[8] the main ideas in the "Three Fundamentals" are the same as those Georg Wallin (the Swedish philologist who studied language and religion in Najd in 1845 and 1848) recorded as fundamental to Wahhabi belief, which he determined by interviewing residents of towns and villages in northern Najd; Edwin Calverley translated and published what he thought to be the main piece of propagation literature circulated during the Ikhwan movement in 1918, and it is again word for word the "Three Fundamentals." "The Three Fundamentals" is reprinted often, sometimes under the name of the author, Muhammad ibn Abd al-Wahhab and sometimes under the name of others.

During his lifetime, Ibn Abd al-Wahhab, in partnership with Muhammad Al Sa'ud, sponsored a revival of religious learning in southern Najd. The village of Dir'iya, which was the center of power of the Al Sa'ud family, became the capital of the new Wahhabi state and the center of learning in Najd. Students from different parts of the peninsula gathered at Dir'iya in order to become learned in the Qur'an, the Hadith, and scholarly works that influenced Ibn Abd al-Wahhab's thought. These students were among the first Wahhabi missionary teachers, sent to the towns of Hejaz, to the deserts of Syria and Iraq, to Hasa, Yemen, and Asir, and to the Bedouin and townsfolk of Najd.[9]

Commentators on Arabia in the nineteenth century tell us that Ibn Abd al-Wahhab's followers carried on his educational initiative after his death, through sermons, proselytizing literature, and missionary activity and kuttab classes, which grew along with Wahhabi territorial conquests. Even in remote areas far from the center of Wahhabi hegemony in southern Najd, the movement to propagate religious learning achieved a degree of success that was noted by foreign travelers. Burckhardt, for example, remarked on the newly gained knowledge of prayer ritual among northern Anayza Bedouin in about 1812:

> The Bedouin until within a few years had not any priests among them, neither mollas not imams; but since their conversion to the Wahaby faith, mollas have been introduced by a few sheikhs, such as el-Teyar, and Ibn Esmeyr, whose young children have learned to write from one of them. The Aenezes are punctual in their daily prayers; they have no Khotbe on Fridays. They observe the fast of Ramadan with great strictness; even during their marches in the middle of summer, nothing but the apprehension of death can induce them to interrupt the fast.[10]

By contrast, speaking of the same Anayza of Syria and Mesopotamia in 1877, long after any trace of Wahhabi political influence had vanished from the region, Lady Anne Blunt remarked that she had never seen a single instance of prayer among these Bedouin.[11]

From this same journey, however, she supplies us with a description of the efforts of the Al Rashid rulers of northern Najd to instill ritual practices among the people of Jouf. "We saw an instance of Ibn Rashid's paternal government, and the first sign of Wahhabism," she wrote. "The midday prayer was called from the roof of the mosque . . . but for some time nobody seemed inclined to move. . . . Then an old man with a sour face began lecturing the younger ones, and telling them to get up and go to pray, and finding precept of no avail, at last gave them the example." When persuasion failed, two soldiers arrived, shouting at the assembled men to get up and go to the mosque, hitting them with the flat of their swords until they obeyed."[12]

So successful was the combination of missionary teaching and political domination that even after the destruction of the Wahhabi capital of Dir'iya between 1816 and 1818 and the Al Sa'ud's loss of control beyond southern Najd, the Wahhabi emphasis on religious learning still persisted in the towns of northern Najd. There, the Al Rashid family and their Shammar tribespeople, who had been converted to the doctrines of Ibn Abd al-Wahhab in the first years of the movement, supported the propagation of Wahhabi beliefs in northern Najd throughout the nineteenth century.[13]

Doughty was particularly impressed by the Wahhabi movement's influence on Bedouin he encountered in northern and central Najd. "The Wahaby rulers taught the Beduw to pray," he wrote. "They pacified the wilderness; the villages were delivered from factions; and the people instructed in letters. . . . No Beduins now obey the Wahaby; the great villages of East Nejd have sent back Abdullah's tax-gatherers [Doughty refers here to the Al Sa'ud's loss of authority in northern Najd]: but they all cleave inseparably to the reformed religion."[14]

The connection between political domination and religious indoctrination was noted by Wallin, echoing the observation Burckhardt had made some thirty years earlier and Doughty was to make thirty years later. "Like most of the tribes which were not forced to adopt the reformed doctrines of the Wahhabiye sect during the period of its ascendant power in Arabia," Wallin wrote, "the Ma'azeh [sic, a tribal group in the Tabuk region] are, in general, grossly ignorant in the religion they profess, and I scarcely remember ever meeting with a single individual of the tribe who observed any of the rites of Islam whatever, or possessed the least notion of its fundamental and leading dogmas; while the reverse might, to a certain degree, be said of those Bedouins who are, or formerly were, Wahhabiye."[15] Alois Musil, like his predecessors in northern Najd, also commented on Wahhabi influences on religious learning. On his previous visit to the Jouf region in 1909, he said, no Bedouin he encountered performed the obligatory prayers, but in 1914 he was surprised to find ritual observance common among them. The change, he said, had to be attributable to the recent conquests of the Wahhabis.[16]

The religious learning propagated by the Wahhabis did not necessarily include knowledge of reading or writing. The objective, at the most basic level, was to learn to perform the prayers; beyond that, the objective was to memorize parts of the Qur'an and Hadith. Neither of these required a knowledge of reading, for the medium of instruction was memorization through oral recitation. Reading, especially at the level necessary to read scholarly texts on religion, was a special accomplishment, which makes Wallin's assessment of literacy in Jouf all the more remarkable. For Bedouin, religious learning meant knowledge of the rituals of prayer and fasting. Even as Burckhardt had noted the attention of Bedouin to ritual practices, he could also say that "all the Bedouins throughout Arabia are equally ignorant. The Wahaby chiefs have taken pains to instruct them; they have sent Imams among the different tribes to teach the children, but their efforts have had little effect and the Bedouins remain, as might be expected, a most illiterate people."[17]

Wallin also commented on the lack of literacy among Bedouin, in spite of their adherence to rituals of prayer, although he also says that the Bedouin

valued skills in composing poetry: "Notwithstanding the prejudices entertained by Islamites, and especially by the Wahhabites, against poetry, that art
is at home in Gebel Shammar; men and women compose verses very often
extempore, and every one, young and old, knows a quantity of songs by
heart."[18] Doughty too, noted that knowledge of prayer rituals and of the
Qur'an did not mean literacy. The only literate Bedouin whom Doughty
ever met was a Bedouin member of the Al Rashid family, who were, in
Doughty's time, the ruling family of Ha'il, and this man had actually been
educated at the court of Al Sa'ud: "No man of the inhabitants of the wilderness knows letters; and it was a new pleasure to me to meet here with a let-
tered Beduwy, as it were an eye among their dull multitude, for he was well
taught and diligent, and his mind naturally given to good studies. This was
one Rashid who had been bred a scholar at er-Riath; but had since forsaken
the decaying Wahaby state and betaken himself to Hayil."[19]

In contrast, reading and writing were reported to be widespread among
townspeople in northern Najd, and there were among them scholars of the
Hadith, judges, and imams who were educated abroad. Wallin found that a
knowledge of religious ritual and literacy appeared to be more common
among Wahhabi villagers in northern Najd than he had seen anywhere else.
"As in most of the Wahhaby villages," he wrote of Jouf, "the youth are instructed in the dogmas and ceremonies of their religion, and the art of
reading and writing is more general among them than even in the Turko-
Arabian towns."[20]

Wallin asked himself the question, "what kind of education would the
most educated Najdi have acquired?" Wallin took as his paragon a man in
Ha'il who had been appointed imam of the great mosque, who he said was
called *khatib* (reader) in Najd. The educated man, he said, was one who studied in Medina, Cairo, or Riyadh. His education would consist of memorizing the whole or part of the Qur'an and the intricacies of the prayer rituals,
and he would be familiar with the legal texts of Ahmad ibn Hanbal. "He
ought moreover to be versed in the controversies between his co-religion-
ists and the other Muslims . . . but this is generally all the literary education
which the Imam possesses, and it was in vain I tried to converse with him
about other branches of Arabic literature, and even in the grammar and obscure expressions made use of in the present language of the Bedawies, I seldom obtained from him satisfactory resolution of my doubts" (p. 70). The
qadi (judge) of Ha'il, Wallin said, also studied the jurisprudence of the Hanbali school, but Wallin found that his library consisted only of works of jurisprudence purchased in Kerbala and that in other matters he was "quite as

ignorant as his spiritual colleague" (p. 71). Wallin adds that it was rare to meet a man with a knowledge of Arabic literature in northern Najd, whose inhabitants, he said, were less instructed in the Islamic sciences than were the people of the "Turco-Arabic and Persian countries, though the art of reading and writing," he commented, confirming his observation about literacy in Jouf, "is very common among them" (p. 71).

Palgrave, who visited Najd in 1862–63, gives a different view of the learning of an educated person. Commenting on his experience in Riyadh, the center of Wahhabi education, he says that the knowledge of an educated person included first the Qur'an and the Hadith but also some historical texts, commentaries on the Hadith, literature (especially poetry), and possibly medicine. Palgrave describes a learned man's library in Riyadh:

> His library was the most copious that I had yet seen in Arabia; it consisted of the works of many well-known poets, among whom were Ebn el-Atiheeyah, Motenebbi, Aboo l-Ola, besides the Divan of Hariri, the Hamasa, and other works of classic Arab literature; along with these, treatises on law and religion by Malekee and Hanbelee authors, commentaries on the Coran, books of travels, . . . [and] geographical treatises, dividing the world into seven regions. . . .
> The most interesting work for me was a manuscript history of the Wahhabee empire, preceded by a general sketch of Arab annals.[21]

From the commentators of the nineteenth century it appears that ideas about what constituted education varied over time, from village to town and from region to region, and between settled people and nomads, although all appear convinced that there was an exuberance for learning in Najd and that it was fueled by the Wahhabis. Expectations for educational achievement also varied between men and women, and one gauge of this difference is the types of schools available. Religious education in Muslim towns normally took place in kuttab (*kutatib*, pl.) schools attached to the mosque. In spite of the apparent widespread ability of Najdi townspeople to read and write, observers also comment on the paucity of schools. Wallin stated that in Ha'il, Jouf, and Jebel Shammar, there were "no public or private schools in the land, nor any lectures of consequence delivered in the mosques. The children are instructed by their fathers in the first principles of religion, and from early years taught to read the Alkur'an and to recite the prayers. Whatever they else possess of lore and knowledge, they acquire from the greatest part by oral communication with the elder, from whose company the young are never debarred in Arabia."[22] Similarly, Sulayman al-Dakhil, who wrote about Najd in 1911, thirty years after Doughty but at the beginning of the Ikhwan Bedouin settlement movement, says that the only teaching offered in Najd towns in general was on a private tutorial basis and that even the kuttab schools common in other Muslim towns were absent.[23]

The only suggestion of schooling funded by public money comes from Doughty, who specifically mentioned four "common" schools that were supported by the state, the male teachers receiving a stipend, meals at the *mudhif*, or guesthouse, of Ibn Rashid, and an occasional new suit of clothes.[24] These public schools, he said, were intended to teach boys up to the age of thirteen how to read, in the literal sense of the word (2:45). Although these schools were not for girls, some still had access to religious learning. "Townswomen of well-faring families, in all the old government of the Wahaby," wrote Doughty, "are taught the prayers, and there are some that have learned to read" (1:279).

As for Unaiza, Doughty described the city as a cosmopolitan place, whose wealthier merchants traveled abroad, spoke other languages, and talked about educating their sons at home and abroad. He also mentioned learned shaikhs who could read books other than the Qur'an (2:386–389) and said that the people of Unaiza far exceeded Ha'il in their appreciation of literature. As for girl's education, Doughty again indicated that some learned to read. After asking a friend to lend him a book to read, his friend, he wrote, "brought me the next day from Unaiza a great volume, in red leather, full of holy legends and dog-eared, that was, he said, 'of the much reading therein of the hareem.' Many of the townswomen can read in the Wahaby countries; and nearly all the children are put to learn their letters: and when a child, as they say, 'is grown to a sword's length,' he is taught the prayers" (2:472).

For such a level of learning to have been general, there must have been some corporate means of educating children, if not in mosque schools than in neighborhood tutorials supported by parents. Whatever the case, it seems clear that whatever educational opportunities existed for boys, the opportunities for girls were fewer. Absent public or mosque-funded schools for girls, their education could only have come through tutors or parents. Modesty values and seclusion practices would also have been a factor in limiting girls' access to learning. From the descriptions of all nineteenth-century visitors to Najd, girls were expected to remain at home after puberty for the sake of propriety. Of Ha'il, for example, Doughty wrote that "girls are like cage birds bred up in their houses; young maidens are not seen abroad in the public streets" (2:45).

Revivalism (1912–1930): A Leveling Influence?

"In that city men live for the next world," wrote Paul Harrison during his first journey to Riyadh in 1917 to open a "touring" medical clinic. "Hundreds are studying in the mosques to go out as teachers among the Bedouin tribes. It is the center of a system of religious education that takes in every village in Central Arabia, and imparts the rudiments of an education to much the larger part of the male population of the various towns. Great efforts are being made now, to educate the Bedouins."[25] Riyadh was then the political center of Najd and eastern Arabia and the center of propagation of the Wahhabi faith and the Ikhwan Bedouin settlement movement. According to Dr. Harrison, at the time of his visit over three hundred Ikhwan missionaries were studying in Riyadh to go out as teachers to the Bedouin.[26]

The educational system of the revival was being administered by Najdi ulama. "Under [the] general direction [of the Al Shaikh family]," wrote St. John Philby,

> the instruction and religious administration of the country was entrusted to a body of Ulama, of whom there were at this time six at Riyadh, three in Qasim, a similar number in the Hasa, and one in each of the other districts or provinces of Najd—some twenty or more in all.
>
> Besides their administrative functions, these Vicars are responsible for the administration of the Shar [sic] Law, and their decisions are binding on the provincial Amirs, who merely sign and execute them, subject of course to a discretionary power of reference to higher authorities—the Shaikhs at Riyadh and Ibn Sa'ud himself—in cases of great interest and importance. They are also responsible for the training and direction of the Mutawwa'in, who enjoy no administrative or judicial functions but are entrusted with the religious instruction of the Badawin, among whom they are distributed in the proportion of one for every fifty men. Beneath these again is a body of *Talamidh* [students] who under the guidance of the Mutaw'wa' aspire one day to be enrolled among them.[27]

Control of the educational system by ulama was appropriate, since education, by definition, meant religious education: "Learning, as Arabia understands it," wrote Hafiz Wahba, Ibn Sa'ud's minister of education in the late 1920s, "consists of interpretation of the Quran, familiarity with the Hadith . . . Muslim Law, the principles of theology, the Arabic language, and Islamic history."[28] Wahba also notes that the ulama of Najd were better educated than those of Kuwait, Bahrain, and Oman when it came to Islamic subjects. He commented, however, that intellectually they were "slavish imitators constantly drawing on the knowledge of their predecessors." Furthermore, he suggested, they are immune to information from outside: "Riyadh enjoys the distinction," he said, "of possessing an Ulema which is outstandingly fanatical and hostile towards unbelievers" (pp. 52–53).

Yet even in Riyadh during the revival, with education being funded by the ruler, religious learning was imparted by rote memorization, not actual reading. Memorization was so well understood as the goal of learning that the word for "reading," Philby tells us, actually meant reciting from memory or listening to another do so.[29] Dr. Wells Thoms observed the methods of Qur'anic education in Riyadh with the clinician's eye and noted particularly how blindness was no impediment to learning, as the rote memory method of Islamic education did not require vision, only a good memory.

> To see a person with normal vision in both eyes here is as rare as to see a one-eyed person in the average city at home. . . . It seems as if most of the priesthood and holy men have poor eyes or are blind. One day I happened to visit the home of the president of the Riadh theological seminary. The seminary was in session in the mejlis of Sheikh Mohammed bin Abdul Lateef, the holiest and wisest of the local clergy. . . . The sheikh sat on a mattress near the coffee hearth, supported by two pillows, stroking his beard and listening to the sing-song recitation of a blind mutowa or religious teacher. Ten others sat around him, of whom three were blind in both eyes, two in one eye, and five had fairly good vision in both eyes. They were learning the "hadeeth" or Islamic traditions.

The text of the Qur'an and Hadith were repeated orally until memorized. "When the student has learned these sufficiently well to be able to repeat by heart a given tradition to cover almost any question that the teacher might ask (for instance if the teacher asked how one should brush his teeth or eat a watermelon, a smart student could repeat right off, 'Prophet Mohammed, upon him our prayers and God's peace, etc. etc.') then he in turn becomes a lesser teacher in one of the twenty-two mosques."[30]

By the end of the First World War, "there was almost universal illiteracy throughout the Peninsula,"[31] Wahba wrote. In the whole Hejaz—the western province of the Arabian peninsula that did not become part of Saudi Arabia until 1924—he said, there had been only two schools that taught reading and writing, and these had been founded only in 1908, while "the whole large province of Hasa contained only one small school, and even that was not built until after the declaration of the Turkish Constitution (1911)" (p. 47). Samuel Zwemer, one of the Arabian Mission founders, gave the Ottomans more credit, for he recorded in 1890 that there were three schools in Hasa, with 3,540 pupils, according to the official Turkish report. Considering that the population of the entire province was put at 250,000, the number of pupils was small, but these students were learning secular subjects and foreign languages, subjects then not taught in Najd. There was also a very substantial mosque school just for boys, Zwemer tells us: "The large mosque with its twenty four arches and porticoes, smooth-plastered and with a mat-spread floor is always full of mischievous youth learning the mysteries of grammar and the commonplaces of Moslem theology."[32]

In the Gulf towns, Wahba says, there were also a few schools teaching secular subjects, such as simple arithmetic, in addition to or in combination with the kuttab schools. In Wahba's opinion all these schools established during the Turkish era employed the kuttab method of teaching by rote memorization and the subjects taught concentrated mainly on theology and literature. These schools, he thinks, "did very little to raise the educational level beyond reducing the number of actual illiterates."[33] In this category he includes two schools established in Bahrain, which taught reading, writing, beginning Arabic grammar, simple arithmetic, and geography, and a school set up by the shaikh of Kuwait and named "Mubarakiyya," after its founder.

Edwin Calverley had better information than Wahba about the schools in Kuwait because as an evangelical missionary he surveyed the educational facilities available looking for a niche in which to establish a mission school. He also knew a lot more about the Mubarakiyya, because this school for boys was founded as a Muslim response to the activities of the Arabian Mission. Calverley had established a school in 1912—actually just a Sunday school class for about six boys—when the editor of a Muslim journal in Cairo came to Kuwait to lecture and said publicly that Calverley's class was a "modern instance" of missionary methods of using schools and clinics to draw potential converts to Christianity. As Calverley recalls the experience, the Egyptian editor urged Kuwaitis to avoid the missionaries and make it unnecessary to go to them by providing their own medical and educational facilities. The result was the founding of the "Muslim Benevolent Society of Kuwait," which established a dispensary (which failed almost immediately after the Turkish doctor hired by the shaikh of Kuwait resigned) and a school, also supported by the shaikh's patronage.

The school, according to Calverley, was a "splendid success" and initially offered geography in addition to Qur'anic studies.[34] It opened with over one hundred students—not a small number given that the school was for Sunni boys only and the town had a total population of less than 10,000. Within two years the school had expanded its curriculum to include additional secular subjects, eventually English, and was so successful in attracting and retaining students that Calverley, still searching Kuwait for students for his own classes, could find only a handful of boys who were not already attending the Muslim school, and these boys were Christians and Jews.[35]

Over the next few years a second school for boys opened in Kuwait. This one failed to prosper, Wahba says, but not because of lack of student interest or religious opposition. The ulama in fact supported the idea of teaching secular subjects. "Its leading spirit produced a kind of 'fatwa' proving that the study of English was in accordance with Moslem tradition, but efficient teachers were not secured and most of its people left. This failure led the school's founder to send some of the young teachers to an endowed Islamic school in Baghdad for further training."[36]

The initiative taken at this early date by at least some ulama in Kuwait toward establishing education in secular subjects marks a critical difference with Wahhabi-dominated areas of the peninsula. It wasn't until the late 1920s, at least fifteen years after the beginning of secular education in Kuwait, that Abd al-Aziz tried to introduce science and other subjects to the curriculum of schools in the newly founded Kingdom of Saudi Arabia. His intention was also to increase the number of schools and to import teachers from Egypt and Syria. He also sent a number of Saudi boys to Egypt to study, in hopes that they would return home as competent teachers. Because of financial constraints, however, by 1931 the expansion and improvement of education had to be halted,[37] but there were other constraints at work as well.

Najdi ulama who controlled the educational system fought the introduction of secular subjects. Hafiz Wahba, as Ibn Sa'ud's minister of education, was familiar with the resistance of the ulama, who, in his opinion, ranked in power as equals with the emirs. In 1930 Najdi ulama protested the addition of drawing, foreign languages, and geography to the curriculum in Hejaz. The ulama based their arguments on the principle that whatever leads to something prohibited must itself be prohibited. They objected to drawing on the grounds that drawing is the same as painting, which can lead to representations of the human form. Foreign languages can lead to learning about other religions and sciences, which might lead to undermining people's faith and morals. Geography was a problem, Wahba says, because the study of the mapping of the world presupposes that the earth is round, when religious scholars have said otherwise. Even though Najdi scholars were better versed in Islamic law than the ulama of Kuwait, Bahrain, and Oman, Wahba said, doctrine was all they knew, and they were profoundly ignorant about everything else (p. 53). In Kuwait and Bahrain and, surprisingly, in Hasa too, Wahba added, communications had already diminished resistance on the part of religious scholars to innovative learning (p. 52).

Teaching and Learning for Girls: Parity with Boys?

Whether the available educational institution was a Qur'anic school or one of the new partly secular schools, whether in the Gulf towns or in the peninsula, educational resources were dedicated mainly to boys. In the atmosphere of religious revivalism in Riyadh one might have expected, since Wahhabi belief recognized women's right to a religious education, that women would attain access to religious learning to a degree comparable with that of men, but this was not the case. Public education under Abd al-Aziz was addressed to men and boys, and public recognition accrued primarily to male educational achievement. One of the most important celebrations in the life of a young boy, for example, was the *khatma*, the recital of a complete reading of the Qur'an. In Riyadh, the khatma, which was celebrated with an exhibition of marching with swords in hand, was the only form of commencement—that is, the only one known to Ameen Rihani—who leaves us the following description:

> They marched up and down the city square, the infantry with
> swords drawn, simulating a charge, followed by the cavalry. Their
> weapons glittered in the morning sun, and their cry: Sami-in,
> lami'in! (hearing and gleaming, we come!) filled the air. No drums,
> no bugles, not a musical instrument of any kind; only the sword and

the Book. It was not the Sultan's army, however, but its raw
material—the principle of its perpetuation.

The Masjid-School boys marched up and down the city square,
the boy scouts, one might say, of Wahhabism; and they were
celebrating the khatmah of one of them who had finished reading
the Koran. Thus do they in Wahhabiland.[38]

Violet Dickson witnessed a private khatma celebration for a young boy
of Ibn Sa'ud's household in 1937, fifteen years after Rihani's visit and years
after the revivalist movement had ebbed. For this occasion, around eight
hundred (male) guests performed a dance with stylized sword movements.
Dickson watched the performance in honor of the new *khatim* from a sec-
ond-story balcony of the Riyadh palace, sitting behind a latticed opening in
company with the women of the royal household.[39]

Girls too were honored for learning the Qur'an, but in a less public
forum. At about the same time that Ameen Rihani was a guest of Ibn Sa'ud
in Riyadh, little girls in Unaiza also celebrated the memorization of a portion of the Qur'an. This celebration, as described by Soroya Altorki and
Donald Cole, was called a *zaffah*, which means simply "procession."

The girl was dressed up for the occasion in gold and fancy clothes
and passed in the zaffah from the house of her teacher through the
nearby streets accompanied by singing. The procession led to her
parents' home, where a reception was held in the women's
quarters of the house. Incense was burned and usually a meal was
served for her teacher, schoolmates, and other female neighbors
and relatives. The zaffah usually coincided with the onset of puberty, at which time veiling and seclusion became mandatory for girls.
Since they had to stay at home from this period on, many forgot
much of what they had learned, although a few who made special
efforts to obtain some reading material were able to develop and
maintain their literacy.[40]

This passage suggests that girls' education was not supported by the mosque
but took place in private homes and only during the years before the onset
of puberty. Any further education for girls would therefore have required
the expense of a private tutor or a helpful relative.

In these Qur'anic schools the goal, as elsewhere, was to memorize the
Qur'an, not to learn to actually read text. Altorki and Cole say that "each

girl had a small wooden board on which a verse from the Quran would be written, and when this verse was memorized, it would be washed off and a new one written" (p. 95). The student could thus learn to recognize certain written words and phrases in context as cues to a Qur'anic verse but would not be able to translate the memorized words or phrases into the functional ability to read other texts in classical Arabic or texts in modern Arabic.

When Philby traveled to Unaiza with Abd al-Aziz in 1918, he made an observation about the educational system there that suggests the goals of learning for boys were only marginally higher than the expectations for girls, although for boys there were Qur'an schools. "The only education in Anaiza," he wrote, "was the 'Quran-teaching madaris.' " Philby listened to the son of his Unaizi host as the boy read for Philby's benefit and commented, "The boy could read or spell out the sacred text with some difficulty, but was unable to write. Our host had two sons, the younger of whom could read while the elder had not even reached that standard—neither could write, and they marveled to hear that my son . . . frequently wrote letters to me."[41]

The Najdi and Wahhabi ambivalence toward the education of girls was a feature common to the whole Gulf region. Every description indicates no publicly funded schools, or few schools, or schools of lesser quality for girls. Before 1911, for example, when the first mission school for girls was opened in Basra, the only other educational facilities for Arab Muslim girls were the "little Quran schools where gabbling youngsters sat cross-legged on the floor, swaying to and fro as they learned the Holy Book by rote."[42] There was also a Jewish girls' school and a Catholic girls' school, and later, in 1914, while Basra was still under the Turkish government, one government-sponsored girls' school for the entire Basra province opened. The school was held in one mud-brick, unplastered room lined with benches to accommodate about twelve students, and the curriculum included the Qur'an, Hadith, arithmetic, Turkish, and needlework.[43] For boys in Basra, in addition to Qur'an schools there were numerous government schools that taught secular subjects. The language of instruction in these schools, however, was Turkish, so they appealed more to the sons of Ottoman officials, according to mission reports, than to Arabic-speaking Iraqis. The language barrier in the Turkish schools drew students to the mission school for boys, where the language of instruction was Arabic, and Turkish, French, and English were offered as foreign-language subjects. The mission school for girls was successful too: in 1925 the mission was operating two schools for girls, and in both well over half the students were Muslims, a fact highlighted in field reports because mission schools usually appealed more to Christians and Jews, even though Muslims were their primary target.[44]

In Bahrain, Qur'an memorization schools were established in residential neighborhoods and commercial districts, and at least some of these schools taught little girls and boys together. More boys than girls attended these schools, however, as the following 1914 description of a school in Bahrain suggests:

> The native school finds itself between other houses. Some are found in the bazaar, amidst the noise and bustle of Eastern trading. . . . The building is generally a small, low, dark, date-sick hut, without windows to let in the light. The dim light inside comes only through a small hole used for the door. . . . The scholars sit on the ground along the wall, with their date-leaf mats beneath them. . . . The number of Bahraini school children is difficult to estimate. There is no roll kept of pupils in attendance, and so the only way of getting an estimate is by observing the size of the different schools. The lowest estimate made by Arabs is eight hundred boys and four hundred girls. The average number in a boys' school is twenty-five. . . . We seldom find more than one teacher in each school. The teacher knows his flock well, for he is generally held in high esteem by the family of the boys. . . . The boys and girls are generally far apart. Most of the boys in these schools come from well-to-do families. The boys of the poorer class are compelled to go out with the parents to help to make a living.[45]

Yet again, in the Qur'anic classes, the method employed was not geared toward actually teaching reading or writing, even in the boys' classes. The mullahs or mutaww'as who taught in the schools "know the Koran perfectly and are fairly well versed in Arabic religious literature," wrote Garrit Van Peursem of the Bahrain mission. The Qur'an

> is the only text-book, although the older boys are taught the Traditions privately. The beginner is started with a small book containing the Arabic alphabet and small words until it runs into the first Sura of the Koran. . . . The method of teaching used in Bahrain is that of endless repetition. . . . Under this method it takes some boys years before they can read the Koran, while others never learn, although

they can quote passages. Some are able to read the Koran but not a newspaper, even when printed in the easiest Arabic.   *(pp. 13–14)*

A description of religious training of little girls in Bahrain written in 1923 suggests that girls began their education late and finished early and that only a few even went to school:

> When about eight years old, only the minority of girls are sent to a neighborhood teacher, generally an old woman, who gathers some fifteen children around her, the boys on the one side, the girls on the other, and teaches them the Koran. Each pupil comes in turn to sit beside her while she points out the lesson, word for word, and then sends the child back to practice with the others till her turn to read with the teacher comes around again. The stick is in frequent use to help both memory and manners of the children.[46]

Until 1919 there were no indigenous schools offering secular subjects for either boys or girls in Bahrain. That year Paul Harrison was stationed in Manama when the ruling family attempted to establish a school to be supported with private funds, and this was to be a school for boys only. A son of the shaikh of Bahrain had gone to England at the expense of the British government, and on his return he invited the merchants of Bahrain to make contributions to an education fund,[47] resulting in the founding of the al-Hidaya School for Sunni boys in Muharraq. Ten years later a second school was built for Shi'a boys in Manama,[48] and the first school for girls was opened.[49] Over the next few years, additional schools supported by private funds were opened, including a few for girls, but the disparity between the facilities available is evident in the numbers of girls and boys attending: in 1931, for example, five hundred boys and one hundred girls were enrolled in these schools.[50] Even in 1951, two years after the first secondary school for girls had opened,[51] there were half as many girls as boys in public schools (4,500 boys and 2,300 girls).[52]

In this vacuum the mission managed for two decades to maintain schools for both boys and girls, and the girls' school continued into a third decade. In 1925 the enrollment in the girls' school was forty-five, and the school offered arithmetic, geography, writing, sewing, English, and the Bible in Arabic ("one Christian, 12 Jews, and 32 Muslims, the latter divided into 17 Arabs, 8 Persians, 3 Negresses and 4 Indians").[53] In 1932, even after the opening of public schools for girls, enrollments in the mission schools more than doubled, to 110 girls and 143 boys.[54] In the same year, however, a Jewish school opened for boys, and all the Jewish students left and the first of many new private Muslim schools also opened. Given the increasing availability of educational options for boys, the mission school could not compete for students, and by 1936 the boys' school ceased to be mentioned in the mission's annual reports. An indication of the limited curriculum and smaller number of schools available to girls in comparison to what was available to boys is that the mission school for girls continued successfully, with over a hundred students each year to the beginning of the 1950s, closing only after the Bahrain public schools finally offered programs for girls beyond the elementary level.

During all those years Qur'an teachers continued offering Qur'an memorization classes. Public secular education had removed some of the cachet from these classes, and, as this 1949 description suggests, for boys and girls alike Qur'anic memorization had come to be taken as preparation before elementary schooling began rather than the object of education in itself: "[The very young boys and girls] sit on the ground or on flat date baskets with their Koran stands, made of two crossed pieces of wood, in front of them, all reading aloud in high-pitched voices. Hajjia sits on a mat near them with her nargileh in front of her and has a puff at the pipe every few minutes while she listens to them. . . . Most of [the children] stay for a few months only ('dalil' as she calls this preparatory period) and then go on to the public schools."[55]

Sarah Hosmon, a missionary physician with the Oman mission, wrote in 1916 about the limited schooling available to girls in Musqat, mentioning also that in the Qur'an schools boys, and boys alone, were taught to write as well as to recite the Qur'an. "A little girl begins her schooling at four years and finishes after four or six months. Of course, some are in school later. I have seen girls in the school at Bahrain until they were twelve years old, but this is not a general rule. When schooling is over they learn to cook, keep house and to sew. As soon as the parents can find a husband for their daughter, they get her married. There are some who marry as young as eleven years and the most of them marry at thirteen and fourteen years of age."[56] Minnie Dykstra, who went to Musqat from the Bahrain mission in 1931, mentions that for years the Musqat mission had tried to offer classes for girls but finally gave up as none would come, and except for a brief period during World War II all the educational work in Musqat was for boys.[57]

For Kuwait, the missionary record is almost silent on the matter of indigenous schools for girls during the early years of the century, and the reason is that there were none until 1916, when one woman who had learned the Qur'an from her father set up classes in her own home.[58] Despite the lack of available classes, the missionaries never even tried to establish a mission school for girls because the idea of girls' being educated, they felt, had not yet been accepted by Kuwaitis, and trying to introduce girls to a Christian education would have been completely impossible. (Anything the missionary literature refers to as a school for girls run by missionaries in Kuwait was nothing more than a class for the few female hospital servants, foreign workers, or patients who were children.) By contrast, there had been Qur'anic schools for boys operating as least as early as 1887 (p. 46), and by the time the first Qur'anic school for girls was set up, the Mubarakiyya for boys (mentioned above) had been open for four years. In addition, Edwin Calverley's mission school for boys was also open, and students were studying English by reading Bible passages and learning Arabic grammar, composition, arithmetic, geography, and history.[59]

Many more Qur'anic schools for girls opened after the first, and by 1926 there were twenty-five, by Calverley's count, along with twenty-seven for boys, eleven for Persians, and one religious school each for Jews and Christians. All these schools, he said, were due to the private enterprise of individuals who set themselves up as teachers, and they taught only scripture. Moreover, Calverley added, when a girl finished her Qur'anic class, she had completed her education (p. 13). In the same year Calverley was writing, 1926, the enterprising wife of a Turkish schoolmaster started the first school for girls to offer nonreligious subjects (reading and writing, embroidery and dressmaking). Other women eventually set up their own private schools as a way to earn an income, but it was only in 1937 that the state assumed responsibility for educating girls and established the first state-funded girls school.[60]

As in Najd, attempts to modernize education increased the disparity between boys' and girls' educational options. The boys Mubarakiyya, in spite of Wahba's cynical assessment of the quality of education offered, operated on a substantial endowment. In 1926, fourteen years after it was founded and the first year there was any nonreligious schooling for girls, the school had a director and six teachers, 220 students in graded classes, and a curriculum that included the Qur'an, traditions, canon law, ethics, Arabic reading, composition, and grammar, along with arithmetic, geography, history, and English. It did not however, pretend to offer more than a primary education. A second school for boys, the Ahmadiya, founded about 1922, was less well endowed financially but offered the same curriculum to 165 students. In addition, Kuwait had a school for orphaned and poor boys supported by a single family of pearl merchants, with a curriculum of history, arithmetic, and the Qur'an. For boys, there were still more options: eight privately run schools that taught arithmetic along with the Qur'an and elementary religious subjects, and also sixteen "mulla" schools, equivalent in terms of subject matter to the girls' Qur'an schools; one Hebrew school; and three Persian schools that offered writing and arithmetic in addition to the Qur'an.[61]

By 1945, eight years after the first state-funded school for girls opened, when the population of Kuwait had become significantly more diverse and oil money was flowing, there were two government schools for girls where, Kuwait missionaries reported, several hundred students were "receiving a good general education."[62] In 1954 Kuwaiti schools had adopted a British-style dress code (plaid dresses for the girls, green jackets and gray trousers for the boys), and the girls' curriculum included intramural basketball along with Arabic, geography, mathematics, history, and science. Still, that same year there were twenty-four schools for boys and only six for girls inside the old city walls.[63]

Reading: A Matter of Propriety?

Even though memorization was the goal of a Qur'anic education, there were still many people who learned to read and write, and a hundred years of commentaries by missionaries and travelers show that some of these literate persons were women.[64] A knowledge of reading and writing could be an asset for a woman, bringing both recognition and income for performing as an imam for other women, as a reader at group religious ceremonies, and as a healer who recites holy words over the sick. The *maulaya* (female teacher; in some places called *mutawwa'a*) was often able to read not only the Qur'an, but other texts as well.[65] In Darain, a Sunni town forty-five miles from Bahrain, for example, women of the Bahrain mission encountered a mutawwa'a who could read the New Testament in Arabic,[66] and Shiite maulayas read the poetic histories of the Prophet's life and the Imam Hussein's death.

The professional reader could also sell her readings for the religious merit of another: "The woman who could read the Koran, and the majority of women never learn to read," wrote Eleanor Calverley, "gains great merit by each completion of the recitation from cover to cover. She can divert this merit to the account of some departed loved one or she may sell it to another person who is willing to pay for the act of reading."[67] According to Edwin Calverley, "a khatmah, a complete reading of the Koran, could be assigned to the account of the dead Muslims from the Prophet down to the Muslimin and the Muslimat, but with special reference to the dead father and forefathers of the man who has the khatmah performed, or who buys one that is performed. The prices in Kuweit vary . . . depending upon the religiosity of the one who says he has completed a khatmah." A maulaya among the Wahhabi could also teach, lead prayers, and read prayers but would not be expected to sell Qur'an readings to raise the account of a deceased person. In fact to offer such readings is abhorrent to the Wahhabis. According to the *Taqwiat al-Iman* (Strengthening the Faith), Edwin Calverley says, the Wahhabis specifically oppose the idea of reading the Koran, giving alms, fasting, or doing other good works for the benefit of a dead person, as this is *shirk al-'adat* (ordinary or customary polytheism): acts thought of as attempts to counter God's judgment of a person who is already dead and to interfere with the direct relationship between the deceased individual and God.[68] Still, the maulaya derived great prestige by virtue of her education.

Why then was a knowledge of reading and writing not sought by parents for their daughters as it was for their sons? One reason had to do with propriety. Everywhere in the Gulf and Arabian peninsula, Wahba tells us, the ability of a woman to write was looked on with ambivalence. "Writing is very seldom taught," he wrote, "and in many parts of Arabia it is generally considered to be a drawback to a woman to be able to write."[69] Abd al-Aziz expressed the ambivalence of society toward women reading in a conversation with Philby: "It is permissible," said the king on one occasion, "for women to read (actually meaning to listen to the reading of) the Quran and scriptural literature, but ordinary reading, and especially writing, is an accomplishment regarded as unsuitable in a woman, though not forbidden."[70] In Kuwait, Calverley wrote that, except in rare instances, the art of writing was not taught to girls. One of her patients gave her this reason: "If our wives knew how to write, how could we prevent them from writing to other men?" "Usually," Calverley added, "a letter (always a formal epistle, at best) must be written by a male relative or a paid scribe."[71]

Some viewed the ability of women to read and write with suspicion, if not alarm. Mrs. Garritt Pennings, writing from Bahrain, commented that "it would be considered a family disgrace if a girl learned to write. Why should she want to write and to whom? Few learn to read well enough to be able to read from any other book, many don't even finish the Koran."[72] According to Dr. Hosmon of the Musqat mission, writing was only for boys; a girl was "sent to a Koran school where she learns to read only the Koran. The boys have one other branch of study, which is writing. Sometimes the girl learns it also, but this is very seldom because here at Maskat, I am told, the girls are not allowed to learn to write, for their husbands are afraid to trust them with so convenient an accomplishment."[73]

This ambivalence about women's reading and writing, added to modesty and seclusion values, contributed to the gap between the educational opportunities for boys and girls, a gap that widened as the era of modernization began.[74] In 1942, the sons of Abd al-Aziz were privately educated by shaikhs who were brought from Mecca especially for them, while their sisters had no such tutors.[75] Until the year of Abd al-Aziz's death in 1953, the same year in which public secular education for boys began, there was still no school for girls of the king's family, and no publically funded schools for girls at all.[76] The question of the appropriateness of educating girls to read and write was not resolved in Saudi Arabia until 1960, and even then girls' education met with resistance that took a few years to overcome.

In every community in the Gulf, as long as knowledge was equated solely with religious learning, education was presumed to be the responsibility of the religious establishment or the family, not of the state. For the individual, then, educational achievement depended largely on one's family resources and the availability of local mosque instructors. Ibn Sa'ud, because he united religion and state and promoted religion for political purposes, was the only ruler in the region before oil money began to flow to put the burden of education on the state. His initial attempt at promoting secular education in the late 1920s was not successful, however, and ultimately Saudi Arabia was among the last of the Gulf states to provide it.

Whether the state, the religious establishment, or private donors sponsored education, for girls the end product was the same. Without exception, in every community in the Gulf and Arabian peninsula, whatever opportunities for education the local community afforded its members, there were fewer for girls than for boys. Where the mosque or the state funded schools, there were fewer available for girls than for boys, and girls were able to attend these schools for shorter periods of time because of social attitudes about girls leaving the house after puberty. Girls' education, especially at a level beyond the kuttab school, necessitated private tutors, and so among girls the disparity in educational achievement ran along class lines more so than was the case for boys. Generally, even when girls had access to educational opportunities, they were not offered the opportunity to learn to read or to write to the same extent that boys were, although neither subject was considered critical to either a girl's or boy's education. Furthermore, because of notions of propriety, girls in general were actually discouraged from learning to read and write.

Under the Wahhabis, women were theoretically entitled to religious learning at the same level enjoyed by men. During the revival, however, the energies of the Wahhabi regime, which sponsored classes, paid teachers to teach and students to learn, and sent missionaries across the land to teach, were directed primarily toward the religious education of men and boys. Still, there is no question that the Wahhabi movement stimulated an appreciation of learning that must have encouraged families to provide religious education for their daughters and therefore increased women's access to learning relative to what had been available before the revival began. Descriptions suggest that many women under the Wahhabis achieved competence in Qur'an memorization, the recitation of prayers, and knowledge of some Hadith literature.

Religious learning, however, was valued everywhere, and the many examples of highly literate teachers and prayer readers among women and the respect they derived from their reputations for being educated testify to the commitment of some families and of society to religious education for girls. While most women couldn't read text, the educational system for both boys and girls hadn't been designed to promote this skill. What it was designed to do—to teach students to recite the Qur'an and Hadith and to pray—it achieved. While missionaries complained of the lack of literacy, they also— as the next chapter shows—complained of women's constant and regular attention to religious worship, a devotion that was precisely what the educational system had been designed to foster.

The disparity between men and women in educational achievement only increased over the first half of the century, as opportunities for secular education offered by the mosque, by private enterprise, and by the state were directed toward the benefit of boys. The disparity between boys and girls in the distribution of religious learning can be seen as a logical reflection of gender hierarchies in the society as a whole, as a means by which these hierarchies could be reinscribed back into society: girls were taught enough to buy into an assigned role, a role in which they were subordinate to men, but not enough to challenge it.

CHAPTER TWO

Prayer, the Mosque, and the Ways Women Worship

"Mosques are for men to pray in," Paul Harrison wrote, after having lived in the Gulf region for fifteen years. "Women are supposed to pray just as faithfully as the men, but they pray at home."[1] Women did pray at home, with devotion and regularity, as mission observers over the years documented in their field reports. Prayer performed exclusively at home, however, does not fulfill the highest standards of orthodox worship, which requires regularity, a knowledge of correct prayers, and, at least on Fridays, praying with a group in the mosque. These are standards that can only be wholly fulfilled by men.

The Wahhabis raised prayer in the mosque to an even higher level of importance than was the case in the Gulf towns: it become the very emblem of the community living according to God's laws, signaling membership in the political community of believers. During the revival era as well as at times during the nineteenth century, the state enforced male attendance at mosque worship. In general, women under the Wahhabis were afforded greater access to religious learning and, unlike their Gulf sisters, had at least limited access to the mosque. Did this mean that these women were able to fulfill their ritual obligations to the same degree as men?

The presence or absence of particular groups of people in the mosque and their physical placement when in it reveal much about the relative positions of men and women in social life. John Bowen has observed that as a social model the power of prayer comes from the fact that it is obligatory and, when performed in the mosque, public. Orthodox prayer, he says, "makes public particular ideas about the arrangement of men and women in social life: about hierarchy, social boundaries and the nature of communication."[2] Hierarchies of gender are obvious to any observer of prayer ritual in the mosque. There is more to ritual experience than what occurs in the mosque, however, and there are competing notions over whose ritual experience is of greater value. Outside the mosque, women have their own ways of experiencing rituals of spirituality and community, from mourning celebrations to the observance of saints' days, votive offerings, shrine visitations, and rituals of spirit possession. Whether Sunni or Shi'a, women in the Gulf region, as well as in the Hejaz—in fact everywhere except in the Wahhabi Najd—have had alternatives to prayer in the mosque or prayer at home. Under the Wahhabis, however, all these alternative rituals were suppressed. This lack of alternatives in the ways women may worship is the great divide that distinguishes the religious and social experiences of women of the Najd.

The Meaning of Prayer

Where Should One Do It and How?

Prayer is the essence of Muslim religious practice. A prayer manual approved by the General Presidency of Scientific Research, If'ta, Islamic Propagation and Guidance of the Kingdom of Saudi Arabia, says that prayer is the first and most important obligation among the five pillars of the Faith, "the line which divides Islam from non-Islam." Prayer is considered to be not only of spiritual significance but also a means by which a believer accumulates merit toward a favorable judgment before God in the life to come. According to Hadith selected for inclusion in this manual, prayer that is faithfully performed and correctly executed will open the gates of Paradise to the believer: "The Prophet said, 'the first thing that the servant of God will be called to account for on the Day of Judgment will be Prayer. If it was good, his deeds will have been good; if it was bad, his deeds will have been bad.' "[3]

The value of prayer in orthodox Sunni Islam is profoundly influenced by the manner in which it is performed and the place in which it is offered. Prayer is best performed punctually, according to a set formula, and not by the solitary worshiper but in company with other Muslims. Islam "requires Muslims to gather together for prayer in the mosques, to get to know each other, to be on good terms with each other, to be loyal and sincere towards each other, and to treat each other with truth and patience." Referring to the Hadith, the manual states that "Islam considers congregational prayer to be twenty-seven times better than solitary prayer, which demonstrates how glorious and important is the act of praying together" (p. 52).

For prayer to be considered communal, the worshiper must pray with at least one other person. If one of these persons is a man and the other a woman, the woman may not act as imam, that is, she may not lead the other in prayer. When both are men, the following rule applies: "If you wish to perform the prayer and there is only one other person with you, the one who is to be led stands to the right of the one who is leading, but not behind him." But if one is a woman and the other a man, the woman "must stand behind that man and not to his right" (pp. 54–55). Even if a woman praying at home has a companion with whom she can join in prayer, her prayers will not quite qualify for the full benefit of public congregational prayer that a man may obtain by praying in larger company in a mosque. "The reward for congregational prayer will be obtained even though there are only two, one of whom is a child or a woman, *although the greater the number the better it is*" (p. 53; italics mine). In fact, however, no matter how many people pray together, only worship in a public forum can fulfill the essence of congregational prayer, which is, as the manual states, the demonstration of the equality of all men before God, "the most glorious of Islamic religious acts, whereby the old and the young, the rich and the poor, the powerful and the wretched, all stand before God with no difference between them, all the same" (pp. 53–54).[4]

Paul Harrison could have been reading from the same prayer manual when he described the worship services with which he was familiar. "Prayers may be performed privately at home but it is reckoned much more meritorious to pray with the congregation in the mosque. In congregational service a leader intones the prayer, and all join in the 'A-min' with which the different paragraphs close. The hundreds of worshippers stand in long rows, and as the leader ends each paragraph, the deep musical 'A—min' of the response sounds almost like the tone of a great organ." In one of the numerous literary moments in which this Christian missionary appears on the verge of conversion, Harrison adds,

> I know of few more impressive sights than sunset prayers in the
> large city mosque, or better still, out under the open sky in the
> limitless desert. Line behind line, they stand and kneel and pros-

trate themselves together. The master is there with his slave. The man who has spent twenty years in the schools stands next to a Bedouin who can neither read nor write. The richest man of the community stands next to one who is just out of jail for debt. No one is surprised, for it is the ordinary thing. It would surprise them to be told that there are places in this world where men persist in their conceits and divisions even when standing in the presence of the omnipotent God.[5]

The observations of Georg Wallin suggest that theory met popular practice in mid-nineteenth century Ha'il as well. Subsequent to his research on religious practice in Najd in 1845 and 1848, Wallin reported that communal prayer was so important to the Wahhabis of Ha'il that it was taken to be one of two pillars of faith:

The two principal tenets of the Wahhaby doctrine, to which the Shammar still unalterably adhere, are the rejection of all saints, even the Prophet himself, as mediator between God and man; and secondly, the necessity of saying the prayers publicly in a mosque, in common with a congregation, and not alone at home, as is the general custom with other Muhammadans. In consequence of this rule every different quarter in the villages is generally provided with a mosque of a smaller size, where the people assemble at the time of the five daily prayers, in order to perform their devotion in common; and in Hail there is besides, a larger one in the palace of Ibnu Alrashid himself, where the whole congregation meets on Friday to make their holy-day prayer and hear the sermon delivered on the occasion.[6]

The mosque, in addition to being the place where ritual obligations were fulfilled, was in a very real sense the place where men learned their religion. It is the site of higher religious training as well as one of the places for Qur'an classes; after the formal prayers, Harrison writes, sermons, Hadith readings, and religious discussions took place, as well as the exchange of political gossip. Wallin described the centrality of the mosque in the religious life of Jouf in northern Najd: "After the prayer of noon the Khatib generally interprets some tradition of the Prophet, or some verses of Alkuran, or explains the Wahhaby doctrine of the unity of God, and the impropriety of rendering worship to saints, this being the principal point of controversy between the Wahhabies and other Muslims" (p. 55). William Gifford Palgrave's later (1862–1863) description of the goings-on in the Grand Mosque in Ha'il mentions informal learning and discussion. Afternoon prayers, he wrote,

> are invariably followed by the reading aloud of a chapter or section selected from some traditionary work, and to this often succeeds a short extemporary sermon or commentary on what has been read. . . . When prayer is over, about half the congregation rise and depart. Those who remain in the mosque draw together next the centre of the large and simple edifice, and seat themselves on its pebble strewn floor, circle within circle; some lean their backs against the rough square pillars. . . . In the midmost of the assembly a person selected as reader, but neither Imam nor Khateeb, who is supposed to be better acquainted with letters than are the average of his countrymen, besides being gifted with a good and sonorous voice, holds on his knees a large manuscript. . . . It contains the traditions of the prophet, or the lives of his companions, or perhaps El-Bokharee's commentaries, or something else of the kind. Out of this he reads in a clear but somewhat monotonous tone. . . . This kind of lecture lasts ordinarily from ten minutes to a quarter of an hour, and is listened to in decorous silence, while all who have any pretensions to religious feeling, and these form of course a large proportion of those present on such occasions, look down on the ground, or fix their eyes on the reader and his volume.[7]

The mosque offered space not only for communal prayer and learning but also for socializing. Not only is prayer "more efficacious and meritorious if performed in the mosque," commented Paul Harrison, but "there is the added attraction of friends to meet."[8] The mosque, he wrote, is the center of town life, with neighborhood mosques serving perhaps fifty to two hundred families, male members only, which fosters, he says, "neighborliness as well as religion." The mosque "serves as an inn where any belated traveler may rest for the night, where the poor who must beg for their living can sleep, and where any man who is sick may rest till he recovers, if he has no better place to go. . . . This function of the mosques as philanthropic institutions is very important. No beggar, no traveler, no stranded sick man need lack for shelter, at least, in any Mohammedan city" (p. 236).

The mosque, then, is the place where obligatory prayer can be most perfectly fulfilled. It is also the town hostel, speakers' corner, public school, and charitable society—in short, the center of community life, and especially so under the Wahhabis. But how did women engage with the center of community life? Clearly the place of women has been a question recognized since the formalization of the Muslim schools of law in the second century A.H., because the question of whether women should be allowed in the mosque is addressed in numerous Hadith, as the following two examples illustrate: "Ibn Umar reported on the authority of the Prophet, who said, 'When your women ask your permission to go to the mosque at night, give them permission.' . . . A wife of Umar used to attend the morning and 'Isha prayers in congregation in the mosque. It was said to her, 'Why doest thou go forth and thou knowest that 'Umar does not like this and is averse to it.' She said, 'What prevents him from prohibiting me?' He said, 'What prevents him is the saying of the Messenger of Allah, "Do not prohibit the handmaids of Allah from attending the mosques of Allah." '"[9]

Because some Hadith acknowledge women's right to attend the mosque, from a theological perspective there should be no barrier to this, and in many countries, such as Kashmir, Indonesia, and Iran and in the Grand Mosque at Mecca in Hejaz, for example, they do. The attitude prevailing in Najd and in the Gulf during the first half of the twentieth century, however, was that they should not, at least not all the time, or, if they do, at least not in close proximity to men. The prayer manual mentioned above addressed the question of women in the mosque this way: "It is permitted for women to attend the congregation in the mosque and their husbands may not prevent them from doing so unless it is feared that harm will come to them. However, it is preferable for women to perform the prayer in the house rather than in the mosque."[10] In this context, "harm will come to them" is a euphemism for women's perceived potential for inspiring harmful behavior in men—*fitna*, or social chaos—by tempting men sexually and distracting them from their spiritual purpose in the mosque.

The Mosque, Political Authority, and the Community of Male Believers

From a theological perspective, individual performance of the five daily prayers is obligatory, and communal prayer in the mosque at least on Fridays is an obligation on the community as a whole. In all Muslim communities, therefore, public scrutiny can act to pressure the individual to attend mosque services. The Wahhabis, however, actually enforced mosque atten-

dance. Both the Al Sa'ud and the Al Rashid ruling families assumed the obligation to enforce communal prayer, in order to signify their legitimacy to
rule over a Muslim community. The rationale for the role of the ruler in an
Islamic government was laid out by Ibn Taimiyyah (d. 1328 A.D.), the jurist
whose writings were most influential on Ibn Abd al-Wahhab's thought:

> Enjoining good is to look after the enforcing of Allah's orders
> regarding prayers, alms, fasting, pilgrimage, truthfulness, honesty,
> obedience to the parents, maintaining close relations with members
> of the family, friendly associations with the relatives and the neigh-
> bours, and the like. It is the duty of any man in authority to order
> all people under his jurisdiction to preserve prayer and to punish
> those who neglect to pray. He is called upon to do that by consen-
> sus of all Muslims. If those neglecting to perform prayer were a
> rebellious group, they should be fought.
>   . . . If those neglecting prayer were individuals, the situation
> would be different. Some jurists say that the individual neglecting
> to pray should be punished by beating or by imprisonment until he
> resume performing prayer. The majority of jurists maintain that
> such an individual is asked first to repent and to resume performing
> his prayers; if he insists on his attitude of refusal to perform prayer,
> he ought to be killed.[11]

Ibn Abd al-Wahhab had used Ibn Taimiyya's theory of the role of the ruler
to rationalize the Al Sa'ud's initial conquests in the late eighteenth and early
nineteenth centuries, so prayer in the mosque became one of the emblems of
political legitimacy during the revival era. At the height of the Wahhabi revival
under Ibn Sa'ud, recorded instances of Wahhabi coercion of men to attend
congregational prayers were legion. Paul Harrison, writing of his 1917 medical tour to Najd, cites the ruler's enforcement of mosque attendance as one
of the elements distinguishing the "fanatical Wahhabis" of "inland Arabia" from
Sunnis elsewhere. "Men pray five times a day in Riadh," he writes. "In the winter the roll is called at early morning prayers, and also at the service in the late
evening. Absentees are beaten with twenty strokes on the following day. In the
summer, duties in the date gardens and elsewhere are considered a valid excuse for praying at home. Only a few years ago, a man absented himself for
some days from all prayers, and was publicly executed for so doing."[12]

After subsequent trips to Riyadh, Harrison again talked about enforcement of mosque attendance: "The roll is called at early morning prayers and any man who is absent is hunted up and hailed before the judge. Sickness is an adequate excuse and if on some account the absentee prayed in another mosque, he is dismissed as blameless, but if he was simply too lazy to get up in time for such early devotions, he is publicly beaten to increase his zeal." Then Harrison told of another death, this time of a man in Riyadh who "decided that he had prayed enough, and absented himself from all prayers for a week," admitting that he was simply "tired of praying so much." "He was executed on a high gallows," Harrison says, "his body left there as an example for the general public. His father, who came to intercede for the foolish boy, was publicly beaten for so far making himself an accomplice in the heinous crime of infidelity."[13]

Ameen Rihani, who was Ibn Sa'ud's guest after accompanying him back to Riyadh from the Uqair conference in 1922, wrote, "At every masjid in ar-Riyadh there is a list-call every day, mornings and evening. And when anyone of the regular attendants is absent a committee is sent to his home. If he is sick, they offer their assistance; if he has overslept himself, they offer their advice; if he is remiss, they pronounce a warning; if he is absent a second time, they give him a lecture and a rating; and if in spite of all this benign tolerance he persists in his remissness, the palm-switch is applied without hesitation or mercy."[14]

In Ha'il men were also punished for failing to attend mosque prayers. British captain G. E. Leachman mentions a beating meted out in 1911 under the Rashid rulers, and Wallin leaves us an observation from the mid-nineteenth century: "The Wahhaby princes keep a strict eye upon assembling the people to the Friday prayer, and there were in Hail many instances of Abd Allah's having severely punished several men for default of attending to the service."[15] According to virtually every foreign observer of the Arabian towns under the Wahhabis, public congregational prayer in the mosque on Fridays was obligatory, and in some towns during certain periods of zealousness, it was obligatory every day for all five prayers.

Did Women in Practice Attend the Mosque?

Neither the elevation of the mosque as political center under the Wahhabis nor the emphasis on the importance of mosque prayer in theological texts tells us whether women actually attended services in the mosque. Harrison—as well as many other missionary correspondents—says that the exclusion of women from the mosque in the Gulf towns was absolute; "only in Oman do they pray in mosques and then not with the men but in mosques of their own." "The Friday services," he adds, "are frequently listened to by numbers of women. They can be seen sitting closely veiled outside the sacred precincts."[16]

Harrison's observations suggest that women wanted to get as close to the mosque as possible, and there was every reason for them to want this, because the mosque was conceived as the place closest to God's ear, the place where God could best hear their voices and answer their needs. Women felt their exclusion, Eleanor Calverley thought, because Hadith known to the person on the street elevated the value of mosque prayer over prayer offered outside. "Prayer in the mosque or public place of worship," she wrote, "is said to bring twenty-seven times more merit to the believer than prayer in other places. Yet Arab women are not allowed to pray within the mosque."[17] For Calverley, the reason for their exclusion had little to do with theology and everything to do with the ideal of women's seclusion taking precedence over the ideal of communal worship in the mosque. In her personal experience, the seclusion of women had in fact been preferred to the delivery of life-saving medical care, and she had numerous times performed surgeries on the floor in patients' homes because a husband refused to let his wife go to the hospital or was traveling and had forbidden his wife to leave the home in his absence.

While in Najd the Wahhabis included women as believers who should attend worship services in the mosque, in practice, the tension between the ideal of mosque worship and the attitudes underlying women's seclusion rendered women's attendance at the mosque an ambiguous proposition. Philby found that women's participation in public prayer in Riyadh was limited to special occasions. In 1918 he described the feast-day prayer ground in Riyadh as a large, bare, oblong space enclosed by a low mud wall with a qibla niche in the middle on the western side. This space, used for congregational prayers only on the great feast days, was reckoned to be large enough to contain the whole male population of praying age in the city. "The women who were permitted to join in the 'Id prayers," he said, "were excluded from the enclosure itself but left to pray on the open ground behind it."[18]

Even this privilege was possibly little used, for in that same year Philby observed the actual 'Id celebration at the end of Ramadan, from the watching for the crescent of the new moon by whole families from their rooftops to the end of the first day's feasting, and what he writes suggests that men alone participated in the public mosque services and celebration: "The whole *male* [emphasis mine] population of the city had gone forth to the special enclosure reserved for the 'Id prayers outside the north-east gate. The service, begun at sunrise and including an address by Ibn Sa'ud, lasted about half an hour. The crowd then streamed back to the palace, where countless trays of rice and mutton awaited the guests in the great courtyard . . . of the palace."[19] The worship service, the description suggests, was primarily if not wholly for men, and except for the distribution of leftovers to beggars after the meal, the public reception that followed was absolutely for men alone.

Philby found something quite different when later in that same year, 1918, he watched the 'Id al-Adhah (Feast of the Sacrifice, the annual celebration that occurs at the end of Pilgrimage season) prayer services in Unaiza. At this service Philby watched women not only in attendance at the service but participating in it as well:

> I noticed a good proportion of women in smocks of greenish-blue and black 'abas. From the south and south-west gates dense streams of people converged on the masjid, where behind the pulpit sat an ever-growing phalanx of men, behind whom at a reasonable distance gathered a similar but smaller crowd of women. . . . The whole congregation rose as the Imam . . . proceeded to his place before the pulpit. . . . In a sing-song chant, as if reciting rather than preaching, the Imam delivered the Khutba or sermon in imitation of the annual sermon on the mount of 'Arafat, which is the culminating ceremony of the great pilgrimage of Mecca. And as he told the story of how Abraham would sacrifice his son Ishmael, the women and even many men among the congregation fell to sobbing aloud in sympathy with a father so God-fearing. . . . The Imam then continued to the end, when there was a wild hurrying and scurrying homeward; but I noticed that the women of the congregation stayed behind after the men had gone and crowded round the pulpit, continuing their devotions in postures of abject humility and adoration. Perhaps there was virtue in touching the very ground and pulpit on which the preacher had stood. And some, as they prayed, sobbed and wept bitterly.[20]

Philby's description brings women into the mosque—albeit in smaller numbers than men—but it also shows a kind of emotional display on the part of both men and women that would not have been acceptable Wahhabi practice. Emotional laments are considered a sign of discontent with God's plan, and the description of women exhibiting reverential behavior toward the pulpit is the epitome of what Ibn Abd al-Wahhab called idolatry. In fact it is the type of behavior he cited as proof that women's ritual behavior needed to be curtailed and controlled.

Philby's experience of women in the mosque for Unaiza's 'Id celebration, however, is not an example of Wahhabi flexibility or openness to women in the mosque. At the time of his visit, Unaiza was the only town in Najd with a mixed population, that is, attachment to Wahhabi beliefs was never complete among the population and possibly even among the majority. Unaiza had just fallen under Wahhabi political dominance, and the town had maintained a spiritual independence that came to an end only with Ibn Sa'ud's takeover of the city. One of the first effects of the absorption of Unaiza was the sanctioning of public festivities. "Formerly, they told me," Philby writes, referring to citizens of Unaiza, "the celebration of the 'Id used to be kept up for three days with dance and song and general revelry, including military displays and dancing by Badu women. But since Ibn Sa'ud's occupation of the Qasim (the central area of Najd) it had reverted to being a purely religious festival of prayer and sacrifice." (pp. 261–262). Philby's experience in Unaiza thus represents a singular documentation of political Wahhabism's effects on ritual practices. It is also a striking example of the way gender affected the ritual observances of men and women.

Commentaries from the nineteenth century on women's place in the mosque under the Wahhabis also suggest that women were allowed to attend mosque services, but only on special occasions. Wallin wrote that women did not attend the small neighborhood mosques in Ha'il, but they did visit the palace mosque, where the ruler and whole congregation meet for Friday services. "At this service," he says, "some scores of women also generally assist, forming rows behind the rest of the congregation; but," he adds, using language that could have come right out of the contemporary Saudi prayer manual quoted above, for "all other prayers it is regarded as more decent for the sex to perform by themselves alone at home."[21] Richard Burton, writing of his experience in the Hejaz not long after Wallin was in Najd, also affirms that the Wahhabis accorded a place for women in the mosque as a religious fundamental, but only at limited times: quoting a Najdi named Khalid Bey he says he met on the Pilgrimage to Mecca, Burton writes that "the Muwahhid on pilgrimage follows his two principal tenets, public prayer for men daily, for women on Fridays, and rejection of the Prophet's mediation."[22]

If attendance at Friday and feast-day prayers was theoretically obligatory for women as well as for men under the Wahhabis, it is not surprising that in practice only men's participation was enforced. This could not have been otherwise, in Najd or anywhere else. In Sunni tradition, menstruating women are exempt from prayer, as well as from making Pilgrimage and from fasting during Ramadan. In popular perception, furthermore, menstruation renders a woman impure for purposes of touching or reading the Qur'an and is generally perceived as actually invalidating women's prayer, because God will not choose to hear her, regardless of where she prays.[23] Muhammad ibn Abd al-Wahhab wrote a chapter on menstruation, and his conclusion is in line with standard Sunni thinking on the subject: the weight of his argument is that women should not pray to God at all so long as any menstrual discharge is visible. Women's prayer is therefore conceived as being not so important to the community's well-being that their presence in the mosque could or should be enforced, and because of their perceived body pollution, women's prayer is even conceived as being less important to God.

Outside the Mosque: How Did Women Pray?

Women's praying at home did not preclude performing prayers with regularity and solemnity. Neither, however, did it attempt to mimic the community experience of men's prayer in the mosque, led by a knowledgeable imam. In the missionary record there are a great many descriptions of women at private prayer. In 1919 Eleanor Calverley related, not without a hint of sarcasm, her impressions of what she took as superficiality in the ritual of women's prayer:

> It is Allah's right to be worshipped by those He has created. Those who fulfill this duty acquire merit; those who do not are laying up trouble for themselves in the future. . . . Prayer must not be undertaken unless the body is ceremonially clean. Some sicknesses are considered defiling, and until the patient recovers he is not allowed to pray. A bandage is often the object of much concern to a devout woman. "How can I pray?" she will ask. "Can I pour the water for my ablutions over this bandage, or will you allow me to take the bandage off?" She could not pray at all unless she had made the prescribed ablutions.[24]

Calverley was however, impressed by the solemnity of prayer on the part of both men and women:

> The prayer . . . is performed slowly and with great dignity, facing
> toward Mecca, the holy city. The worshipper stands, if possible
> upon a choice rug, or at least in a clean place. At sunset, one comes
> across praying Moslems on the seashore, on the sail-boats beached
> along the water's edge, on the verandahs of the hospital, and in al-
> most every conceivable place. . . . In the midst of a social call upon
> the missionaries, Moslem ladies will excuse themselves, and, select-
> ing a rug in the room, will perform their prayers in quietness and
> solemnity while their hostess waits. *(p. 6)*

Women's faithful performance of obligatory prayers impressed all the missionary commentators. Even in situations in which the prostrations of prayer were injurious, such as when a patient was recovering from surgery, women—of all social situations—took their obligations literally. Sarah Hosmon of the Oman mission station operated on an enslaved woman in the seaport town of Sibe who was suffering from trichiasis, a disease that caus-es the eyelids to curl inward. "Just before I left," Hosmon wrote, "I had to do a second eyelid for Heela and as I put on the dressings I took special care that everything was absolutely clean and dry, for she got her other dressings soaked with blood and I wondered why. I soon learned the cause when prayer time came around. . . . When she had to pray, because she could not use water on her dressings, she rubbed her hand in the sand and then over her face. After she had put her head to the ground five times a day, of course the fresh blood would ooze out of the wound on to her dressings!"[25]

Anecdotes such as these about women and their devotions were being cataloged in the Gulf towns at the time Wahhabi religious fervor was at its height in Najd, and Philby in Riyadh was also taking notes. Painting himself as a voyeur, he admits watching from the roof of his home and recording the activities—including prayer—of women from the neighboring house:

> All of a sudden, as the sun sank behind the rugged rim of Tuwaiq,
> the whole city would burst into discordant song as countless
> Mu'adhdhins uttered the call to prayer from the dumpy minarets—
> curious turrets with an irregular upward projection at one, usually
> the northern, corner. Immediately there follows a bustle of
> people—*men only of course*—in the streets, at first dawdling and

later hurrying to the mosques. Then there is silence, broken only by the Allahu Akbars and Amins of the praying congregations, while on the roofs the women too go through all the motions and prostrations of the prayer, *though always single and silently.*[26]

In 1878 Lady Anne Blunt, the only woman foreign traveler to the Najd in the nineteenth century to leave a written record, also commented on women's ritual prayer outside the mosque. In Ha'il only ten years before the establishment of the Arabian Mission, Lady Anne was visiting the wives of Muhammad ibn Rashid, emir of Ha'il, along with "a few friends and a vast number of attendants and slaves."[27] Just as Calverley described, when prayer time sounded, all the women "got up and went to say their prayers in the middle of the room" (p. 237).

Even where such large groups of women gathered for the purpose of saying obligatory prayers, women are described as praying individually and usually in silence. At the mission clinics, for example, the space available virtually duplicated the mosque setting: a spacious walled courtyard was open to the public from all walks of life, including patients, their servants, retainers, and relatives, and, more accommodating than the mosque, the clinic provided a screen to separate men and women, creating space that was exclusively female. Yet at prayer times women invariably separated themselves to perform their devotions silently and alone.

The manner of prayer of Bedouin women mirrored that of townswomen. Dickson's observations among the Ajman and Mutair of eastern Arabia in the 1920s and 1930s show Bedouin men and women to be regular in their prayers, but with men in the mosque and women outside it. The mosque of a Bedouin encampment, Dickson says, is a line drawn on the ground with a half-circle in the middle simulating a qibla. "The Bedawin is very punctilious in his prayers. Whether in camp or on the march, he solemnly prays five times a day according to Muslim rule. If possible he prays in company, as there is more virtue in this than praying alone."[28] Bedouin women, Dickson says, pray regularly also. For example, "little Hussa bint Salim al Muzaiyin learnt her prayers at the age of twelve, and at thirteen and a half prayed regularly five times a day. Her mother Amsha was equally careful about her prayers" (p. 185). Yet even in a Bedouin encampment where all are related, women prayed apart from the men, Dickson adds, and usually in the privacy of their tents. The situation was the same with Al Murrah Bedouin in the 1970s, for, according to Donald Cole "the Al Murrah and other Bedouins of Saudi Arabia since the time of the Ikhwan movement, strictly observe the five prayers."[29] However, the women, he says, prayed individually in their part of the tent, while all the men gathered at the mosque, which was just a line drawn on the earth to the east of the tent (p. 127).

In descriptions of Bedouin at obligatory prayer, there is but one possible exception to the practice of men praying in the mosque and women outside it. In the *hujar*, the Ikhwan settlements of former Bedouin, one report indicates that women as well as men were obliged to be present in the mosque for the five daily prayers and sermons. "The Imam of the mosque took the attendance of all those who were late or absent and, after the sermon, he went to their house to determine the cause, marking their shoes with a special sign to indicate their laxity. These persons were required to explain their behavior before the Imam if they were absent once, the governor (*hakim*) if twice, and a convocation of the people if thrice."[30] It is exceedingly doubtful, however, that these formerly Bedouin women really did pray regularly in the mosque with men and that their attendance was monitored. For one thing, women are exempted from performing prayer when menstruating, so there are times when women should not be praying at all, let alone in the mosque. Second, segregation practices were extremely strict in the hujar, so strict that in al-Artawiyah, the first Ikhwan settlement, each house had its own well because women were not allowed to use a public well (Habib p. 53). Furthermore, women were not allowed in the marketplace, according to the governor of the town: "Even today no woman is allowed in the market to shop. Instead, the women congregate at the steps of the large mosque where the merchants bring their wares, and then take orders. The merchants deliver the merchandise to the customers' home. Even today the sound of a woman's voice is not allowed to be heard in the streets, and when one woman desires to call the attention of another in public, she claps her hands."[31]

One might find it curious that such a draconian attitude toward women's separation would prevail among Bedouin, who are accustomed to women doing much of the labor for family subsistence and selling their produce in market towns. Furthermore, a kind of equality between Bedouin husbands and wives was repeatedly noted by missionary writers, among others, who met them in the markets of Kuwait and Hasa. Perhaps the attempt to segregate women rigidly in the Ikhwan settlements is a reflection of the converts' zeal to fulfill the Wahhabi ideal of women's total body covering and separation from unrelated men.[32] Bedouin, having converted to this sterner version of the faith and wishing to exemplify the principle of community living according to God's laws, might well have taken women's public invisibility as an emblem of their conversion.

Nineteenth-century observers also noted the regularity of women's obligatory prayer in Najd under the Wahhabis. Wallin commented that "the Wahhaby women are very punctual in observing the religious duties, and while in other Arabian lands I can scarcely remember having seen a woman perform her devotions at home, far less in a mosque, I saw the greater part of those in Gebel Shammar and Algawf [Jouf], very punctually go through their five daily prayers."[33] At the time, Jouf was, Wallin says, a staunchly Wahhabi town, with a chief shaikh in every quarter with his own mosque (p. 147).

Doughty records that every home in Ha'il had its own "praying-stead":

> In the palm ground without [Hamud's] kahwa, he has (in their town manner) a raised place for prayers; this was a square platform in clay, with a low cornice, bestrewn with clean gravel, and so large that a coffee company might kneel in it and bow themselves to the ground. . . . In all the house-courts at Hayil, and in their orchard grounds, there is made some such praying-stand; it may be a manner of the reformed religion in Nejd, and like to this we have seen prayer-steads in the open deserts defended from the common by a border of stones. Every such raised clay masally, littered with pure gravel, is turned towards the sanctuary of Arabia.[34]

Were these praying-steads in private homes special pieces of consecrated ground for women's daily prayers? They may have been used by women but were undoubtedly not constructed for their special use, for they were situated in the most public space in the house, at the entrance to the men's reception room. If they were intended for the private use of women, would they not have been situated where women might use them in private? Lady Anne Blunt's description suggests that the royal ladies of the palace in Ha'il did not have a praying-stead of their own, as they performed their prayers in the same room where they were already congregated to socialize.

Nineteenth-century descriptions of Bedouin women at prayer show women praying less regularly than men, sometimes only on special occasions, but again always singly and outside the mosque. Doughty wrote that "in the nomad tribes women are seldom seen to pray, except in ramathan [*sic*], the month of bodily abstinence and devotion; they are few which know the prayers; I suppose even the half of the men have not learned them. . . . Women pray not as the men, falling upon their faces; but they recite the form of words with folded arms and kneeling" (1:279). Bedouin, Doughty observed, gathered together outside their booths and formed rows, reciting the prayers and performing the appropriate rakahs, and when the shaikh was present, he says, he joined the men, not attempting to take the place of an imam, because, Doughty wrote, "All the Moslemin are equal in the performance of their religion." As for women, however, "such few of the nomad hareem as are taught, kneel down in the religious month before their beyts, to say the formal prayers; and seldom at other times is any woman seen praying" (1:558).

Outside the Mosque: Ritually Imperfect Prayer

Whether in the nineteenth or twentieth century, in Bedouin or town communities, in Wahhabi regions or not and whether performed inside a mosque or inside a home, prayer performed correctly and in unison with others is prayer that is most highly valued by the community as a whole. Women replicate the actions of men but in ways that are ritually imperfect: women's prayer at home is performed either alone, in the company of children, or with whomever is present, such as visiting friends and family, and even when in the company of others women have tended not to pray in unison. Women offer prayers irregularly, being exempt from prayer when menstruating and after giving birth, and are less likely to use correct formulas because they are less educated than men and pray without benefit of an imam to guide them. Prayer at home is not an experience of the mighty and the low, rich and poor, standing shoulder to shoulder as an emblem of mankind's equality before God, as the prayer books say. It is not an occasion to meet and socialize with others whom one wouldn't otherwise meet, nor is prayer at home an occasion to connect with the political life of the larger community. Prayer that is outside the mosque, whether the mosque is a line in the sand, a building, or a specially designated place in the home, is valued less according to the highest standards of orthodoxy and of the community as a whole.

Women's prayer at home cannot be other than ritually imperfect. How can solemnity or regularity be guaranteed? How can segregated women know the correct words to say, or the correct way to say them, when they have less access to religious learning than men do? Without the guidance of an educated imam, something the mosque provides for even the least educated male, women outside the mosque are less likely to know the correct words to say or the correct timing of prostrations and other ritual motions of prayer. The solemnity, the silence, the unison, and the language of prayer are instilled through practice and reinforced through public performance. Those who participate in mosque prayer share in a culture that cannot be replicated at home.

Spirituality and Community

Women's Rituals for the Prophet's Birthday, Votive Offerings, and Celebrations of Mourning

In spite of their exclusion from the experience of mosque culture—indeed, perhaps because of it—women have engaged in rituals of spirituality and community outside the mosque. In Bahrain and Kuwait, in Basra and Musqat, and in towns of the Hejaz as well, women have come together to celebrate the Prophet's birthday, saints' days and feast days, to make votive offerings in exchange for favors from God or the saints, and to mourn, not only the deaths of martyred saints but those of their own loved ones. Given women's separation from the mosque, these rituals may have been the most significant experience of religious ritual for women, and given the limitations imposed by modesty and separation values, these outside-the-mosque rituals may also have represented the primary venue for women to experience community outside the family.

Missionary women observed or participated in some of these rituals and recorded their experiences. Fanny Lutton, for example, had already spent seventeen years working in Musqat and Bahrain at the time she wrote about what she called "women's prayer meetings" in Manama around 1913. These were different for Shi'a and Sunni, she says, as Sunni women gathered for religious "meetings" only to celebrate an 'Id, such as the Prophet's birthday (*moulid annabi*) or the breaking of the fast of Ramadan (*'Id al-fitr*). Shi'a women, on the other hand, were always meeting, she says, as often as twice a week. The Sunni women's meetings she describes, called "readings" (*qira'a*), took place in private homes in the neighborhood and the focus of each meeting was on listening to a textual narration appropriate to the feast day being celebrated.[35]

After attending a reading of a biography of the Prophet in celebration of the Prophet's birthday, what struck Lutton most was the festive atmosphere and the way the religious purpose of the gathering appeared subordinate to the event as a social occasion. Women and children, she says, arrived dressed in new clothing, in colors of bright purple, orange, green, and magenta, and adorned with necklaces, earrings, nose rings, and finger rings, as well as jeweled ornaments and jasmine and bunches of sweet-smelling greens in their braided hair. For the occasion, hands were also colored and decorated with yellow and black dyes.

The participants sat on the floor, Lutton says, facing a line of about ten readers who sat in a prominent place, leaning against the wall, each taking a turn at reading. "I could not say that any of the audience paid any attention to what [the reader] was reading," Lutton comments. "Visitors were coming in all the time and saluting one another as they took their places. The women would say, 'How is your condition? How is your evening? How are your children?' and many more of the same inquiries, and this was often repeated three times over. The reader never stopped, but went on reading as if the whole audience were hanging on her words. . . . At stated times the whole assembly would respond, 'Oh God!' " (p. 16).

As the reading continued, servants (always referred to in missionary correspondence as "slaves" if the person doing the serving were black) dressed in handsome silk dresses served coffee, pouring it into tiny handleless cups that were passed out to the guests. Meanwhile, children made noise as their mothers scolded them, visited with each other, and drank coffee, and all the while, Lutton says, the readers never paused. So pronounced was the social—as opposed to the reverential—character of the gathering, that when Lutton sent her report for publication in *Neglected Arabia*, she asked her readers to imagine such a thing "in your own land"—refreshments, scolding, noisy children, coming and going—while a religious "reading" was going on (p. 16).

Visitation at shrines and tombs was an integral part of women's religious experience in the Gulf region, in particular among the Shi'a. Tombs and shrines dedicated to holy people were (and are) favorite locations for vowing rituals—also called votive rituals—although these rituals can take place anywhere, such as in a private home. Wherever they take place, however, they also serve as a social occasion. Vowing rituals are occasioned by a personal life crisis, such as illness or infertility, or by a pressing personal desire, perhaps to regain a lost love or to give birth to a male child. In the ritual, the supplicant asks a saint or deceased holy person for his or her intercession with God to have a wish fulfilled; in return for the favor, the supplicant promises to give something to the saint or to do something on his or her behalf (the "votive offering").

In 1911, while Fanny Lutton was still assigned to the mission station in Musqat, she attended a vowing ritual and afterward wrote about the happy social affair occasioned by the vow. Lutton describes a gay company of women dressed in silks and copious gold jewelry who had been invited to meet at a shrine on the edge of town, a crumbling building situated close to a number of holy graves. The woman making the vow circled around one of the graves while trying to engage in negotiations with the saint buried there. In return for granting her wish, the woman promised the saint she would come back to the shrine with a gift of sweets. Immediately after the circling, she served coffee and sweets. Then a sheep was killed right over the shrine, and the sacrificial animal became the main course for the picnic lunch that followed.[36]

Shrines used for women's vowing rituals are located all across Bahrain Island. In the early years of the century, the Shi'a religious establishment supported them, and the religious shaikhs who oversaw their maintenance administered the donations given on their behalf.[37] There were also shrines used for vowing rituals in Kuwait, and Violet Dickson visited one on the island of Falaika off the coast and left this description of the physical site:

> Today there exists a surrounding wall plastered over with white lime from the base rocks up to about six feet above the floor of the shrine. The inner side of the wall is splashed and smeared with henna, but not handprints. In the centre of this enclosure there is a small phallic shrine about three feet in height, with a square base and pointed top in which a flagpole stands, with pieces of green silk flag and black dots of thin veil hanging limply to it in the bright sunlight. A small opening in the base of the altar permits incense to be burnt on charcoal embers. A strong perfume of rosewater exists, and smashed on the rocks below the shrine are the remains of green glass rosewater bottles of Persian origin.
>
> At times, pieces of women's hair can be found tied in a piece of black veiling to the flag pole, and before the surrounding wall was plastered over clumps of women's hair could be seen tucked away among the rough stones. This custom I would say is done possibly to fulfill a vow made on some previous visit or else to atone for some sin—as is done by women on the great Pilgrimage to Mecca. On the steps leading up to the shrine were stains of blood where sacrifices were frequently being offered, again in fulfillment of vows.[38]

The ground around the shrine, as Dickson describes it, was all sacred, for nearby was a tomb with a small tower in which incense was burnt. The islanders knew it, she says, as the tomb of a saint whose body had washed up on the shore nearby. Because the body had appeared to be that of a Bedouin, the villagers called it the tomb of Muhammad al-Badawi. The holiness of the site was important, because the point of performing a vowing ritual at a shrine is to be physically as close to the spirit of the holy person as possible or close to the location of some event important in the holy person's life, so that the wish of the person making the vow will have the best chance of being heard. Dickson says that the tufts of hair tied in veiling and tucked among the stones were the fulfillment of previous vows. More likely, however, the hair was not the gift promised in exchange for the saint's granting a favor but the supplicant's attempt to establish a personal connection with the saint and to seal the bargain she had just made. For these purposes, personal mementos, including strips of cloth torn from clothing, notes, hair, and even metal charms, are commonly left at shrines and other holy places, from the magnificent silver tomb of Imam Reza in Mashhad, Iran, to saints' shrines in Greek Orthodox churches, to holy graves in rural villages such as the one Dickson describes.

Vowing rituals at shrines, celebrations of the Prophet's birthday, and other moulid gatherings in Muslim communities throughout the Middle East are very well known because they are still an integral part of women's religious experience and also because they have been recorded and analyzed in numerous works of recent anthropology. Historical examples, however, are far less copious, and even less so for the Gulf and Arabian peninsula than for other regions. Available historical examples, however, do show that women in the Hejaz also performed these rituals.

C. Snouck Hurgronje, who wrote his book on Mecca at the time the earliest missionaries of the Arabian Mission were getting established in Bahrain and Musqat, describes the public side of women's participation in the celebration of the Prophet's birthday. On the day designated for the Prophet's birthday, he says, the women of Mecca, dressed in their finest clothes, came to the mosque for the sunset prayers and afterward attended a procession to the Prophet's birthplace, where a reading from the life of Muhammad was performed. The site designated as the Prophet's birthplace is a shrine where prayers are offered and favors are asked, but here the ritual was a public celebration, endorsed by orthodox authority and attended by both men and women. Women were also in the mosque, a striking contrast to what the missionaries say about women's practice in the Gulf. Hurgronje, however, was quick to point out that women who attended prayers in the mosque were not usually Meccans but foreigners.[39] Whatever the case, women did go and were clearly allowed to join in the public celebration at the shrine of the birthplace.

In the Hejaz, there are numerous earlier historical examples of vowing rituals and saints' day celebrations. Burckhardt witnessed the moulid an-nabi celebrations in 1815, in Medina, where the Wahhabis had damaged the

Prophet's mosque and outlying tombs of the Prophet's companions and saints. He too comments on the ritual participation of women, suggesting that women's role was directed toward shrine visitation, while men's was to visit the mosque. The Prophet's birthday could be considered a national festival, he writes, when all businesses were shut and men assembled in the mosque for a moulid, a reading from the life of Muhammad, while women visited the Prophet's tomb.[40] Burckhardt also had some other things to say about the practice of seeking intercession. For example, once a year, at Ramadan, families traveled to the saints' cemetery of Medina, sometimes remaining for several days, and at Jebel Uhud, a site for seeking intercession and fulfilling vows of sacrifice, he says, crowds from town prayed to "Abu Bekr, Omar and Sittna Fatima" (2:269–270). In about 1853, Richard Burton visited the same places in Medina and described in more detail the vowing practices at the holy spots and saints' tombs, especially the tomb of Fatima, the Prophet's daughter, which was, he says, crowded with "female 'askers,' who have established their Lares and Penates under the shadow of the Lady's wing."[41] In other words, women had come to Fatima's tomb to ask a favor of the saint, having brought with them useful household implements because they planned to stay a while. (Burton adds the interesting note that the revered Fatima is known as al-Batul, the virgin, the same title given to Mary, mother of Jesus, by Eastern Christians, adherents of Greek and Monophysite Orthodox, and Catholics alike [1:327–328].)[42] In 1925 and 1926 the Wahhabi regime destroyed all the cupolas, domes, and architectural embellishments over these same holy graves. During the 1931 Pilgrimage policemen were assigned to the cemetery to discourage emotional displays of reverence, and women, but not men, were entirely excluded from even entering the cemetery grounds.[43]

Rituals of seeking intercession were performed not only by urban people but by Bedouin as well. In the Syrian desert, Burckhardt encountered the performance of votive rituals by Bedouin men and women of the northern Anayza:

> There are few Bedouin tribes within whose territory, or at least
> within a little distance from it, the tomb of some saint or reverend
> sheikh is not found, to him all the neighboring Arabs address their
> vows. These tombs are usually visited once a year by great numbers
> of Arabs, who there slaughter the victims they had vowed during
> the preceding year. These vows are made with the hope of obtaining
> male issue, or a numerous breed of horses or camels. The day of

visiting the saint's tomb becomes a festival for the whole tribe, and all the neighbors. The women then appear clothed in their finest dresses, and mounted upon camels, the saddles of which their husbands take great care to adorn.

Burckhardt adds that at these tombs "the veneration in which these Bedouins hold a saint almost borders on idolatry. They certainly believe that they can influence heaven in their favour, both here and in the other world." In Burckhardt's time, the Wahhabis' presence was still felt in this area where the northern desert of Arabia merges with the desert of southern Syria, and he adds "Against this superstition, and the killing of victims in honour of saints, the Wahabys have exerted themselves in sermons."[44]

These nineteenth-century examples make it clear that vowing rituals at shrines and tombs were a part of the religious life of the community in which women participated along with men and one that persisted even during the Wahhabi iconoclast interlude at the beginning of the nineteenth century. In missionary records at the opening of the twentieth century, when it came to the Sunni population of the Gulf towns, these rituals performed by women appear to have been organized privately and carried out in intimate associations of family and neighborhood, while women's "reading" ceremonies took place at select times, paralleling official orthodox holidays celebrated by men in the mosque. For Shi'a women, veneration of the saints in community with other women was the sine qua non of ritual practice.

Shi'a Women and the Celebration of Mourning

At the top of Fanny Lutton's list of ways she thought Sunni and Shi'a women were different from each other was their distinct styles of group ritual. The Shi'a observed days of mourning throughout the year but especially at Ashura, which, she says, "the Sunnis utterly ignore and ridicule."[45] Shi'a women, she says, met in Bahrain as often as every Thursday and Friday afternoon for commemorative readings (p. 14). These celebrations, collectively called *taharim*, occurred at slated times on the religious calendar to commemorate the deaths of saints or important historical religious figures, such as Zain al-Abidin, the Virgin Mary, the Prophet Muhammad, and Fatima al-Zahra.[46] Both men and women participated in these ceremonies, but separately. The men's ceremonies took place in a publicly supported "funeral house," called a *ma'tam*, while the women's rituals usually took place in a private home in a room designated as a ma'tam, which Lutton says "is attached to the houses of the wealthier class."[47] Some idea of the extent of Shi'a investment in these mourning celebrations is suggested by Fu'ad Khuri's 1980 study of society and politics in Bahrain, in which he says there are about five hundred ma'tam buildings, about fifteen hundred ma'- tam women's groups, and one thousand ma'tam groups for men.[48] Even Wahhabi Hufuf, the main town of Hasa in Saudi Arabia, in 1955 had at least one ma'tam, called a Husainiya, for Shi'a mourning celeberations.[49]

The major commemorative ritual took place in a celebration called 'Ashura, on the tenth day of Muharram, designated as the day on which Hussein, son of Ali and Fatima, the Prophet's daughter, was killed at Kerbela. During the first nine days of Muharram, Shi'a women's gatherings for commemorative readings occurred daily in Bahrain, corresponding to the men's meetings in the ma'tam houses. Fanny Lutton described the women's readings from the vantage point of a self-described barely tolerated outsider, sitting alone with her back pressed against the wall, but even from this jaundiced stance she conveyed the community spirit and the pathos mixed with joy that characterized the mourning celebration.

Lutton arrived to find that pipes (*ghalyun*) had been prepared with hot charcoal and tobacco for the women to smoke during the ceremony. (She had never seen a Sunni woman smoke, she says, and had never seen a Shi'a gathering where women were not smoking.) Like a social gathering, participants came and went, including the readers. When the reading began two women readers were sitting at the front of the room, a handful of mourners sitting before them. Participants arrived throughout the reading, Lutton wrote, all wearing the dark blue chador draped over the head and covering the whole body. The casual arrivals and departures of the women did not match Lutton's expectations for a religious ceremony, and she commented that by the time the reading was finished, twelve readers sat at the front and over fifty women were crowded before them, but as the crowd dispersed, more women were still coming in.

The reading concerned the story of the death of Hussein and was actually read from a book in the rhythmic style of poetry, not recited from memory.

> Some of the women wept from the beginning of the meeting to the finish. At times the women would beat their breasts, swaying their bodies backwards and forwards and calling out 'Hosain, Hosain' over and over again. . . . In the midst of all this wailing and reading the pipes were placed in front of these women, and through the cries were intermingled the gurgling sounds of the pipes, all over

the room. Women kept on coming in, greetings were exchanged. Some were shouting to their unruly children in angry tones. . . . Through it all the reader went on, never stopping for a second, not even raising her eyes from the book.[50]

In 1919 Mrs. James Cantine attended a women's ma'tam in Basra, and she too captured the mix of pathos with joyful sociability. "It was wonderful to see," she writes, "how the women gave expression to sorrow, despair and anger . . . as they were guided by [the reader's] dramatic reading of the sad story. In one place in particular, where it tells that Hussein's enemies refused to give him a drink of water when he lay dying on the battle field, she had them wailing and shrieking and beating themselves in a most frightful manner."[51]

The Shi'a of Bahrain, Rene Harrison wrote in 1918, mourned the death of Hussein for the entire month, wearing black and draping their homes with black flags. She too commented that "the women beat their breasts and wail and weep real tears over the death of their beloved Hussein," but she also comments that women actually were included in the public procession of ritual mourning for the death of the imam: "On the ninth day of the month a bier draped with gaily colored cloth was carried through the streets on the shoulders of four men, followed by a number of men *and women* beating their breasts and crying; this in honor of the nephew of Hussein who was murdered on that day."[52] The culmination of these ceremonies was reached on the tenth day with the 'Id al-Ashura parade, in which the roles of Hussein's female relatives were filled by male participants.

On the morning of this day a big parade was held. . . . First came the standard-bearers carrying black flags, an emblem of mourning, and the Persian flags. Following these were two companies of about twenty men each, brandishing swords in the air and occasionally gashing themselves on the forehead and chanting. . . . These men wear new white garments to display the blood from their streaming wounds to the best advantage. The body of the procession was made up of men and boys representing different relatives of Hussein who were taken prisoners, some of whom were killed. Two camels, one of them bearing the son and daughter of Hussein and the other bearing his sister, headed this division.[53]   *(pp. 13–14)*

Women were not absent from the procession, even if they played no specific role. A photograph of the Muharram procession in Bahrain reproduced in *Neglected Arabia* in 1908 clearly shows women walking alongside and closely following the procession.[54] Paul Harrison's discussion of the Ashura ceremonies also reports women walking alongside the procession, but he places women at the men's readings as well, where they "sit on the outskirts of the meetings and join in the weeping and wailing that accompany the recital."[55]

The Shi'a mourning ceremonies can appropriately be called celebrations, because, in spite of the ritualized expressions of grief, the chest beating, and the retelling of the tale of blood and martyrdom, the story ends in joy and catharsis. "Suddenly the reading ends," writes Paul Harrison, "and every one is happy and cheerful again. The sudden passing of the emotional storm is as striking as its intensity" (p. 226). What with the mythology surrounding the Hussein story and the manner in which its commemoration takes place, the mourning celebration is actually a time of community bonding and the affirmation of hope, a time of spiritual rebirth explicit in the text of the Shiite passion play.

Dr. Sharon Thoms of the Bahrain mission gives an account of the passion play he witnessed around 1907. The drama, Thoms says, begins with the "resurrection, when Gabriel hands the keys to Paradise to Muhammad, saying that he shall be intercessor for his fellow creatures," but it culminates with the angel Gabriel's anointing of Hussein as God's chosen intercessor, who will deliver mankind to Paradise.

> Gabriel appears, and addressing Hussein, speaks words of consolation, on which the whole fabric of the Shiah religion rests: "Permission had proceeded from the Judge, the Gracious Creator that I should give into thy hand this key of intercession. Go and Deliver from the flames every one who has in his lifetime shed but a single tear for thee, every one who has in any way helped thee, everyone who had performed a pilgrimage to thy shrine, or mourned for thee, and everyone who has written tragic verses for thee. Bear each and all with thee to Paradise." Then the sinners entering Paradise say: "God be praised! By Hussein's grace are we made happy and by his favor are we delivered from destruction. By Hussein's loving kindness is our path decked with roses and flowers. . . . We were thorns and thistles, but are now made cedars owing to his merciful intercession."[56]

The Muharram story of martyrdom so closely parallels the Easter story that when Fanny Lutton, a Christian missionary, asked herself why women bothered to come together for these ceremonies every week when they are repetitive and do not offer "a crumb of comfort or anything to help them along their dark and cheerless journey," she should have been able to answer her own question. The Christian Holy Week services, especially as ritualized in Catholicism, could have been a model for Ashura. On Good Friday, the suffering of the martyred Jesus is commemorated in the performance of the stations of the cross, when the supplicant follows in mournful prayer each painful event in Christ's walk to Golgotha: here is where he was spat on and struck on the head; here the crown of thorns was put on his head, causing blood to flow; there he called for water and was given sour wine; finally, he is crucified, nails driven through his hands and feet, suspended in the air, left to suffocate, bleeding, and then a spear is driven through his heart.

Even the ritual duplication of the physical suffering of the martyr has a parallel in Christian tradition. The Christian Penitents of New Mexico and some Catholics in the Philippines actually reenact the crucifixion, minus only the last spear thrust, and men vie to play the role of Christ, because to relive Christ's suffering is to feel as one with Him, and it is an honor in the eyes of the community. Afterward, all this reenacted suffering culminates in Easter, the third day after the crucifixion, when Christ rose from the dead and was taken up to heaven, and in Christ's resurrection is the promise of everlasting life for all who believe in Him. Easter is the Great Feast in the church calendar, the day of greatest joy, the joy of rebirth that came out of blood and denial and suffering.

In the Shi'a processional of mourning, men vie to produce the most blood, the most tears, the loudest thump on the breast, the most frenzied grief, while women participating in the commemorative readings and those following in the public procession cry and beat their chests as well. In the end, however, after the sharing of grief, there is the shared experience of renewal, along with coffee and sociability. Here Fanny Lutton got it partially right when she recognized the social aspect of the ritual gathering: "I could not help thinking the chief attractions are the pipes and coffee and any little bits of gossip they hear at these meetings."[57] But the sociability was an integral part of a larger spiritual experience, one that—like the rituals of Holy Week—engendered passions and promised hope, and one that could not be experienced except in community with other women.

The Wahhabis and Women's Ritual Practices

In 1899 Samuel Zwemer, the founder of the Arabian Mission, wrote *Arabia: The Cradle of Islam*, his compendium of information on Arabs and Islam in Arabia, with an eye toward laying the groundwork to expand Christian mission stations into Hasa and Najd. His information was based on his then nine years of living in Bahrain and traveling to every town from Hufuf to Basra and from Kuwait to Musqat. Always interested in the Wahhabis, whom he thought held the key to "inner Arabia," Zwemer talks about the ways they differed from other Muslims. The Wahhabis, he says, offered no prayers to the Prophet, walis, or saints, and neither did they visit their tombs for that purpose; they did not celebrate Muhammad's birth, and they forbade women to visit the graves of the dead.[58]

Ibn Abd al-Wahhab believed in controlling ritual practices in order to uphold the absolute oneness of God (*tawhid*) within the community of believers. Upholding God's oneness meant rejecting the notion that any being, whether spiritual or human, or any inanimate object, could possess godlike powers. In his view, the belief that God's powers were shared was manifest in any ritual action in which a supplicant asked a favor of God by appealing to an intermediary or invoked the name of an intermediary to do the favor directly (as in the Christian invocation, "Holy Mary, mother of God, pray for us sinners . . ."). Performing such rituals as praying to the Prophet to intercede with God or bypassing God altogether by asking a favor directly of the Prophet or a saint or invoking the spirit of a holy place, Ibn Abd al-Wahhab thought, was simply polytheism (shirk).

Guided by this concern for respecting God's Oneness, the Wahhabis pejorated or tried to eliminate nearly every ritual exercise that did not conform to orthodox Sunni practice, in effect, nearly all the group ritual practices performed by women in the neighboring Gulf region and the Hejaz. They banned celebrations of the Prophet's birthday because in eulogizing the Prophet the rituals threatened to deify him. When Ibn Taimiyya, the intellectual ancestor of Ibn Abd al-Wahhab, issued a fatwa condemning all new festivals as bid'ah—innovation—he cited the celebration of the birth of the Prophet as an example. Ibn Taimiyya's contemporary, Ibn al-Hajj, along with later scholars, vigorously criticized the participation of women in the birthday celebration in particular.[59] Prayers at saints' tombs, in which women in particular try to negotiate with saints as if they possessed godlike power, were also forbidden, along with vowing rituals.

Also forbidden by the Wahhabis as contrary to both theory and traditional practice include the use of amulets for protection against the evil eye, because using an amulet presupposes belief in the power of spirits to do harm and the power of an inanimate object to thwart it, independently of the will of God. Fortune-tellers, in the Wahhabi view, commit shirk (polytheistic acts) because knowledge of the future belongs to God alone; similarly, witchcraft of any kind is considered an attempt to trespass on the terrain of God's omnipotence. Other chronic offenders include mystics such as Sufis and dervishes, who, by claiming to seek unity of themselves with God, challenge the uniqueness of God's powers and the oneness of God's being. For the same reason, possession ceremonies such as the Zar, in which a ritual expert attempts to communicate with a spirit that has taken possession of someone's body, would be unthinkable under Wahhabi rule: not only did engaging a spirit challenge God's omnipotence, but the ritual of appeasement employed music and dancing, which, in the view of Wahhabi ulama, were acts inconsistent with the custom of the Prophet and thus disallowed under any circumstances. The Shi'a were the worst offenders because of their veneration of the Prophet's family, the custom of praying to the imams at shrines, and especially because of the Ashura mourning celebration that elevates Imam Hussein to the level of redeemer and is therefore the very definition of shirk. Paul Harrison sampled the opinion of a "puritan Wahhabi" who happened to be in Manama at the time of Ashura, asking him whether such a procession could occur in "inland Arabia." "Such a thing," the Wahhabi replied, "would not be permitted in all the country of Ibn Saoud. Men guilty of such an enormity would be killed."[60]

Ibn Abd al-Wahhab forbade both men and women to participate in any of these rituals, but this proscription did not affect men and women equally. First, men still had the mosque, where they were daily invited to perform correct worship together. Second, women were considered uniquely susceptible to particular types of polytheistic rituals because of perceived weaknesses in their nature that needed to be controlled. Mourning, for example, was generally proscribed, but only women's mourning practices were specifically forbidden. "Four undesirable customs still persist in my ummah from pre-Islamic times," writes Muhammad ibn Abd al-Wahhab, citing Hadith in his *Kitab at-Tawhid*: "Pride in the noble achievements of one's relatives, attack of weak genealogies, seeking rain through the stars and bewailing the deceased."[61] Displays of emotion on the occasion of a death are undesirable for both men and women, not only because the mourner might ask the deceased for a favor with God, but also because grief indicates that the mourner is questioning God's will. Women, however, unlike men, were categorically excluded from attending funerals and from accompanying bodies to cemeteries, not only in Ibn Abd al-Wahhab's view but in Sunni Islam generally. One Hadith on women and funerals says, "The Prophet saw his daughter Fatima and asked, 'Why are you going out?' She replied, 'I have come to the people of this house and invoke mercy for their deceased one.' He then said, 'If you went to the grave you would not see Paradise until your father's grandfather sees it.'" In a second Hadith, women are chastised for wanting to go to a funeral: "The Messenger of Allah found some women sitting, and asked them what they were doing. They answered that they were waiting for a funeral. 'Did you wash the deceased person?' he asked. They answered, 'No.' 'Will you carry the bier?' 'No,' they answered. 'Will you assist in placing the corpse into the grave?' and they said, 'No.' Whereupon he responded, 'Then go back home, and you will not be rewarded for your conduct.'"[62]

The reason for women's exclusion is that they are considered to be less able than men to control their emotions and, if given the opportunity, are likely to transform prayer *for* the dead into prayer *to* the dead. Because women lack the emotional restraint that men possess, explains a biographer of Ibn Abd al-Wahhab, their compassion for the dead person can escalate into reverence and veneration, and this, he says, is polytheism (p. 151). It is also women who are more likely to want to pray at grave sites, and in the *Kitab at-Tawhid*, Ibn Abd al-Wahhab expressly singled out women in the strongest terms to be prohibited from visiting shrines: citing Hadith, he writes that "the Apostle of Allah cursed women who visit tombs and people who build mosques over them and hang lamps to light them."[63] Women's mourning—not men's—is potentially so pernicious that a woman who mourns deserves the ultimate sanction in the hereafter: "If the bewailer-woman does not repent before her death," writes Ibn Abd al-Wahhab, quoting Hadith, "she will rise on the Day of Judgment covered with a dress of liquid tar and a cloak of leprosy."[64]

While the Wahhabis theoretically also enjoined men not to return to the grave for prayer after a burial, they did allow them to return for visitation. In fact this is not only not forbidden; it is recommended. "What [our religion] permits is tomb visitation and this is recommended because the believer who stands at the grave recalls to mind that all that there is in the Universe shall vanish, and the countenance of Allah alone shall endure."[65] "If [a] man punctually visited graves with good intention and genuine feeling, and to strengthen his spiritual relationship with those who died before, his faith would grow, his creed would be purified, and in this case [he] would be more averse to crime and forbidden acts, for faith and iniquity never go together" (p. 150). During the height of the Wahhabi revival in the 1920s, grave visitation was, in practice, a male privilege of which even Abd al-Aziz took advantage. The sultan of Najd, Philby tells us, used to go regularly to the cemetery on the outskirts of Riyadh, accompanied by his father, the learned imam Abd al-Rahman, and visit the graves of his ancestors. Philby also noted while participating in the rites of Pilgrimage in 1931, that women were barred from entering the cemetery in Medina except to be buried. "Alive, they are debarred from making visitations, which for men are an established part of the Madina ceremonial programme and include, of course, visits to the tombs of such ladies as have a recognized niche in Islamic history. For women, the practice is to stand in a small cemetery outside the Baqi'a [the name of the cemetery at Medina] limits but over-looking them and thence to make the customary salutations."[66]

Sunni women in the Gulf towns did not attend funerals either, again because they were supposed not to possess the restraint men possessed. But there women performed commemorative ceremonies and mourned for their dead at home, sometimes with demonstrative wailing and sometimes in quiet prayer with neighborhood and family. Shi'a women actually followed funeral processions to the grave, weeping, and if the deceased was a women, lowered the body into the grave;[67] they also engaged in the feast-day commemorative readings and vowing rituals discussed earlier in this chapter. And, as the following chapters discuss, the Zar possession ceremonies were extremely popular among Sunni women of the Gulf.

Did the Wahhabis Actually Eliminate Women's Rituals?

While there is no question the Wahhabis enjoined women from engaging in demonstrative mourning, attending funerals, praying at grave sites, engaging in Prophet's birthday celebrations, or offering vows to saints, it is unknown to what extent these rituals had been practiced before the movement began and to what extent they were actually suppressed. Available sources indicate that rituals performed by women were certainly practiced in Najd in the eighteenth century, as their performance was precisely the evidence the founder used to justify the need for religious revival and to define the purpose of his movement. According to Uthman ibn Abd Allah ibn Bishr, the nineteenth-century chronicler, at the time of Ibn Abd al-Wahhab, vowing rituals performed at tombs, shrines, and sacred objects were common in Najd. He wrote, for example, that people sought intercession with God at the grave of a blind hermit who had lived on alms and wandered unmolested through the desert near Dir'iya because they believed the man had survived by God's protection and was thus blessed. At Dir'iya there was also a cave in a hill thought to be the grave of a young girl called Bint al-Amir to which men and women came seeking the deceased girl's blessing.[68] The historian of the Wahhabi movement, Uthman ibn Abdallah Ibn Bishr, gave the following description of what were viewed as polytheistic practices in eighteenth-century Najd:

> At that time polytheism had become widespread in Najd and else-where. The belief in trees, stones, tombs, and buildings over them, and in the blessings to be had from tombs and in sacrificing to them had increased. [Also] belief in seeking the help of the jinn and in sacrificing to them, and in placing food before them and putting it in the corners of the houses to cure the sick, and belief in the good or evil power of the jinn had increased. [Finally] belief in oaths to other than God, and other polytheistic actions, both major and minor, had increased.[69]

The pervasiveness of these practices was probably exaggerated, because their existence was used as a rationale for the conquests of the Al Sa'ud family, which would purify Islam of these acts of polytheism. The elimination of heterodox ritual practices become an objective with each new conquest. For example, votive shrines and tombs of saints that had become popularly incorporated into rites of Pilgrimage were smashed when the Wahhabis conquered Mecca at the beginning of the nineteenth century, rebuilt after the Turks drove out the Wahhabis, and destroyed again when the Wahhabis retook the Hejaz in 1926. The shrine at Kerbala was also destroyed when the Wahhabis briefly drove into Iraq at the opening of the nineteenth century. The *mahmal*, an elaborate litter that traveled from Cairo to Mecca leading the annual procession of pilgrims from Egypt, was intercepted in 1926 and turned back as a forbidden object of veneration and because it was accompanied by music,[70] which the Wahhabis consider contrary to Sunna.

In spite of these dramatic episodes of iconoclasm and tomb destruction, the historical record doesn't allow us an unobscured vision of Wahhabism's impact on women's actual ritual behaviors. Religious tracts alone, furthermore, are no measure of common practice, as there can be a stunning gulf between professed attachment to religious doctrine and religious practice in daily life. In addition, ritual behaviors are inventions that can be discarded or adapted in response to changing needs, and what evidence we have suggests that enforcement of doctrines suppressing heterodox rituals varied over time and among different ethnic populations and geographical regions. In Unaiza, for example, certain 'Id rituals were ordered stopped by Ibn Sa'ud when he took over the city, yet at the same time women attended feast-day services in the mosque, crying openly. Women's moulid celebrations (celebrations of saints' days) that were discouraged during Ibn Sa'ud's conquest of the Hejaz enjoyed a revival during the 1980s. The Zar, which was virtually a fad among fashionable ladies in Mecca in the late nineteenth century reappeared among rural women in the Mecca region in the 1970s.

It can be assumed that celebrations of the Prophet's birthday were being performed in Hasa in 1913 at the time of Ibn Sa'ud's conquest of the province because the sultan forbade their performance, yet the celebrations were being performed, along with Ashura processions, in 1980 when King Khalid tried to suppress mourning celebrations in the wake of the Islamic Revolution in Iran. Despite the Wahhabi ban on ritual celebrations of the Prophet's birthday, the occasion has been co-opted by the Saudi regime as a national holiday. Today there is also a national day of praying for rain in Saudi Arabia, which is officially sponsored even though the prayers evoke the intercessory powers of the Prophet. Performance of the rite was not only rationalized but promoted by ibn Abd al-Wahhab. As his biographer explains: "Supplication through the Prophet was practiced during his lifetime in prayers for rain, and after his passing away the practice was confirmed by the silent agreement of the Companions as is obvious from a tradition ascribed to 'Umar in which he said, 'Whenever we suffered drought we used to invoke the intercession of our Prophet and rain would then fall; now we invoke the intercession of the Prophet's uncle.' This is legitimate invocation, and it excludes every other practice."[72]

In the prayers for rain, incidentally, we have the only description of a public ritual practice in which men and women shared equally, written by Ameen Rihani who was in Dir'iya with the Sultan of Najd to attend the occasion, which took place in 1922. Men and women, he says, came out and filled the wadi where the prayer took place. "There was no kneeling or prostrating but only an invocation pronounced by the Shaikh of the village and repeated after him by the people. It was very impressive."[73]

The information on prayer and the ways women worship assembled on these pages suggests that whatever the level of religious learning and ritual piety within a given society, Bedouin or settled, Wahhabi or Gulf Sunni or Shi'a, anything men did, women did less well or had less opportunity to do it well according to that society's own standards. The ability to read or recite holy text from memory, for example, was a highly valued achievement for both men and women and was a prerequisite for correct obligatory prayer, but everywhere boys had greater access to religious learning than did girls. This lower level of religious learning meant that women did not perform the prayers with the degree of correctness in language or form that men acquired through classroom study and experience in the mosque. The Wahhabis carried the ideal of religious knowledge for all believers to a higher level of social importance, knowledge being the sine qua non of correct practice and correct behavior, yet communities dedicated far more resources to men's learning than to women's, especially in the higher religious sciences.

In the ritual traditions of Sunnis, Shi'a, and Wahhabis in the Arabian peninsula region, there is no instance of women participating fully in mosque services. To the contrary, in the Gulf towns, women were excluded entirely from the mosque. The Wahhabi ideal was that each person, man or woman, be part of the community of believers and individually responsible for fulfilling ritual obligations with regularity. In fact public fulfillment of these obligations became the hallmark of Wahhabi society, particularly during the twentieth-century revival. Even under the Wahhabis, however, this ideal did not lead to women being brought into the mosque where the most correct form of worship could occur, as modesty values militated against their attending. For this reason, it is likely that the small number of women who did attend services were of low social status.

As long as women pray at home, the ideal cannot be fulfilled: at home, obligatory prayer takes place in the earthy reality of women's everyday lives, surrounded by noise, crying babies, pots on the stove, and the demands of little ones too young to understand or care that their mother's attention should be elsewhere. At home, when a woman prays, she prays alone; when other women are present, they do not join in a solemn assembly as do men in the mosque, praying in unison in a place where they are separated from the world of mundane things. And even women's solitary prayers cannot be offered complete and correct as prescribed by orthodoxy because their prayer goes unheard by God when they are ritually unclean.

In the Wahhabi Najd, the marginality of women in relationship to the orthodox tradition was magnified because of the importance attached to prayer in the mosque in the Wahhabi political community. Women were not excluded but were encouraged to attend on Fridays and feast days only and then to remain at the back. At the same time, in Najd during the Wahhabi revival, men were actually required to attend, and their attendance was enforced, while women's was not. And for modesty reasons, most women performed the daily prayers at home, even on the feast days and Fridays,

The inability of women's prayer to be complete by orthodox standards is one reason why participation in alternative, heterodox rituals is so compelling. Alternative rituals offer the opportunity for women to play leadership roles denied them in the orthodox tradition. Seeking intercession allows women to express agency on their own behalf. In vowing rituals women can try to bargain with God or a saint and to come away with hope. Furthermore, these rituals are group experiences: feast-day celebrations, vowing rituals, and taharim meetings provide a legitimate means of counteracting the social isolation that results from the practice of seclusion. At the same time, these meetings in respectable homes suggest that the rhetoric of total seclusion for upper-class women is not supported by the activities in which women actually engage.

Women's meetings for ritual prayer and sacrifice, I suggest, are more than social occasions for which ritual provides a pretext. The ritual and the sacrifice (whether offered as a meal, as in the shrine picnic, or as simply the serving of coffee or food) create bonds of obligation among those who participate, and these bonds are forged into networks of women's communities. The way these communities come together and are carried forward by the ritual bond is highlighted in the Zar societies I discuss in a later chapter: in order to participate, one had to reciprocate in kind, and therefore each Zar association took on the character of an exclusive club.

In Najd, where the Wahhabi influence has remained paramount as a political force since the time of the founder, it appears possible that women's rituals were virtually snuffed out. Whether snuffed out or merely suppressed, with the persistent hegemony of a political leadership that used its identity with Wahhabi Islam as a means of legitimizing its authority, the institutionalizing of Wahhabi Islam in the state bureaucracy, and state-sponsored missionary efforts throughout the kingdom, whatever quiet practices may have remained could only have been carried out under a cloud of suspicion and official disapproval.

It is likely that the strongest impetus for women to avoid practicing rituals condemned as polytheistic would have come from women themselves. The values that underscore the ban are values to which women, as members of their own society, would want to subscribe, particularly since they are articulated as positive moral principles that apply to society as a whole. When these values were applied in practice to men, even missionaries anxious to expose Islam's weak points had to admit that Wahhabi principles were channeled into the morally positive action of men gathering for group ritual in the mosque. What is less apparent, however, is that when applied in practice to women, the positive moral principle represented a negative judgment against women's nature and a constriction or elimination of ritual practices that women may legitimately perform. Women, in effect, in embracing the highest moral principles of their own society, were also embracing a system that undermined their capabilities and minimized the avenues by which they could take an active role in connecting with society as a whole.

CHAPTER THREE

The Healing Power of Words

Ink, Spit, and Holy Speech

During the first quarter of the twentieth century, there were no indigenous practitioners of Western medicine in the Arabian Gulf region. In the opinion of Arabian Mission physician Paul Harrison, there was no local medical tradition of any kind. Harrison, who first went to Bahrain in 1909 as a young graduate of the Johns Hopkins University Medical School and who practiced medicine throughout the Gulf region for most of his professional career, claimed that "there are no doctors in Arabia, neither doctors trained in schools nor inheritors of tradition handed down from father to son or from master to pupil by word of mouth." "In twelve years' experience," he wrote, "I have never seen the most elementary beginnings of anything that could be termed a medical profession in any part of Arabia. Its only medicine consists of a generally diffused knowledge of some useful remedies and the kindly ministrations of the Arab women to the sick of their own household."[1]

In spite of the absence of what this American physician would have called a medical profession, there were still individuals, many of them women, who possessed specialized knowledge of the healing arts. One of the reasons we know about these Gulf practitioners is that Dr. Harrison and his mission colleagues wrote about them. In the course of trying to dispense Western medicine, they discovered the importance of cultural context in the delivery of medical care: they had to deal with the results of local practitioners' techniques and the expectations of their patients concerning causes and cures for their diseases, and these were not always compatible with the medicine the missionaries were trained to practice.

The missionary records show that healing practices in the Gulf, as elsewhere in the world, were inseparable from religion, philosophy, and ideas about the body's relationship to the local environment. Acquiring specialized knowledge was therefore seen as a prerequisite for recognition as a medical practitioner, but, as elsewhere, access to this knowledge was controlled and distributed unevenly between men and women. Men and women thus employed different healing techniques, specialized in different ailments, and were perceived by patients as being worthy of different levels of respect.

In the Gulf region during the early twentieth century, this dichotomy meant that male practitioners claimed specialized religious knowledge in order to prepare writings for amulets, utter healing words correctly, and prescribe what were called Prophetic medicines. Women claimed knowledge of practical experience and heterodox rituals, prescribing herbal cures and homemade amulets as prophylactics against disease and votive offerings to facilitate the intervention of the supernatural. Women could also utter healing words, but only to the level of their expertise. In spite of their preponderance in the day-to-day practice of medicine, women's skills were held in less esteem, and their access to the best medicines was limited. Whatever the training of the healer—man or woman, Western missionary or Gulf practitioner—the treatment was keyed to the expectations of the patient.

What Do Patients Think Causes Illness, and What Do They Expect the Healer to Do for Them?

According to medical missionaries throughout the Gulf region, patients generally attributed both the cause and the cure of disease to spiritual intervention. Missionary physicians represented their patients as convinced that God was all-knowing, a being who intervened personally in the life of the individual, who planned out each person's life in advance and was responsible for his or her fate. When illness occurred, it could therefore only have happened because God willed it to occur. However, witchcraft and malevolent spirits, including Satan and pesky impish creatures called jinn, could intervene to cause illness.[2] Because the existence of these spirits and the power of witchcraft was validated in the Qur'an, the possibility of their being a part of the disease process could not be denied; even so, because of His omnipotence, God was never off the hook. He was always ultimately responsible for disease or misfortune, and because he was the designated responsible party, patients' response to illness was problematic. If God had predetermined what would happen, wouldn't seeking medical care be a challenge to his judgment? Wouldn't it be a denial of his omnipotence?

"Apparently," would have been the missionaries' answer. In each of the Gulf stations, as in Hasa and Najd, where the mission doctors took medical tours, they complained that patients' resignation to their fates was an obstacle to the delivery of medical care. During one of these tours in 1949 in villages near Hufuf, for example, mission physicians were not allowed to treat trachoma in the eyes of children. According to Ida Storm, the wife of a missionary physician who worked as her husband's assistant, not one woman would let the doctors treat her child, even after being told the child would go blind if left untreated. "The women would say," she wrote, " 'they are in God's hands. If he wishes them to go blind, God is good; if he doesn't, they will not go blind.' They shrug their shoulders," she wrote, "saying, 'God is merciful,' and they take the babies away without medicine."[3]

In spite of what the missionaries said about their patients' acceptance of illness as a judgment from God, it is not true that sick people in general did not seek to be cured. In fact the sick came in droves to the mission clinics. In Bahrain, in Musqat, and in Kuwait, patients took a number and waited their turn to be seen, sometimes all day, and during medical tours into Hasa and Najd more patients sought medical care than could possibly be accommodated. Even after taking in account the possibility that medical reports inflated the missionaries' patient loads, the numbers of those treated in the second year of operations in Kuwait are respectable: the Kuwait Medical Report just for women in 1913 indicated fifty surgical operations and 2,877 treatments given to "town Arabs, both rich and poor, Bedouins, Persians and Negroes," as well as to thirty "Jewesses."[4]

The absolute necessity of accepting God's will without complaint is bedrock in the ideological frame of the Wahhabis. In Ibn Abd al-Wahhab's *Kitab at-Tawhid*, which was circulated widely during the revival of the teens and twenties, even mourning for the dead is taken as a statement of unbelief.[5] Ibn Abd al-Wahhab reasoned that God afflicts individuals with illness not for the sake of punishment but for their ultimate salvation and affliction is, in effect, a blessing in disguise: "Whenever Allah wishes a person well," writes Ibn Abd al-Wahhab, quoting Hadith, "He hastens to send him punishment in this world, and whenever He does not, He postpones the punishment to the Day of Judgment." "Affliction is directly proportional to the reward," he adds. "If Allah loves a people, He vests them with affliction. If they accept it, Allah is pleased with them and rewards them accordingly. If they resent it, Allah will be displeased with them accordingly" (pp. 103–104). Yet even the most prominent proselytizer of stoic Wahhabism, Ibn Sa'ud, called for the missionary doctors to treat not only himself but his family and retainers as well, and the first time this occurred was in 1914, in the very heat of the Wahhabi revival.[6]

Ibn Sa'ud was hardly being cynical about his professed religion when he sought out medical care from the American doctors. To the contrary, while the Qur'an and Hadith do assert God's predeterminism, they also explicitly open the door to the use of healing techniques of all kinds. Recitations from holy books were in fact at the heart of Arabian medical practice, prescribed in the Qur'an itself: "And We reveal of the 'Quran that which is a healing and a mercy to the believers, and it adds only to the perdition of the unjust."[7] A great many Hadith prescribe medicaments to consume, perfumes to smell, and herbs to brew; cures for constipation, back pain, scorpion sting, and infestation by jinn. There are also Hadith laying out formulaic expressions to exorcise bad spirits and undo witchcraft, and prayer prescriptions to pronounce over the sick.

The question of taking medicines in defiance of God's plan was taken up in the medieval era when the Hadith and Qur'anic verses related to healing were collated and integrated with elements of the Greek Hippocratic corpus into a science of Prophetic medicine. One of these texts, *Prophetic Medicine*, by Ibn Qayyam Al Jawziyya, resolved the contradiction with an illustration from Hadith, justifying the taking of medicines in spite of predestination on the grounds that the taking of medicines to alter predestination is itself predetermined by God. "Do you know of an amulet we can use or a healing medicament or a precaution we can take that could repel [the path] of predestination?" the Prophet is asked. "All these things," the Prophet answers, "are pre-ordained by God."[8] What this tradition means, Al Jawziyya explained, is that when a person seeks treatment, he does so only because God has preordained that he would, and therefore seeking a cure is permissible. Being cured is furthermore possible only if God intervenes to assure that the cure employed is compatible with the disease, for "Whatever a disease that may be, Allah has created a medication for it, regardless of the fact that some men may come to know what this medication is and others may not" (pp. 16–17).[9] If the healing "weren't preordained," he says, "then the treatment would be in vain" (p. 18).

Patients, in short, could be receptive to any remedy, with the understanding that the outcome of medical treatment is ultimately in the hands of God. The patient goes to the doctor hoping that he or she knows the precise remedy God created for the patient's particular ailment and understanding that the medical treatment provided will only work if God has already decided that it will.

The *Kitab at-Tawhid* also approves all medical treatment, provided it is done correctly, the sole criterion of correctness being that treatment take place without supplication to any power except that of God. Ibn Abd al-Wahhab's concern was that the person asking to be cured or doing the curing not strike a deal with the evil spirit perceived to be behind the illness; rather, the person should go over the spirit's head and deal directly with God. Malevolent spirits, he writes, can be countered, but only by reciting verses from the Qur'an or any "legitimate prayers." Opening the door very wide to any and all techniques of healing, Ibn Abd al-Wahhab adds, "One may also use pharmaceutical preparations."[10] In fact he says, "Whatever is useful has not been forbidden" (p. 84).

In Najd under Ibn Sa'ud, it can be safely assumed that at least among the political elite medical treatments were considered legitimate in practice as well as in theory (although this chapter will show that certain treatments were more legitimate for men to perform than for women). Ibn Sa'ud and his father took pride in their knowledge of both Prophetic and Hippocratic medicine, which Dr. Harrison thought to be the common knowledge of the unlettered man on the street. Ibn Sa'ud even complained to Dr. Mylrea, the physician he consulted in 1914, of the current lack of interest in studying these sciences.[11] At the same time, he imported Syrian doctors trained in France to be on call for his family.

Such openness to every known type of medicine on the part of the educated elite should caution against overstating the importance of religion in motivating individuals in their choices about medical care. Scriptural interpretation is not the same as individual belief, and even if faith in God's predeterminism were etched in the mind, it would not necessarily predetermine individual choice. Parallel or contradictory belief systems exist simultaneously in every society, and people act on those beliefs: sick people go to faith healers after mainstream medicine has been exhausted, for example, or choose faith-healing instead of it; they light votive candles in church as an extra precaution while undergoing conventional treatment; an athlete might carry a good-luck charm when competing but would not substitute the charm for physical training; and a traveler's decision to place a St. Christopher medal in his car would not preclude his choice to use a seat belt.

It is also entirely possible that missionaries overstated predeterminism as a motivation for refusing treatment because they misinterpreted what their patients were telling them: certainly, there were situations in which the physicians mistook words that were a polite refusal of *their* medical treatment for a refusal to accept *any*. In one of her reports to mission headquarters, Eleanor Calverley lamented the problem of "Arab fatalism" and told of an instance in Kuwait in the early 1920s when a woman brought a baby nearly blind with eye ulcers to the mission hospital. She had criticized the mother, who had already tried a homemade remedy, for not having brought the baby sooner, and the mother responded that she had not because "Allah ketebt alayha [*sic*]": God had willed her not to.[12] This episode, however, does not necessarily indicate that the mother rejected treatment because of religious beliefs; she was, after all, at the mission clinic asking for help. Rather, it suggests that she believed she had other health-care alternatives in local healers, which she had already explored, and that the American clinic might not have been her first choice.

And why should it have been? Until the missionary doctors set up their clinics, Western medicine was quite unknown in the Gulf, and where the clinics' work was known it was the subject of rumors. There were even occasional fatwas advising people to stay away from the missionaries and *khutbas* (mosque sermons)—in Kuwait, at least—warning against going to the Christian doctors who dispensed Christian prayers each morning along with medical advice.[13] In any case, even at its best, Western medicine had its limits when the first missionary doctors arrived in the Gulf around 1909. The physicians knew about bacteriology, and knew how to use anesthesia and perform some surgeries such as Caesarean sections, appendectomies, and removal of cysts and tumors. They could set bones and knew to use sterile instruments and clean water, and how to inoculate for smallpox and avoid contagion. They could dispense cough mixtures, aspirin, iodine, quinine, diarrhea medications, and laxatives and could diagnose common diseases. But during the first years of the mission there were no sulfa drugs, and there were no antibiotics at all until after World War II, when penicillin became available in commercial quantities.[14] Mission programing further-more put evangelizing ahead of good medical practice: young people grad-uated from medical school and went, without a residency, to seminary and then to the field for a year of full-time language study. Of all the medical missionaries, only Mary Allison admitted in writing that the time lapse was starting to cause her to forget what she had learned in school. A latecomer to the mission who began her practice in the 1940s, Allison candidly ad-mitted years after the Arabian Mission closed, "The treatment was neces-sarily inadequate. I specialized in omnipotence and learned my trade at the expense of the poor."[15]

Despite all this, when the missionaries set up their clinics in the Sunni and Shi'a towns of the Gulf and in touring stations in Wahhabi-controlled Hasa and Najd, the legitimacy of medical care was not at issue, regardless of what patients are reported to have said about fate. God's role in the course of illness was considered paramount, and supplications to God were the sine qua non of the healing process, but beyond that, any technique that held out hope for a cure—God willing—was welcomed.

The Healing Power of Words

"The best of all remedies," according to Hadith, " is the Quran."[16] Because spiritual intervention was perceived to be the ultimate cause of illness, words from the Qur'an were employed both as an antidote to illness and a prophylactic shield in its prevention. One method of conveying the Qur'an's goodness on behalf of the sick person was to recite parts of it over him or her, and professional readers were employed for this purpose.[17]

Professional readers were both men and women. For men, reading over the sick was ancillary to other occupations, such as being an imam in a mosque, a Qur'an teacher, a judge, an officiant at marriage ceremonies, or a scholar of the higher religious sciences. Because the higher education in re-ligion required for these occupations was the prerogative of men, male read-ers were perceived as being more highly skilled than women readers. Many women employed to read over the sick could actually read text, but their numbers were small. And even with the ability to read, women readers could not have competed with male religious scholars for prestige in the profession because they were not eligible for study of the higher religious sciences, and even with the basics of Qur'an and Hadith learning, they could never aspire to one of the prestigious public offices for which their education qualified them.

Women readers were invariably described as "old" in missionary records. Age was an important prerequisite for the profession, as women's prayers—the very medicine the reader administers—are invalid if said while one is menstruating. Because age also mitigates a woman's potential for causing fitna, being "old" also would allow her physical mobility and respectability, both necessary for her to visit the sick in households outside her neighborhood or family.[18] "Old" also implies widowhood. Women readers, like women who practiced other professions, were often people who had to earn a living.

The clientele of professional women readers were other women and children. Although they faced competition from more highly esteemed male readers—missionary records offer numerous examples of women patients' preference for the services of male readers (the favorite concubine of Ibn Sa'ud, for example, brought a blind mullah to read over her daughter every night at bedtime)[19]—women readers achieved status in their communities. As with medical practice in the United States in the early nineteenth century, a time when the profession's reputation suffered from inadequate science and the lack of fixed qualifications for its practitioners, the healer's professional status attached not to her success rate in curing patients but to the social status of the patients she was able to attract.

In Najd, women healers were known as *mutaww'at*, and their treatment of the sick was called "reading" (*qira'a*).[20] In Bahrain, the woman reader was called *maulaya*. A missionary nurse in Bahrain, Cornelia Dalenberg, described the schedule of one particular Shi'a maulaya who carried the honorific title of *hajjia*, not, Dalenberg tells us, because she had made the Pilgrimage to Mecca, nor because she had made the pilgrimage to Najef and Kerbala, but because she had learned the Qur'an and was a professional reader. "Every day," Dalenberg wrote, "she goes from house to house, here to read over a sick baby, there to read a bad spirit out of a girl."[21] Hajjia had learned more than just Qur'an recitation, for she also performed readings for the *ta'ziya* (literally, "consolation"; ritual and drama performed in commemoration of the martyrdom of Hussein) held in the ma'tam.

Reading holy words from scripture as a method of healing is universal. In the Gulf region this method had been observed and recorded in different social contexts for more than a century previous to the missionaries' arrival and continues to be used up to the present. The Al Murrah Bedouin, for example, deal with insanity by taking the patient to religious functionaries in Hufuf who perform special readings of the Qur'an over the afflicted person, according to Donald Cole, the "reader" being anyone who has memorized some lines from the Qur'an.[22] Doughty, whose experience predates Cole's by some hundred years, also commented on the use of holy words as a method of curing mental illness, which the Bedouin, Doughty indicated, attributed to possession by jinn. "Every disease asketh a remedy," Doughty wrote, "and there are also exorcists for the mejnuns in Arabia. . . . By reading powerful spells out of the scripture of God over those sick persons, they would have us believe they can put in fear and drive out the possessing demons."[23]

Ink, Spit, and Holy Speech

The pharmacopoeia of Qur'anic words included not just the uttering of words but also physical extensions of them. Words were conceived as capable of communicating their goodness to patients when written down on paper and buried, worn, or consumed through drinking the ink with which they had been written or the saliva of one who had uttered them.

A medicine derived from the goodness of Qur'anic words that was in use in Kuwait was the saliva of a male believer. This medicine was uniquely designed for the benefit of women and children, because the saliva of men was viewed as better able to communicate goodness than the saliva of women. Men were more likely to know the proper words from the Qur'an, and, in the Gulf towns, they alone prayed in the mosque, the place closest to God's ear. Women patients therefore believed, according to Eleanor Calverley, that the saliva of one who had worshiped in the mosque had greater healing power than the saliva of one who had worshiped at home.[24]

In 1918 Edwin Calverley, a missionary in Kuwait, watched as the saliva of men who had just completed prayers in the mosque was collected. A group of women, he wrote, were huddled about the entrance to the mosque with cups and bowls in their hands, and as they left the men spat right into the cups that were held out to them. "Some . . . spat into one cup after another, —into every cup that was put near them." Calverley made a project out of trying to understand the meaning of what he had seen. Everyone he asked (primarily the male students in his English classes) was familiar with the saliva offering. "Those people with the cups and bowls," he was told, "have some friend or someone in their family who is sick, and they are collecting the spittle of the men who have just finished their prayers for their sick ones at home."[25] His students also told him that the use of saliva for healing purposes was widespread all over the Arabian Peninsula, including in Hasa and Najd and all the towns along the Gulf.

In her twenty years of medical work in the Gulf, Dr. Eleanor Calverley saw her patients actually swallow this medicine many times. "Someone comes in bearing a cup containing a contribution of saliva from the mouth of a man who has just finished worshipping in a mosque," she wrote, "and they say that it has great healing power if swallowed by the one in pain."[26] During an epidemic of smallpox in Kuwait, Mrs. Stanley Mylrea was present when a request for saliva was made, and she recorded the incident in a quarterly report to mission headquarters: "I was once spending the day at the house of a mullah or learned man and there came a knock at the door. My hostess called out, 'Who is it?' and the answer came, 'I want the Mullah—my child is ill.' It was a woman at the door, with a glass of water in her hand, and she wanted the Mullah to read over the glass and spit into so that she could give it to her child as medicine."[27]

Hafiz Wahba, Ibn Sa'ud's Egyptian-born education minister who spent a decade in Riyadh in the 1920s and traveled throughout the Gulf towns, describes a similar method of transmitting the healing power of words. A remedy, "particularly popular for chronic ulcers," he wrote, "is for a relative of the patient to stand at the door of the Mosque with a cup of water or clarified butter, into which each member of the congregation breathes as he comes out, some in addition reading a verse or two of the Quran or reciting a prayer for the patient's recovery. The contents of the cup are then drunk by the patient."[28]

The local healer with the most popular practice in Kuwait in the 1920s was a man with the title *sayyid* who used water as the medium for transmitting God's words to the patient. According to Harold Dickson, this man "had remarkable powers of healing." Dickson wrote that Sayyid Yasin would take a cup of water, "go through the form of spitting in it without actually doing so, then tell the patient that he had but to drink the water and all would be well." "Some might call it faith healing," he wrote, "but Sayyid Yasin described it as the hand of God working through him. He would place his hand on a patient's head and say, 'Believe in God and He will cure you of your ill. Go in peace.' "[29]

The use of spit as medicine was controversial, and Edwin Calverley learned from his students that at least one shaikh who tried to oppose the practice was expelled from Hasa, a fact also mentioned by Hafiz Wahba, who names the expelled shaikh.[30] Calverley concluded that in Kuwait the local mullahs promoted the distribution of spit for use as medicine because they could charge a fee for it.[31]

The saliva cure could not have been a transient phenomenon of the period, because about thirty-three years before the Calverleys arrived in Kuwait Doughty had encountered spitting as a cure "everywhere" he went in Arabia. Doughty wrote that he was twice asked to deliver the cure himself because he was known to be able to read: once he was asked to spit into the sore eyes of an infant, and once Mutair Bedouin in Qasim asked him to spit onto some bread and salt that would be delivered to someone who was ill.[32] Doughty also described saliva used to cure a sick camel. The healer, Doughty wrote, "sat with a bowl of water before him, and mumbling. There upon he spat in it, and mumbled solemnly and spat many times; and after a half hour of this work the water was taken to the sick beast to drink— Spitting," Doughty adds, "we have seen to be some great matter in their medicine" (2:184).

In Doughty's opinion, reading, enhanced by the spit of the reader, was the ultimate medical cure among the Bedouin of Najd whom he visited (1:359). When someone has been wounded, he wrote,

> They know nothing better than to "read" over him . . . some spells
> they have learned to babble by heart of words lifted out of the
> Qur'an; the power of "God's Word," . . . they think, should be able to
> overcome the malignity of venom. Some wiseacre "reader" may be
> found in nearly every wandering village; they are men commonly of
> an infirm understanding and no good conditions, superstitiously
> deceiving themselves and not unwilling to deceive others. The
> patient's friends send for one, weeping to be their helper; and
> between his breaths their "reader" will spit upon the wound, and
> sprinkle a little salt. . . . All availeth less, they think, than the "Word
> of God," were it rightly "read"; upon their part, the desert "readers,"
> without letters, acknowledge themselves to be unlearned.
>
> (1:358–359)

In all of Doughty's numerous recorded observations of reading and spitting as a method of cure, every reader, regardless of his being unable to actually read from the Qur'an, some unable even to recite Qur'anic verses correctly from memory, was a man.

In addition to saliva from the mouth of one who had uttered holy words, healing power could be communicated through the ink with which holy words had been written. The "ink" commonly used was water dyed with saffron, although ink for medicinal purposes could include other ingredients. (For example, a recipe from the tenth century calls for tree sap, water, salt, gum arabic, grilled nuts, iron sulfate, honey, and carbon black.)[33] Words would be written on paper, pottery, or parchment and then washed off with water that was collected for administration to the person who was ill.

Both the Calverleys and Hafiz Wahba witnessed the consumption of ink medicine.[34] Eleanor Calverley, in describing the very first time she was allowed to help deliver a baby in Kuwait, writes that an ink-and-water drink prepared by a mullah was brought to the patient when her labor became difficult, and the patient drank it.[35] Hafiz Wahba, in his discussion of Arabian medicine, also says that the ink cure was a popular treatment for "many chronic ailments, particularly nervous ones." Lines of the Qur'an were written on a plate, he says, plain water or rosewater was poured over the writing to dissolve the ink, and then the water was given to the sick person.[36]

Like the spit medicine, ink medicine was known historically throughout the region. A full century before the arrival of the first missionary doctors to Kuwait, Burckhardt, who visited Anayza Bedouin in the Syrian desert and also traveled to the Hejaz, wrote that the Bedouin "have great faith in the efficacy of certain words written on slips of paper which the patient swallows with avidity."[37] The ink cure was still in use among other Bedouin forty years after the mission doctors first described the ink cure in their quarterly reports. Violet Dickson, who lived in Kuwait from the time of her marriage about 1918 until her death, observed the preparation of a treatment for headache by a mutawwa' (here, simply teacher, reader, or healer). She was visiting a family of Al Murrah Bedouin in 1964, when a reader from another tribal group, the Manasir tribe, was making a house call, having been summoned from Qatar especially to administer an ink cure for headache.

"While I sat there," Dickson wrote, "he was performing the magic ritual known as mahu which would cure Salah's headaches. On his lap he had an enamel bowl, and by his side a coffee-cup containing a mixture of saffron and water. With a twig, which he dipped into the cup, he was most carefully painting patterns inside the bowl commencing from the bottom." The holy man drew a pattern in the shape of the number three sideways around the lip of the bowl, and then another series of patterns of circles, dots, and lines above the first.

When these were completed, he poured water into the bowl, until it was about half-full, and slowly swirled it round until all trace of his patterns had disappeared and the water was coloured yellow. This he now poured carefully into a bottle, and then repeated the process. I was told that Salah would later be given some of this water to drink and the rest would be rubbed on to his body. . . . The women told me that the signs were taken from the Quran. . . . The Mutawwa' had remained for twenty-two days and they had paid him Rs. 300.[38]

The mutawwa' was a healer with a professional specialty. His methods, however, did not require actual writing or even reciting specific Qur'anic words from memory, and, as with Doughty's reader, he may not have been able to read at all. The key to his success lay in the expectations of his patients, who believed that, if there was to be a cure at all, it would come through the healing power of holy words or, in this case, holy symbols. As Dickson wrote, the people who came to the mutawwa' for treatment believed the symbols he used to have emanated in some way from the Qur'an.

Medicine or Filth?

In the first quarter of the century, people in the Gulf region did not perceive the ingestion of spit (and ink as well, depending on its composition) to be as counterproductive in curing illness as it would appear later in the century, when the principles of contagion and germ theory were more commonly known. Before the discovery in Europe of the organic bases for the transmission of disease—which was made only in the 1860s and did not become generally known in Europe and the United States until the 1870s and 1880s—the distinction between dirt and cleanliness was less clear, and the purity of substances that would today be understood as filth was determined by cultural rather than biological factors.[39] Historically, substances that would be understood today as filth have been used as medicine across cultures. In the Greek Hippocratic corpus, for example, substances such as animal feces, saliva, and other bodily fluids were prescribed as medicine, particularly for women's ailments. In the Gospel according to Mark, Jesus heals a blind man by spitting in the man's eyes; in the Gospel according to St. John, by mixing his spit with dirt and applying the mud patty to the man's eyes.[40] The ambiguity over filth and medicine can be seen in the method of vaccination performed successfully in the Ottoman Empire and emulated in Europe long before the organic basis for contagion was understood: a smear of pus from an infected sheep was spread into an open cut on a healthy one. Even after the discovery of bacteria as the conveyor of disease the lines between filth and purity are not so clearly drawn: penicillin, for example, is made from mold cultures; many vaccines are made from weakened forms of the microorganisms that cause the ailments they are meant to prevent.

An Islamic principle for defining what is and what is not dirt is empirical and open to reason and scientific observation: substances are pure unless proven otherwise. Spit, in the Gulf of 1918, had not been proven impure: not only was it not known to carry disease-causing bacteria, given an infusion of Qur'anic words, it was known to be capable of conveying goodness by virtue of the Prophet's example. Thus in 1918 saliva from the mouth of a person saying prayers would have been perceived by patients and healers alike as a potential source of medicine prescribed in the Hadith. When Calverley asked his night-class students for the reasoning behind the spit cure, they knew immediately a Hadith that would explain it: "Aisha said that the Prophet told a sick man, 'In the name of Allah, the earth of our land and the saliva of some of us cure our sick, by God's grace.' "[41] Calverley added that an aphorism commonly known in Kuwait conveyed the same meaning: "The saliva of a believer will cure a believer" (p. 16).

The saliva cure appears in the medical prescriptions of Al Jawziyya's book of Prophetic medicine. In one Hadith the Prophet's companions spat directly on the wound of a scorpion sting, as they recited, "Praise be upon the sustainer and cherisher of the worlds," and when the Prophet saw what his companions had done, the story goes, he approved.[42] Spitting infused the goodness of the words directly into the wound or into a medium to be consumed by someone who was ill and thus taken directly to the source of the illness. Al Jawziyya explains the process as an exorcism, which works through an exorciser's heart and mouth. If accompanied by some of his spittle and breath, Al Jawziyya says, the healing act is more efficacious (p. 215). Spit mixed with prayer can also be useful as a deterrent to illness, he explains, and he relates the following: "When the holy Prophet went to bed, he used to expectorate in his hands, saying, 'Say, He is God, Alone,' and recite the muawithatain verses [verses asking God for refuge]. He would then wipe his face and every part of his body that could be reached" (p. 220).

Al Jawziyya also lays out a rationale for a cure that employs salt (a "natural element") together with prayer (a "spiritual element"), which Doughty also described. He relates a Hadith in which the Prophet, stung on the finger by a scorpion, tends the wound by pouring salt mixed with water over it, reciting at the same time "God is One" along with the verses for seeking refuge from harm in God (p. 217).[43]

At the opening of the twentieth century, the state of public health in the Gulf region would have been a challenge to the skills of any competent healer. Infant and child mortality was extremely high everywhere in the peninsula, and adults rarely lived beyond fifty years.[44] In addition to childhood diseases, such as German measles, mumps, and chicken pox, there were epidemics of cholera, smallpox, and plague, as well as chronic dysentery, malaria, and tuberculosis, probably caused by the ingestion of camel's milk. Widespread venereal disease was complicated by malnutrition, and a standard practice employed by midwives during birth sometimes caused the unborn child of the subsequent pregnancy to be trapped in the mother's womb, bringing death to both. During an epidemic in Riyadh in 1919, "one hundred people a day were dying," Paul Harrison wrote, and "the bodies were carried out . . . two to a donkey and ten to a camel."[45]

In spite of the presence of so much serious disease, whether the local healer was a man or women, the prestige accorded to the healer was qualified by the medical profession's limited ability to bring relief to the sick. As a profession, Gulf medicine in 1920 could be compared to the profession in the United States right up to the mid-nineteenth century: a survey carried out by the American Medical Association in 1851 showed that medicine was at the bottom of professional choices of graduates from the top U.S. colleges and was viewed by some with disgust.[46] Until near the end of the century medical education had no standardized training programs or examinations; neither were there even approved apprentice programs.

This is not to say that Gulf physicians, like American physicians, did not experience success, as some healing techniques were not without positive and tangible effects. These techniques included exorcism and prophylaxis, as well as herbal brews, bone setting, and surgical intervention, which will be discussed in the following chapters. But the person who healed with holy words also experienced success. The ink, spit, and holy speech methods of healing were of value for their placebo effect: if the person being treated believed that the holy words would work he was likely to feel that they had.

The placebo effect is not to be underestimated in considering what respect would have been rendered to the healer. Since the will of God and the intervention of malevolent spirits figured prominently as causes of disease, patients would have wanted what the reader, as well as the exorcist and the hijab writer, could give them. They would have wanted and expected the treatments that the Prophet prescribed, however ineffectual or harmful some might perceive them to be. Women and men practitioners were judged according to the expectations of their patients, and so both derived a certain prestige that was otherwise unwarranted by their skills. Given patients' views of the causes of their misfortune, for all practitioners of the healing arts in Arabia, the missionary doctors included, the ultimate absolution for incompetence, poor judgment, ignorance, and bad results was the patient's willingness to deflect responsibility for the outcome from the acts of the healer to the vicissitudes of fate and God's will.

If one is looking at differences between men and women as healers, however, women's professional practice carried less prestige. The professional reader did occupy a respectable position in the towns, because she was educated and performed a recognized service among other women. At the same time, however, she was invariably described as old; as someone who was not in a guardian relationship to a man or who was beyond the age at which she needed to be guarded. The woman reader would have had to be old to establish her credibility as a healer, for her prayers, the very medicine she had to offer, would have been invalidated were she to be menstruating. Assuming that the normative state for women was to be under the guardianship of a man, the professional reader was in this one sense abnormal, like most of the women healers and midwives discussed in the following chapters: they were poor, or Bedouin transient in town society, or former slaves, or foreign, or widowed. These were people who worked because they needed to.

When men engaged in healing with holy words their activities were performed on a perceived higher level of skill, even when, sometimes, they were unable to read at all. The perception of men's possessing a higher level of skill was held by women patients as well as by men, for, given the option, women tended to choose a male reader over a woman. This only makes sense, since the man who was a reader was in fact likely to be better educated. Furthermore, the titles bestowed on male scholars—imam, or mullah, or sayyid—certified their competence to practice medicine in a way that "hajjia" and "maulaya" do not.

Men also had direct access to the best medicines: because men pray in the mosque, the place that is closest to God's ear, their very spit carried the goodness of the holy words uttered in the mosque. The ink cure, too, was prepared by men and given by women to the sick of their households to drink. The examples given by the missionaries and other commentators furthermore suggest that even where the professional healer was an illiterate among illiterates, the person esteemed for his recitations, his spit, and his ink preparations was also likely to be a man.

A similar gendered division of skills and perceived difference in level of expertise also characterized American medicine in the first decade of the twentieth century, when the first mission clinic was established in Kuwait. During the latter half of the nineteenth century, women's medical schools opened in the United States, and the number of women physicians increased between 1880 and 1900 to 5.6 percent nationally, while in Boston the proportion of women physicians increased to over 18 percent (p. 117). The elite schools, however, were for men: Paul Harrison graduated from the nation's premier medical school, Johns Hopkins, a college that did not open its doors to women until 1890 when a donor offered funds earmarked for women's medical education (p. 117). After 1906 the regulation and upgrading of medical schools forced the closing of poorly rated schools, which included nearly all women's medical colleges, and the near-exclusion of women from most of the good colleges that remained (p. 124). After 1910, even when women were admitted to the better medical schools, their admission was limited by a 5 percent quota that remained until affirmative action policies came into effect in the 1960s (p. 124).

The mission bureaucracy in the United States also devalued women's practice of medicine in a very tangible way: women medical missionaries were paid less than their male colleagues, and their tenure in the mission terminated if they married someone not employed by the mission. By contrast, wives of missionary doctors, even wives who were full-time homemakers, were automatically put on the mission payroll.

The ink, spit, and holy speech methods of healing discussed in this chapter are a paradigm for women as healers and as patients in general and for the perceived quality of medicine they were deemed capable of delivering. Communicating the goodness of holy words to the sick person was the singular orthodox method and the first line of defense against illness, but it was still just one of many healing methods in common use. When women engaged in preventive medicine and healing techniques based on exorcising, appeasing, or getting communication from spirits, the most highly skilled practitioners were, again, men, but most practitioners were still women, and their patients included just about everyone. The exception was the Zar. The following chapter looks at healing techniques by engaging spirits.

CHAPTER FOUR

Engaging Spirits

Prophylaxis, Witchcraft, Exorcisms, Trial by Ordeal, and Zar

Missionary observer Eleanor Calverley recorded in 1919 that the women of Arabia not only have "faith in Allah, but they believe also in jinns, in demon possession, in enchantments, and all kinds of charms and magic."[1] Calverley, a Protestant missionary doctor, like her medical counterparts in the Gulf, saw magic as something different from the healing that comes through faith in God, and as less preferable. Magic—the use of spells, charms, and ceremonies aimed at imposing one's will on nature, on others, or on the spirit world—may be effective, but it is different from prayer, for prayer follows correct procedure and invokes the help of the right God. The difference between prayer and magic is therefore not an objective fact, says Jacob Neusner, but a matter of personal judgment about whose procedure is correct.[2] For Sunnis of the Gulf and for Shi'ites, the line between prayer and magic was elastic, but to the Wahhabis of Najd, the line was impermeable: when one engaged the spiritual world in hope of a cure, one had to do it through proper prayer, and this prayer had to be addressed directly to the ultimate spirit, God, and to God alone.

Calverley's hospital in Kuwait drew patients who were Bedouin, villagers, and townspeople from Najd to Basra, and they came with their own interpretation about the cause of their disease and their own ideas about what they expected the doctor to do for them. Patients sometimes assumed that malevolent spirits had been at work on their bodies and were responsible for their illnesses. Given the absence of information about the organic basis of disease, this diagnosis made sense. As mentioned in the previous chapter, in the Qur'an and in Hadith literature, Satan, witchcraft, impish sprites called jinn, and amorphous spirits exist in the world and intervene in the life of the individual to precipitate misfortune. Because their existence is validated in infallible sources, these malevolent spirits cannot be denied, and their machinations must be countered in some way. The malevolence of spirits, for example, could be deflected away from a potential victim through prophylactic applications of holy words and by decoys, disguises, or branding; once ensconced in a body, malevolent spirits could be exorcised through spells or more branding performed while uttering holy words. Spells could also be used in sympathetic magic to direct a malevolent spirit to go after a chosen victim. Similarly, spells could be used to tap into the latent animate characteristics of inanimate objects and enlist them in discovering truth or foretelling the future or in injecting emotions of love or hate in another person.

Both men and women healers specialized in spirit engagement, but, as in the case of reading, they practiced their professions on different perceived levels of skill and social acceptability and catered to different clientele. Spirit engagement was commonplace in the Gulf towns but was at the same time considered vaguely suspicious or downright disreputable unless performed by a recognized practitioner who used only holy words and knew the "right" way to proceed. Under the Wahhabis, spirit engagement was and is theoretically intolerable but still practiced to a limited extent. When a healer or magician engaged the spirits, however, the act was treated as less intolerable when performed by a man. When performed correctly by a man, in fact, it could be a profession. In contemporary Saudi Arabia, spirit engagement is not just theoretically intolerable, witchcraft and the use of amulets are illegal: in 1996, in fact, a person was executed in the Kingdom of Saudi Arabia for practicing witchcraft.[3]

Amulets, Decoys, and Disguises: Women Guard the Household

In the Gulf region, jinn, Satan, spirits, and the evil eye were thought to be lurking everywhere, even in the ground, awaiting the opportunity to inflict misfortune or illness. Around 1909 Samuel Zwemer, the founder of the Arabian Mission, described the most common method used to deflect these malevolent forces: the amulet (hijab). An amulet is a passage from scripture used as a prophylactic shield against harm or the container that holds the holy words. "The most common things used as amulets are a small Quran suspended in a silver case," Zwemer wrote, "words from the Quran written on paper and carried in a leather receptacle; the names of Allah or their numerical value; the names of Muhammad and his companions." An amulet can also be in the form of a charm, such as a piece of jewelry, often gold with turquoise stones. The charms used for protection, Zwemer writes, include "precious stones, with or without inscriptions; beads; old coins; clay images; the teeth of wild animals; holy earth from Mecca or Kerbala in the shape of tiny bricks or in small bags. When the Kaaba covering at Mecca is taken down each year and renewed," he adds "the old cloth is cut up into small pieces and sold for charms."[4]

Dickson writes that Shi'a tribal people in Iraq commonly wear amulets, usually in the form of a pouch containing a little scroll with a verse from the Qur'an. Dickson also says that this is only true of non-Bedouin: Bedouin tribes, he says, "especially if tainted with Wahhabism, look upon charms as wrong."[5] Nurse Cornelia Dalenberg, who first arrived at the Bahrain mission station in 1921, wrote in her memoirs that she "often saw blue beads, animal teeth, or other charms hung around [children's] little necks or heads to ward off evil. Amulets containing verses snipped from a copy of the Koran were almost always present in sick rooms, or even hanging above baby cradles."[6] Hafiz Wahba wrote that "prophylactic treatment by means of quotations from the Quran . . . is practiced a good deal all over Arabia, and in the Hejaz and Bahrain children are often heavily laden with amulets and talismans, one perhaps to ward off envy, another to guard against the evil eye, another to protect against jinns, another to ensure long life to the wearer."[7]

The verses of protection (*ayat al-hifdh*) in the Qur'an, Zwemer writes, are considered the most powerful deflectors of evil and are the verses most commonly written into amulets. Examples Zwemer gives include, "The preservation of heaven and earth is no burden unto Him," "God is the best protector," "They guard him by the command of God," "We guard him from every stoned devil," and "A protection from every rebellious devil."[8] The same holy words written into the amulet are spoken as formulaic expressions to invoke God's protection against malevolent spirits. Wahba gives some examples of these expressions: "I take refuge in the word of God from every devil or unseen thing, and from every evil eye. In the name of God I protect you from everything that may harm you, from any evil that may befall you, from any living person, and from any jealous eye."[9] Wahba's examples are holy words (dismissed as incantations by some missionary writers) because they are taken from Hadith. Formulaic expressions of holy words for prophylaxis are actually prescribed in *Prophetic Medicine* for protection in specific instances, as, for example, when one is traveling or staying in a strange house. Some expressions are to be repeated in the morning for all-day protection; others in the evening for overnight safety.[10]

Learning the correct holy words to utter or write to invoke God's protection is knowledge that must be acquired. Other techniques of prophylaxis come from custom and the imagination. These are techniques improvised by women, premised on the assumption that, while the spirits are always lurking to cause harm, by nature they have human limitations on their ability to see and hear and therefore can be fooled. One way to fool a lurking spirit was to set up a decoy to deflect attention away from an intended victim. Nurse Dalenberg attended the delivery of a women in Amarah (lower Iraq) who had previously given birth to seven children, all of whom had died. This is how she described what she saw on the day following the birth of this patient's healthy child: "When I looked into the baby's cradle it looked as if two babies were lying side by side. . . . Staring up at me was the head of a long-dead fish, dressed in baby garments. The fish had been dried and salted many months before and then dressed in the traditional hood and swaddling bands, just like any Arab baby. . . . The bundle next to the fish twisted a bit, and I could see it was the woman's baby, dressed almost like the fish." The mother told Dalenberg not to touch the fish, which, the mother explained, was a certain variety especially prescribed to fend off the evil eye.[11]

Another method of protecting infants was to trick the malevolent spirit into thinking the intended victim was not a worthy object of envy. One missionary in the Gulf described the technique of dyeing a baby's face to disguise its healthy looks.

> I sometimes find that some female relative, before the baby is a day old, has taken it to the market to the dyer's shop to have its face dabbed with indigo dye, and a cloth dabbled with the same dye is laid over its face to keep the evil spirit away as he is being carried through the streets. Seven colors are really necessary, but because of the high price of dyes, indigo has to do the work alone. It is very important to do this soon after the baby is born, before neighbors and friends come in to look at him and cast the evil spell of "chebsa" [*khabisa*: confusion, getting things messed up] on him. With the

dyed cloth over his face, the baby is laid in his basket with a knife beside him and charms sewn all over his hood and the front of his dress. Then a dish of water containing an egg, a blue bead, "the mother of seven eyes" because it has seven little depressions in it, and a nail are placed just outside the door. This dish with its contents is supposed to detract [*sic*] the visitor's attention from the new baby inside the house. Why all these pitiful precautions? Because the mother has lost so many of her children. . . . The mother will go to almost any lengths to save this one.[12]

Spoken words were also used to confuse a malevolent spirit and deflect its attention away from the intended victim. Praise of a child, for example, had to be avoided for his or her own protection; instead, the child would be insulted, to make the spirit think he or she was not worth attacking. Dr. Calverley describes a patient's well-intended greeting of her infant daughter: she spat three times in the direction of the baby's face, saying how undersized, pale, and sickly she looked.[13] Dorothy Van Ess of the Basra mission writes that "tribal and village" people would give their children names such as Dog, Garbage, Angry, or She-Doesn't-Belong-To-Us to indicate that they were not worth the attention of a malevolent spirit.[14]

Both men and women used amulets to prevent illness, although the missionary sources discuss amulets, as well as decoys and disguises, exclusively in terms of women. These were people inventing ways to exercise some influence over forces of chance and nature that were beyond their control, who did not have the educational tools to go about it the "right" way. By contrast, in these same sources, those who prepared the amulets, the only prophylactic technique that required training, were in every instance men. Zwemer in fact clearly stated that it was men who deal in amulets and women who buy them: "It is very important," Zwemer explains, "that the one who writes the amulet be a holy man in the Moslem sense of that word,"[15] and this person needed to be trained in the "science" of amulets. He had to know, for example, the correlation between the particular names of God he intended to write and the corresponding diet he, the writer, needed to follow before committing the names to ink (p. 8). Verses of protection were written for the hijab "with great care and with a special kind of ink" and were "sold for a good price to Moslem women and children" (p. 7). The hijab writer with accreditation was thus at the top of the hierarchy of producers of preventive medicines. It was Zwemer's understanding that there was no religious objection to the use of "charms and spells" so long as one employed only the correct method, with God's own words or words addressed directly to God alone (p. 7).

In the Gulf region, a knowledgeable practitioner producing recognized holy words for use as hijab could therefore have a respectable profession. But this was not always the case. Given the largely illiterate society of the Gulf, there was always the potential for fraud in the hijab-writing profession. Hijab writers were sometimes one and the same as the street vendors who promised magical cures using symbols and who claimed to achieve reversal of misfortune through witchcraft and exorcisms. Such people were considered, in Zwemer's words, "traveling dervishes who grow rich in trading upon the superstition of the common people" (p. 9). Wahba called men who dealt in hijabs and "prey upon the credulity of the ignorant" "charlatans" and "Moorish."[16] The choice of adjectives is telling, in that Doughty had used the words "Moghreby hakim" to describe the magicians and hijab dispensers he had encountered in Najd forty years earlier. "All the Aarab would have hijabs sooner than medicaments, which they find so unprofitable in the hands of their hareem," he wrote. Hijabs were marketed, Doughty says, as being designed to counter specific potential calamities, such as possession by jinn or wounding by a lead bullet, and there were all-purpose hijabs to keep one safe in time of danger. "The Moors, or Occidental Arabs," he wrote, "are esteemed in Arabia, the best scriveners of these magical scriptures," for "it is always in the people's faith," he added, "a Moor who is master of the magical art."[17] The words suggest that hijab writing was viewed with suspicion, and the purveyors of hijabs considered outsiders, even subversives. Wahba and Zwemer were talking about the Gulf and Hejaz. Doughty, however, was talking about the Wahhabi Najd, and about Bedouin, more than a generation before the Wahhabi revival began. He was talking about a religious environment in which virtually all techniques of spirit engagement were, theologically speaking, acts of polytheism, and practiced under a cloud of suspicion if not under threat of death.

In the revival era in Najd, overt practitioners of healing through engaging spirits were so few that Wahba thought them not to exist. "There is a brisk market for charms and spells for the treatment of disease," he wrote, "and practitioners of these arts reap a good harvest from all parts of Arabia *except Najd*."[18] "In Najd, although there is a widespread belief in magic and its evil effects," Wahba added, "there are no actual 'practicing' magicians" (p. 43).

Why the Wahhabis Forbid Engaging Spirits and Why Women Are Implicated

The Wahhabi religious environment and the use of religion as an arm of political expansion at the time Wahba lived in Riyadh account for the difference he observed in Najd. Chroniclers of the Wahhabi movement claim that charlatans who preyed on people's credulity and prescribed "magical" cures were commonplace in Najd before the movement's ascension in the eighteenth century:[19]

> The Bedouins, when they stopped in the towns at the time of
> [harvesting] fruits, had with them men and women treating the sick
> and prescribing medicine. And if one of the people of the town was
> sick internally, or in one of his members, its people would come to
> the practitioners of that group of Bedouins, asking for medicine for
> his disease. And they would answer, "Sacrifice for him in such and
> such a place either a completely black lamb or a small-eared goat,"
> thus speaking as if with authority before those ignorant people.
> Then the practitioners would say to them, "Do not mention God's
> name when you sacrifice it; and give the sick person this part of it,
> and eat from it such and such, and leave that part." And perhaps
> God would cure the sick person in order to lead them on and to
> deceive them; or perhaps the time had come for him to be cured.[20]

The Wahhabis were critical of fraudulent healing practices, but the real thrust of their opposition was directed against healing and prophylactic techniques that engaged spirits directly. And anyone who recited unholy spells, disguised a victim's attractive qualities, attempted to deflect a spirit's attention with a decoy, or placed a charm on the potential victim as a shield against evil was engaged in negotiation with the spirit and in effect attributing power to it that the Wahhabis say should belong to God alone.

The desirability of ending spirit engagement in all its forms is at the core of Wahhabi principles, and the amulet is the epitome of the kind of spirit engagement the movement proposed to stamp out. "Whoever . . . wears an amulet . . . has nothing to do with me or my religion," wrote Muhammad ibn Abd al-Wahhab, quoting the Prophet in his *Kitab at-Tawhid*, his catalog of ways to commit *shirk*, or polytheism.[21] Other Hadith he cites support this condemnation: "Whoever destroys an amulet or talisman worn by anyone has earned as much as if he had liberated a slave" (ch. 8, p. 29); "Whoever wears a talisman has committed shirk" (ch. 7, p. 26).[22] While acknowledging that there was disagreement among scholars over whether correctly prepared amulets containing exclusively words from the Qur'an—such as Zwemer mentioned—were permissible, Ibn Abd al-Wahhab said they were not permissible under any circumstances, and he sealed his argument with the Hadith, "They [the Companions] used to reject all amulets whether containing Quranic verses exclusively or otherwise" (ch. 8, p. 29).

In addition to amulets, Ibn Abd al-Wahhab forbade theurgy (*al-ruqa, al-'aza'im*), that is, the invocation of any kind of supernatural agency (except God) in human affairs, especially to cure illness.[23] This includes witchcraft (*at-tiwalah*), which, in the *Kitab at-Tawhid*, is synonymous with sorcery (*al-jibt*), one of "seven grave sins," that are, according to the Hadith, punishable by death (ch. 24, p. 77). The definition of sorcery is so broad as to include any act in which the perpetrator claims to know things that are unknowable or to perform deeds that require supernatural powers. In the chapter "Varieties of Sorcery," *al-jibt* is conflated with witchcraft and includes "listening to the voice of Satan," astrology, "conveying false rumours," and making a knot and blowing on it. The fortune-teller (*al-'arraf*) joins the list of the condemned, along with the person who listens to fortune-telling and believes it (ch. 26, pp. 81–82). "Soothsayer," in the masculine, is the name used for the priest, astrologer, fortune-teller, or other who claims knowledge by use of "omens." This is a man who claims to know not only the future but the unknown or unknowable, such as the location of stolen items and stray animals (ch. 26, p. 81).[24]

Ibn Abd al-Wahhab did not single out women as being more likely to be responsible for witchcraft, but in the scriptural sources he used to validate condemning these acts women are usually the culprits. In sura 113, verses 1–5, a prayer for protection from fears proceeding from the unknown, the potential evildoer is in the feminine: "In the name of Allah, the Beneficent, the Merciful: Say, I seek refuge in the Lord of dawn, from the evil of what He has created, And from the evil of the utterly dark night when it comes, And from the evil of those who blow on knots [*al-nafatat*], And from the evil of the envious when he envies."[25] "Those who blow on knots" is a reference to "witches," who, in popular culture, are capable of causing evil by tying knots in a cord while spitting and uttering curses.[26]

Ibn Abd al-Wahhab also did not present sorcery as a woman's crime. In the Hadith he selects, however, both men and women are sorcerers, but only women are executed for the crime, and they are executed under the command of a rightly guided caliph, no less: "Bajalah ibn 'Abadah reported that 'Umar ibn al-Khattab issued the following command: 'Execute every sorcerer and sorceress.' So Bajalah continued, 'We killed three sorceresses.' " Under the command of one of the rightly guided caliphs, according to this story, only female perpetrators were killed. After citing this Hadith, Ibn Abd al-Wahhab adds a piece of supporting evidence, and again the perpetrator is a woman: "It has been established that Hafsah commanded [the] execution of a slave woman who sought to charm her."[27]

Theoretically, because Sunnis generally subscribe to the Hadith Ibn Abd al-Wahhab cites, his admonitions could apply to Sunnis of the Gulf as well, but there is no evidence to suggest they did or that the government of Kuwait or Bahrain ever took these proscriptions literally. In Najd, however, the government of Ibn Sa'ud enforced Wahhabi prohibitions, if selectively. The ulama elite of Najd during the revival period took these prohibitions seriously, not just because they are grounded in the words of the Prophet, but because they took for granted the existence of spirits confirmed in the Qur'an as potentially destructive forces in the world to be reckoned with.

The Ulama of Najd
Literal Interpretations of Scripture

According to Hafiz Wahba, the Wahhabi ulama in his time did not avoid or suppress the passages in the Hadith and Qur'an that affirmed the existence of spirits but rather took them as literal truth as opposed to allegory.[28] Acceptance of the literal truth of Qur'an and Hadith, including the anthropomorphic passages and passages that are subject to interpretation, is so basic to Wahhabi philosophy that it is incorporated into the testimony of faith. In his 1974 book *Islam: The Religion of Truth*, the contemporary Saudi scholar Al Umar devotes a section to "the true testimony":

> I testify that there is no God but Allah. I testify that Muhammad is
> the messenger of Allah. I testify that Paradise and hell-fire are true,
> that the Judgment-Day is certainly to come, that Allah will raise up
> people after their death to reckon and requite them for their deeds.
> I testify that whatever had been mentioned by Allah in His book
> [the Qur'an] or through the traditions of His Prophet Muhammad
> is true.

May I call on everyone to believe in this testimony, declare it openly and behave according to its meaning, because this is the only way for salvation.[29]

Al Umar shows how seemingly meaningless passages in the Qur'an can be interpreted literally. He explains sura 51, verses 56–57 ("I have not created jinn and men [mankind] except that they should serve me. I desire of them no sustenance and I do not desire that they should feed Me") by virtually repeating what the verses say: "In these verses, Allah stated that He had created the jinn and mankind to worship Him alone, and that He is All-Independent, and not in need of any provision or food from his bondsmen."[30] Similarly, he explains the following Qur'anic verses concerning resurrection by reiterating the verses themselves: "From the earth We created you and into it We shall send you back and from it will We raise you a second time"; "And he strikes out a likeness for Us and forgets his own creation. Says he: Who will give life to the bones when they are rotten? Say, He will give life to them Who brought them into existence at the first, and He is cognizant of all creation."[31] The explanation for the verses lies in the verses themselves. As Al Umar says, "In these verses, Allah, glory be to Him, informed mankind that He created them on the earth as He had created their father Adam from dust before. He will raise them up from their graves, and bring them to account to requite them for their deeds. Allah refutes the false pretexts of the unbeliever who denies resurrection and finds it strange that rotten bones could be revived again. The verse states to such unbeliever that Allah who had created these bones before out of naught is certainly able a priori to reproduce them again" (p. 11). In other words, these Qur'anic verses do not have to be explained; they make sense simply because they are the word of God.

Wahhabi scholars' resistance to interpreting anthropomorphic verses from the Qur'an as well as to discussing predestination and participating in philosophical speculation about the meaning of such verses, is rationalized in Hadith on the grounds that these are matters about which the Prophet kept silent, thus discussing them would represent innovation.[32] Ahmad Abd al-Ghafour Attar, another Saudi scholar who writes on the life and thought of Muhammad ibn Abd al-Wahhab, explains the literalism in Ibn Abd al-Wahhab's interpretation as grounded in the practice of the Companions, who "avoided discussing matters only Allah knows, displayed aversion towards people who talked such matters over, and kept to the strict wording of the Quran and the verses definite in meaning. They took the Quran and

its contents for granted, without asking why or dwelling upon matters belonging to the realm of metaphysics, and so did not fall into error or go
astray" (p. 114).

In Wahba's opinion, the ulama of Najd were profoundly ignorant about
the physical world and incapable of skepticism regarding the anthropomor-
phized beings validated in the Qur'an and Hadith and their potential for in-
terfering in the life of humans. In Wahba's opinion, in fact, they were not
even well educated in Islamic scholarship. He writes that "very few of the
Arabian ulama have a complete knowledge of the Arabic language and its literature, of rhetoric, etymology or elocution, and not one of them knows
Moslem history properly. Historical knowledge is limited to the Life of the
Prophet, and the Caliphs to the end of the Abbasid Dynasty, and, in ancient
history, to Tabari and Ibn Alathir." Furthermore, Najd had virtually no scholar of religion who, in Wahba's opinion, was thoroughly versed even in the
Hadith or jurisprudence.[33]

Literal acceptance of the Qur'an and Hadith combined with lack of information about the physical world allowed the intellectual leaders of Najd
to presume a reality that conformed to their own expectations regarding the
animate qualities in inanimate objects and the existence of Satan, jinn, and
angels with a personal interest in the daily affairs of humankind. Wahba gives
numerous examples. In the late 1920s, he writes, Shaikh Abdullah ibn Blai-
hed, a highly respected Najdi scholar, argued that lack of a common language would be no barrier to communication between the inhabitants of
Mars and the people of earth because Satan would impersonate the Martians
to make fools of the people of earth. This scholar also raised questions about
the earth's being spherical (p. 52), and years after the landing of a manned
spacecraft on the moon, Shaikh bin Baz, then director of the General Presidency of Religious Research, proclaimed the earth to be flat.

To the scholars of Najd in the 1920s (but not to the establishment scholars of the 1980s and 1990s), technology was innovation, and innovation was
to be avoided because anything new was considered to be contrary to the
practice of the Prophet and his companions. Hafiz Wahba relates the following experience he had in 1928 in the company of Shaikh Abdullah ibn Hassan Al Shaikh, who later became chief qadi. On a trip to Medina, the shaikh
expressed his conviction that modern inventions such as the wireless were
the work of the jinn. He added that he had been told by an eyewitness that
wireless telegraphy would not work until there had been a sacrifice to Satan,
and to support this contention he quoted stories of human beings who employed the devil. Shaikh Abdullah later accompanied Wahba to the wireless

station at Medina in order to inspect the station for traces of sacrificial offerings such as bones, horns, or wool (p. 58).

Wahba also relates that when the wireless station in Riyadh began operations, the ulama took to sending agents to visit the station to look for demons, and the wireless operators reported that some of the younger scholars
were asking them when Satan visited the station, whether his headquarters
were in Mecca or in Riyadh, how many children Satan had, whether they
helped him in his evil work, and whether he used the station to communicate
with them. They even tried to bribe one of the operators to give them the
truth about Satan, offering in exchange not to reveal the operator's name.
(Ultimately, Wahba adds, it was recognition of the practical necessity of the
wireless and not a change in the religious leaders' vision of reality that led to
its acceptance: in 1932 there was a revolt in the northern Hejaz, and later in
the same year a rebellion in Asir, both of which were dealt with expeditious-
ly because of the speedy means of communication that the telegraph provided [p. 60].)

Other observers of Najd record similar examples. Mrs. Louis Dame,
wife of an Arabian Mission doctor, was in Riyadh when the first telephones
were being installed in the king's palace. By 1933 the palace at Riyadh, including the harem buildings, was fully wired, and even slaves were using the
telephone for casual conversation. However, when the telephone lines were
first being installed, she writes, some ulama grew suspicious and went to the
king to voice their objections. Recounting an incident that has been retold
by visitors to Najd many times since, Mrs. Dame writes that the king succeeded in assuaging their concerns by inviting them to read the Qur'an over
the telephone, the successful transmission of holy words proving that Satan
was not on the line and that God did not disapprove.[34]

It was not just the insular religious leaders of Najd who took for granted
the power of spirits to intervene in people's lives. Recognition of a spirit
world populating the world of humans has a long history not only in religion
but in classical works of geography, poetry, prose fiction, medical texts, and
oral epic, and over the centuries a belief in the existence of a world of spirits has been infused into the common culture shared throughout the Gulf region and beyond.[35] What made a difference in Najd was the paucity of knowledge about the physical world to offer balance and the Wahhabi movement,
which cut off debate and speculation over other modes of interpretation.

The literalism of the Najdi scholars had practical implications not only for
the introduction of technology into Saudi Arabia but also for the types of
healing practices that could be legitimately practiced and the qualifications of

those who could be designated legitimate healers. Because the spirit world existed as a perceived fact of nature, healing practices that engaged the spirits also had to have existed in Najd, and so they did, despite the absolute negation of spirit engagement in the philosophy of the Wahhabi movement. It would be impossible to determine the extent to which theological texts produced by the movement's founder were integrated into Wahhabi missionary education, much less the extent to which the message of these texts was heard and put into practice by its intended audience. Wherever Ibn Sa'ud took control, however, his regime took measures to suppress ritual practices that would qualify as shirk according to the *Kitab at-Tawhid*, condemned the use of amulets, and condoned the execution of individuals for witchcraft and fortune-telling. For the healing profession, the consequence was that only those practices that conformed to accredited standards could be practiced openly or at least with respectability. Decoys, disguises, amulets, and spells recited without correct words—practices commonly available to women—were not accredited, but other methods employing correct words and a particular kind of education were. These included Prophetic medicine, Greek medicine, midwifery, and the recitation of verses from the Qur'an or any prayers prescribed by Ibn Abd al-Wahhab himself.[36] What this meant is that—with the exception of midwifery—the respectable healer with a profession was more likely to be a man.

Witchcraft:
Woman as Cause and Cure of Disease

Witches are conceived primarily, though not exclusively, in the feminine. Their craft, *Prophetic Medicine* explains, involves "the influence of wicked spirits and the reaction of natural forces on them."[37] Certain types of inferior people are their victims: "Bewitchment disseminates its influence in feeble hearts and lustful souls hanging on sordid things. Thus, bewitchment mostly affects women, boys, nomads and persons lacking the faith and trust in Allah and whose part in Prophetic invocations and prayers is reduced" (p. 153). Unfortunately, women, who are likely victims, are also least able to administer proper treatment, for the antidote to witchcraft is Qur'anic prayer, limited access to which is precisely the failing that renders women susceptible to witchcraft in the first place: "One of the most useful remedies of bewitchment is the Divine medicament. . . . The repulsion of their impact would be the use of an element that resists them such as the laudation of

Allah, the verses and prayers that invalidate their acts and influences" (p. 153). Thus, according to the most prestigious text of Prophetic medicine in circulation, women are all at once the perpetrators, victims, and incompetent healers in a disreputable transaction.

One of the most popular uses for the skills of the witch was the love spell. In fact Ibn Abd al-Wahhab had described witchcraft as the use of some substance to make a man fall in love with a woman or a woman with a man.[38] In 1935 the shaikh of Kuwait, discussing how Bedouin women were always wanting to purchase spells to regain their husbands' love, explained to Dickson how spells worked: a successful love spell, he said, required the wife to remove a hair from her husband's head or beard when he was asleep and give it to the spell maker, who would put it in a concoction, mixed with some object from the wife's body, for the husband to drink.[39]

The principle behind the love spell, as Zwemer explained, was "animism": the notion that the soul or spirit of a person rests not only in the heart but also pervades special parts of the body, such as the blood, hair, teeth, saliva, sweat, tears, and nails. Thus the essence of a person can be communicated to others by spitting, blowing, blood wiping, and touching or through the manipulation of clippings from a person's hair or nails.[40] For this reason, according to Zwemer, in Arabia, Bahrain, and Kuwait, as well as in Egypt and North Africa, fingernail clippings were carefully gathered up, wrapped in a piece of cloth, and then buried. This custom of stowing away nail clippings is mentioned in Hadith, he said. In Bahrain, according to Zwemer, a special order in trimming the fingernails was observed, and, as the nails were wrapped and buried, one would say, " 'Hatha amana min 'andina ya Iblis yashud ana al Rahman [*sic*],' meaning, 'Oh Satan, this is a safe deposit from us as God is our witness.' "[41]

Animism explains why spit from the mouth of someone who is at prayer (discussed in the previous chapter) could have curative power, in the same way that spit from the mouth of Jesus—a holy man imbued with the essence of God, who is God himself in Christian tradition—cured blindness.[42] It also explains why applying a woman's milk to her husband's eyes (milk in the eyes was a cure for eye sores) was forbidden, according to Dickson: the milk would transfer something of the essence of the wife to the body of her husband, making the two of them as mother and child. Similarly, no woman, he says, "should allow her husband ever to taste her milk, however small the quantity. This was 'unlawful' according to the Shari'ah law, or so said the *Mushaiyikh* or Holy Priests of Najd."[43]

The transference of essences could work in combination with sympathetic magic, by which an action on a representational object is believed to produce a corresponding effect on the object represented: the pin in the chest of a replica of the intended victim dressed in a piece of cloth belonging to the victim or with a strand of hair attached, for example, or tying a knot in a rope and blowing on it while uttering curses and the victim's name. These techniques of witchcraft could be applied to communicate hate as well as love, illness as well as cures, pain as well as pleasure, and bonds of affiliation as well as disaffiliation, and the medium could be almost any substance. In 1919, for example, an evangelical missionary in Bahrain wrote about a Shi'a woman whose daughter had converted to Christianity. Wanting her daughter to return to Islam, she removed some dirt from a Shi'a cemetery, mixed it with kettle black and red dye, and buried it on the grounds of the Christian mission. By transferring the dirt, she was transferring the spiritual essence of the cemetery to the Christian mission ground where her daughter experienced her conversion and where she came for Sunday services, in hopes of compelling the girl to return to Islam.[44]

Anyone who practiced sympathetic magic or applied the principle of animism could be thought of as a witch, but, as mentioned above, witches were usually women. Women versed in the methods of *sahr*, witchcraft, Dickson says, were thought to possess special talents for preparing *saqwa*, poisons, as well as love potions.[45] They were the same people, he says, who knew how to cast and avert the evil eye and how to make and break spells, who were skilled in herbs, midwifery, fortune-telling, dream interpretation, and divining truth (p. 329). They were therefore people who were thought capable of causing as well as curing disease. Certainly, they were people to be feared as well as sought after. Like professional readers, they were often older women without men, such as widows and spinsters, but did not have the readers' education, and they tended to be rural, Bedouin, poor, of African extraction or Sulubba, that is, belonging to the outcast tribe of the desert (see appendix). Sulubba women were so closely associated with witchcraft, Dickson tells us, that when something unfortunate happened to a prominent person, the common rubric would be to say "It must be a Sulubba woman who has cast a spell on so-and-so" (p. 517). One could buy the services of such women, called *sahhara*, he writes, in nearly every summer encampment and town where small groups of Sulubba made themselves available for employment as tinkers and metalworkers (p. 534). Still, the practice of witchcraft must have been the specialty of few: in the seventy years of missionary documents, witchcraft is rarely mentioned, though the writers were interested in chronicling everything they could learn about Arabian women and had daily contact with rural and urban poor.

Dickson and Wahba both took an interest in stories about the practice of witchcraft, and while the reliability of these stories as representations of actual events is doubtful, they still offer valuable insights into social attitudes. Some of these stories show that because women were presumed capable of witchcraft, they were also vulnerable to accusations of performing it, and that women who were accused were usually low-status persons or women without a man's protection. One of Dickson's stories, for example, tells of the 1936 murder of an Ethiopian girl encamped with a Bedouin family on the outskirts of Kuwait. The girl was in an intimate relationship with her owner, whose sister resented the relationship and decided the girl must have bewitched her brother. The sister enlisted the help of a man—in fact a personal friend of Dickson—who subsequently arranged for the beating death of the Ethiopian girl and justified to Dickson what he had done on the grounds that the girl was a witch and deserved to die.[46] A similar story of Dickson's tells of a Mutair shaikh diagnosed with tuberculosis at the Kuwait Mission hospital, who decided his illness was the result of a spell cast on him by his wife, and after his death, the shaikh's brother murdered the wife in revenge (p. 535).

Other stories suggest that women were thought capable of causing illness just by being women. Wahba writes, for example, that in 1922, after the marriage of Abd al-Aziz to a member of the Al Rashid family, the Sultan developed a small boil on his lip which became inflamed, and a high fever. All known Najdi methods of treatment were tried, Wahbi writes, including prayer, reading the Qur'an over him, and cauterization, but without success. According to Wahba, the bride was subsequently divorced, on the grounds that she must have brought the ill luck that cause the boil.[47] In this there is an echo from Doughty, who had observed that "men too often ascribe their slow and obscure maladies to 'witchcraft of the hareem,' " and suspected that women were capable of poisoning their food or drink.[48]

Dream interpretation was also a skill that women who performed witchcraft were supposed to possess, and a few of these stories show that the interpretation of dreams to foretell the future was a desirable skill even in Riyadh, at least when practiced by a man, but a criminal act of witchcraft when practiced by women. According to Wahba and Philby, 49 Abd al-Aziz was a believer in the significance of dreams, and some of the ulama of Riyadh were specialists in interpreting them. "Abd al-Aziz often spoke to me of his dreams," wrote Wahba, "which he asserted invariably came true. For instance, he once dreamed that Sultan Abd al-Hamid was dressed in rags and a short while later the Sultan was dethroned. On another occasion he dreamed that King Hussein (of the Hejaz) rose from his chair and made Abdul Aziz sit in his place—and later Abdul Aziz, of course, did indeed displace Hussein on the throne of the Hejaz."[50]

Dickson, who devotes a chapter of *The Arab of the Desert* to "Dreams and their Interpretation," writes that Abd al-Aziz was known to have employed for many years a professional dream interpreter in his palace in Riyadh, a man named Shaikh Abd al-Aziz al-Nimr, and to have sought his opinion after every dream.[51] However, in 1937 a woman in Riyadh who interpreted dreams was labeled a "witch" and executed, according to Dickson, who claims the story to be based on reliable information.[52] The woman, who belonged to the Utaiba, claimed that she learned through a dream that in three years Abd al-Aziz would be dead, that his death would be followed by internecine strife, and that she herself would be slain in five days. On the fifth day after the woman revealed her dream to her sons, a party of armed camel riders appeared at the woman's tent, bade her come out, and and shot her dead. According to the story, she was killed for being a witch, not for the future she foretold, as one of the riders is reported to have said, "The King's orders are strict, and his arm is long where witches are concerned" (pp. 368–369). As an interpreter of dreams, the slain woman probably lacked the essential skill of tact which Shaikh al-Nimr must have possessed, but what makes this fanciful story compelling is the woman's vulnerability—that as a woman, she could be accused of witchcraft and mudered for doing the same things that a man could do as a profession.

A witch-hunt that occurred in Najd during the late 1920s and early 1930s under the auspices of the Riyadh ulama and the Ikhwan illustrates again men's credulity in the powers of witchcraft and women's vulnerability to accusation. According to Dickson, around 1929, a woman spell-weaver of the Utaiba tribe who was "known all over Najd and Northeast Arabia," including Kuwait, was slain by the Shaikh of the Utaiba, Sultan ibn Humaid, at the Ikhwan stronghold of al-Ghatghat[53] (al-Ghatghat was then one of the most fanatical of the Ikhwan hujar, the agricultural settlements of former Bedouin who joined the army of Abd al-Aziz). Another incident was recorded by Hafiz Wahba, who says that an elderly woman, also from an area near al-Ghatghat, claimed to cure people by magic, and was executed by ibn Bijad, one of the three leaders of the Ikhwan rebellion. This execution, Wahba makes a point of saying, was carried out after consulting the ulama.[54]

In 1932, while Hafiz Wahba was still in Riyadh, the ulama there were being consulted about yet another woman who had been accused of, among other things, witchcraft, and the King had ordered her to be brought to Riyadh for questioning. "If the allegation turned out to be well-founded she would no doubt have been executed," wrote Wahba (p. 44).

The occurrence of executions for witchcraft makes sense in Najd during the revival period. The Saudi leadership was using Wahhabi Islam as a justi-fication for conquest and as a means of arousing the fighting loyalty of newly settled and newly converted Bedouin. Because Wahhabi Islam is opposed to precisely the sort of spirit engagement that witchcraft entails, it is reason-able that those who engaged spirits in healing, or causing sickness, or truth seeking, astrology, fortune-telling, or any of other acts forbidden by the Wahhabis would be a likely target for suppression. Given the political con-text, suppression of witchcraft in the 1920s would have been an opportuni-ty for Abd al-Aziz and his following to demonstrate a commitment to the re-ligious ideals they claimed to be struggling to make a reality.

Spirit engagement practices in Najd were probably suppressed during the first period of the Wahhabi movement, because putting an end to these practices was the justification used for the Wahhabi political expansion in the first place. Witchcraft remains a crime against religion because God alone must be addressed when seeking a favor from the supernatural, and the use of magic implies a usurpation of powers that should belong only to Him.[55] But acts represented as magic and witchcraft in one form or another go on all the time, and not all magicians or witches are punished; in fact most of the time none are. Repression occurs at certain times in response to politi-cal crises or other pressures: as I. M. Lewis has suggested, the existence of marginal cults plays a role in the definition of ideological boundaries; they are a way religions define and redefine orthodoxy.[56] The eighteenth-centu-ry Bedouin healing practices were suppressed as a means of defining the or-thodoxy of the then-new Wahhabi movement and of justifying its political expansion; the suppression of witchcraft in the 1920s was a way to assert the ruler's commitment to orthodoxy while appealing to the fanaticism of his new Bedouin Wahhabi converts during a period when religion was again being used as a vehicle of expansion. A more recent event also illustrates how ideas about witchcraft can be manipulated for political purposes: the execution of a person for witchcraft in 1995 occurred not because witches were suddenly operating in Saudi Arabia but because the orthodoxy of the royal family had been impugned by political dissidents. The king, in particu-lar, had been accused of consulting an astrologer (an act expressly forbidden in the *Kitab at-Tawhid*), in an attempt to undermine his credibility as a ruler of the Muslim state. Allowing an execution for witchcraft to go forward provided a way to demonstrate the royal family's commitment to orthodoxy in a politically harmless way, satisfying one level of society that justice had been done while not alienating other constituencies, such as those who would see the execution as nonsense but would also be uninterested in the execution of one of society's nobodies.[57]

Exorcising Malevolent Spirits:
Cautery with Words and a Bad Taste in the Mouth

There is no basis for cautery as a method of exorcism in the Prophet's Hadith, but in popular practice, it was generally the favored technique, a way to chase malevolent spirits causing emotional or physical illness out of the body. In the recorded instances of exorcism by cautery, by far the majority of technicians—but by no means all—were women who were rural, Bedouin, or urban poor, and often of African extraction, and the majority of patients were rural, Bedouin, urban poor, and children, the sorts of people who were also the primary users of missionary health care.

Exorcising a malevolent spirit from the body required a combination of two actions performed simultaneously: making the site in the body where the spirit resided so uncomfortable that the spirit would flee, and the reciting Qur'anic words.

In Harold Dickson's record of Bedouin medical techniques, he describes the treatment given in 1939 by a Kuwaiti village woman of African extraction to an Anayza Bedouin who was camped outside the town of Kuwait. The patient had initially consulted one of the Kuwait mission doctors, Dr. Mylrea, who attributed the patient's symptoms to a brain tumor and pronounced the condition hopeless. The woman healer shaved the Bedouin's head and burned a cross from ear to ear and from the nape of the neck to the forehead. At the end of the burning process she uttered words from the Qur'an and then ordered the spirit out. Dickson, who had boundless faith in the resourcefulness of the Bedouin, marveled to find the patient, whom Dr. Mylrea had clearly misdiagnosed, in a healthy condition weeks after the time the doctor had told Dickson he would be dead.[58]

Another healer, an elderly woman of Jahra, the agricultural village near Kuwait, who was known for her cures with cautery, used what Dickson called the standard Bedouin method. First, two small brands were made on the left wrist with tent pins. Follow-up treatment required similar branding on the right wrist. The next step, in the absence of improvement, required branding on the underside of the tongue, which, Dickson comments, caused swelling and terrible pain (p. 445). The exorcism could be modified to suit particular cases. One case, for example, involved a young girl with symptoms of a severe gastrointestinal ailment whom Dickson thought to be dying of tuberculosis. The girl was cured after a single visit to the healer in Jahra, who determined the patient would not benefit from branding, for she was afflicted with multiple jinn of a type that would flee with just a stern warning from God (pp. 442–448).

Burning the body with the heat from molten lead was another method of chasing a malevolent spirit out of the body. This technique Dickson describes as specifically performed by Bedouin, and while he does not mention the practitioner, he says that it was used for either men or women afflicted by a spirit. A bowl of cold water containing a pair of scissors, a woman's comb, the head of a woodcutter's chopper, a small needle, a sail maker's bodkin, and a round yellow pebble was placed on the patient's head. About a pound and a half of molten lead was then poured into the water, and during the few seconds that the bowl was held on the head, the spirit was forced straight out of the patient and lodged into the objects inside the bowl (p. 160).

Cautery was also a cure for madness caused by jinn, and in a case that occurred around 1935 Dickson mentions the exorcism of a young man he believed to be demented by frustrated love but whose family believed had been seized by jinn when he inadvertently walked over a grave. The family tried treatment at home to start, cauterizing the boy on the head, neck, and back, but when this failed to restore the boy's sanity, they took him to "a wise old woman who had promised to get rid of the spell from him for a sum of money." Her technique: reading passages from the Qur'an over him day and night (p. 150). The boy wasn't cured, but his condition improved, Dickson says, when he married the sister of the woman he loved.

Exorcisms were performed not just by professionals but also by loving hands at home. Mrs. Van Vlack of the Basra station reported that to correct a delay in teething, mothers would place a bad-tasting object inside a child's mouth on the theory that the jinn lodged at the back of the throat who were preventing the teeth from coming out would be repulsed by the bad taste.[59] Ruth Jackson, who spent years as an evangelical missionary in the Shatt al-Arab of southern Iraq, recorded in 1926 witnessing an attempt to exorcise spirits in a marsh village. She was performing her own reading, from the

Bible, when a young women fell into a convulsive fit. Jackson watched as the husband and brother of the women backed off, not knowing what to do, and the women present took charge in what appeared to be an attempt to cut off the path of the evil spirit entering the victim through her mouth: "A Persian woman brought a stick and broke it as close to the girl's mouth as she could," Jackson wrote. "The girl seemed to be strangling. Another woman brought scissors and kept opening and shutting them across her mouth as though to cut her breath. They all believed the attack to be due to jinn or evil spirits." The afflicted girl came out of the convulsion quickly, and then the men came back and asked the missionary to continue reading. "They have a custom of reading the Koran over the sick, especially to cast out demons, and perhaps they thought the act of the reading going on there would help whether they listened or not."[60] She might have added, "whether the holy words being read were from the Christian Bible or the Muslim Koran."

The employment of exorcism appears to have been universal across social classes. Dr. Storm was once called to the house of one of the shaikhs to treat his son and heir and was taken by the shaikh himself to the women's area, "a wretched, bare room next door to the stables. The sick child lay on the matting which covered the earthen floor. The mother sat by helplessly moaning while an old slave woman assiduously waved an incense burner over the baby, intermittently striking the floor with her fists. Now and then she would spit on the child and recite verses from the Koran. The other slaves sat about wringing their hands and calling upon Allah."[61] The child was receiving the spit and holy words treatment in combination with what appears to have been a scare technique to chase off the bad spirits. The efficacy of the method must have been established, because when Storm decided that the child needed an immediate injection, the women attendants were opposed. It took an argument before the shaikh prevailed and Storm was able to treat the child, "amid the black looks of the women" (p. 10).

Trial by Ordeal

Trial by ordeal was a means of determining the guilt or innocence of an accused person used by Bedouin and townspeople alike in the Gulf and in Najd before the Wahhabi revival. The trial worked through the animistic belief that inanimate objects have the ability to absorb characteristics of animate beings and communicate to the knowledgeable observer what those characteristics are. In a trial by ordeal God is not a party to the judgment, and God does not speak through the medium. Judgment is determined by powers already existing in the medium—whether fire, lead, grain, or other instruments—that are activated and interpreted by the judge through his specialized skills. Conducting a trial by ordeal therefore requires skills similar to those necessary for the performance of witchcraft: the technician needs to know how to manipulate an inanimate substance as a medium for transferring knowledge or thought from one person to another.

In Kuwait the judges held the honorific title "sayyid," and the sayyid acted as a consultant, taking on private cases as well as those referred for adjudication by the ruler. Edwin Calverley, of the Kuwait mission, wrote that there were several Shi'a sayyids in Kuwait. Calverley attended numerous trials and says that the sayyids used one of a number of established mediums to elicit truth. One method was reciting curses over grains of wheat. The accused would then have to swallow the wheat, and "if the grains stuck to his throat," Calverley wrote, "his guilt would be evident. But if he could swallow them, his innocence would be proved."[62]

Another sayyid, he wrote, used a leavened dough test, in which all the suspects took a portion of dough in their fingers and worked it. Those whose dough worked well were proven innocent, while the one whose dough crumbled was guilty. Another method of trial by ordeal was particularly appropriate to women, says Calverley, because their faces could be covered during the procedure. This method required inserting the fingers of an accused person into molten lead; the lead would stick only to the fingers of the one who was guilty. Calverley does not mention what happened to the fingers of the guilty party (or of the innocent) after being dipped into molten lead.

Calverley witnessed a trial performed in 1918 by a Sunni sayyid in Kuwait that was being carried out for the benefit of three Najdis accused of stealing money. All three had agreed to come before the sayyid and "lick the fire" to prove their innocence. The trial began by inserting a coffee-stirring spoon into hot charcoal. When the sayyid thought the spoon was hot enough, he called for one of the suspects to come and squat before him, face to face, and then requested that he stick his tongue as far out as possible. The sayyid then took the spoon out of the coals and struck his own bare heel once or twice with the red-hot bowl. Then with the other side of the bowl he struck the outstretched tongue four times. He then performed the same procedure on each of the other two suspects. Afterward, the sayyid inspected the three tongues and determined which tongue bore the *nishan*, the sign of guilt (p. 6).

Because the process is supposed to work by evoking powers other than the power of God, trial by ordeal is another ritual act that contravenes the Wahhabi insistence on the Oneness of God and was consequently banned during the revival period, particularly by the Ikhwan-settled Bedouin. John Habib, writing about the Bedouin army of Abd al-Aziz, was told in a 1968 interview held in al-Ghatghat that trial by ordeal had been practiced by former Bedouin before they became Ikhwan and joined the *hijra* settlements that Ibn Sa'ud established for Bedouin who were converted to Wahhabism and became part of his standing army. The practice had been long established among Bedouin of Najd and throughout the region and continued to be practiced in the Gulf towns during the revival period.[63]

In the early nineteenth century, Burckhardt, visiting Anayza Bedouin in southern Syria, wrote that when a case was brought up that the qadi could not unravel, the litigating parties went before the "mebesshae [*sic*]" a chief judge, who subjected them to the ordeal.

> This judge directs that a fire should be kindled before him; he then
> takes a long iron spoon (used by the Arabs for roasting coffee), and
> having made it red hot in the fire, he takes it out, and licks with his
> tongue the upper end of the spoon on both sides. He then replaces
> it in the fire, and commands the accused person first to wash his
> mouth with water, and next to lick it as he has done; if the accused
> escapes without injury to his tongue, he is supposed innocent; if he
> suffer from the hot iron, he loses his cause. The Arabs ascribe this
> wonderful escape, not to the Almighty Protector of innocence, but
> to the Devil.[64]

Lady Anne Blunt described a trial by ordeal used by Anayza Bedouin in northern Najd to settle a child custody dispute between a mother's current husband and the family of her former, deceased husband. The issue was to establish the truth of the mother's claim that her current husband was the child's father. The woman received a judgment in her favor after she endured having a live coal placed on her tongue.[65] Doughty wrote of diviners who were sought out to determine who was responsible for some criminal act, and in all cases the professional diviner was a man. One of these was a *mandal*, one who prophesies or receives visions by looking into a reflecting surface, such as a mirror or a bowl of water.[66] Another diviner performed a reading to discover what had become of a missing child, resulting in the discovery of the child's body buried in a neighbor's house.

The woman who owned the house, Doughty wrote, was subsequently executed (2:395).

A hundred years before Doughty and Lady Anne were in Najd, Carsten Niebuhr reported a case of trial by ordeal in Jeddah. The objective of the trial was to discover who had stolen a sum of money. A shaikh gathered together a number of suspects, who were all servants in the house from which the money had been taken, lined them up, and recited a prayer. Then he "made each of them take into his mouth a bit of folded paper, telling them, that they who were innocent might swallow it with safety, but that the guilty person would be choked by it. They all swallowed the paper, save one, who, being thus surprised and embarrassed, confessed the theft, and made restitution."[67]

Edwin Calverley noted that the sayyids of Kuwait who specialized in trial by ordeal did not occupy a position of respect among the religious establishment and were not allowed to preach in any of the mosques in town in spite of having received years of formal education. These sayyids can be compared to healers whose techniques evoked spiritual powers or some latent power in objects instead of appealing directly to God. And even though all used well-established techniques that appealed to popular belief and were in popular demand, they practiced their professions under a cloud of suspicion. Under the Wahhabis, the sayyid's skill—like that of the witch—was ultimately banned. Wherever trial by ordeal was practiced, however, it was practiced openly as a profession, and all sorts of people, including women, tribal leaders, and heads of state, chose to make use of the trial judge's skills and accredit the results. In every case, the judge, or sayyid, in a trial by ordeal was a man.

Zar:
A Healing Fellowship for Women

"[The Zar] provides [women] with a great deal of fun and excitement, and gives them distinction and authority which otherwise they would not have," wrote Minnie Dykstra in 1918.[68] Mrs. Dykstra, who was assigned to perform educational work with the Bahrain mission, had set out to investigate the curious complaint of some patients at the mission clinic that they were "under compulsion," (*tahta al-darura*), suffering with an ailment the American doctors were not skilled in healing. What she discovered were organized group healing societies in Bahrain that centered on relief from possession by a spirit called the Zar. The Zar was an invisible being who entered into the body of a man or woman, being masculine if the body it entered was a woman's and feminine if the person entered was a man. The etymology of the word, Mrs. Dykstra presumed, is the Arabic word for "visitor" (colloquial *zaar*, *zeeraan* in the plural; *za'ir*, *za'irun* in classical Arabic), and the word was used both as the name of the spirit and the ceremony to engage it. (Snouck Hurgronje thought the word to be of Ethiopian origin, but it may well have been an Arabic loan word adopted into Amharic and reintroduced into Arabic by the Ethiopian slaves who were the leading Zar performers in the Gulf.)[69]

Not only in Bahrain but in Cairo, Mecca, Kuwait, and virtually every town in the Gulf during the first quarter of the century there were societies composed of individuals, primarily women, who believed themselves possessed by the Zar, and there were, in addition, Zar "clinics" open to the public. The point of these Zar gatherings was to obtain relief from the symptoms of possession; the point was healing, whether from a physical or a psychological illness. Possession by the Zar, Mrs. Dykstra writes, would manifest itself in attacks of melancholy, hysteria, anger, excess foolish talk, delirium, fainting, convulsions, or symptoms of illness that could not be diagnosed or did not respond to medical treatment. Alternatively, the Zar could make itself known by making demands of the person whose body was being occupied, such as requiring him or her to dress in a particular way. A man, for example, might be told to dress as a woman, or, more rarely, a woman to put on an item of men's clothing. Or the Zar might simply command an otherwise healthy person to perform a certain act on pain of being killed. For example, in the Bahrain mission hospital, a patient explained the abrupt absence of her mother, who had been sleeping by her side, by saying that she had arisen during the night and returned to the desert because the Zar who possessed the mother had ordered her to leave at once. Usually the demands of the Zar were benign, but they could also be expensive: a woman could be forced by her Zar to demand from her husband new clothing, new jewelry, or new furnishings for the house, which had to be acquired or some calamity would befall her. Most commonly, the Zar demanded that a feast be served and specified what types of food and the quantity desired.

Zar possession was not the same as possession by the sort of malevolent spirits whose existence is validated in the Qur'an, nor was Zar possession grounded in Islamic tradition. Malevolent spirits that cause disease have to be exorcised for the healing process to take place; the Zar, however, must be appeased. The Zar practitioner wants to establish communication with the Zar, to find out what it wants and temporarily satisfy it so that it will leave the body of the possessed person, at least for a time. People possessed by malevolent spirits, Mrs. Dykstra writes, were usually considered to be objects of commiseration, but those possessed by the Zar became eligible to join a fraternal order of people who were chronically possessed and who met regularly to satisfy the wishes of the Zar.

Groups of individuals who claimed to have the Zar followed the authority of their own leader; men being led by one known as abu az-Zeeraan, and women by one known as umm az-Zeeraan or shaikhat az-Zar. The shaikha was an older woman, or as Mrs. Dykstra observed, a black woman, and one who was herself possessed by multiple zeeraan. The umm or shaikha held a position of great honor, she writes, for she had the skill of communicating with the Zar. She was a paid professional and treated with deference by everyone who attended her Zar ceremonies.

When someone was believed to be possessed, the shaikha was consulted. Ordinary people could consult the shaikha at a public clinic, but wealthy women sought private consultations, and the shaikha would then organize a Zar ceremony to be held in the possessed woman's home. To this ceremony would be invited those in the same society and of the same sex who also had or had had zeeraan. Music was critical to the performance, and the shaikha usually had her own troupe of musicians and dancers. (Mrs. Dykstra noted that all the Zar musicians in Bahrain were black.) Zar ceremonies usually began with the inhalation of incense by the possessed, followed by music, dancing, feasting, and the sacrifice of a ram whose blood was consumed or dripped over the possessed one.[70]

A Zar ceremony attended by Mrs. Dykstra in Bahrain extended over several gatherings, each one becoming progressively more elaborate in the quality of food served to the guests, the complexity of the ritual, and the fee of the shaikha. The first gathering began with an initial feast of rice prepared with syrup, accompanied by at least ten side dishes, including such items as peanuts, raisins, nuts, melons, and dates, with one dish for money for the shaikha. Before the feasting began, the possessed person was "covered with a large cloth, and under this cloth [were] placed three incense burners filled with hot coals and incense, and until this incense [was] burned out of all of them the covering [was] not removed." The ability to tolerate the incense, Dykstra writes, was supposed to be evidence of the presence of the Zar. Then rice on a tray with other food was brought in, and the Zar was asked whether it were satisfied. This question, Dykstra explains, set the stage for the next gathering, for the Zar would likely say that some other special food was required, such as rice and lamb, and that new clothes, jewelry, or furnishings had to be purchased.

The second feast that she attended began the same as the first, except the musicians played the drums while the shaikha and visiting company got "down on their knees and crawl[ed] towards the one possessed, making grunting noises as they [did] so." This was kept up for a long time, until all were under the influence of the zeeraan and got communication from them. The climatic feast, she wrote, was called *kabsh*, "ram," because a ram was to be sacrificed, and at this feast the fee of the shaikha was substantially increased. Mrs. Dykstra describes what happened this way:

> After the dinner the leader begins to chant the testimony of faith, "la illah illa allah wa Mohammed rasoul allah" [*sic*], all the others joining in the chorus, and this exercise is kept up for about an hour, and all the while their bodies are swaying back and forth in rhythm to the chant. After this is ended the whole company get down on their knees and go through the crawling, grunting exercise which is kept up until they are exhausted. After a little rest the musicians begin their playing and do not stop until the next feature in the program, which is riding the ram. . . . The ram to be ridden is decorated with "*mashmoum*" [musk][71] and the rider is the one in whom the zaar is.

The ram was ridden, pulled, and prodded twice more and then killed by the shaikha. Dykstra described what happened next:

> The head of the ram is held over a large tray or dish, for not a drop of blood must be spilled or wasted. When the beast is killed, a glass is filled with the blood and into it is put some saffron and some sugar and the Zar drinks while the blood is warm. Three or four others of the company then strip the Zar and give him the blood bath.
>
> The possessed person is bathed to remove the blood and dressed in new clothes and new ornaments, while the sacrifice is being prepared. As with the blood so with the body; not a hair or bone or any entrails must be spilled or thrown away. The entrails and the feet are boiled separately, but the skin, turned inside out and tied, is cooked with the rest of the body including the head, When all is cooked, a portion is brought to each table (the table is a large mat spread on the floor) . . . and all the rest of the food is placed around the central dish. A stick, which has been bathed in the blood of the

animal, is placed before the Zar. When all is in readiness, the leader asks the Zar, "Is everything here that you want?"

The objective of the ritual was finally achieved when the shaikha extracted an agreement from the Zar that for now at least it was satisfied and would depart.[72]

In Bahrain, all ethnic groups and social levels were represented in the Zar societies, although Dykstra thought that Sunni Arabs and the black population constituted the majority of the participants in the Zar groups. "The Baharanes [the Shi'a peasants of Bahrain][73] believe in Zeeraan," she wrote, "but they are much more quiet about it, and if they have many gatherings for them it is kept quiet. There is one woman of this class, who are Shia, who is an umm, but investigations show only this one, while the Arabs and negroes have many."[74] Even among the ruling class in Bahrain, "sometimes there are people who have the zeeraan but who are ashamed to be known as such. . . . These wear a ring with the simple engraving, *en-nasru min allah wa fathun qareeb* [sic], meaning 'victory is from God and deliverance is near.' This signet ring must receive a bath of blood before it becomes efficacious, and so a fowl must be killed and the stone soaked in the blood." There are others still in Bahrain who deny the Zar altogether, she adds, thinking it foolishness and financially wasteful (p. 17).

The private Zar ceremony was an indulgence of the wealthy, but the Zar also visited the poor, who could attend public rituals. Even Bedouin women sometimes claimed to have zeeraan. At the Bahrain mission hospital, for example, a woman patient was removed by relatives who claimed the American doctors' inefficient was ineffective because it did not address the cause of the illness, which they believed was visitation by the Zar.

The Zar cult was practiced in Kuwait as well as in Bahrain. In 1918 Edwin Calverley counted about twenty places where public Zar rites were conducted regularly,[75] and in addition to these there were unknown numbers of private Zars conducted in women's homes. As in Bahrain, the shaikhat az-Zar was usually, if not always, a woman of African extraction, he says, and the musicians were also Ethiopians and Nubians.[76] The patients and other participants in the Zar, however, were both rich and poor, Sunni and Shi'a.[77] In a letter written to his dissertation mentor, Duncan Black Macdonald, Edwin Calverley wrote that the Zar performers played the drums and a stringed instrument, called a *tambura*, and the chief dancer in their troupe wore a wide belt of "*athlaf*," goat hooves.[78]

In the late nineteenth and early twentieth centuries, the Zar cult could be found virtually everywhere in the Arabic-speaking world, including

North Africa, except possibly in Najd. In Egypt, the shaikhat az-Zar were Ethiopian, Sudanese, and Egyptian, and those possessed were both Christian and Muslims, poor and wealthy.[79] The Zar was so thoroughly enmeshed in the life of the women of Cairo that a missionary resident in that city wrote, "The woman missionary in Egypt, to take a single point, who does not know about the Zar, cannot have really known the women of her district, does not intimately touch their lives, and cannot fully help them."[80] The cult of the Zar was also practiced all along the Batina coast of the Gulf, in the fishing villages of Musqat and Oman. Bertram Thomas attended a Zar ceremony in 1927, which was presided over, he notes, by a black woman. The participants were nearly all women, he says, and they danced along with the patient into a state of ecstasy until the Zar identified itself as male or female, made its wishes known, and then switched sexes.

> This cult of the Zar, though not found in the desert, flourishes
> throughout the fishing villages of these coasts; and although enlight-
> ened Muslims scorn it as a heresy, and a pious Wali will sternly
> forbid it in his area on religious grounds, hoi polloi have from some
> dim antiquity clung to its sensuous rites. . . . It is presided over by
> a priestess, or witch, or medium, whichever you will, who is not
> infrequently an old negress, and who shines in the sobriquet of
> Umm az Zar.[81]

In late-nineteenth-century Mecca, the Zar was integrated into the social and emotional life of women of all nationalities, wrote Snouck Hurgronje, who spent six months there in 1884–85. Hurgronje discussed the groups in Mecca who met to obey the commands of their Zar, giving an account of their shaikha and their cult practices that is similar to the descriptions of these groups' activities in Bahrain, as well as in Egypt.[82] In Mecca, he writes, the Zar is an affliction known especially to women ("males are generally immune from them"), and the "struggle with the Zar exemplifies the saddest and gayest sides of the lives of the Mekkan women" (p. 101). When a woman is afflicted, "learned men, doctors, and in general most of the men are always inclined to employ either medicine or else orthodox religious exorcism of the Satanic powers; the female friends and relations, on the other hand, advise unconditionally the calling in of an old woman who is versed in dealings with the Zar, a shaikhat az-Zar, and they in the end overcome all resistance" (p. 100). As in Bahrain, Kuwait, and Egypt, the Zar visited women of every nationality and religious persuasion, but the leaders and performers were nearly always people of African extraction. In Hurgronje's opinion, in fact, the Zar had been introduced into Arabia by "Abyssinian slaves" (p. 100).[83]

The Zar in Najd

In the period of the Wahhabi revival, there is no evidence of Zar performances in Najd. If these performances were in fact absent, as seems certain, the Wahhabi movement alone is sufficient to explain why. Given the ideology of the Wahhabi revival and the politics supporting it, there are very sound reasons to assume that Zar performances would have been suppressed: the Zar ceremony is addressed to a spirit—and not an official, Qur'anic spirit—so the ceremony would have been perceived as an affront to the unity of God, the very definition of shirk. Second, the ceremony employs dancing and music. The Wahhabis disapprove of both, and in Riyadh, at least during the revival, music and dancing were prohibited. Third, participants' striving toward a state of ecstasy is similar in method to Sufi zikr ceremonies, which the Wahhabis specifically condemn. Bearing in mind that in the 1920s smoking was a whipping offense in Riyadh, and individuals were said to have been executed for repeated absences from prayer call, it is highly unlikely that a shaikhat az-Zar would have performed before a public audience in Riyadh more than once.

The absence of the Zar is a powerful statement of the ideological penetration of political Wahhabism and its capacity to enforce compliance, because social conditions in Najd were otherwise ripe for the Zar to have taken root. East African immigrants and their descendants were ubiquitous in all the towns, villages, and Bedouin encampments under the control of Ibn Sa'ud, and references to newly imported African slaves are frequent in missionary writings on Najd, where the trade in enslaved people, especially from Ethiopia and Sudan, continued into the 1950s. Furthermore, wherever the Zar has been documented, including in the Gulf towns and Mecca, it was Ethiopians and Sudanese who were reported to be the ritual experts of the Zar performances, and Ethiopian women were very numerous in domestic service in Najd, physically in a position of influence, living and working intimately within Arabian families. Because they were outsiders, these women could fill professional roles as healers, midwives, and spell makers, and one would expect therefore that these same Ethiopian women would surely have brought the Zar into Najdi households as they did in Mecca and in the Gulf.[84]

Another reason why conditions were ripe for the Zar in Najd is that the ritual appeals to women who experience physical isolation, and physical separation of women has been a constant feature of Najdi town society, noted by every commentator from the nineteenth through the mid-twentieth centuries. One source of the ritual's appeal to segregated women that has endured over time, noted in missionary correspondence as well as in works of more recent anthropology, is that the Zar provides the core for a community of women. It offers not only a means for isolated women to experience greater sociability but also a way to challenge authority and to compensate for exclusion from formal religion,[85] and for these reasons Gulf women participants viewed the Zar as a positive experience.[86] When Minnie Dykstra attended Zar ceremonies in Bahrain in 1918 she noted that the ritual appealed to women far more than to men and commented that "there does not seem to be the least desire or effort on the part of those possessed to be freed from their zeeraan. This, perhaps, is due to the fact that it provides them with a great deal of fun and excitement, and gives them distinction and authority which otherwise they would not have."[87] The anthropologist I. M. Lewis only echoed Dykstra's opinion when he suggested that spirit possession generally appeals to women in societies that exclude them from social, religious and political affairs. "Women's peripherality, is," he wrote, "a general feature of all societies where men hold a secure monopoly on power positions and deny their partners effective jural rights," and "it is secluded and excluded wives who are regularly subject to spirit possession."[88] Many studies, in fact, show that women who are most subject to physical segregation are also those most attracted to Zar societies, and these are primarily affluent women who can afford to maintain seclusion.[89]

A Zar Revival:
Antidote to Isolation and Depression

The Zar has proven to be adaptable to new situations over time, attracting different groups of people, and holding different meanings for its participants. In 1945, for example, the Zar craze had ebbed in Kuwait but had not disappeared, for there were at least two public Zars held regularly.[90] In the 1970s the Zar was experiencing something of a revival, although no longer with the social cachet that it once possessed. A look at the women drawn to the Zar again reaffirms its appeal as an antidote to feelings of isolation and depression. In Mecca, for example, it is tribal women from the rural districts who joined Zar groups and who also became the target of condemnation as a result. A pamphlet published in Mecca by a Wahhabi shaikh in 1976 complains about the Zar ceremonies on the grounds that the Qur'an prohibits entering into contact with "jinn" and goes on to identify "women who believe in Satan" as the culprits who encourage others to attend the Zar.[91]

In Kuwait the Zar has also resurfaced, specifically as an activity of socially marginalized women, who are, like the Zar adherents in Mecca, tribal. In her study of the Zar in Kuwait, Zabaydah Ashkanani shows that today, as before, all the ritual specialists are former slaves and their descendants.[92] Membership in a private Zar society is no longer an elite activity but one confined to women who find themselves physically isolated in suburban housing and socially marginalized because they have not received the kind of education as their children and husbands. These women suffer from depression, loneliness, and loss of identity, experiencing headaches, loss of appetite, dizziness, nervousness, and nightmares. Either because of lack of education, inclination, or family support, they have been unable to adjust to the changing environment that came about with modernization. (Interestingly, these women, Ashkanani tells us, generally pursued the same course of medical treatment prior to attending the Zar that their counterparts sought during the missionary era: the first line of treatment was calling in a man to read Qur'anic verses; that failing, the women sought out local healers who tried other methods and then diagnosed spirit possession.)

Kuwait was a small town until around 1950, and women's freedom of movement depended on their being chaperoned by servants or older women; they were also confined by men, by the veil, and by the walled structure of their homes, but the proximity of other houses, including the houses of siblings and other close relatives, made possible extensive visiting in other women's homes and a widespread community support group that was the center of their lives. The new city plan for Kuwait, however, moved families outside the crowded old town into homes on large lots that separated families and destroyed neighborhoods. Nuclear family dwellings replaced extended family units, eroding parental authority, distancing siblings from each other, and forcing married couples to depend on the resources of their own company.

The elimination of traditional space has left some Kuwaiti women, in particular women of late middle age who are of rural origins or came of age too late to take advantage of public education (80 percent of Kuwaiti women were illiterate in 1980), isolated in the midst of affluence. Most of these new Zar participants suffer from double alienation: they are *'asil*, or pure-blooded tribal people, who, in the era before modernization, possessed the ultimate status: they were the aristocracy among Arabs by virtue of birth. Today, however, education, money, full Kuwaiti citizenship, careers (even for women), political influence, and the ability to speak foreign languages are far more important in determining status. For these women the "Zar is an opportunity to express their feelings of alienation and confusion, and to receive a feeling of solidarity and of belonging" (p. 229).

It is not coincidental that the new participants in the Zar in both Kuwait and Mecca tend to be tribal women: at least one study suggests that tribal women are less likely to go through the educational system and enter the workforce than are nontribal women and that the tribal family structure that values segregation for women is more resistant to change.[93] It is precisely this problem of alienation, of segregation, of disconnectedness from avenues of self-reliance, that suggests the Zar should have found an audience among women in Najd, and the explanation for its absence is most surely Wahhabi Islam with its connection to political power.

Engaging spirits as a method of healing declined in the Arabian peninsula as a result of Wahhabism and the political hegemony behind it. The Wahhabis designated the One God as the only source of supernatural power, disenfranchising all the saints, spirits, jinn, and angels of their intercessory powers and condemning healers, witches, and fortune-tellers who sought to engage them or negotiate with them.

Virtually all women known to us who claimed specialized knowledge to engage spirits were in some way anomalous. They were women in ambiguous positions in society or, by virtue of age, race, poverty, or ethnicity, marginal to the politically and economically dominant classes. The Arabian women whose association with spirit engagement has been recorded include black women, especially those of foreign origin. Black women who engage spirits are not just servants who can be controlled but individuals perceived to possess powers to help or harm or to control others; when old or unmarried, they are dangerously independent of men's control. Witches and healers are also elderly, whatever their ethnicity, and perceived as being beyond the capacity for sexual provocation and thus not needing to be under a man's control; they include Sulubba, from the most demeaned of social groupings, people who are Bedouin but not tribal, who engage in manual labor and eschew all the claims of independence that are the pretense of tribal Bedouin, and their women do not subscribe to the modesty values that are the sine qua non of honor in tribal society.

All these women have taken on a role beyond daughter, wife, mother, and their extensions, nurturing and homemaking. They are all in some way out of order in society. Like indentured women who are mothers of free-born children in the homes of their former masters, they cross social boundaries. Simply by being what they are, such women are the objects of suspicion. They evoke feelings of unease and fear in others. The perception that they are capable of engaging spirits therefore may be a product of their ambiguous position alone, and when they actively attempt to do so, their machinations can be perceived as being toward evil ends.

The same cannot be said to be uniformly true of the men who engage spirits. Some indeed held ambiguous positions in society or were in some way marginal to it. The Moorish readers, for example, were foreigners or were perceived as being foreigners. However, if some of the men known to engage the supernatural were in ambiguous roles, others also possessed knowledge and skill that held society's respect: the mandal, the diviner, and the medium in the trial by ordeal were hired and paid money for their skills, and the results they produced were considered valid for determining judgment by recognized authorities. Abd al-Aziz's dream interpreter was one of the most influential of the ulama in Riyadh. The trial-by-ordeal judge in Kuwait presided over cases referred to him by the ruler, even though he was not allowed to preach in any of the mosques. When a diviner in Unaiza discovered the body of a missing child, the guilty person revealed by his discovery was executed. The skills of such men were openly performed and publicly acknowledged, and, far from being persecuted or ignored by established authorities, they were patronized by them.

In the arena of spirit engagement, then, men and women who performed similar tasks were viewed differently, and similar tasks, when performed by a man, were carried out on a perceived higher level of proficiency. When men engaged spirits, they tended to be perceived as being more in control of what they did, as having acquired some special skill that could be worked toward wonderment, the discovery of truth, or some positive good. In contrast to men, women tended to be perceived not so much as possessing acquired skills as being possessed by some uncontrollable internal power that could do harm. When women claimed the ability to undo the work of the evil eye, cast out jinn, prepare potions, or interpret dreams, even other women could suspect them of also being agents of the evil eye or practitioners of witchcraft even when they were performing the role of healer. Even outside Najd, where spirit engagement practices were not so heavily disparaged on religious grounds, such practices and the women who performed them were viewed with suspicion.

From the viewpoint of society at large, women's handle on the supernatural could sometimes be associated with the evil that women were supposed to do to men, especially their ability to manipulate them for their affection or their pocketbook, to use them as the objects of their predatory sexuality, or to kill them. The fears and suspicions that such preconceptions evoked were difficult for women to dispel or control, and thus any woman, once accused of witchcraft, was vulnerable to a man's retribution. (It is worth noting in this context that we have no examples of male dream interpreters or spell makers being murdered for real or imagined offenses.) Thus while women's association with the spirit world can be viewed as a source of power or status, it can also be viewed as a symbol of vulnerability and weakness.

However low the prestige of the healer who engages the spirits in society at large, practitioners were judged by their patients according to the patients' expectations for relief, and patients did sometimes experience positive benefit from treatment, such as temporary relief from pain while experiencing the additional pain of cautery or the placebo effect that could occur when the patient expected to feel improvement after an exorcism. Like Christians who accept exorcism as a legitimate means of healing because in the Bible Jesus cured epilepsy by casting out demons, the patient in the Gulf knew for certain from the Qur'an that evil spirits existed and could be the cause of illness.

In fact the results of treatment in terms of relief from symptoms could in some cases be irrelevant to the prestige of the healer, so long as the healer performed according to recognized standards of procedure and the procedure appeared to be related to the patient's understanding of the cause of the disease. The amulets, decoys, and disguises employed in the Gulf were theoretically no different from a method used as a prophylaxis at almost the same time in rural Rhode Island. During a period in the late nineteenth century when tuberculosis carried off one in six persons, the bodies of some who died of the disease were exhumed and decapitated. The skull was placed inside the ribcage and the body reburied, on the theory that the dead, who were thought to rise from the grave and sit on the chests of family survivors while they slept, thus causing the tightness in the chest and coughing of blood so characteristic of the disease, would be unable to climb out of the grave once dismembered.[94] Like placing a fish decoy in bed with a child, or pinning an amulet on a child's clothing, or burning a cross on the patient's head to scare off the demon inside, this was a means of responding to a disease according to the way its genesis and transmission were understood.

The difference in the social posture of men and women who engaged spirits held true whether in the Gulf or Najd, whether Sunni, Shi'a, or Wahhabi. Doughty provided examples from Unaiza and Khaibar, and I have also cited examples from Riyadh and Kuwait, from the deserts of northern Najd and Syria. The Wahhabi movement, however, had distinct effects on the relationship of women to spirit engagement. First, the Wahhabi movement specifically identified women as those who are vulnerable to practicing shirk because of their emotional deficiencies and emphasized and sometimes enforced controls that the Qur'an and Hadith already place on women because of this deficiency: women must not attend funerals, offer vows at graves, or weep demonstrably in response to death, for example. Second, the Hadith and Qur'anic verses that Ibn Abd al-Wahhab and his scholarly followers selected to explain the prohibition against shirk, sorcerous practices, the use of talismans, and excessive mourning tend to identify women, as distinct from men, as most likely to indulge in such acts, in some cases with evil intent. Third, the Wahhabi movement also underscored the ambiguous position of those women who were actually associated with engaging spirits: the definers of orthodoxy demanded acceptance of the literal truth of the anthropomorphic passages in the Qur'an and Hadith yet at the same time most strongly condemned any attempts to engage the beings believed to cause the harm. This contradiction made the position of such women even more ambiguous and thus perceived as more dangerous and so rendered them more vulnerable.

The contradiction in the position of woman healers was magnified by the Wahhabis' targeting of unorthodox practice, which made the practitioner seem more powerful at the same time that it made her more vulnerable. As mentioned above, marginal cults provide a way for orthodoxy to define itself, but "the price centrality pays to marginality for providing this service," Lewis says, "is, in effect, the ambiguous power it cedes to the latter."[95] However useful, he says, those who fail to conform, who persist in ritual behaviors contrary to what orthodoxy prescribes, thus possess some actual negative power that must be controlled. In condemning spirit engagement practices, orthodoxy in effect accredits those practices and gives them an appeal they might not otherwise deserve based on their own efficacy. Therefore, just as these marginal practices attract those who need the services they can perform, they become the likely and necessary target of suppression. While the acts of the sorceress or witch would have been disparaged in the Gulf as well as in Najd, in the Wahhabi Najd alone they would have been specifically condemned, and the practitioner punished.

The Zar is a special case. The ritual experts of the Zar, like most other professional healers, are primarily women and are in some way marginal to established society. Zar leaders, however, have status that can be measured by the clientele they attract and can be the magnet for social gatherings of the elite as well as the common people. In addition, the Zar method, when practiced regularly in a society of fellow sufferers, could be very successful as a healing technique, especially for depression, anxiety, and psychosomatic ailments. In fact the symptoms of possession as described in early missionary sources and in contemporary studies are consistent with chronic depression: tiredness, fainting, fits of crying, and sense of purposelessness. As a method of healing, especially for depression and its psychosomatic manifestations, the Zar was probably among the more successful techniques performed by local practitioners. Like other rituals in which rational control is temporarily abandoned, the Zar was believed to produce powers of healing, the energy to command, and access to truths that rational effort could not produce.[96] Women could find relief and enhanced self-esteem in the Zar ritual, because there they could express themselves in ways otherwise not open to them or acceptable in the larger society.[97] The ritual performance was also an opportunity for women to play at possessing power by playing at being men, dressing up as men and speaking in men's voices, as the sex of the spirit was usually identified as the opposite of the person being possessed.[98] The possessed person can also exercise influence over her husband and manipulate him to do something she wants by claiming that the Zar threatens some disaster for failure to perform.[99]

Associations formed through the Zar could also be the core of a community for women who were otherwise isolated. In places where the segregation of women has a high social value, communal rituals constitute what is perhaps the one legitimate venue for women to engage in group activity outside the family and the one avenue toward status independent of the family. For urban, elite women of the Gulf, group rituals such as the Zar probably provided the only destinations where women could legitimately experience community in a circle of relationships outside the family.

The experience of community can be critical for women, emotionally and psychologically, and it is worth repeating here that the ritual expert, as Hoch-Smith and Spring observes, creates "a 'community of sisters' by acting upon female physiology. The midwife, the medium, and the healer are the archetype of nurturance *in relation to* their patients. . . . Relationships built on the healer-patient tie and the ritual expert-to novice tie crosscut ties based on kinship, friendship and residence. Ritual validates bonds between women."[100] But virtually all the avenues for communal ritual activity practiced in the Gulf were absent in Najd because the Wahhabi movement precluded the Zar and suppressed the vowing rituals, celebrations of the Prophet's Birthday, visits to saints' shrines, and moulid ceremonies, along with the public and private Shi'ite celebrations mourning the death of Hussein. In Najd it is actually possible that, before the start of public education for girls in 1960, there was virtually no place for a townswoman to experience community outside the social circle sanctioned through the family. This extreme isolation must have made a critical difference in women's life experience, while the practice of isolation itself must have reinforced the religious and cultural attitudes that undergird it.

CHAPTER FIVE

When Words Fail

Surgeries, Smells, and Salt Packing

Commentators on Arabia and the Gulf never tired of harping on Muslim fatalism and the refusal of the Muslim to accept medical care when offered. "The Moslem is a fatalist," wrote Minnie Dykstra of the Bahrain mission, "and in all new-fangled ideas such as inoculation and modern medical treatment, he practices, to his own hurt, this slogan, 'We trust in God.'"[1]

Clearly, however, "the Muslim," as every commentator on medical practice also illustrated, could be entirely practical when it came to seeking cures and applying healing techniques. During a 1919 epidemic, Ibn Sa'ud—the Wahhabi chief—sent for Dr. Paul Harrison to come to Riyadh, where, Harrison wrote, a hundred people a day were dying of influenza.[2] In spite of local antagonism toward the missionary practitioner of unfamiliar medicine, Harrison found even Ikhwan receptive to his treatments: "The Ikhwan," he wrote, "will not be such a very difficult proposition. In three-weeks time they have learned that it is permissible to take the Kaffiri medicine and even submit to operations." As early as 1913, after an initial year of being ignored by the Kuwaiti population, the Gulf missionaries had reported success in courting patients: in that year the Kuwait Woman's Medical Report stated that the physician had not experienced "a single rebuff"; Eleanor Calverley reported again in 1917 that no patients refused to take their remedies.[3]

Theologically speaking, as I discussed in an earlier chapter, the patients were on solid ground in trying out missionary medicine, as well as all other kinds of medicine. "Every disease has a remedy," goes the Prophet's Hadith, and the skill of the physician was in knowing what one correct remedy corresponded to a patient's particular disease. God, however, remained in the picture, for God would not show the correct remedy to the healer unless He had already predetermined that the person using it would be cured.

Most patients who encountered the missionary doctors were probably not much concerned about the potential contradiction between God's predetermination of their fate and their quest for a cure. The Arabian patient, in any event, had a choice, just like the American patient does when he chooses between seeking help through the orthodox medical canon and looking for treatment through Christian Science, acupuncture, or holistic medicine. The use of medicines and techniques of healing were all around them, and they had at their disposal the benefit of experience and observation to know that human intervention could and sometimes did have an effect on illness. Healing specialists employed herbs, inoculation, quarantine, cautery, massage, bloodletting, and bonesetting; they performed circumcisions and other surgeries and aided in birthing. They also employed techniques drawn from the Prophet's Hadith and still other healing practices derived from the Hippocratic corpus of the ancient Greeks by medieval Arab physicians. Moreover, knowledge about the Prophet's prescriptions as well as Greek medicine was so widely diffused in Arabian society that even the most unschooled patients went to the clinics armed with diagnostic information, expecting the American physicians to prescribe cures that corresponded to what they thought was the source of their illness.

Given the option of all these potentially efficacious treatments, patients might have verbally expressed a belief that God predetermines everything, but—as shown in the previous chapters—they acted as though they believed that destiny was negotiable and God could be persuaded to change His mind. Furthermore, when holy words failed or were left unsaid, there were always practical remedies available to try.

Midwifery

Midwives were invariably women, and were often also skilled in the use of herbs and other healing techniques. That only women would treat other women during this intimate procedure might appear to be a given, but this

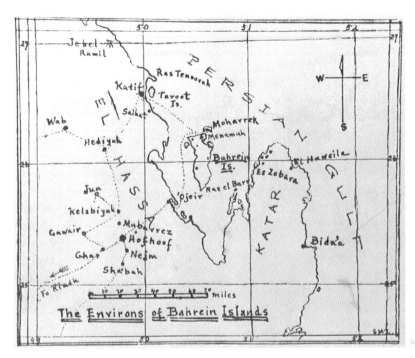

Map, "Environs of Bahrein Islands," showing routes of missionary medical tours to the mainland. Published in *Neglected Arabia* 80 (January–March, 1912).

A group of Zar musicians and dancers, photographed about 1918 in Bahrain.

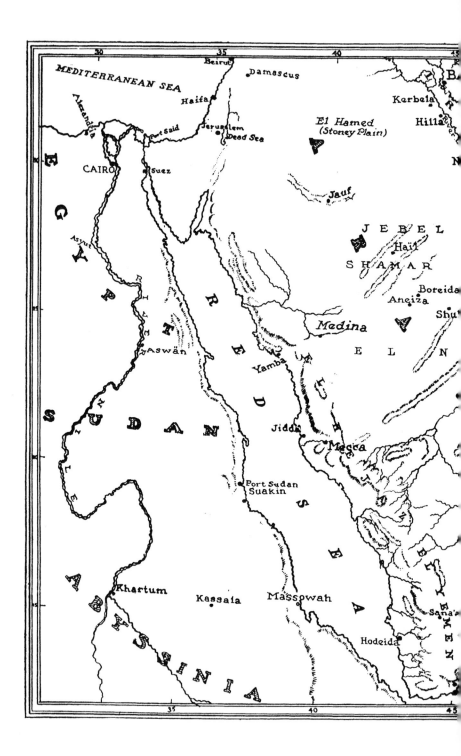

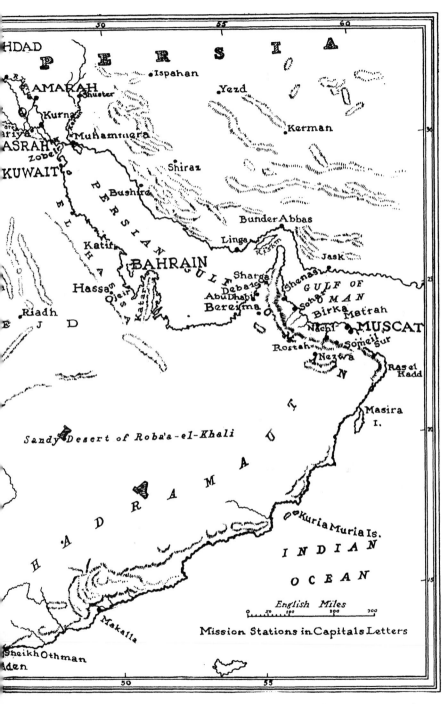

Map of Arabia from *The History of the Arabian Mission* by Alfred Dewitt Mason and
Frederick J. Barny (1926, New York). Courtesy Board of Foreign Missions, Reformed
Church in America.

Mrs. Bessie Mylrea and Dr. Eleanor Calverley conducting gospel services at the Arabian Mission Clinic in Kuwait, 1918.

Women and girls of Kuwait, photographed about 1927.

Missionary Letters and News from Arabia

APRIL—JUNE, 1904

The Arabian Mission Hymn*

SONG.　8s & 5s.

I.

There's a land long since neglected,
　There's a people still rejected,
But of truth and grace elected,
　In His love for them.

II.

Softer than their night wind's fleeting
　Richer than their starry tenting,
Stronger than their sands protecting,
　Is His love for them.

III.

To the host of Islam's leading,
　To the slave in bondage bleeding,
To the desert dweller pleading,
　Bring his love to them.

IV.

Through the promise on God's pages,
　Through His work in history's stages,
Through the cross that crowns the ages,
　Show his love to them.

V.

With the prayer that still availeth,
　With the host that still prevaileth,
With the love that never faileth,
　Tell His love to them.

VI.

Till the desert's sons, now aliens,
　Till its tribes and their dominions,
Till Arabia's raptured millions,
　Praise His love of them.

J. G. Lansing.

---

* This being the *Fiftieth* number of our Quarterly it is appropriate to print once more the mission hymn which is the Marseillaise of our campaign against Islam. We invite all our contributors to sing it with us.

The Arabian Mission Hymn, "the Marseillaise of our campaign against Islam," as published in *Neglected Arabia* 50 (April–June, 1904).

"Missionary sisters Miss Rachel and Miss Ruth Jackson and students at their girls' school in Basra," published in *Neglected Arabia* 134 (July–September, 1925).

"Four Ikhwan patriarchs," photographed in Hufuf in 1924 by Dr. Louis Dame.

"Women of Musqat," probably photographed by missionary Elizabeth Cantine, then stationed in Oman. Published in *Neglected Arabia* 54 (April–June, 1905).

THE ARAB WOMEN CLEANING RICE

"Arab Women Cleaning Rice," photo probably taken in Basra, 1907. The women are using cloth noseplugs as protection against disease-causing smells. Published in *Neglected Arabia* 66 (January–March, 1908).

LEFT: "Women of Matrah carrying water," published in *Neglected Arabia* 173
(October–December, 1935). RIGHT: "Woman carrying fuel" (dried animal dung);
her clothing suggests she is Najdi. Published in *Neglected Arabia* 222 (Winter 1950–51).

Servants in the household of Ibn Sa'ud, 1933, photographed by Elizabeth Dame.

"Louis and Elizabeth Dame of the Bahrain mission in Arab Costume," published in *Neglected Arabia* 176 (January–March, 1934).

A family group in Kuwait. Probably a staged photograph, as the child is in rags and the parents are well dressed. The caption on the photo as it appears in *Arabia Calling* 216 (Spring 1949) says that "the little girl is carrying on her head a bundle of Guild Box clothes just given her."

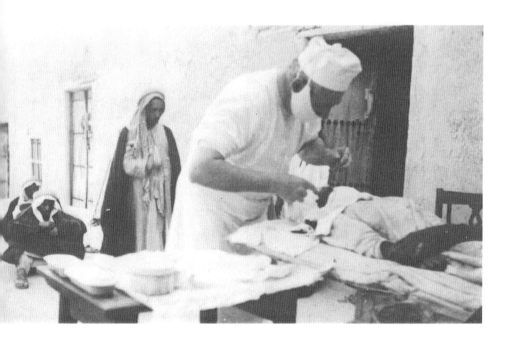

Above: Dr. Louis Dame operating on a patient on a veranda in Hufuf, 1931.

Left: A wounded Bedouin patient at the Kuwait hospital. He has a cloth plug in his nose to prevent inhalation of sweet smells that might prevent his wounded arm and hand from healing properly.

ABOVE: Balcony of chief of police's home in Riyadh where mission doctors were quartered during a medical tour in 1933. The cloth screen was erected for the privacy of women while male guests were in the courtyard below.

RIGHT: A well-dressed patient with her children at the Kuwait hospital.

Women's bazaar in Unaiza, 1924.

Booths for women sellers in the women's bazaar in Qatif, a town on the Gulf coast, 1923.

The congregation gathered for the 'Id al-Fitr prayer service at the end of the month of fasting (Ramadan) in Bahrain, 1928. The photographer comments that there are only a few women present, and they are all far to the back of the assembled congregation (in foreground of photo).

At the end of the mosque service, the photographer tells us, the women left first and went off to the cemetery for prayer and a picnic, where he photographed them en route.

A young woman of the Rualla Bedouin, about 1928.

A Bedouin family of the Al Murra tribe photographed by Dr. Harold Storm near Hufuf around 1933.

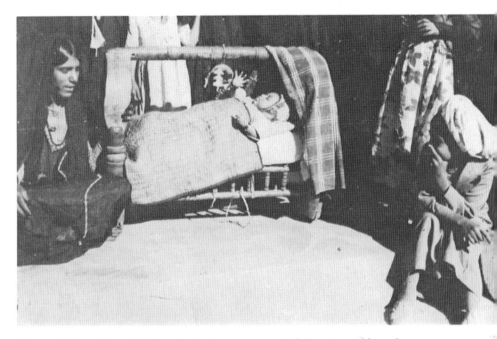

A Persian baby in his cradle, Kuwait. Amulets on cap, on baby's wrist, and hung from cradle. Taken around 1934.

A friend of the mission with his two wives and their children, Kuwait, about 1934.

Women and children at the Kuwait mission hospital, about 1934.

Crowd attending a Shiite Muharram procession, Bahrain, 1908. Women in foreground following the procession.

is not always so. In the United States during the early nineteenth century, for example, male midwives dominated the profession among middle-class women, who thought men more competent in light of developments in the knowledge of anatomy and the introduction of forceps.[4] Occasionally the midwife, always described as old, was also thought to be skilled in the use of spells and exorcism.

Only in rare instances was a missionary doctor called to attend a normal birth. Usually, Eleanor Calverley wrote, she would be called only after a midwife had exhausted all methods and given up hope, and then only in the most extreme cases, when disaster had already occurred. The first time she was called was to an emergency, when the mother had been in labor for four days, and a servant begged Calverley to help as the woman was dying. When she arrived at the home, however, no one would open the door to her, and she never knew whether the woman had already died or if the family had decided not to allow her to attend the birth.[5] Four years after opening her practice in Kuwait, Calverley reported that she had had five obstetrical patients with normal deliveries, "three Muslims, one a daughter of Shaikh Mubarak, and two Jews."[6]

One source of opposition to the missionary doctor's intervention was the midwives, who resented their competence being questioned and also feared the threat Western medicine posed to their livelihood. Often were the times, Calverley reported, when she would arrive to help in a most desperate delivery at the invitation of the husband and find herself the focus of a pitched verbal battle among the midwife, female relatives, and the spouse. The midwives had reason to feel threatened: their skills were so limited that most labors could just as well have been attended by female relatives of the mother alone, as they most often were. In 1944, thirty years after Calverley first assisted in a normal delivery, Mary Allison, a doctor in Kuwait, reported that women usually went to their mothers' homes to deliver their babies. "Her mother and an older woman sit with her during her ordeal," Allison wrote. "Wisely they do not interfere with the process in any way so the cases do not suffer the complications of unskilled hands and most cases get along fairly well."[7]

Family members treated the process of giving birth as a collective experience. Always, according to nurses and doctors of the Arabian Mission, numerous female relatives, or relatives along with a midwife, attended the woman in labor, offering verbal encouragement and joining in the mother-to-be's ejaculations of pain. Usually the woman went through her labor in a squatting position, and in the course of a normal birth, the midwife offered moral support and physically helped to prop the mother up. Calverley described a normal delivery she attended in the home of a pearl diver who would not allow his wife to go to the hospital. When Calverley arrived the mother-to-be was already in labor, attended by her mother and aunt, and she was squatting on a pile of sand with "two old midwives" supporting her, one sitting in front and the other supporting her from behind.

The purpose of the sand was hygiene, because it could absorb blood and other fluids and then be discarded, and it was quite suitable to meet the needs of the woman in labor since she did not intend to lie in it but to squat over it. Calverley, however, thought the woman in labor should lie on her back on a mattress, in the position that was then preferred according to American medical practice and had brought along her waterproof sheeting so that the one mattress in the house, which its owner had wanted to keep clean, could be used. The midwives were resentful, Calverley thought, that the "Engliziya" had been called and particularly resentful that the woman in labor was being told to lie down. As the labor progressed, Calverley wrote, many other women entered until the room was quite crowded with well-wishers. Someone brought an amulet in a small leather case to hang around the patient's neck, and another brought some medicine to drink, the ink washed off a piece of paper on which a mullah had written a verse from the Qur'an.[8]

The skill of the Arabian midwives did not extend to surgical intervention during birth. Rather than performing a simple episiotomy, a midwife would allow the flesh to tear, and afterward she would not suture the wound to repair it. If an unborn fetus died in the womb, the midwife would try prayer and amulets while the mother died of infection caused by the decomposing body of her unborn child. A breech birth was also a challenge to the midwives' skills. In 1949, the American nurse, Cornelia Dalenberg, responded to an emergency appeal to attend a birth on Sitra, an island southeast of Bahrain. Dalenberg was taken to a date garden, in which there was an enclosure around several huts with cows and chickens inside. One of the huts was crowded with people: Dalenberg counted fifteen exiting from the hut to make room for her to enter. Inside she found a girl lying on a mat, with her baby partially born, all but the head, and already dead for many hours. "The head remained in the birth canal and its little neck had been horribly twisted and lacerated by attempts to pull it free," Dalenberg wrote. "All night she had lain in this condition. The exhaustion of the poor girl-mother, the amulets tied around her arms and legs, the Quran by her side and the smell of herbs cooking in a small pot over a hole in the ground, all these things told of her night of agony and of the fruitless attempts of her relatives to help her." "We cleared a space around her and got to work. I had encountered this problem many times in the hospital and in other situations, so I knew that the basic approach was to flip the baby up over the mother's stomach and ease the head out along the natural upward curve of the birth canal."[9]

Dr. Calverley had no way of estimating the infant death rate during normal delivery, because her experience was almost entirely with the abnormal. She was certain, however, that it must have been very high. One of the reasons for this was the midwife's practice of packing the birth canal with coarse salt, to serve as an astringent, immediately after the birth. The process was extremely painful and caused the postpartum woman to experience great thirst, which was exacerbated by the midwives' refusal of water because they believed, according to Dalenberg, that drinking water while the salt was being absorbed into the body would hamper the absorption process (p. 29).[10]

This treatment did have one positive result, as the incidence of puerperal sepsis (infection during the period of confinement after birth) was rare. The importance of mitigating the danger of puerperal sepsis should not be dismissed, as infection after childbirth caused a high incidence of mortality in women even in industrialized countries. In the United States, for example, 2.7 out of every 1,000 women died of childbed fever in the 1920s.[11] The long-term results of salt packing, however, were pernicious. The inflammation of the tissues caused by the salt set up a condition that produced partial or complete atresia, the closing of the birth canal by a gradual growing together of the tissues. The initial result was pain during intercourse and possibly the inability to engage in intercourse at all. If atresia occurred and the woman became pregnant, she would experience protracted labor because the baby could not push through. The baby was then likely to die, and the mother, weak from long labor, might die as well. It was also possible that the baby might force itself out, tearing the mother's body and causing fatal injury. "Very often she is rendered an invalid," wrote Ida Storm in 1949, "subject thereafter to a life of severe suffering, and since she is usually of no use thereafter to her husband, her divorce is swift and inevitable."[12]

The missionary records on salt packing give only a partial view of the extent of the practice, because mission doctors attended so few births. Still, they documented the technique in Kuwait, Bahrain, and Hufuf,[13] and also in

Najd, where during a five-month medical tour, according to the 1935 annual medical report of the Bahrain hospital staff, seven operations to correct atresia of the birth canal were performed. The salt-packing procedure was probably not in use in the royal palace in Riyadh, at least in 1942, because at that time a Syrian midwife had been brought down from Damascus to care for the women of Ibn Sa'ud's household.[14] In any event, the technique passed into history with the introduction of birthing in hospitals, probably by the 1960s. Interviews I conducted in May 1996 with the nursing staff of the obstetrical unit of the Saudi Arabian National Guard Hospital in Riyadh revealed no encounters with the effects of the salt-packing technique.

Circumcision

Even though there are many references by missionary doctors to atresia of the birth canal as a result of salt packing, there is literally no specific reference in all the years of missionary correspondence and medical reports to female circumcision. Female circumcision is an operation performed for the purpose of inhibiting sexual arousal and discouraging sexual intercourse before marriage. The operation may involve slicing off all or just the tip of the clitoris (clitoridectomy), or it may involve a more radical procedure in which the clitoris is completely excised, the labia minora are entirely or partly removed, and incisions are made in the labia majora and then pressed or stitched together to cover most of the vaginal opening (infibulation). Either type of surgery is visually apparent to even the untrained eye and could not have been overlooked by a physician attending an obstetrical or gynecological patient. The missionary doctors therefore either never encountered the operation or were squeamish about reporting it. Occasional comments in missionary records, however, may refer obliquely to the practice: Amy Zwemer, working in the Bahrain mission hospital, commented delicately in 1911 that a patient's husband threatened her with divorce "unless something happens which only a surgeon's knife can accomplish."[15] Similarly, Anna Harrison, traveling in Hasa with Dr. Storm, who had been called to save a woman in childbirth, wrote that "in the interior of Arabia women still live according to the strictest laws. Age old customs had made this woman unable to be delivered of her child."[16] Even though the preference for home birthing and women's modesty values would have limited the doctors' exposure to evidence of the operation, the fact that there is no specific reference to the surgery by observers who were looking for customs to complain about suggests that if female circumcision were practiced at all it was confined to particular areas or groups of people who didn't frequent missionary clinics.

It is in fact certain that the operation was performed by some peoples in the Gulf and Najd region in spite of the lack of references by missionary doctors, and evidence suggests that both the radical and limited surgeries were performed. Based on accounts by male inquirers and recent anthropology, the operation appears to have been performed primarily, but not exclusively, on tribal women, especially Bedouin tribal women. Dickson, whose information comes from asking questions of Bedouin women, says that the operation was not performed on Bedouin of northeast Arabia, northern Najd, or Kuwait but was performed on girls in the town of Basra and among some of the Shammar (of southern Najd), as well as the Manasir on the Gulf coast and the Muntafiq settled and shepherd tribes in the Kuwait-Iraq region. He also says that the *Kauliyah*, or Gypsies, of Iraq, circumcised their young girls. A woman specialist from one of these tribes was paid to perform the surgery, Dickson says, and he describes the less radical of the procedures, which, he says, was explained to him in 1933 by women of three different tribal confederations, the Mutair, Anayza, and Shammar. The operator would pass a needle and thread through the clitoris, stretching the clitoris outwards with the thread and cutting it off as close to the body as possible.[17] The operation was not a cause for celebration, Dickson relates. "Among certain Shammar families, the operation was done quietly and without fuss. Only the female members of the family were told," his Shammari informant said, "and not even the neighbors knew about it."[18]

Philby, whose information on the subject comes from men's banter, relates having been told that female circumcision was not performed on girls in Najd towns but that it was indeed practiced by some Bedouin tribes. "Ibn Jilam told me that the practice is almost confined to the nomad elements of these tribes (the Manasir on the Hasa coast, and by most of the Oman tribes) and is a relic of the old pagan days of Arabia—it is not known among the Murra, who like true Najd tribes regard it as disgraceful."[19] (Philby was writing after the Wahhabi revival, which resulted in the conversion of the Al Murrah, who may have regarded anything prerevival as "the old pagan days.")

On the other hand, during his journey through the Empty Quarter in 1932, Philby heard that female circumcision was practiced among some of the largest and noblest Najd tribes, including the Al Murrah:

His [Abu Ja'sha's] strong subject was sex, and he loved to poke fun at Salih by dilating on Manasir practice in the matter of female circumcision. "Take it from me," he said, "they let their women come to puberty with clitoris intact and, when a girl is to be married, they make a feast for her circumcision a month or two before the wedding. It is only then that they circumcise them and not at birth as do the other tribes—Qahtan and Murra, Bani Hajir, ay, and 'Ajman. Thus their women grow up more lustful than others, and fine women they are too and . . . hot! But then they remove everything, making them as smooth as smooth, to cool their ardour without reducing their desire.". . . "And if they make a feast for such occasions," I asked, "do they perform the ceremony publicly as with boys?" "God save you! No," he replied, "but the girls are dealt with in their tents by women who know their business, and get a dollar or so for the job. They are expert with the scissors, the razor and the needle, which are all used for the operation." The Dawasir do not practice female circumcision nor the townsfolk of Nejd; and some of the northern tribes do, while others do not.[20]

Philby's confidant was describing the more radical procedure, infibulation. The age at which the operation was performed among the Manasir is likely to have been just before puberty, sometime between the ages of nine and eleven, as after puberty girls were considered eligible for marriage. In other regions where the procedure is documented, girls were usually circumcised around the age of seven, not at birth.

Female circumcision was also practiced at one time by women of the Al Saar, a nomadic tribal group that travels in the Empty Quarter, according to Aisha Almana, who conducted interviews with members of this tribe in the late 1970s.[21] She was told that mothers and grandmothers of her informants had been circumcised but that the procedure was no longer practiced. Almana attributes the practice among the Al Saar to the tribe's exposure to Yemen tribes, who are said to practice female circumcision. This is certainly possible, although it is also possible that female circumcision is the product of African influences, as the practice is very widespread in Ethiopia, Somalia, and Sudan, from whence a great many people were brought into Arabia as slaves and transported by Bedouin inland through Musqat. Because of the reported circumcision among other Bedouin, however, the practice could also have been indigenous.

Almana says that female circumcision is virtually nonexistent among other nomadic tribes in Saudi Arabia. This could have been true in the 1970s when she did her research, in spite of the commentaries of Philby and Dickson: in my May 1996 interview with the nursing staff of the obstetrical unit at the Saudi Arabian National Guard Hospital, (the National Guard is made up of former Bedouin), only one of the nurses participating in the interview had encountered female circumcision, and this was but one instance of a thirty-five-year-old woman with a partial clitoridectomy. A Shi'ite woman from Hufuf, however, told me in 1994 that Shi'ite village women in Hasa still have the operation.

Unlike female circumcision, circumcision of young boys is a standard procedure that, although not mentioned in the Qur'an, is considered to be obligatory for males in Islam. Also unlike female circumcision, the operation, which involves only removing the foreskin of the penis, does not affect sensual pleasure or hamper the functioning of the organ if successfully performed without complications.

According to Dickson, in Kuwait the surgeon was a professional called from outside, who was known as al-Hindi (the Indian), and Dr. Mary Allison, a contemporary of Dickson working in Kuwait, would later write that a local barber performed the procedure. Dickson describes an unceremonious surgery: al-Hindi "arrives on the scene and with an ordinary razor cuts off the child's foreskin."[22] Doughty had described what appears to be a clinically safer and less painful method: the operator draws the foreskin through a hole cut in a stone shard, ties it off with a thread, and then slices through it with a razor.[23]

When al-Hindi was called to operate at a private home for a fee, neighborhood boys from families too poor to hire him themselves would turn up to be circumcised at the same time. Unfortunately, because of a lack of proper sanitary precautions, such as sterilizing the razor used to cut off the foreskin, the wounds sometimes became septic and failed to heal properly. In 1931 the mission hospital in Kuwait was caring for dozens of cases a year that resulted from this procedure.[24]

The operation to remove the foreskin of a boy's penis was a joyous occasion, marked by a feast in the boy's honor and performed in the presence of the family circle. In Najd towns and in Kuwait, Dickson says, the feast followed seven days of rejoicing. The days of celebration, Dickson tells us, were—surprisingly—looked on by women and girls as their particular feast, and each evening women of the neighborhood and relatives were invited to the boy's home for dancing, music, and sweets. Professional prostitutes even came, he says, and entertained for free to "gain merit and favor from the Almighty." The circumcision signaled that a boy had become "a proper Muslim" (pp. 175–176).

What did the circumcision of a girl, performed quietly without public ac-knowledgment, mean to the girl on whom the operation was performed and to her family? Almana says that Al Saar women considered it a means "to cleanse a woman."[25] (The idea of cleansing, or purification, is used to refer to female circumcision in Egypt and Sudan; Doughty also reported that the word was popularly used to refer to male circumcision.[26] The most common con-temporary colloquial term is *tahara*, "ritual purification.")[27] There is a religious rationalization for the operation in a number of Hadith. In one, the Prophet is reported to have said that if one does circumcise, one should not destroy, "for not destroying the clitoris would be better for the man and would make the woman's face glow."[28] It is highly doubtful, however, that religious significance was attached to the operation in Arabia, since the procedure was not univer-sally practiced and, where it was practiced, appears to have been in most places precipitously dropped with the arrival of modern medicine. Curiously, the surgeon for both male and female circumcision was not a religious spe-cialist but a barber, a family member, or a complete outsider to the commu-nity. Dickson makes a point that the circumciser hired for women was a spe-cialist from one of a few particular tribes, even if the person being circumcised belonged to a different tribe, and the name al-Hindi suggests that the male cir-cumciser was an Indian. (Doughty wrote that the circumciser was either a member of the family or a tradesman from the Sulaib, the nontribal, low-sta-tus tinkers who followed the tribal Bedouin to perform odd jobs.)[29]

The parallels between the male and female operations do not go far: male circumcision was an occasion for joy and public celebration with reli-gious blessing, while female circumcision was a quiet event, treated even by those who initiated the surgery as if it were something shameful and of con-cern only to the women immediately involved.

Bad Smells and Sweet Perfumes

To patients at the Kuwait mission hospital, who came from as far away as Riyadh and Hejaz, smells figured prominently in the causes of illness. The mission doctors were constantly asked, "Will it matter if I take a whiff of perfume or smell the aroma of our cooking?"[30] An individual who came for treatment might also attribute a condition to some smell that he had en-countered recently.[31]

In general, the Dicksons observed, foul odors were considered to be car-riers of disease, while good odors were viewed as beneficial. Healthy people used unscented nose plugs to exclude bad smells, and one particular bad smell that the nose plugs were designed to exclude was that produced by a menstruating woman. The Bedouin, when he came to town, Dickson writes, was particularly on the lookout to protect himself from the "smell of a woman" or of a man who has just had intercourse, and he kept his nose plug in place until he left town.[32]

While the belief was that good odors were usually beneficial to the health, if one already had a wound, an ulcer, or a cancer, it was thought that good odors could cause it to fester. When Elizabeth Dame of the Bahrain mission went on a medical tour to Riyadh, she wrote that "Shahida," the Armenian concubine of Abd al-Aziz was distressed when Dame offered her a bar of perfumed soap as a gift. (Dame christened her "Christina" when she talked about her in her report to the Mission Board on the Riyadh trip because Shahida had been born a Christian.) She was ill and asked Dame whether she would be harmed by the soap as she had already inadvertently smelled it.[33] Abd al-Aziz would have shared her concern, as Wahba comments that the sultan himself frequently discussed the power of perfumes over wounds.[34]

The belief in the power of smells to promote or prevent healing was so firmly held that the heavy loss of life in the Ikhwan attacks on Jahra in October 1920 was attributed by Kuwaitis to indulgence in the smell of musk. In those attacks, the Ikhwan lost eight hundred in the fighting and nearly eight hundred more who died of wounds. The story current in Kuwait to explain the high mortality, according to Dr. Mylrea of the Kuwait mission, was that "when the enemy was looting Jahrah . . . , a quantity of musk was found and the Ikhwan, not knowing exactly what it was, and thinking it to be harmless perfumery, wrapped it up with the spoils and saturated all their stuff with its pungent and penetrating smell. . . . The Ikhwan wounded had inhaled musk, therefore their wounds had festered and therefore they had died." "To the man of Kuwait," commented Dr. Mylrea, "this is a straight example of cause and effect and admits of no argument."[35]

In order to prevent fragrant odors from accidentally reaching the nostrils, Bedouin people, in particular, tied asafetida or garlic into the ends of their headdresses or into rags that they stuck in their noses, according to Wahba, "so that they, or rather their wounds, may not smell perfume."[36] As Edwin Calverley observed, "The strong and unpleasant odor, they say, saturates the brain, so that sweet odors will not affect it."[37] Thus it was a common sight to see a Bedouin coming into Kuwait with his nostrils stuffed up with dirty bits of rags[38] or walking along with a very dirty end of his headdress stuck into his nose. On one occasion, Edwin Calverley approached a Bedouin in Kuwait to ask why the ends of his headdress were in his nose, and the man responded silently, Calverly comments, by lifting his *thobe* to his knees, displaying a bad sore on his leg, as if this would make the reason self-evident.[39]

Another common belief in Kuwait, according to the Dicksons, was that there was "one particular smell, different in every case," that could cure a particular disease. It was a problem, however, "to find the one and only smell which would be effective." Violet Dickson writes that she knew a falconer who was ill, and every possible thing was brought before him to smell, such as fruit, flowers, vegetables, and cooked food. When all those smells failed to cure him, various people, including children, young women, and old women, but apparently no men, were made to pass before him, but he still did not get better.[40]

The notion that smells affect the health was widespread in the region. In Doughty's experience, perfumes were actually part of the Bedouin woman's store of medicines,[41] and he observed Bedouin using nose plugs. "The Aarab stop their nostrils where is the least thought of any infection," he wrote, "which they can imagine to be as a kind of ill-odours in the air. In Semitic cities we find some nice opinions of this kind, as that aphorism of the Damascenes, 'Who is lately vaccinated, should smell no flesh-meat'; . . . good odours they esteem comfortable to the health. . . . The Aarab make therefore nose-medicines, little bunches of certain herbs and odours, to hang a day or two in their nostrils, and in the nostrils of their camels."

The notion that bad smells are harmful and good smells helpful is common across cultures. The connection between odors and disease was still unresolved in the United States at the opening of the twentieth century, when the mechanisms by which infection is transmitted were still unclear. During an epidemic in Providence, Rhode Island, for example, sanitary officials were "preoccupied with vague miasmas like 'sewer gas' " as a possible source of contagion fumigated the air around the city sewage plant.[42]

Herbs, Concoctions, and Practical Cures

The importance of smells to the healing process was one reason that the herbal specialists who prepared the nose remedies were believed to possess important information, and these herbal specialists were usually women, as indicated in virtually every twentieth-century account of the dispensing of herbal treatments in the missionary record. This accords with Doughty's earlier observation that "the Aarab are cured in their maladies by the hareem, who have all some little store of drugs, spices and perfumes, fetched from Medina, and their grandam's skill of simples, which are not many to find in their desert diras. The nomads had little expectation of better remedies in the hands of Khalil (Doughty's name for himself in Arabia), which were dearer 'government medicines' and strange among them. They bade me show my drugs to the hareem who, they supposed, would certainly know them."[43]

Herbs and other medicaments used in healing were commonly known and available in every bazaar.[44] Traditional methods of healing with herbs and other concoctions were sometimes successful, either because of the medicinal value of the herbs and methods employed or as a result of the placebo effect arising from the belief that such treatment would help. In the available accounts (which often, unfortunately, fail to specify the herb used), in virtually every anecdote relating to application of herbs, concoctions, and curative techniques, a woman is the practitioner to be praised or blamed. Mrs. Van Vlack of the Basra mission, for example, wrote that a technique used by mothers to speed up the growth of teeth was to rub on a child's head the juice of a certain fragrant herb mixed with water and vinegar. If applied when cold, teeth were supposed to appear in three days. Strong black coffee given to a child was supposed to help him or her to start speaking.[45] According to Hafiz Wahba, a leading Kuwaiti named Ali al-Fahd Al Khalid claimed that at one time he had an ulcer on his leg that an American doctor in Basra had been unable to treat successfully and indeed had thought so hopeless that he advised Al Khalid to have the leg amputated. On his return to Kuwait, Al Khalid met an "old fellah woman" who offered to cure his leg. She dressed his wound with some ointment made up of some herbs, and within two weeks his leg was healed.[46]

Traditional remedies sometimes caused problems far worse than the ones they were intended to cure. For example, a favorite remedy for the crying infant was to steep a few seeds from a plant known as *khashkhash* (poppy) in boiling water and to spoon-feed the liquid to the baby. This remedy was used in Mecca, according to Snouck Hurgronje, to quiet a hungry baby whose mother's milk had failed or who was ill.[47] In Kuwait Eleanor Calverley learned of the custom of dispensing opium to infants to keep them quiet after a helper she had hired to care for her infant daughter resigned, and Calverley's baby suddenly suffered severe, life-threatening diarrhea and dehydration, which Calverley discovered were symptoms of withdrawal. To save her baby's life, Calverley put the baby back on opium and withdrew the drug gradually.[48] While the drug allowed an infant to sleep through the din created by many people living in one small room, Calverley said, in unmeasured doses it could make an already weak child too weak to suckle or cause the child to suffer addiction and possibly die.

The near-blindness in the eye of King Abd al-Aziz, Wahba tells us, was the result of a treatment applied by a woman healer. In 1923, in an incident Wahba witnessed, the king's eye had become inflamed after the application of a mixture of antimony and powdered pearls. The king's private physician, a French-educated Syrian doctor, was unable to cure the inflamed eye, and a woman skilled in traditional healing methods with a great medical reputation was called in. "Her diagnosis," Wahba wrote, "was that it was a common disease and very easily treated; she prescribed the insertion of a few drops of the milk of a Negress nursing her first child. She also applied a powder which she said she had prepared specially, and promised the king that in three days his eye would be completely cured." The king was so impressed by her promises and her reputation that he allowed her to treat him, Wahba said, but after a week the eye developed an ulcer and became swollen, so a doctor from the Kuwait mission was asked to come. When he arrived in Riyadh he found the king's face tremendously swollen, his eye the size of a baseball, and his lips so swollen that he could hardly speak.[49]

The idea that the milk of a Negress nursing her first child has a particular medicinal effect is another example of the animism underlying some medical practices in Arabia. The theory behind the cure is that the bodily fluids of a particular person can communicate something of his or her essence to another person. Dickson says that there was a Bedouin custom of washing the wounds of a man hurt in a *ghazzu* (raid) with urine. "But to gain the best results, it must be urine of young braves, not of elderly men."[50] The same notion underlies the Islamic prohibition against marriage between two people who are brother and sister "in milk," meaning that they are unrelated by blood but were suckled by the same woman as infants.[51]

Medicines believed to have healing properties include copper sulfate crystals, which were used for treating trachoma, and mercury, inhaled with tobacco smoke, which was the specific for treating the secondary lesions of syphilis. The caul (a part of the amnion) of a baby donkey, dried and soaked as needed, was applied for the healing of wounds.[52] Camel's urine also had medicinal uses: Philby reported seeing camel's urine gargled by a Bedouin to cure mouth sores.[53] (Burckhardt, a hundred years earlier, had reported seeing fresh camel's urine drunk as a cure.)[54] Harrison noted that senna was a popular laxative much in use, constipation being a chronic problem attributable, he thought, to the heavy fat-and-meat diet.[55] (Doughty, who carried dried rhubarb to sell as a laxative, reported that the leaf of the colocynth was used for the same purpose.)[56] Hemorrhoids, Harrison noted, were also a very common problem because of the constipation, one that was cured by a procedure he described as "hideously painful" but in "considerable vogue in Arabia." The patient was given a violent purgative so as to cause the hemorrhoids to extrude, and a corrosive paste containing arsenic was then placed over the extruded mass. While waiting for the hemorrhoids to fall off, the patient, Harrison says, could find relief by sitting in the cold Gulf waters, where the salt water would act as an astringent.[57]

All kinds of common herbs were steeped and taken as medicine. A wild bush called *al-ja'ada* provided a useful purgative, wrote Dickson, and *ram-ram*, a wild flowering plant, was used for mouth sores.[58] For ulcers and sores a favorite remedy was a plaster made of camel fat, dates, and salt. After the birth of a child, Bedouin women and townswomen of Najd and Kuwait employed alum to reduce the size of the vagina (p. 173). An herbal plaster containing arsenic, Dickson says, was prepared and used by women as a depilatory.

Bedouin mothers applied *kuhl*, or antimony, to their children's eyes to prevent eye sores (p. 507),[59] and a mother might treat her child's sore eyes by putting a few drops of her milk into them. If the patient were a man, a woman's milk was also prescribed, as long as it was not his wife's, for reasons explained above (pp. 513–514). Bedouin mothers treated scabies of the head with various concoctions of clarified butter and charcoal, and measles was treated by giving only certain foods and preventing the child from smelling certain other foods (p. 507).

"Much in demand in Arabia," wrote Wahba, "are rejuvenating medicines, and people arriving from India, or traveling inland from the coast, particularly doctors, are at once assailed with demands for potions of this kind."[60] Treatments offered for impotency included shark's meat and essences of iron and steel, and Dickson wrote that Arab townsmen believe that to have connection with a black woman made a man sexually strong if he was suffering from disability.[61] Harrison was asked for a cure for impotency so many times that he counted preoccupation with sexual prowess to be a prime reason for what he considered to be stagnation in Arab society.[62]

Local remedies in Riyadh included antelope flesh, which, if eaten, was believed capable of drawing a bullet out of a wound, according to Wahba, and this was actually used as a last resort when other methods of extraction had failed; the meat was dried and stored for future emergencies and Abd al-Aziz, Wahba says, used to quote many stories in support of this intervention. Other local remedies, according to Wahba, included treating measles in children by keeping the patient in a completely dark room and starving him or her for a time.[63]

Massage performed by women was a treatment used to alleviate colic and other forms of stomach distress noted by nineteenth-century observers. After Doughty had given laudanum powder to a man suffering from "flux of the bowels," he then "saw a remedy of theirs for the colic pain, which might sometimes save life after drugs have failed. The patient lay groaning on his back, and his sister kneaded the belly smoothly with her housemother's hands (they may be as well anointed with warm oil); she gave him also a broth to drink of sour milk with a head of (thum) garlic beaten in it. At midnight we sent him away well again."[64] Carlo Guarmani, during his 1863–64 journey in northern Najd, was given the same treatment by two Utaiba women who had found him unconscious and massaged his stomach with oil until he awoke.[65]

It is possible that the use of maggots as a method of treating infection in wounds was known to Bedouin of eastern Arabia. On two separate occasions documented by missionary doctors, patients came to the hospital with raw, open battle wounds in which living maggots were crawling. The missionary doctor assumed that the maggots had hatched in the uncleaned, uncovered wounds. In one of these cases, however, the lance thrust that had caused the wound had occurred three days previously, too short a time for blowfly larvae to have hatched. It is therefore possible that the maggots were intentionally placed in the wound as a known means of promoting healing. In the West, physicians discovered in the late nineteenth century that maggots prevent wounds from becoming infected, the assumption being that the insects eat away dead matter. Only recently has it been proven clinically that maggots can actually cure infection by eating bacteria, which are then killed by an antibiotic in the maggot's saliva.[66]

Surgery, Inoculation, Contagion, and Bonesetting

A few surgical techniques for common conditions were known in the Gulf. One of these was a treatment for trichiasis, a condition that accompanied the more advanced stages of trachoma, a contagious viral disease that causes seep'age from the eyes and nose that attracts flies and fingers, which helps to spread the infection to others. Scarring on the inside of the eyelid eventually causes the eyelids to turn inward, so that the lashes scrape painfully against the cornea until the eye is destroyed. One method of treatment was to pluck out all the eyelashes to prevent the scraping, and tweezers for the treatment of trichiasis were a standard piece of equipment among Bedouin women and townswomen alike.

The surgical method of correcting the effects of trichiasis involved cutting a superficial incision along the edge of the affected lid, and inserting two sutures at both edges of the lid. A stick about an inch long was secured with sutures to the cut edge of the lid and left in place for about six weeks to prevent the wound from closing. When the stick was removed, the wound finally healed, creating a ridge of scar tissue along the edge of the lid that counteracted the contraction on the inside formed by the trachoma and thus prevented the lashes from turning inward.[67] A Bedouin boy who came into the Kuwait mission hospital with badly infected eyes after this surgery described his operation to Harrison as one performed by a friend with an old knife.[68]

To prevent hemorrhage during surgery, incisions were normally made with a red-hot knife. As noted in the previous chapter, amputation was concluded by dipping the stump in boiling oil; after an amputation for punishment, this procedure was carried out in the public square.[69] Bone fractures were treated by immobilizing the injured limb according to a somewhat implausible method described by Harrison: the patient was laid on the sand and stakes were driven into the ground along the sides of the fractured limb, which was tied into place with cords. The patient then remained lying on the sand under a tent for about three months.[70]

Techniques of inoculation and quarantine to prevent contagion had been known in Arabia since the opening of the nineteenth century. Sheep-raising Bedouin had developed a means of inoculation for anthrax, according to Harrison. At the first sign of an outbreak of the disease, the lungs of a diseased animal were cut out and allowed to putrefy slightly, and a piece of the putrefied lung would be rubbed into a small incision cut in the ear of a healthy sheep. When inoculation was performed in this way, nearly the whole herd could be saved, Harrison said; without it, nearly every animal would have been lost.[71]

Inoculation for smallpox, according to Burckhardt, was well known among the Anayza, who learned of the technique—which, he says, was performed only by men—from the peasants of Syria. "Whenever a man or child is attacked by it, a tent is pitched for him at a considerable distance from the camp, and he is attended by only a person who has already been affected with the disease." The Arabs of the interior, such as the Shammar, he says, knew nothing of inoculation.[72] By the time of Doughty's journey, however, vaccination for smallpox was well-known in northern Najd and also in Hejaz. A Syrian vaccinator had already visited Taima, Ha'il, Qasim, and Unaiza and left a convincing legacy, Doughty thought, because Bedouin he met who claimed to have been vaccinated expressed confidence they were safe from ever catching the disease.[73] In the early twentieth century, in the Kuwait area, Bedouin segregated smallpox victims and also practiced inoculation. The method used more often killed than cured, Dickson says, as the serum was taken directly from one smallpox victim and applied to another.[74]

In spite of the use of inoculation and quarantine among some Bedouin, in the early part of the twentieth century neither was well understood or accepted in the Gulf towns. The ulama of Najd, as well as those of Bahrain, were debating its use when Wahba was in Arabia, and its increased use in Najd, wrote Wahba, was due to the efforts of Abd al-Aziz.[75] The sultan had taken an interest in vaccination subsequent to the Riyadh influenza epidemic of 1917–18, according to Philby, who sent for a supply of vaccine. "One objection to vaccination," he noted, "was the fact that fresh supplies are not always available, and disaster had not seldom ensued from the use of old lymph by the many quacks who made their living out of the people's need."[76]

In the Gulf, even during epidemics of smallpox and plague, it was difficult for the mission doctors to make their patients understand the role of contagion in the spread of the disease or accept vaccination. In one home to which a mission doctor was called to attend a small child with smallpox, a sibling of the sick child was crawling among the covers under which the child lay dying.[77] In another home, one in which a man had four wives, three had died of the disease. Each wife had had her own apartment, and one of these, being far more commodious than the others, was an object of jealousy among the wives. When the occupant of this apartment died,

Eleanor Calverley wrote, her rooms were immediately occupied by a second wife, who subsequently became ill, and then when this wife died, the third had been pleased for a chance to possess the best rooms in the house (p. 142).

Greek Medicine as Folk Medicine

There is a "puzzling matter in treating Arabs," wrote Mrs. Stanley Mylrea. "There are cold and hot diseases. Arab medicine was taken from the old Greek doctors. We are made up of four elements—phlegm, blood, sweat and bile." Patients would come into the Kuwait hospital and ask the doctor, "Is it a problem of too much heat or too much cold?"[78] What the patient wanted to know was what he should eat in order to restore the correct balance in his body. "Heat" and "cold" in this case have nothing to do with the foods themselves, explained Paul Harrison, but with their effects "upon the human body or to conditions of the body itself. Coffee, for instance, is hot and dry."[79]

At the opening of the twentieth century, some aspects of the principle of polarity from the Hippocratic corpus as interpreted through Arabic medical texts had become, in Harrison's words, the "common property of everyone." That Greek medicine would be known and applied by ordinary people in the Gulf when modern Western medicine was becoming the standard for society's elite is not unusual. "Folk medicine and lay healing typically include ideas and practices taken over from professional and authoritative sources," writes Paul Starr. "Popular culture develops partly by a process of 'cultural sedimentation.' Like a residue of the past, the theories and remedies of learned traditions filter down to the lower classes, where they remain even after the learned have abandoned them."[80] In Arabia, the learned had not entirely abandoned Greek medicine: Abd al-Aziz, Wahba wrote, "often criticized modern physicians for not being familiar with the theory of the Four Elements, which he used to debate with them at great length," and, he added, the king's father, Imam Abd al-Rahman, also had a wide knowledge of medical principles, many derived from the works of Avicenna and Da'oud of Antioch.[81] Texts on Greek medicine in Arabic were still circulating in 1923 in Kuwait, when Mrs. Mylrea obtained a copy for translation in *Neglected Arabia*.

According to the principle of polarity, Harrison explains, cold, heat, dryness, and moisture are the basic properties of nature. These combine to produce the four humors in man: yellow bile, black bile, phlegm, and mucus. The proportions in which the basic properties are combined in a person produce the individual temperament, determining whether one is, for example, lazy and dull-witted or energetic and bright. Combined in faulty proportions, the basic properties may bring about an imbalance in the four humors, causing disease or discomfort, and thus restoration of health requires restoring a proper balance of heat and cold, wet and dry.[82]

Treatment focused on the patient's symptoms, which were regarded as the disease itself,[83] and the skill of the medical practitioner was in the knowledge of the nature of the imbalance and the properties of foods to consume in order to correct it. The knowledge of Greek medicine encountered by Arabian Mission physicians in the clinic was at the simplistic and fuzzy level of folk wisdom, but the literature behind this folk wisdom required specialized study to master. The kind of complicated information the physician needed to treat a patient is illustrated in the version of the *Medicine of the Prophet* (Tibb an-Nabbi) produced by the fifteenth-century Egyptian Jalal ad-Din Abd ar-Rahman as-Suyuti, a text that is a compendium of medical properties of foods, remedies for certain conditions, and theories as to the cause of illness interspersed with commentary from the Prophet's Hadith. As-Suyuti writes, for example, that the

> signs of a fever which is due to spleen [as opposed to bile, phlegm, or blood] are a livid complexion . . . and excessive insomnia. At the onset of the fever, the urine looks like barley water. The best foods when treating this kind of patient are those which produce wetness and induce sleep. The best food, in terms of both quality and quantity, is a drink made with one ounce of one of the above mixed with half an ounce of sugar. The constitution should also be made to flow by using decoctions. The patient should be fed on kids' flesh, fresh fish and pulses.[84]

A cross-check of the properties of foods listed in the text confirms that fresh fish is cold and wet, as opposed to salted fish, which is hot and dry. And while as-Suyuti prescribes the flesh of a kid because it "is evenly balanced" between hot and cold, wet and dry, he also advises that the Prophet said, "Be kind to goats, and leave them alone, for the goat is indeed one of the animals of the Garden" (p. 98). As for pulses, barley is useful because it is cold and dry, and barley water "cools down heat as it dispels it" (p. 72). As-Suyuti adds a quote from Hippocrates, saying that "barley water is 'both sticky and smooth' " and is "the best food for treating hot diseases" and then confirms the benefits of barley with a Hadith from Aisha, which says that whenever the Prophet suffered from a fever he would prescribe barley soup (p. 73).

Remedies Prescribed by the Prophet

Al Jawziyya's medieval book *Prophetic Medicine*, which I discussed earlier in this book, is one of several texts of the medieval science of Prophetic medicine, which is based on the curative prescriptions that are included in the Hadith, the authoritative accounts of the Prophet's life. Certain herbal treatments, for example, are prescribed in Hadith, such as "Be careful of nigella, for verily in it is healing from every disease except death, and if it were possible for anything to drive away death from the sons of Adam it would be nigella." Another Hadith became the rationale for the use of the natural purgative senna as a laxative: "Be careful of senna and honey, for in them is a cure for every disease except death."[85] The application of Prophetic treatments is not so straightforward, however, as for almost every Hadith offering a type of treatment there is also an authorative Hadith that contradicts it or offers an alternative. One Hadith advising treatment for scorpion sting, for example, says that salt combined with linseed oil makes a good ointment, while another has the Prophet saying that the harm of the sting should be countered with recitation of the words "I seek refuge with the perfect words of Allah from the mischief of what He created."[86] Another Hadith prescribes spitting on the wound while reciting Qur'anic words, and still another prescribes pouring a mixture of salt and water on the wound, while reciting verses from the Qur'an related to seeking refuge.[87]

In some respects, the remedies were harmless and could even be helpful, such as the prescription of salt and water for a wound. In other ways, however, Prophetic medicine had the pernicious effect of deterring patients from seeking more efficacious treatments because any contradiction between Hadith prescription and modern medicine could be elevated to the level of contradiction with religion. In the opinion of Hafiz Wahba, even a discussion that raised questions as to the efficacy of certain remedies recommended in the Hadith might be taken as heresy.[88] W. Norman Leak, a Cambridge scholar who joined the mission staff in Kuwait for a year in 1923, wrote in *Neglected Arabia* that all patients possessed some level of awareness of these Hadith prescriptions and presumed them to be efficacious whether they worked or not, at times undermining the authority of doctors of Western medicine at the clinic. "If you tell a patient," he wrote, "that he may eat anything he likes he looks at you askance and is at once reminded that you are an unbeliever, for has not the Prophet said, 'The stomach is the seat of disease, and the mainstay of treatment is diet?' "[89]

Prophetic medicine, furthermore, sometimes encouraged patients to rely on God instead of seeking any medical treatment. Leak noted that everyone on the street knew the Hadith that prescribes honey for any physical ailment and then associates piety and trust in God with the means to a favorable outcome. "A man came to the Prophet and said, 'My brother is complaining of his stomach,' so he said, 'Give him some honey.' The man came a second time and the Prophet said, 'Give him some honey.' Then he came a third time and the Prophet said, 'Give him some honey,' but the man said, 'I have done so and he is no better,' and so the Prophet said, 'Believe in God and disbelieve your brother's stomach. Give him some honey.' So he gave him some and he recovered" (pp. 3–4). With this kind of tradition in their minds, Leak commented, healers would continue their hopeless treatments and patients would seek further help only when all hope was gone.

Other Hadith prescriptions Leak thought actually dangerous. For example, scarification, which is the opening of an incision in the flesh as a means of bloodletting, was widely practiced and believed to be superior to venesection, which involves opening a vein. Scarification, however, often brings on infection, as well as unwanted scars, and is painful. Even so, it remained the prevailing method of bloodletting because the Hadith records that the Prophet said, "Healing is in three things, a spoonful of honey, the scratch of a scarification, and the burn of a cautery."[90] Defenders of the practice would persist in employing scarification even after admitting its harmful effects and the painfulness of the procedure, Leak wrote, and they are "reduced to finding its superiority in this painfulness, for, say they, if it were very simple people might get into the habit of blood-letting too frequently and so weaken themselves thereby."[91]

Another persistent but less harmful practice promoted in Hadith literature was illustrated in an experience Edwin Calverley had while having tea with a Kuwaiti friend. A fly fell into the cup of Calverley's friend, who took his spoon and shoved the fly to the bottom of the cup and then scooped it out and threw it away. Calverley placed a fresh cup before his guest, but, Calverley wrote, his guest said that having dunked the fly he would have drunk the tea anyway, because "the wing on one side of a fly carries disease and the wing on the other side carries healing, but we do not know which is which, so to be sure to get the healing, we push the fly all the way in before we take it out." Calverley went to his students in search of the supporting Hadith and found, "The Apostle of Allah said, 'If a fly falls into a vessel of any one of you let him immerse all of it and then throw it away, for, verily, in one of its wings is healing and in the other is disease.' "[92] The idea in Hadith that both disease and its antidote lie within a single source was incorporated into the stock of knowledge even of desert healers (I mentioned an instance earlier in connection with a homegrown method of inoculation for anthrax): Doughty had encountered a healer at Medain Salih who had the head of an adder in his hand and was trying to figure out which of the snake's horns contained the venom and which the antidote.[93]

The most common method of treatment practiced in the Gulf, and one that is both validated and forbidden in Prophetic medicine, was cautery. Cautery was "in great vogue," wrote Paul Harrison. "All manner of complaints are treated by branding the over-skin of the affected part, or indeed sometimes the skin of some other region. The underlying idea, of course, is counter irritation, and frequently the practice is very beneficial." Harrison thought the temporary relief from pain brought about by counterirritation outweighed the harm caused by burning the flesh, for this graduate of Johns Hopkins Medical College added, "I have used it myself for the treatment of a painful pleurisy with good results," and "for the pains of chronic rheumatism it is doubtless of real benefit, as also for many other chronic troubles."[94]

Like Harrison, Gulf healers used cautery to divert the sufferer's attention from one source of pain by creating another, even though this use of cautery is explicitly forbidden in *Prophetic Medicine*. Al Jawziyya's book actually relegates cautery to the treatment of last resort because the pain caused by the burn can be worse than the pain it is intended to mitigate.[95] Hadith also discourage the use of cautery in testimonials by companions of the Prophet who claim they tried cautery as a counter to various diseases and observed that the treatment simply had no benefit (pp. 75–76). The one use for cautery approved in *Prophetic Medicine* is as a means to stem the bleeding from amputation (p. 76), which in the Gulf region was usually done by dipping the bleeding stump into a vat of boiling oil.

Even though Hadith quotes the Prophet as saying, "I forbid my community to use cautery" (p. 60), another Hadith lists cautery along with honey and scarification as the three sources of healing. Gulf practitioners either didn't care about a religious justification for its use or chose whichever tradition suited their purpose, for missionary doctors like Harrison found cautery in use for every kind of ailment, including infectious diseases, wounds, and abscesses. Jaundice was treated by cauterizing fingers and toes, ordinary stomach ache by burning the skin over the pain,[96] and malaria by cauterizing the abdomen. Dr. Storm of the Bahrain mission reported caring for a twelve-year-old boy with a spleen enlarged from chronic malaria who had eighty-six distinct brand marks on his abdomen.[97] Rabies was also treated by cauterization, and there was a special form of cautery used for the treatment of spear wounds: "A fire is kindled in a small hole in the ground. When it has abated, the wounded limb is placed in the heated ground in a particular way, a complicated procedure but one which is often followed by a cure."[98] In addition to specific diseases or injuries, any pain or swelling in any part of the body could be treated with cautery. A child in the Mason Memorial Hospital in Bahrain suffered an injury to the soft cartilage in the knee, and an abscess had burrowed up along the bone and opened. On his knee were found "twelve open sores made by the red-hot head of a boat nail, right along the seat of the pain, and they were nicely placed three in a row in four orderly lines."[99] Storm noted that, like the application of herbs and concoctions, cautery was "usually done by an old woman in the village or tribe. She takes a nail or piece of iron and after it is red hot she applies it to the painful or swollen part."[100]

The widespread knowledge of Hadith benefited all medical practitioners in the Gulf, whether local people or foreigners, men or women, even if this knowledge did not benefit the patient. First of all, the Hadith tradition helped to legitimate the role of women as doctors and nurses treating men, which was being debated in Kuwait during Leak's 1923 visit. Leak says that the precedent for women treating men was established, discoursively at least, in a narrative relating how women accompanying a raiding party with the Prophet gave men water to drink and helped to bring the dead and wounded back to Medina.[101] In addition, the person who prescribed a Hadith treatment was insulated from blame if the treatment failed because of the divine source of the remedy. In fact the inclination to resign oneself to Divine Will implicit in Prophetic medicine also exonerated medical practitioners from blame for poor results in the minds of their patients, a reality of medical practice not lost on the mission doctors.

There is no reason to expect that practical healing techniques, Prophetic prescriptions, or Greek medicine were used or applied differently under the Wahhabis in comparison with their use in the Gulf towns. From a theological perspective, there would be no reason to expect a difference: the Wahhabis were concerned only with avoiding negotiation with spirits and correctly approaching God but were otherwise open to any type of treatment, including Western medicine. As early as 1914, when the Ikhwan colonies were still being settled, Ibn Sa'ud welcomed Western medicine—even from missionaries—after Ikhwan soldiers picked up malaria during their conquest of Hasa.[102]

The experience of Western medical personnel with indigenous healing techniques and medical sciences in these regions shows that medical knowledge filtered down to different levels of awareness across society. There were scholars who studied books on the Prophet's remedies and Greek medicine, mostly the Greek medicine already incorporated into the science of Prophetic medicine; there was a general awareness on the part of ordinary people concerning certain remedies prescribed in Hadith for certain types of ailments, as well as ideas about causes of ailments and corresponding cures derived from Greek medicine; and there was folk wisdom gained from experience and observation of any and all healing techniques, as well as other information detached from its source in the words of the Prophet, and these were the common property of all.

For reasons of differential access to knowledge, as shown throughout this book, it would be men who would most likely have been professional dispensers of the remedies derived from the indigenous medical sciences. But there were absolutely no such professionals mentioned anywhere in the seventy years of records I have covered. Within this tradition of indigenous medical sciences there were not even professional dispensers, or pharmacists, who stocked herbal remedies along with advice. This shows us that indigenous medical sciences were at a dead end by the opening of the twentieth century, even before the introduction of Western medicine into the region. There was sufficient respect for these sciences to influence decisions on an individual level, but not enough evidence of efficacy to allow this type of knowledge to support a profession.

Unlike the medical sciences, practical healing techniques had no sourcebook and thus no standards of accreditation, and for this reason the professional application of these techniques should have had no gender. In practice, however, the most common procedures were sex specific: men exclusively performed circumcision on male children, and women performed female circumcision and midwifery. In all situations recorded by Western observers, the woman practitioner is described as "old" or foreign or is in some way perceived as an outsider, just as I noted in an earlier chapter about professionals who engaged spirits. But here a similar observation can be made about men who performed circumcisions, as the operator was perceived as an outsider. On the other hand, even at this level of healing practice, the recorded instances of inoculation, bonesetting, and other surgeries were performed by men.

The concentration of examples I have found of healing professionals being rural people treating rural people suggests that the more educated town population recognized the limits of local healers' skills and relied instead, as Harrison said, on the women who applied the herbs, massage, the tweezers, and "kindly ministrations" to the sick of their own households. Certainly people in general—men and women—were aware of current ideas about the effects of smells, the benefits of honey, and the uses of cautery and herbs, for example, and applied this information to themselves or to family members as they chose.

But what about the midwife? She occupied perhaps the one position in medical services that could truly be called a profession. She faced no competition from men, but she also had limited skills to intervene positively in the birthing process during an abnormal birth. For this reason, the midwife was not always called, her place at times assumed by women relatives. Still, the midwife offered moral support during labor, and in spite of the perverse effects of salt packing, the procedure prevented pelvic infections after birth. Such infections were virtually unencountered by the missionary physicians, a fact noted with professional interest, because in the United States puerperal fever was the single largest cause of death among childbearing women in the early years of the twentieth century.[103]

Even in the United States, the skills of the midwife were limited. As American medicine began to professionalize in the early years of the century and physicians began attending births, any professional intervention became suspect because techniques were being introduced that were experimental and potentially harmful. "Twilight sleep," a narcotic containing morphine and an amnesiac drug, scopolamine, for example, was being given to women in labor, and the routine use of forceps and unnecessary cesarean sections were also becoming hazards of giving birth in a hospital.[104] In the United States, women who delivered at home, not in a hospital, used a "birthing stool,"[105] squatting in a position considered best by advocates of natural childbirth today, the same position that women of the Gulf used with the aid of the midwife, but a position missionary doctors thought crude and uncomfortable and wanted to correct by having women lie on their backs on their beds.

The respect midwives received in Arabia would have been commensurate with the practical results of their skills as understood by their patients. The good of preventing puerperal infection was recognized, for example, while the consequent harm of causing atresia of the birth canal was not: until Western missionary health-care workers began giving pelvic examinations to women in the Bahrain area around 1910, the connection between salt packing and atresia was unknown and therefore could not have reflected badly on the skills of the midwife.

The midwife was furthermore usually the same "old woman" skilled in the use of herbal medicines and techniques of healing that were not without some positive effect. Some of the herbs employed, senna as a laxative and opium as a sedative, for example, are drugs that can do what the midwives intended them to do. Cautery does stem bleeding, and as a counterirritant may distract the patient from the pain of the original complaint. Eyelash removal for trichiasis provided immediate relief from discomfort and prevented blindness. Even some of the techniques of healing associated with the supernatural, such as exorcism of jinn, and the inert medicaments such as honey prescribed in Prophetic tradition, were of value for their placebo effect: if the person being treated believed that they would work he or she was likely to feel that they had.

In the 1920s and 1930s, as Western medicine was being accepted in both the Gulf and Najd, the only source of overt resistance came from professional midwives. And the overwhelmingly positive response to the missionaries' medical efforts during those years justified the midwives' fears and resentments toward Western medical practitioners, whose presence rapidly undermined their profession. Perhaps the openness of women to Western medicine tells us something about the prestige associated with the role of healer at home. Such openness suggests that women with reputations to preserve within their families had little stake in the preservation of traditional medicine.

Community, Gender, and the Spiritual Experience

Women in Sacred Space, Women in Social Space

During the early twentieth century in Najd and in the towns of the Gulf, the mosque was the place where men prayed. Women were at the back, outside the mosque enclosure, or not there at all. What does their marginality to the mosque tell us about women's religious experience? What does it tell us about women in community with other women or about the hierarchical relationship between men and women in their ability to feel themselves in communication with God?

Dale Eickelman and James Piscatori remind us that "proximity to the centre [of sacred space] is assumed to invest persons or institutions with greater sanctity and thus religious or political legitimacy." They also remind us, however, that this assumption presupposes there is only one center, when the reality is that there may be many. [1] The peripherality of women to the mosque in fact reveals only one part of women's ritual experience. In the Gulf towns, women's ways of worship were varied and adaptable to everyday needs and could offer women outside the mosque the experience of community for which the mosque is designed. Outside the mosque, women had neighborhood prayer meetings to celebrate the Prophet's Birthday or to ask God for favors. They made votive offerings at shrines and cemeteries, where they gathered with friends and family and established personal links with God's intermediaries. These women-centered rituals were performed in Kuwait, Bahrain, and Musqat, in Mecca, Cairo, and villages in Palestine and along the Gulf coast, and in all these places, as well as in Nile villages and towns in North Africa, women also participated in performances of the Zar. Shi'a women participated in mourning ceremonies to commemorate the death of Hussein and other figures in the historical hagiography of Shi'ism. Though performed separately from men, these were not exclusive to women but were mainstream rituals, in which the whole Shi'a community engaged.

Where did the Wahhabis of Najd have a place for women-centered rituals? They condemned these out-of-the-mosque group rituals because they interpreted them as acts of polytheism. The Wahhabis expressly forbade celebrations of the Prophet's Birthday and other types of moulid ceremonies as well as praying at shrines, sorcery, and any kind of negotiation with the supernatural. They also specifically condemned the zikr ceremonies of mystics, which involve ecstatic chanting, singing, and dancing, as well as music in general, and thus it is likely that Wahhabism was also responsible for the nonappearance or suppression of the Zar in the lives of Najdi women. Also forbidden were healing practices that involved engaging spirits, the use of prophylactic medicines such as amulets, and fortune-telling, demonstrative wailing at funerals, and praying at grave sites.

The opening of the mosque to women under the Wahhabis should have advanced their integration into the ritual life of the community's spiritual center. Women's presence in the mosque, however, was limited by both convention and decree, at a time when men were required to attend daily, sometimes for all five prayers. They were to attend on special occasions only, such as feast days and on Fridays, and to stand at the back or outside the mosque enclosure. In practice, attitudes about modesty and women's predatory sexuality militated against their being in the mosque at all. In effect, women's presence in the mosque was treated conceptually and in deed as less important to the well-being of the community than the presence of men.

The importance of religious learning for men and women alike so that each person could pray and behave correctly should have facilitated women's ability to communicate with God directly and should have compensated for the paucity of ritual options. Women were in fact given better access to religious learning than was previously available, and this learning was a critical asset in getting oneself heard by God. Like women in the Gulf towns, some learned to read text as opposed to simply memorizing it. But also as in the Gulf towns, the ability actually to read text and especially the ability to write were suspect in women, and the educational ceiling to which women could aspire was far lower than the heights accessible to men. Moreover, in fostering prayer in the mosque by men and not by women as the ultimate expression of communal piety, the Wahhabi movement virtually defined the best prayer as prayer performed by men.

Outside the mosque, there was no alternative center anywhere that allowed women to experience in the same way that sense of community advocated as critical to wholly fulfilling the ritual requirements of obligatory prayer. Ideally, in the mosque there is a congregation. Men of all races and social classes stand shoulder to shoulder before God, pray together, and listen to the sermon, and some stay after to talk. The fellowship forged among men in the mosque cannot be duplicated by women, nor can prayer performed alone at home re-create the prestige and sanctity of prayer in the mosque. Women, however, can still experience sisterhood through all kinds of group ritual practices that become the sacred center for those who perform them.

Eickelman and Piscatori note that "religious communities, like all 'imagined' communities, change over time. Their boundaries are shifted by, and shift, the political, economic, and social contexts in which these participants find themselves" (pp. 4–5). What better example of these shifting boundaries than the landscape of women's rituals? Local contexts not only brought about differences between women's ritual experience in the Gulf and Najd but also, over time, reconfigured the boundaries of women's ritual space even under the political authority of the Wahhabis. It is clear, for example, that some of the rituals the movement proscribed existed in the eighteenth century in Najd because their performance was the rationale Ibn Abd al-Wahhab used to justify his reformation and to define its purposes, and that the performance of some of these persisted afterward. Engaging the evil eye is one of these, as amulets were used by Bedouin women in northern Najd in the late nineteenth century and by women in Ha'il in the mid-twentieth.

Saints' tombs in Medina were frequented by women making vows in the 1850s, half a century after these tombs were destroyed during the first Wahhabi conquest of the Hejaz; in 1931, after the tombs were again destroyed and Ibn Sa'ud was in full control of the city, women were still making vows to the saints buried in the cemetery although they were barred from entering the cemetery grounds. Women's moulid celebrations that were discouraged in the period of Ibn Sa'ud's conquest of the Hejaz enjoyed a revival in the 1980s. The Zar, virtually a fad among fashionable ladies in Mecca in the late nineteenth century and in Bahrain and Kuwait in the teens of this century, reappeared among rural women in the Mecca region in the 1970s and also in Kuwait in the 1980s, and some vestige of Zar performances echoes even in Najd in the music played at women's wedding parties.

The point that there are no definitive limitations on actual ritual behaviors by individuals in any given region or time must be emphasized. Culture travels with people and knows no borders. Despite attempts by Abd al-Aziz to control the movement of people into Najd in the 1920s and 1930s, he could no more restrain outsiders from coming in with their cultural baggage intact than contemporary authorities can control which satellite TV programs or videos people choose to watch in their own homes, nor could he homogenize the already eclectic communities that came under his dominion. Furthermore, some ritual behaviors, such as deflecting the evil eye by substituting insult for compliment, are embedded in language and are such a part of everyday expression as to be immune from theological judgment.

That said, however, the effects of Wahhabism on women's ritual experiences are undeniable. Wahhabism reconfigured women's experience of community through ritual, placing their focus back on a single sacred center that in reality they were not invited to enter. Because of the persistent hegemony of a political leadership that used its identity with Wahhabi Islam as a means of legitimizing its authority, and because Wahhabi practice was promoted, institutionalized, and coerced by the state, even where women's heterodox rituals were not actually snuffed out, they could only have been performed under a cloud of suspicion and official disapproval.

The loss of ritual activity is a loss of women's space, space outside one's home, in the homes of others, in cemeteries, in public meeting halls, and at shrines. It is the loss of space created wherever women's rituals take place and the space in streets and alleyways that are followed to get there. To lose ritual space is also to reinforce boundaries that are both socially conceived and physically circumscribed, and in Najd the cultural ideal of women's place being equated with her own home came close to a reality in social practice. Certainly, in a region where sex segregation characterizes social relations between men and women, ritual experience also plays a central role in the experience of community; in Najd, the narrowing of women's ritual space could only have narrowed their experience of community and their sense of legitimate social space as well.

Conclusion

Gender, Access to Knowledge, and the Healing Experience

Absent awareness of a scientific basis for the causes and cures for disease, the efficacy of medical treatment is fundamentally dependent on perceptions of power. What, after all, is the difference between a miracle performed through rites of established religion and magic but a subjective decision as to which method is accredited and will work?[2] It is a near-universal that men in society possess authority and determine what constitutes orthodoxy in religion. Where women possess power it is either power extracted through a relationship with a man, which is respectable (as Neusner reminds us, normalcy is defined as women being under the control of men),[3] or it is something, as Michelle Rosaldo suggests, abnormal and dangerous, threatening to the right order of things. What is out of order is the witch's, healer's, or midwife's unorderly relationship to male power.[4]

Women's practice of healing reflected this power differential. Before the widespread acceptance of modern medicine in the Gulf and Arabian peninsula in the mid-twentieth century, healing practices and the theory behind the causes and cures of disease were similar to those in Europe up to the opening of the twentieth century. Both wellness and disease were perceived as coming from God, and so knowledge of religion—that is, knowledge of the best means to communicate with God—was the sine qua non of medical practice. If one wanted the very best medicine applied in the most effective way, therefore, the person to see was a man. Men were more likely to carry the right honorific titles than were women; they had better access to religious learning than did women; and while many women acted as readers for other women, men were perceived as being more likely to know the right prayers to recite and the remedies prescribed by the Prophet. Because men were more likely to know how to write, the best amulets to be used as prophylactics against disease and the best ink medicines washed from holy words were prepared by men. Men also had access to the mosque, the place closest to God's ear, the place where even the spit of a man who had freshly uttered prayers possessed healing powers.

At the same time, the efficacy of practical curative techniques was recognized, the understanding being that no cure would be effective unless God had willed it so. If one wanted a stomach massage, an herbal purgative, cautery for a bleeding wound, or removal of eyelashes inverted from trichiasis, the person to see was usually a woman, but these techniques could be performed by anyone, with the exception of surgeries for circumcision and midwifery. In either case, because the intervention of the supernatural was understood as a cause of disease, even those who applied practical curative techniques sometimes employed prayers, charms, chants, decoys, disguises, and spells to exorcise, deflect, or negotiate with the spirit believed to be causing the ailment.

Where women employed magic or healing techniques not sanctioned through established religion, they could become suspect. This is true everywhere, and for men as well, but Wahhabism had a particular effect on the use of magic in healing, one that was strikingly similar to the effect that Protestantism had on the use of magic in Europe. As Keith Thomas has shown, Protestantism promoted only one supernatural force, God, and denied the efficacy of holy water, holy relics, icons, talismans, and crucifixes in promoting healing; in particular, it denied the role of priests, saints, and spirits as intercessors with God.[5] Wahhabism also denied the use of amulets and incantations (except prayer addressed directly to God), votive offerings at shrines, and also any kind of negotiations with saints or spirits, because seeking intercession implied an attribution of God's powers to others and a denial of God's oneness. Both reformations, in denying the use of magic in healing, were defining magic as the incorrect practice of their theological opponents (the Catholic Church, in the case of Protestantism) and correct practice as what they did themselves. But in denying "magic," they were also denying techniques of healing accessible to the laity. Under the Wahhabis, this meant, especially, many of the techniques available to women.

Just as the rise of Protestantism contributed to the rise of witch trials in Europe and America, Wahhabism made witchcraft a crime, and one that was identified as something women in particular do; also deemed criminal was the use of amulets, which women in the Gulf applied liberally to the clothing of their children. The Wahhabis also condemned music and dancing as incompatible with Sunna, so that the women's healing cult of the Zar that was an integral part of women's lives in the Gulf towns was excluded on moral as well theological grounds. In both the Gulf and Arabian peninsula, women could, of course, pray directly to God in supplication, just as men could, and women could act as readers over the sick on behalf of children and other women. With less access to religious education, limited access to the mosque, and the impediments to getting God's ear caused by women's body pollution, however, their ability to act as healers was undermined. Women's healing practices were furthermore sometimes tainted by ideas in common currency that women could be themselves the cause of disease. Because the women healer was invariably described as old, poor, or some kind of outsider, she could also be vulnerable to the suspicions that fall on women who are not under the control of a man.

From the viewpoint of patients' regard for the healing profession, the profession had several factors in its favor. First, because the outcome of treatment was perceived as being already predetermined by God, the healer was unlikely to be held accountable for poor results (a benefit noted with relief by missionary doctors). Second, because the body can be counted on to heal itself at least sometimes, any practitioner could have a success story to his or her credit. Furthermore, the placebo effect of otherwise ineffective treatment is not to be discounted: if a patient expected that a prayer recited over his or her head would draw out the evil spirits causing a headache, he or she was likely to feel that it had.

In Najd the prestige of healers in general was circumscribed by prohibitions on innovative ritual techniques that employ magic and intercession or are intended to defraud the patient, but Wahhabi theology is welcoming to all kinds of practices that promote goodness and healing. This openness meant that there was no theological barrier to the introduction of modern medicine in Saudi Arabia, just as there was no barrier in the Gulf, even when doctors from the United States with limited skills came as strangers to practice an unknown kind of medicine at the turn of the century. Nor was there resistance anywhere on the part of the healing profession (with the possible exception of midwives), which tells us something about the prestige that had been attached to women as healers and to the healing profession in general. Some professional healers who use traditional medicine still continue to practice, including Zar performers, and folk healing techniques are still applied in the home, but with the introduction of modern medicine, the traditional healing professions were quickly brushed aside.

Where in any of the healing techniques practiced in Najd or in the Gulf was there a "community of sisters" centering on "relationships built on the healer-patient tie" as identified by Hoch-Smith and Spring?[7] Only in one instance does evidence of this sort of community appear, and that is the Zar. Only in the groups that met for the social/healing Zar rites have we seen communities of women exist by virtue of women's own choice, that incorporate members who are not family relatives, that women attend sometimes without family approval and even in spite of male disapproval. In all the other examples of women healers, the healer is a sole practitioner; there is not a single mention of a midwife's or healer's apprentice. In spite of the lack of evidence of apprentice training, however, there must have been informal instruction on some level, or there would have been no healers. And what of the crowds of women who gathered to be present during the labor of a sister, daughter, or neighbor? What of the reader who used correct holy words to elicit God's blessing on the sick? There is no reason to think that bonds of sisterhood were not solidified among women through sharing in the birthing process, through the offering of prayers, and also through bedside care given by women to the sick of their own households.

Embedded in the rationale for the physical placement of women in society and for their limited access to the resources of the community were conceptual hierarchies of gender. These conceptual hierarchies have been apparent even where not explicitly stated throughout this discussion of religion and healing, from the question of whose presence in the mosque is important, to who goes to funerals, to who gets to be a healer, and who gets called a witch. These hierarchies that touched on women as learners, as professional healers, and as ritual communicants in the past have been transformed into positive, specifically Islamic values in the present, where they continue to inform ideology, daily practice, and even law. How this happens is explained in the following pages.

Saudi Arabia, 1998

I began this look into women, religion, and healing in the Gulf and Arabian peninsula as a detour in my attempt to discover whether there is something in Wahhabism that can help us understand the tenacious culture of women's separation and dependence in contemporary Saudi Arabia. What I found is that the ritual prohibitions of the Wahhabis affected men and women differently. These prohibitions, impacting as they did on women's agency as healers, ritual officiants, and participants, created an experience for women in Najd that was distinct from the experience of women in the non-Wahhabi towns of the Gulf. What, if anything, can these differences in historical experience tell us about the present? The answer to this question can be found by looking at gender—the way society conceptualizes categories of people based on sex difference—at the construction of legitimate space, and, of course, at the hegemony of Wahhabi ulama as official interpreters of religion for the kingdom as a whole.

The Trajectory of Gender from Past to Present

In October 1998 rumors began circulating in Saudi Arabia that the kingdom's consultative council was considering allowing women the right to drive cars. This could be seen as a major directional shift: only eight years before, women who drove cars in Riyadh as a political statement about their right to obtain licenses were fired from their jobs, publicly humiliated, and deprived of their passports. The fatwa issued at the time by the head of the Supreme Council of Religious Scholars furthermore suggested that for women to drive cars entailed dangers incompatible with Islamic values about protecting women. A look at the rumored conditions to be imposed on women who would drive today, however, reveals how little the cultural premises on which rules restricting women have changed: A woman could only obtain a license if there were a proven need for her to drive; only professional working women would qualify, such as physicians and teachers; and all drivers would have to be over the age of thirty-five. These specially designated people would only be allowed to drive to and from work, and no woman would be allowed to drive after dark. As yet unaddressed is the visibility problem a woman would experience behind the wheel, given that modesty standards currently presuppose her entire face would be covered.

These conditions are perfectly compatible with the gender ideologies that rationalize forbidding women to drive in the first place. "Woman" as a category is today conceived as residing at the heart of the home, as possessing a nature suited to motherhood and nurturing, as serving as the guardian of family honor, as being one to be honored *by being* protected; at the same time, historically in religious interpretation and in popular culture, "woman" is conceived as intellectually and emotionally weaker than men, her destiny determined by nature, and her nature a source of temptation and social chaos if left unchecked. Whether needing protection or control, acting as mother or temptress, honored or perceived as a threat to honor, whether viewed in the soft light of the former or the harsh glare of the latter, the end product in terms of rationalizing social restrictions on women is the same: women are to be kept separate from men and under a man's control.

The ruling family sanctions restrictions on women not because "this is how they are," but because the restrictions governing women's lives appeal to their broadest constituencies as people in Saudi Arabia generally identify with the ideologies underlying them. The continuity in gender ideologies over the past twenty years is undeniable, and they are the same ideologies that have prevailed at least since the period of the Wahhabi revival at the opening of the twentieth century. The values and practices that underscore the contemporary preoccupation with women's separation are therefore not merely modern inventions extracted selectively from Scripture and its interpretations and manipulated for political purposes. They come out of a more distant past, where they were nevertheless inventions extracted selectively from Scripture and its interpretations and manipulated for political purposes, in both cases for the benefit of Wahhabi rulers. The only difference is that the issues around which these attitudes and practices get promoted have changed.

During the early twentieth century, when Abd al-Aziz was promoting Wahhabi Islam and using it as a means of unifying his newly conquered territories, shaikhs were not issuing fatwas about women driving or being in the workplace or traveling without chaperones, because these were not the contested issues of the time. Then, the contested issues related to the establishment of correct ritual practice, signified by adherence to obligatory prayer (in the mosque for men) and the elimination of rituals of seeking intercession, and these were everyday rituals among Shi'a and Sunni, Bedouin and settled, men and women, everywhere around the peninsula where Wahhabi hegemony was not established. Incorrect practice was defined as something done by groups the Wahhabis despised, such as Shi'a or mystics, but also as something done specifically by women, or as something associated with women, or as something to be condemned only if done by women. Women were associated with engaging spirits by placing amulets on children's clothing. Being excluded from the mosque, they were also marked for seeking intercession through votive offerings at shrines, or caves, or special trees. Women, perceived as being emotionally weak, were similarly perceived as likely to challenge God's judgment by weeping demonstrably at grave sites or imputing to spirits power that belong to God alone by practicing witchcraft, telling the future, or healing by incantation, acts all equated with polytheism.

At the same time, women's modesty was defined according to the principle of the Hanbali school, reiterated by Ibn Abd al-Wahhab himself: all of a woman's body is *awrah*, meaning her body is entirely sexually provocative and private, and therefore it is not permitted for women to be seen by unrelated men.[1] As for covering the face, the texts are ambiguous, but in practice and according to parochial interpretation what should not be seen includes her face, except when she is praying at home or in the company of a close relative, such as a brother, father, or son.[2] There is no way of knowing whether local custom influenced religious interpretation or religious interpretation dictated what became custom, but it is certain that historically the more conservative opinion prevailed in Najd. Descriptions by missionaries, visitors, and local commentators amply illustrate that the more conservative Hanbali ideal came close to reality in Najd during the revival period and earlier, and these commentators unanimously noted the greater conservatism in women's covering in Najd than what was customary in the Gulf towns. Ibn Sa'ud himself personally sent 'abayahs and face veils to the women medical missionaries before they set out to open a clinic in Riyadh, with a word of advice about Najdi propriety. Hamad al-Baadi described the modesty and seclusion of women this way:

> Women's mobility outside their home was reduced to the absolute minimum. Modesty of attire was forced on all women. We have no reliable data on whether pre-Wahhabi Arabian sedentary women veiled their faces or not. . . . Wahhabism however, considered the facial veil (ghita) to be a required part of the Islamic hijab and in the towns and villages where Wahhabism ruled, the veil became complete; a woman above ten or eleven years of age would not venture outside her home unless fully covered from the top of the head to her heels with an 'abat, a black cloak worn over her regular clothes. She held the top of her abat with one hand leaving a crack in it in front of one eye to allow her to see her way. Below the abat she also covered her face with a light and porous piece of black cloth called the shailah or ghutwah. The number of layers of the shailah a woman wore often expressed her degree of modesty (sitr). There were not many occasions to wear the abat, anyway, as the Wahhabis preferred that women never venture into the public sphere except under utmost necessity.[3]

Ideas about keeping women separate and the attendant attitudes about women's weakness of mind and emotion and capacity for provocation were also affirmed by their limited presence in the mosque when daily prayer in congregation was required for men. Women were also to attend, but only on Friday and on the 'Id, and when they attended, they were to be at the back, even outside the prayer enclosure. More usually, they were not there at all.

Religious knowledge was valued and promoted for men and women alike, as all citizens of the Wahhabi state were challenged to "know God and his Prophet" in order to live their lives in conformity with God's laws. This respect for learning had been fostered in the contemporary era and became a critical component in the arguments for introducing secular education for girls in 1960, when the idea was passionately and sometimes violently opposed. As in the past, however, accommodating women's capacity for intellectual achievement has been treated as less important to the well-being of the community, a disparity reflected today in the unequal educational facilities and options available to girls and women.

All the gender constructions to define women's roles in society employed by ulama and state at the present time were deployed throughout the early twentieth century: the rigid segregation in contemporary Saudi Arabia and all the attendant attitudes about women's intellectual and emotional insufficiency, their dependency on men, and their being a provocation to them come out of the past, where they were employed to further the Wahhabi movement's insistence on correct ritual practice. Fatwas issued by the most influential contemporary shaikhs reiterate, without modification, positions on women expressed in Ibn Abd al-Wahhab's *Kitab at-Tawhid* and in his commentaries. Women are not to pray at graves, says Shaikh ibn Baz (deceased 1999), Grand Mufti of Saudi Arabia and the kingdom's most influential religious scholar for the past twenty-five years, because they "become a trial for others" because of "their little patience and great grieving that overcomes them" and also because "they are a temptation or trial for the living because the woman is *awrah* and by her going out and being visited by men she is not related to she becomes a trial and may lead to a great sin."[4] A woman should not pray in the marketplace as her house is best for her, but if she needs to pray in a marketplace she may do so provided there is a concealed place for her, but "a man must perform the obligatory prayers in the mosque in congregation" (p. 113).

In the opinion of Shaikh Abu Abdullah ibn Uthaimin of Imam Muhammad bin Sa'ud Islamic University and member of Saudi Arabia's Supreme Council of Senior Ulama, women, by definition, cannot compete with men intellectually: "Even a wife who studies in the Shariah College may not lead a semi-illiterate husband in prayer. . . . Allah has divided society into two parts, men and women. Based on that, women are not included in the generality of the Prophet's statement, 'The Imam of a people is the most knowledgeable of the Book of Allah' " (p. 129). "Women are a place for fulfillment of desire," and even their voices can be a temptation for men (p. 338). Although the voice is not awrah in itself, the senior ulama advise that women should not mix with unrelated men except out of absolute necessity and that when doing so they must avoid flirtatious speech (pp. 338–339). For the same reasons, and because "men are the protectors and maintainers of women, because Allah has made the one of them to excel the other," a woman should not leave her home without her husband's permission (p. 339). For the sake of keeping a woman "safe" she should furthermore never be alone with a chauffeur, unless he is her guardian (p. 341).

The pejoration of women's capabilities—moral, intellectual, and emotional—and affirmation of their dependence on men that are overtly stated by opinion makers in the context of contemporary challenges have been overtly stated all along under the Wahhabis in the context not of side issues but of matters of defining importance in the Wahhabi worldview, and they have been confirmed with the authority of scripture. These attitudes about women furthermore have been reified in popular daily practice and consciously instilled through agencies of the state, from missionaries to mutawwa'in to ulama.

Daily Practice and Ideology:
Constructing and Deconstructing Legitimate Space

The significance of daily practice in confirming or mitigating these gender ideologies cannot be overestimated. In the Gulf towns, gender ideology was very similar to attitudes about women under the Wahhabis. This is to be expected, given that Sunnis and Wahhabi Sunnis refer to the same Hadith and, with Shi'a, to the same Holy Book, while the political and intellectual elite were of the same Arabian tribal origin. In the Gulf towns, however, writing gender ideology into policy and enforcing proscribed behaviors was not an objective of the state to the same extent that it was under the Wahhabis, and daily practice did not conform to it. If women were thought emotionally weak, without agency, dependent on men, and sexually provocative and were excluded from the mosque, these same women, whether Shi'a or Sunni, poor or affluent, had access to ritual support groups.

Equally important, the practice of these rituals incorporated a larger area of legitimate space for women on the conceptual level as well as on the physical. Ritual practice incorporated space in streets and cemeteries, at shrines, in private homes, and in public meeting halls—places that were sometimes even funded by the religious establishment—as space appropriate to women for their use. Ritual practices created legitimate destinations that were not otherwise sanctioned in societies where women were expected to justify excursions outside their homes. In Kuwait and Bahrain, ritual practices by women contradicted the rhetoric of the seclusion ideal. If respectable women were going out and participating in ritual associations, cultural understandings must have been operative that rationalized or overlooked the discrepancy between the seclusion ideal and the social reality of women's daily lives. Ritual destinations in effect appropriated territory for women that was both physical place and idea of place.

The inverse is also true. Under the Wahhabis the absence of ritual space represented a minimizing of physical places where women could legitimately go and hindered their ability to congregate and establish friendships. Some readers might respond to this suggestion by saying that the opposite is the case, because in the absence of alternatives and given large families and strict sex segregation, women lived their lives embraced in a society of other women. That society, however, was composed largely of women in the family, and in the best of circumstances family relationships are complex, fraught with emotion, and characterized by hierarchies and dependencies, complete with legal implications. I remember my young friend Nuf, born too soon to have gone to school, who lived with her two children on the second floor of a house she shared with her husband's first wife and their children. Nuf had never seen the suq nor her husband's sporting goods shop, never left her home, located in a walled compound with her husband's brothers' houses, each separated from the other by walls, except to visit her mother on Fridays, and was not on speaking terms with the cowife. It was dormitory living with a one-day sign-out for good behavior and no parietals, except for the husband's daily visit to drop off groceries. Young Saudis who travel and go to school might find Nuf's living arrangement bizarre, but in 1980 these arrangements were touted as the ideal in family closeness, and the seclusion of wives and daughters upheld as the paragon of virtuosity. Family relationships, even when less complicated than Nuf's, are precisely the kinds of binding relationships from which ritual and healing associations can provide a refuge.

Associations based on ritual and healing cross-cut bonds of family, neighborhood, and class and offer opportunities for bonding among individuals on other-than-family terms such as common needs and interests. Removed from family scrutiny, ritual associations provide opportunities for consciousness-raising, as women share personal problems and improve in their lives. (Consider, for example, how the consciousness-raising sessions of the 1970s in the United States transformed marital rape and wife battering from private family matters into crimes.) These associations are opportunities for assuming an individual identity as a friend, confidante, ritual specialist, or ritual communicant and for feeling part of a community of other women. Ritual associations offer a good time, even if not a spiritual experience. (As Fanny Lutton tells us about women's prayer societies, "I could not help thinking the chief attractions are the pipes and coffee and any little bits of gossip they hear at these meetings.") The endurance of ritual associations in the region over time, especially Shi'a women's public mourning celebrations, moulid ceremonies in Hejaz, and the recent revival of the Zar in Kuwait and Mecca, testify to the appeal of such bonding experiences outside the family and their positive implications for the individual who participates. In the utter sparseness of Najd towns, where the vast majority of townswomen were shut out from trade and the mosque, with servants and male family members acting as intermediaries between the household and its necessities, group ritual practices would have loomed large on the landscape of women's lives

The opening of girls' schools was truly a revolutionary moment in Najd. The act of going to school, of having a legitimate destination outside the home, of being with others outside the family, even outside the neighborhood, created opportunities for female associations that two and a half centuries of Wahhabi domination had denied. Until the opening of girls' schools, the absence of ritual space allowed the ideal that virtue resides with the woman who stays at home to conform more closely with the reality of women's lives. When the ideal and practice are one, practice reinscribes ideology, and each validates the other. The major shift in Saudi Arabian society today, after two full generations have experienced educational, social, medical, and technological development, is that ideology and practice are quite suddenly no longer the same. Women out in society doing whatever they are doing are redrawing the conceptual boundaries of where women's legitimate space ought to be.

Tribalism Revisited

Contemporary restrictions on women and the gender ideologies behind them are not merely the legacy of interpreters of religion and the daily practice they inspired. They are fully compatible with the particular tribal-Najdi culture that dominates in Saudi Arabia: this continuity in gender ideology is reinforced by the fusion of Wahhabi Islam with the values of family, honor, and patriarchy that stem from the country's tribal legacy. Since the tribal explanation for the persistence of sex segregation and male control is so well known and accepted, however, I will again address it here.

In the tribal family, it is said, the aspirations of the individual tend to be subordinated to the best interests of the group because the reputation and economic well-being of the two are inseparable. Implicit in these values is the idea of family as the repository of honor, the first and last refuge of the individual, his ultimate base of support as well as the source of his vulnerability. Tribal families are also said to be hierarchical: elder males on top and women at the bottom. Tribal culture, to use Fu'ad Khuri's words, "is endogamous, exclusive, and non assimilative. Not only does it repulse the outsider, it also prevents the departure of the insider."[5] The tribal family resists out-marriage and encourages marriage back into the family (preferably to a first cousin on the father's side), and by resisting the incorporation of outsiders into its society, the tribal family encourages group solidarity. By virtue of this exclusivity, the tribal family acts as a time warp for social values, building a wall of insulation against normal processes of assimilation and change.

These tribal values and customs are often presented as immutable rules of desert life by writers such as Dickson and Musil and have been incorporated into nearly every modern political and historical work on Arabia. This list of tribal family values, however, sounds to me trite—too pat—even as I write. While it is true that these tribal values have acknowledged significance in family organization, they are neither so absolute as presented nor so impermeable to change. Those who read Doughty know that poverty, estrangement from family, wanderlust, and other circumstance could sometimes bring about racially and tribally mixed marriages. The family is furthermore supposed to embody a model of hierarchy between men and women that, from a distance, appears to be uniform across society because it is institutionalized in legal codes of the state and in Islamic family law. In actual practice, however, families are families, composed of people with different ideas about how they want to live their lives, and so the model of hierarchy that applies to one family may be irrelevant to another. As mentioned in the prologue, furthermore, the endogamous quality of tribal marriage that presupposes gender hierarchy is being undone by money, mobility, and the opportunity for personal choice.

Gender ideologies that can be identified with tribal values gain legal force in Saudi Arabia only when they can be rationalized as being rooted in Islam. Yet even when incorporated into religious law these tribal values are unevenly applied and subject to personal discretion. One woman trying to travel without a mahram might be turned away at the airport, for example, while another merely producing a letter of permission will be allowed to go on her way. Scholarships for study abroad may be denied to women generally for the sake of women's protection but available to someone in the right field of study or maybe to someone with the right connections. A divorced woman is subject by law to losing custody of her children, but in practice the families of the husband and wife may negotiate a custody agreement without ever lodging a case in court. One family will insist on full hijab, while another will discourage it on principle. Some women veil out of fear of the mutawwa"s insults, while some who are of distinguished families know that the mutawwa' would fear approaching them.

The disparity between actual practice and cultural ideologies—whether promoted through religious interests or filtered through tribal society— must be taken one step further. These ideologies rationalize legal or structural restrictions only, such as the mahram rule, debarment from high political office, and the inability to lead mosque prayers or pursue divorce in the same way available to a man. Yet even these restrictions are flexible over time: three Muslim countries have had women heads of state, for example; Saudi university women have organized their own congregational prayer in their own mosques; and most Muslim countries have experimented with modifying Islamic family laws. In fact the same person who cannot drive herself to work because she is a woman is as likely to be a powerbroker in her family or in her profession as she is to be the powerless domestic adjunct that ideology would seem to prescribe.[6] The bottom line is that gender ideologies, whether stemming from tribal values or inscribed in religious text, cannot be seen as fixed conditions that will rule the future.

Where Is Momentum for Change?

The elasticity built into social practice that I've just described has the effect of producing a buffer of tolerance for some privileged individuals. Tolerability, however, does not explain the lack of resistance to legal restrictions on women. These restrictions are largely unchallenged because the culture that undergirds them remains fundamentally unchallenged, even by women activists. So protected is the culture within Saudi Arabia that even those who campaign to liberalize the role of women present their suggestions for change not by challenging the cultural values that underpin the existing system but by trying to work within it. In newspaper articles, for example, women ask for more opportunities to work, but they couch their requests with deference to culture. Instead of asking for the right to drive so that women have a way to get to work, they ask for the government to provide transportation;[7] they ask for more work opportunities for women not by challenging men's (divinely ordained) role as providers for women but by pointing out that women sometimes have no men on whom to be dependent.[8] Instead of raising the specter of sex integration in the workplace or challenging the Hadith-inspired ban on women in high office by asking that women have seats in the consultative council,[9] they ask for a mechanism through which the council can consult women about their own priorities.[10]

The strategy of some activists on behalf of greater work opportunities for women is to join the front ranks of cultural defenders. These women co-opt the rhetoric of male conservatives, according to Mai Yamani, and assume the mantle of total-body covering. They even go one better by wearing black gloves to cover their hands and black stockings to hide their feet, in addition to the double wrapping of black veiling across the face and the 'abayah that most women wear when outside their homes. They also avoid perfumes, makeup, the corrupting influence of satellite television, and music and dancing, which—true to the letter of Wahhabi ideals—are pleasures not sanctioned in Shari'ah.[11] Learned in the Qur'an and Hadith, Yamani says, these women tend to be university educated and employed in banks, schools, and private enterprise. What they want is the right to work and be educated equally with men, but they do not challenge religion or cultural values; they do not challenge male guardianship or women's inequality in inheritance, she says, nor do they advocate a right to drive a car or work in a mixed-sex environment. Instead, they try to get what they want by expressing loyalty to religion and cultural values, using their ability to refer to the Qur'an and Hadith, the same sources used by conservative men, but reinterpreting models of behavior to suit their own agenda (p. 279).

Defense of the culture is also a natural reaction to criticism from the outside, but it is an expression of sincere belief as well. One reason is that members of a society naturally feel an affinity with their own society's cultural values and a sense of loyalty to them. The other reason is that social attitudes about women's subordination and defective nature are reformulated in popular mass culture into positive images of the ideal Muslim woman: she has become the heart of the home and the mother of a new generation; she is not excluded from the mosque but relieved of the responsibility of attending in favor of her higher calling, domesticity; her modesty is not an impediment but a badge of honor; she is not confined to the home but has complete freedom to do whatever she likes, so long as her obligations to family come first. In other words, negative stereotypes of women incorporated into religious texts in the past have been transformed into positive qualities to which young women would want to aspire.

A Prognosis

The rulers of the Saudi state could unilaterally initiate a rethinking of legal restrictions on women, but there are few incentives for them to do so and plenty of disincentives. As mentioned earlier in this work, the state is constrained by the fiction—adopted by Ibn Sa'ud during the period of the creation of the modern state and taken up by the present generation of rulers—that Saudi rule is legitimated by its willingness to implement Islamic law and rule in conjunction with the ulama who define what Islamic law is. The reality is that the Supreme Council of Senior Ulama is made up of employees of the state, not partners in power with it, but as individuals with particularly conservative viewpoints they are still influential arbiters of public policy who cannot be ignored. A case in point occurred in 1994, when the council succeeded in forcing the government to withdraw its participation in the United Nations Population and Development Conference held in Cairo because aspects of the conference platform were objectionable (birth control, abortion, co-education, and equality between men and women, which, the Council said, is against God's law and the law of nature).[12] The rulers responded by replacing some members of the council, but this did not change the outcome: the weight of public opinion remained supportive of the conservative opinion these particular ulama espouse.

The Islamic scholars currently in power have a following today but may be the architects of their own marginalization in the future. Today, the majority of married adult women are raising children and investing in large families: the fertility rate in Saudi Arabia is among the highest in the world, at 6.4 children per woman. While the majority of adults are children of illiterate women, half the population is under fifteen years of age. With near-universal public education for boys and girls, within the next generation the vast majority of the Saudi population will have no living role models of the completely dependent wife and mother who cannot read and who has never left her home without a guardian's permission. By then, even if most women are still not working outside the home, a social revolution will have already been completed: as I have already said, the act of going to school, the fact of having a legitimate destination outside the home, the experience of forming associations outside the family, and having the educational tools to manage one's own affairs are completely radical alterations that impact on the power asymmetry between men and women and on their domains of social space.

Economic incentives are pushing the social revolution even further. Saudi women have been inching themselves into the workforce, even as restrictions relating to sex segregation have severely limited the opportunities available to them and have not been lessened even to alleviate the financial drain on an economy vastly overburdened with foreign workers, some of whose positions could be filled by Saudi women. In 1996, for example, a woman high-tech entrepreneur formed a venture capital company with a mission to invest only in high-tech startups that agreed to an affirmative action policy for hiring women. In government circles in Riyadh, she told me, the idea for her company was warmly received. In practical implementation, however, she could not get the approvals necessary for hiring women.

How long can a society afford to chase capital away in the name of sex segregation? In discussions with faculty and administrators at the women's branch of the Institute of Public Administration in Riyadh, I was told that there must be 35,000 women high-school graduates in Riyadh alone looking for work. This was in 1996, and two years later one estimate had it that nationwide there were 130,000 job seekers coming onto the market annually, both men and women. These people are seeking jobs out of economic necessity, not out of boredom: with a population growth of 4 percent and the number of citizens doubling in the next generation—not to mention a severe decline in the price of oil—the days of cradle-to-grave subsidies for all citizens are over.

There will be a point at which the attitudes about women's dependency and deficiencies given currency in religion will become incompatible with what most—not some—people experience in their everyday lives. The Saudi sociologist Abubaker Bagader suggests that economic realities have already brought about a shift in social attitudes, at least among graduates of secular universities. Today, he says, male university students consider a college education a vital asset in a potential marriage partner because an educated woman is thought able to contribute to the income of the family. By contrast, he says, in a survey of university students he took in 1980 almost 70 percent of men sampled said they would not marry a college-educated woman. Even more students responded that they neither wanted nor expected their wives to hold a job, claiming that any interference in the family budget on the part of the wife is a threat to their authority and status as men.[13]

Education, employment, and an appetite for economic prosperity are clearly transforming social values that sustain women's dependency on men, at least among the Western-educated and moneyed elite. At the same time, however, the global experience of women in relation to the kind of economic downsizing that is occurring in Saudi Arabia today does not offer hope for a corresponding decrease in the institutional restrictions hindering women's ability to work. In fact, when employment opportunities shrink, women are usually the most vulnerable to unemployment as preference in allocating jobs goes to men, whom society considers to be the real family breadwinners. In times of economic hardship, societies may furthermore take refuge in traditional values, and promoting tradition in the guise of domesticated womanhood can be a compelling instrument the state can use to relieve pressure on scarce employment opportunities.[14]

Saudi Arabia is today a different place from what it was before education became available to men and women and before articulate voices rose to challenge the religious scholars' monopoly on definitions of traditional values. Nevertheless, the predominant meaning of these values still incorporates a hierarchy of gender and entails the generalized exclusion of women. With Najd and the Wahhabi movement as moral exemplar and guiding political force for the kingdom as a whole, the seeds of women's exclusion and their subordinate place in the hierarchy have been well sown.

The Scene of the Action for
Getting God's Ear

Najd and Her People

Najd is the central region of the Arabian peninsula, a highland plateau separated from the Gulf by a nearly waterless desert on the east, with the Empty Quarter to the south and the Nafud to the north. To the west, Najd is separated from the Hejaz by a ridge of mountains running 950 kilometers (around 570 miles) from north to south. The plateau is itself divided into three regions whose towns appear isolated when viewed from the air, like widely separated islands in an ocean of rock and blowing dust: Ha'il in the north, Buraida and Unaiza in Qasim, and Riyadh, capital of present-day Saudi Arabia, in the south. Najd is an extremely arid land, with no perennial rivers and insufficient rainfall for dry farming. In oasis pockets, however, water is obtained by tapping aquifers, some as deep as ninety feet, by means of a laborious, animal-driven lift mechanism known as a *jalib*, which has made small-scale agriculture and village life possible.

The people of Najd are often presumed to be culturally homogeneous. One reason is that the land in which they live is so isolated, politically as well as geographically. Local rulers remained autonomous from foreign control throughout most of the eighteenth, nineteenth, and twentieth centuries, when the Gulf experienced centuries of Portuguese, Dutch, French, and British interference. Even when the Ottomans declared nominal control over towns in eastern Arabia in the sixteenth century, local rulers continued to control Najd. The only time Ottoman forces proceeded into Najd occurred between 1816 and 1818 in response to the Wahhabi takeover of Mecca and Medina. Even after the total devastation of the Wahhabi power base at Dir'iya, however, with the destruction of orchards and the starvation that followed, the Ottomans did not remain in Najd but withdrew to Hejaz.[1] Even in 1871, when the Ottomans occupied Hasa, setting up a Turkish garrison that remained until 1913, and proclaimed the deposition of all Sa'uds and Najd a sanjak under an appointed *mutasarrif* (governor), they never extended their rule to Riyadh (p. 255).

In the twentieth-century revival era, the al-Sa'ud family in the south and the al-Rashid rulers of Ha'il were able to control their borders to the extent that few foreigners could have safely entered their territories without obtaining safe conduct from the appropriate ruler. Even after Ibn Sa'ud incorporated the eastern province, Ha'il, and the Hejaz into his realm, Najd still retained a unique territorial integrity. Until the late 1930s, according to missionary guests of Ibn Sa'ud, the king's personal invitation was a necessary prerequisite for any foreigner who wanted to enter Najd, whether Pakistani drivers and car mechanics, missionaries, or oil company employees.

The presumed homogeneity of Najdi people stems not just from the region's geographic and political isolation but from the large number of Bedouin in the population thought to be the stock, even the source, of the settled population and also thought to embody the prototype of Najdi culture. Although there are no accurate statistics, it is possible that at midcentury as much as half the population was tribal Bedouin and all these Bedouin were tied to some extent to the life of the towns. Nomadic people, even those who herd camels in the distant desert nine months of the year, have to have some connection with a town or oasis village because they need the products and foods that the towns and oases can provide, such as tent pins, herding equipment, fabrics for clothing, fodder for cattle during drought, copper kettles for cooking, and coffee pots, as well as dates, flour, coffee, tea, cardamom, and rice, which could be purchased in exchange for butter, yarn, woven tent cloths, sheep, camels, wool, and hides. Most Bedouin families are actually part-time village dwellers, herding sheep and goats close to a reliable water supply, or the family is divided, with only some members tending camel herds while others tend gardens and livestock in the village.[3]

In spite of the numerical dominance of Bedouin and the physical insularity of Najd, during the early twentieth century the people of the region were not quite so homogeneous as was once thought. The towns and the larger oases were mercantile centers, where merchants and caravaneers came and went, married, and had children, and many of these were from outside Najd, especially from Syria, Yemen, or Iraq. The towns were also manufacturing centers. Throughout the nineteenth century, most of the artisans were foreigners or people of foreign extraction, such as black Africans, Yemenis, Syrians, and Jews of Najran. Unaiza, for example, was a commercial center whose merchants traded with Jeddah, Mecca, Damascus, Basra, Baghdad, Egypt, and Bombay. The town of Buraida was the center for the camel trade, where merchants came to purchase camels and horses and artisans manufactured the saddles, bags, rope, and other gear necessary for herding. The Qasim had a laboring class that traveled abroad at different times and seasons in search of work. These Qusman traveled to Egypt to work on the digging of the Suez canal, for example, and some annually traveled to the Gulf to dive for pearls in the spring, returning in the fall with their earnings.[4]

From al-Aflaj, in southern Najd, where most of the agricultural laborers were freed blacks, many of these laborers made the journey to the pearl fisheries on the Hasa coast in hopes of returning after a few years with enough savings to enable them to marry and set up house.[5] Pilgrim routes through Najd brought Persians, Afghans, Baluchis, and Indians into Ha'il, Riyadh, and the towns of Qasim. The population of Ha'il, even though the town was dominated by Shammari tribesmen who spent part of the year in the nearby desert, was sprinkled with a variety of peoples representing the areas with which the town traded. Furthermore, in the agricultural oases and in all the towns, many of those who served as date gardeners, farmers, artisans, and even princely functionaries were enslaved people originally from Ethiopia and Sudan and their progeny. All these nontribal people brought with them a cultural orientation different from that of the Bedouin and the politically dominant tribal families.

Even within Bedouin society there was diversity. In addition to noble and non-noble tribal groups, there were groups of Bedouin people dwelling in Najd who were not tribal at all. These included the low-caste Sulubba (pl. Sulaib) who were famed as hunters and desert trackers and believed (perhaps fancifully) to be descendants of the Crusaders. These poorest of desert peoples traveled under the protection of the tribal groups whom they served as tinkers, blacksmiths, arms repairers, woodworkers, and sometimes as barbers and surgeons. The Sulubba were not Wahhabi, possibly not Muslims, and have been observed enjoying music, song, and dance and as not practicing the sex separation characteristic of tribal Bedouin.

There were also nomadic groups composed of blacks who had been freed by their Bedouin owners and continued to live as a separate nomadic community rather than settle in an oasis. Doughty mentions traveling peddlers called *sayadin*, who carried wares to sell to Bedouin on the back of asses.[6] Finally, continuously traveling through the deserts of Najd were members of the 'Uqail, the guild of camel dealers, which included people of African descent, Turks, Qusman, Persians, and defected Egyptian or Turkish soldiers.

One area where there was clear homogeneity among most people of Najd was their adherence to Islam as interpreted by the eighteenth-century scholar Muhammad ibn Abd al-Wahhab. With the exception of the religiously mixed town of Unaiza, the settled society of Najd was uniformly Wahhabi in all the areas under control of both the Al Sa'ud and Al Rashid families. As a result of the early twentieth-century religious revival, many Najd Bedouin converted to Wahhabism and joined Ikhwan agricultural settlements supported by Ibn Sa'ud. There they could exercise their parochial interpretation of religious law in the exclusive comfort of like-minded persons, while also making themselves available to fight as soldiers on behalf of Ibn Sa'ud's expansion.

Ibn Sa'ud's adoption of Wahhabism effectively converted political loyalty into a religous obligation. According to ibn Abd al-Wahhab's teachings, a Muslim must have presented a *bay'ah*, or oath of allegiance, to a Muslim ruler during his lifetime in order to be redeemed after his death.[7] The ruler, in turn, is owed unquestioned allegiance so long as he leads the community according to the laws of God.[8] How is the ruler to demonstrate that he leads according to God's laws? Like his ancestors, Ibn Sa'ud did it by creating the appearance of ruling in consultation with ulama and by supporting a morals police force as a demonstration of his willingness to enforce correct behavior.[9]

Correct behavior, according to the Wahhabis, is exemplified in the Qur'an and the Sunna of the Prophet, and calls for the avoidance of innovation (*bid'ah*) in matters of worship.[10] According to Ibn Abd al-Wahhab, the individual is not only enjoined to conform to correct practice in his own behavior, but he is responsible for encouraging the conformity of his neighbor as well; as the Qur'an says, "You are the best of nations raised up for [the benefit of] mankind; you enjoin what is right and forbid the wrong."[11] The Wahhabi emphasis on conformity makes of external appearance a visible expression of inward faith. Therefore, whether or not one conforms, behavior becomes a public statement about whether or not one is a true Muslim. Because one's adherence to the true faith is demonstrable in tangible ways, the eyes of the Muslim community can visibly judge the quality of one's faith by observing his outward actions. In this sense, public opinion alone can become a regulator in individual behavior.

The desire for conformity with Sunna is a universal Muslim ideal. In fact, the fundamental tenets of Wahhabism, being conformity in behavior, knowledge of the Qur'an and Sunna, upholding the unity of God and the rejection of polytheistic ritual practices (*shirk*), are technically indistinct from those of Sunni orthodoxy.[12] What has made the Wahhabis' striving for conformity unique is their political capacity to enforce compliance on themselves and on others, and their literal, and sometimes very parochial, interpretations of what constitutes right behavior. To the Wahhabis, for example, performance of prayer that is punctual and ritually correct and that emulates the practice of the Prophet must not only be urged, but was in the past publicly required of men. Consumption of wine is forbidden to the believer, since wine is literally forbidden in the Qur'an, but under the Wahhabis, all intoxicating drinks and other stimulants, including at one time tobacco, are also forbidden by extension. Modest dress is prescribed for both men and women in accordance with the Qur'an, but the Wahhabis specify the precise type of clothing that should be worn, especially by women, and also forbid the wearing of silk and gold.[13] Forbidden also, in conformity with Qur'an and Sunna, are gambling, usury, eating pork, fornication, sodomy, sorcery, divining the future, and swearing an oath by invoking any name other than that of God.[14] Music and dancing have also at times been forbidden, as have loud laughter and demonstrative weeping. The circumcision of males, a near-universal among Muslims although not mentioned in the Qur'an, is a requirement, as well as shaving the mustache, trimming the nails, plucking out pubic hair and hair from the armpits.[15]

The desire to conform to the practices of the Prophet makes the opinion of learned scholars concerning the minutiae of human endeavors one to be sought after. May one wear perfume or make-up or pluck one's eyebrows? How may one correctly caress one's wife, punish the offending, or cleanse one's body? Should a believer shake a nonbeliever's hand? What constitutes final divorce? How can one make up missed prayers? May a postmenopausal widow leave her home during her mourning period?[16]

The Wahhabi insistence on conformity in dress and behavior has magnified the visual impression of homogeneity among Najdi people. It should be noted, however, that conformist behavior was never entirely uniform. In 1856, for example, a revival was going on in southern Nejd and Wahhabi partisans in Hasa destroyed the looms of silk weavers and even ripped clothing decorated in gold thread off wearers' backs, but when Pelly visited Riyadh in 1865 the Wahhabi chief himself wore green cashmere, while his private secretary smoked a cheroot. At the same time that ibn Rashid and his entourage wore silk clothing with gold jewelry and gold-embellished swords in Ha'il, Wahhabi scholars in the town took pride in dressing simply in coarse fabrics. And at the very time a new cycle of religious renewal in the 1980s inspired many to divest themselves of material luxuries, and, in the name of modesty, to shorten the thobe and forgo the aqal that holds the headcloth in place, luxurious living had become the unapologetic pursuit of the moneyed class.

Historically, however, the pressure to conform to what was essentially a regimen of abstinence, leveled on a very poor people living in a stark land, certainly molded a common outlook toward life, as illustrated in this tale told by Ibn Sa'ud to Ameen Rihani: "A traveller in the East came one day upon a people who live in huts and dig their graves in front of their doors. 'You are poor, that is evident. But why do you dig your graves before your doors?' [the traveler asked]. The hut-man replied, 'To be always near our God, for he is all we have.' "The sultan added, Rihani tells us, "Such are the people of Najd."[17]

Kuwait

Kuwait was a tiny walled town ("Kut" is a garrison, "Kuwait" the diminutive) of little interest to either the Ottomans or the British until it became the prospective terminus for the German Berlin-to-Baghdad railroad. To forestall the extension of German control with the building of the railway, Britain concluded an agreement with Kuwait's Shaikh Mubarak by which Mubarak surrendered his country's foreign relations to British control in exchange for British support of Mubarak's rule and that of his heirs. This agreement, similar to Britain's arrangement with the Trucial States and Bahrain, resulted in the appointment of a British political agent to Kuwait in 1904, the establishment of a dispensary, and the opening of steamer service to Kuwait by the British India Steam Navigation Company.[18] Just as in Bahrain, it was the British presence that facilitated the entry of American missionaries to Kuwait in 1910 and as a practical matter made it possible for the missionaries to live there with their families. In addition to providing the necessary leverage to gain residency, British steamer service brought medicine and food supplies and delivered the mail.

Kuwait and its outlying oasis villages, Jahrah and Zubeir, were in many ways cultural extensions of Najd, being populated by people of Najdi Bedouin extraction and surrounded by seasonal Bedouin encampments.[19] Like the towns of Najd, Kuwait City was a mercantile center for goods needed by neighboring Bedouin. It was also the entrepôt for goods being transferred by camel caravan into the Najd, and the prosperity of the town was in part due to trade with the interior, to which enormous quantities of piece goods, rice, tea, coffee, and sugar were exported.

Kuwait's population, however, reflected the two directions toward which the town turned: the desert and the sea. The sea-born transport trade out of Kuwait delivered dates from the Basra district to India, South and West Arabia, and East Africa and was carried out by Persian, African, and Omani seamen. Annually about thirty sailing boats left Kuwait each year in October and returned the following August with firewood and building lumber. Pearl fisheries extending along the coast from Kuwait to Bahrain brought Asian and European traders to Kuwait and divers from Hasa, Najd, and other Gulf towns.[20] In the first quarter of the century Kuwait was home to people from the surrounding Gulf area, including small numbers of Indian and Persian merchants, a tiny number of Jews, and many Persian laborers. While most of the population were Sunni Muslims, there were also Shia and Wahhabi sympathizers, and the town was home to Sufi fraternities. The huge presence of foreigners so apparent during the Gulf War of 1990–91 was the recent product of oil and development, but at midcentury Kuwait's population of 160,000 was still predominantly Arab and of tribal descent.[21] Dickson tells us that Kuwait was then known as "Najd by the Sea," and so monolithic, tribal, and Nadji did Kuwait appear to the American missionaries in the teens of this century that they spoke of Kuwait as the training ground for their eventual penetration of Najd.[22]

Bahrain

The modern state of Bahrain is a cluster of thirty-three islands located off the Hasa coast about two hundred and eighty miles from Kuwait. On the largest island, also called Bahrain, is the main town of Manama. In Western writings, the name "Bahrain" was and continues to be used indiscriminately to refer to both this town and the island on which it is located.

The politically dominant elite is Najdi in origin, as Bahrain's ruling family, the al-Khalifa, trace their origin to the Anayza tribal confederation, as do the Al Sabah of Kuwait and the Al Sa'ud of Saudi Arabia.[23] The population of Bahrain as a whole, however, reflects the diversity of peoples on both the

Persian and Arab shores of the Gulf. Peasant cultivators are Shia who consider themselves to be the original inhabitants of the island.[24] Some Shia trace their origins to Hasa, and others to different villages in Bahrain,[25] while Sunnis have two traditions about their origins: some trace their origin to Najd and follow the Hanbali school of Islamic jurisprudence; others (the "Hawala") trace their origins to different places in southern Iran but claim genealogical descent from Gulf and Arabian tribes and follow the Shafi'i school. Unlike the Shia, who also claim Persian origin, they are arabized and absorbed into the urban Sunni population (pp. 3–4).

Bahrain was not only home to a far more heterogeneous population than was either Kuwait or Najd but had experienced foreign occupation and foreign interference more directly and for a far longer time than Kuwait did. The Portuguese controlled the islands for around a hundred fifty years, followed for short periods of time by the Dutch, Persians, Omanis, Wahhabis.[26] British hegemony in the Gulf lasted almost two hundred years and was at its height during the period of the Wahhabi revival in Najd, when the Arabian Mission was also at the height of its activities.[27]

British interest in the Gulf focused on British possessions in India and on keeping the sea and land routes open for British commercial and strategic interests. In 1861 Bahrain signed a treaty recognizing a British protectorate over its territory, similar to the treaty signed by rulers of what is now the United Arab Emirates; this treaty also provided for the suppression of the slave trade (p. 14), and in 1892 Britain signed an exclusive agreement with the shaikh of Bahrain that banned any sort of relations between his government and other foreign powers.[28] During and after the First World War, Bahrain was used as the meeting point for British Naval forces in the Gulf.

Over the years the impact of these treaty obligations on society was significant. One result was the alienation of some indigenous groups from local government jurisdiction. The British retained authority to adjudicate disputes among foreigners and between foreigners and Bahrainis and to extend British protection to any foreigner as if that person were a British subject (p. 938). Initially, this British prerogative was of little significance because the label "non-Bahraini" applied only to some forty Jewish merchants, the agents of a German pearl trading house, American missionaries, and freed blacks. Later, however, the treaty obligations came to signify the alienation from Bahraini control of Hasawiyyas, Kuwaitis, Persians, Omanis, Indians, Gulf Christians, individuals who claimed Turkish citizenship, and others who were permanently or temporarily living in Bahrain. Eventually, in 1905, the government of India claimed authority even over native Bahraini Shiites, on the grounds that as Shiites justice would be denied them in a Sunni court (pp. 938–942).

The protection of foreigners under British aegis invited European interference and facilitated the establishment of Western institutions, including trading companies and the Arabian mission. The English political resident, for example, effectively made the presence of the missionaries possible by mediating unofficially with the ruler on their behalf. In 1893 the Arabian Mission's founder, Rev. Zwemer, reported to the British resident at Bushire that the qadi of Bahrain had ordered him off the island and proclaimed that no one was to rent him a shop or buy books or take his medicines. The resident, Zwemer claimed, intervened on his behalf, and official opposition came to an end, although soon afterward shots were fired at the mission house, and again the British resident had to intervene to secure the safety of the missionaries. "The English protection in this respect counts for a great deal," Zwemer wrote, "as popularly India law is held applicable to non-Moslem residents."[29]

Under the treaty obligations, Bahrain also lost control over the types of goods that could be imported, even in the case of goods that offended Islamic dietary rules. In 1900, for example, a German firm tried to import liquor into Bahrain. When the shaikh published an edict prohibiting alcoholic beverages, the government of India responded by adding a caveat to the edict, stating that the shaikh's interdiction would be allowed only on the grounds that it should not be interpreted as preventing Europeans from importing liquor for their own consumption.[30] British intervention caused a certain amount of the resentment experienced by the mission, but it was only because of the security Britain provided that the work of the U.S. mission, in all but its proselytism of Muslims, flourished.

Prologue

1. Eleanor Abdella Doumato, "Gender, Monarchy and National Identity in Saudi Arabia," *British Journal of Middle East Studies*, 19, 1(1992).

2. Al-Zaid, Dr. Abdulla Mohamed, *Education in Saudi Arabia: A Model with a Difference*, trans. Omar Ali Afifi (Jeddah: Tihama, 1981).

3. Circular issued by Saad ibn Mutrafi, director, Haiat al-'amr bil ma'roof, Jeddah, no. 1039, January 9, 1979; circular issued by Abdullah ibn Muhammad al-Dubaikhi, general supervisor, Hai'at al-amr bi al-ma'ruf, Eastern Province branch, no. 178/6/T/129/1, September 13, 1982.

4. *Al-Jazirah*, no. 2738, January 28, 1980.

5. *Al-Da'wah*, no. 767, November 20, 1980.

6. Hamad I. al-Salloom, *Education in Saudi Arabia*, 2d ed. (Beltsville, Md.: Amana, 1995), p. 67, and Javid Hassan, "Saudi Women Given Green Light in Hotel Industry," *Internet ArabView in English* (February 28, 1997), quoted in FBIS-NES-97-070, March 11, 1997.

7. Saudi Arabia, Ministry of Planning, *Third Development Plan (1980–1985)* (Riyadh, 1980), table 3-7, "Projected Civilian Employment in Saudi Arabia (1399/1400 to 1404/05)," p. 98. In 1980 the percentage of women in the workforce was 7.3 percent; Hassan, "Saudi Women," gives the figure of 5.5 percent for the mid-1990s.

8. Eleanor Abdella Doumato, "Women and Political Stability in Saudi Arabia," *Middle East Report*, July 1991, pp. 34–37.

9. *Arab News*, November 14, 1990.

10. Doumato, "Women and the Stability of Saudi Arabia."

11. Margot Badran draws out the eclectic mix of influences leading to the awakening of a feminist consciousness in Egypt, and these include Egyptian women's education, which led to their ability to articulate ideas about their condition as women, as well as their exposure to European women and to the publishing of Syrian Christians in Egypt. Margot Badran, *Feminists, Islam, and Nation: Gender and the Making of Modern Egypt* (Princeton: Princeton University Press, 1995).

12. Lila Abu-Lughod, *Veiled Sentiments: Honor and Poetry in a Bedouin Society* (Berkeley: University of California Press, 1988).

Introduction

1. Paul Harrison, *The Arab at Home* (New York: Crowell, 1924), p. 264.

2. Judith Hoch-Smith and Anita Spring, eds., introduction to *Women in Ritual and Symbolic Roles* (New York: Plenum, 1978), p. 19.

3. Rosemary Reuther, ed., *Religion and Sexism: Images of Women in Jewish and Christian Traditions* (New York: Simon and Schuster, 1974), p. 9.

4. Denise L. Carmody, "Judaism," in *Women in World Religions*, ed. Arvind Sharma (Albany: State University of New York Press, 1987), p. 195.

5. Hoch-Smith and Spring, introduction to *Women in Ritual and Symbolic Roles*, p. 2.

6. Sebastian Brock and Susan Harvey, trans. and eds., introduction to *Holy Women of the Syrian Orient* (Berkeley: University of California Press, 1987); and Susan Harvey, "Women in Early Byzantine Hagiography: Reversing the Story," in *That Gentle Strength: Historical Perspectives on Women in Christianity*, ed. Lynda L. Coon, Katherine Haldane, and Elisabeth Sommer (Charlottesville: University Press of Virginia, 1990).

7. Hoch-Smith and Spring, *Women in Ritual and Symbolic Roles*, p. 14.

8. Michelle Zimbalist Rosaldo, "A Theoretical Overview," in *Woman, Culture, and Society*, ed. Michelle Zimbalist Rosaldo and Louise Lamphere (Stanford: Stanford University Press, 1974; reprint, Stanford: Stanford University Press, 1993), p. 32.

9. Qur'an, sura 2, verse 60: "And as for women advanced in years who do not hope for a marriage, it is no sin for them if they put off their clothes without displaying their ornaments" (M. H. Shakir, trans., *The Quran*, 5th ed. [Elmhurst, N.Y.: Tahrike Tarsile Qur'an, 1988]).

10. Carmody, "Judaism," p. 194.

11. Jacob Neusner, "Thematic or Systematic Description: The Case of Mishnah's Division of Women," in *Method and Meaning in Ancient Judaism* (Missoula, Mont.: Scholars, 1979), p. 99, quoted in Carmody, "Judaism," p. 195. Sura 4 of the Qur'an is also entitled "Women" and contains regulations relating to female sexuality.

12. Hoch-Smith and Spring, *Women in Ritual and Symbolic Roles*, p. 15.

13. Elizabeth Fernea, "Saints and Spirits" (Granada TV, 1977), and "Some Women of Marrakech" (Granada TV, 1976).

14. Fatima Mernissi, "Women, Saints and Sanctuaries," *Signs: Journal of Women in Culture and Society* 3, no. 1 (autumn, 1975): 101–112.

15. Hoch-Smith and Spring, *Women in Ritual and Symbolic Roles*, p. 14.

16. See, for example, Elizabeth Fernea and Robert Fernea, "Variation in Religious Observance Among Islamic Women," in *Scholars, Saints, and Sufis: Muslim Religious Institutions since 1500*, ed. Nikki Keddie (Berkeley: University of California Press, 1972); Zubaydah Ashkanani, "Zar in a Changing World: Kuwait," in *Women's Medicine: The Zar-Bori Cult in Africa and Beyond*, ed. I. M. Lewis, Ahmed al-Safi, and Sayyid Hurreiz (Edinburgh: Edinburgh University Press, 1991), pp. 219–229; Susan Sered, *Women as Ritual Experts: The Religious Lives of Elderly Jewish Women in Jerusalem* (Oxford: Oxford University Press, 1992); Rosemary Reuther and Eleanor McLaughlin, eds. *Women of the Spirit: Female Leadership in the Jewish and Christian Tradition* (New York: Simon and Schuster, 1979); Nancy Falk and Rita Gross, eds., *Unspoken Worlds: Women's Religious Lives in Non-Western Cultures* (San Francisco: Harper and Row, 1980).

17. Sered, *Women as Ritual Experts*, p. 28.

18. I. M. Lewis, *Religion in Context: Cults and Charisma* (Cambridge: Cambridge University Press, 1989), p. 43.

19. Al-Zubaydah, "Zar in a Changing World," pp. 222–223.

20. Karl Keating, *Catholics and Fundamentalism* (San Francisco: Ignatius, 1988), as quoted in John A. Coleman, S.J., "Catholic Integralism as a Fundamentalism," in *Fundamentalism in Comparative Perspective*, ed. Lawrence Kaplan (Amherst: University of Massachusetts Press, 1992), pp. 78–79.

21. Lewis, *Religion in Context*, p. xi.

22. Rev. J. P. Searle, D.D., "After Twenty Years: As to Beginnings," *Neglected Arabia*, no. 68 (January–March 1909): 6.

23. C. Stanley G. Mylrea, "A Council of War," *Neglected Arabia*, no. 88 (January–March 1914): 3.

24. James Cantine, "Sharon J. Thoms, M.D.: An Appreciation," *Neglected Arabia*, no. 85 (April–June 1913): 3.

25. Eleanor Calverley, "The Arabian Secret Service," *Neglected Arabia*, no. 11 (January–March 1913): 11.

26. "Report of the Arabian Mission for 1914," *Neglected Arabia*, no. 93 (April–June 1915): 10.

27. Ameen Rihani, *Maker of Modern Arabia* (Boston: Houghton Mifflin, 1928), p. xvii. Abd al-Aziz took the title "Sultan of Nejd and Its Dependencies" after annexing Jebel Shammar in 1921, and in 1926, after taking the Hejaz, he assumed the title of king.

28. Paul Starr, *The Social Transformation of American Medicine* (New York: Basic, 1982), p. 115.

29. Theodore Gosselink, interview in Providence, R.I., 1989.

30. Cornelia Dalenberg, *Sharifa* (Grand Rapids, Mich.: Eerdmans, 1983), p. 7.

31. Paul Harrison, "The Tour to Riadh," *Neglected Arabia*, no. 104 (January–March 1918): 4—5.

32. Paul Harrison to Edwin Calverley, May 18, 1918, Bahrain, Persian Gulf, Edwin Calverley Papers, Hartford Theological Seminary.

33. Paul Harrison, *The Arab at Home* (New York: Crowell, 1924), pp. 68–69.

34. Josephine Van Peursem, "A Christian and a Moslem Deathbed," *Neglected Arabia*, no. 101 (April–June 1917): 7–9.

35. Mrs. James Cantine, "Arab Women and the War," *Neglected Arabia*, no. 108 (January–March 1919): 22–23.

36. Samuel Zwemer, "The Arabian Mission Field Report," *Neglected Arabia*, no. 3 (July 1–October 1 1892): 6.

37. Patricia Hill, *The World Their Household: The American Woman's Foreign Mission Movement and Cultural Transformation, 1870–1920* (Ann Arbor: University of Michigan Press, 1985), p. 174.

38. For the missionary experience in China, see Jane Hunter, *The Gospel of Gentility: American Women Missionaries in Turn-of-the-Century China* (New Haven: Yale University Press, 1984).

39. "Women's Appeal," Cairo Conference, April 4–9, 1906, quoted in Annie Van Sommer and Samuel M. Zwemer, *Our Moslem Sisters: A Cry of Need from Lands of Darkness Interpreted by Those Who Heard It* (New York: Revell, 1907), pp. 9–10.

40. Hill, *The World Their Household*, pp. 3, 1.

41. Gerrit Van Peursem, "How Can the Medical Work Best Help the Evangelistic?" *Neglected Arabia*, no. 97 (April–June 1916): 10.

42. The Arabian Mission, *Quarterly Letters from the Field* (January–March 1900): 12.

43. Hill. *The World Their Household*, pp. 25–26, pp. 116–117, p. 174; see also Hunter, *Gospel of Gentility*, p. 177.

44. Hill. *The World Their Household*, p. 42.

45. Rev. Alfred Dewitt Mason and Rev. Frederick J. Barny. *History of the Arabian Mission*. New York: Board of Foreign Missions, Reformed Church in America, 1926, p. 215.

46. Eleanor Calverley, "One of the Least of These—His Sisters," *Neglected Arabia*, no. 96 (January–March 1916): 8.

47. Eleanor Calverley, "Beauty for Ashes," *Neglected Arabia*, no. 110 (July–September 1919): 8–9.

48. Mary Bruins Allison, *Doctor Mary in Arabia*, ed. Sandra Shaw (Austin: University of Texas Press, 1994), p. 77.

49. The marginalization of women in the medical profession is discussed by Judith Barrett Litoff, *American Midwives: 1860 to the Present* (Westport, Conn.: Greenwood, 1978; reprint, Westport, Conn.: Greenwood, 1985), and in Starr, *The Social Transformation of American Medicine*.

50. Three Western travelers preceded Harrison's visit to Riyadh in the twentieth century: a Danish traveler, Barclay Raunkiaer, who spent two days in Riyadh in

1912; Captain G. E. Leachman, who stayed for a week later in the same year; and Captain W. H. Shakespear, the British political agent in Kuwait, who spent three days in Riyadh in 1914.

51. Brent, *Far Arabia*, p. 73.

52. Margaret Tidrick, *Heart-beguiling Araby: Englishmen in Arabia* (Cambridge: Cambridge University Press, 1981), p. 28.

53. See Mea Allen, *Palgrave of Arabia* (London: Macmillan, 1972).

54. Benjamin Braude, "Palgrave and His Critics, the Origins and Implications of a Controversy: Part One, the Nineteenth Century—the Abyssinian Imbroglio," *Arabian Studies*, vol. 7, ed. R. B. Serjeant and R. I. Bidwell (London: Scorpion, for the Middle East Centre, University of Cambridge, 1985), pp. 97–138.

55. Charles Doughty, preface to the second edition, in *Travels in Arabia Deserta*, 2 vols., 3d ed. (London, 1936; reprint, New York: Dover, 1979), 1:33, 31.

56. Quoted in Tidrick, *Heart-beguiling Araby*, pp. 152–153.

57. Robert A. Fernea suggests that Doughty's language captured the flavor of Arabic as Doughty heard it: "When I read *Travels in Arabia Deserta* today I hear Arabic being spoken, not the formal Arabic of the Quran or even that of the educated urbanite, but rather the country speech which is all Doughty and I ever learned. . . . While the present ethnographic fashion is to provide long statements from native speakers, no one in recent times has approached the success of Doughty in translating the emotive and the semantic properties of conversation" ("Arabia Deserta: The Ethnographic Text," in *Explorations in Doughty's Arabia Deserta*, ed. Stephen E. Tabachnick (Athens: University of Georgia Press, 1987), pp. 216–217.

58. Dervla Murphy, introduction to Lady Anne Blunt, *Pilgrimage to Nejd: The Cradle of the Arab Race* (London: Murray, 1881; reprint, London: Century, 1985).

59. Barbara Tuchman, *A Distant Mirror: The Calamitous Fourteenth Century* (New York: Scribner, 1978).

60. Lila Abu-Lughod, "Fieldwork of a Dutiful Daughter," in *Arab Women in the Field: Studying Our Own Society*, ed. Soraya Altorki and Camilia Fawzi El-Solh (Syracuse: Syracuse University Press, 1988), p. 158.

1. Women and Religious Learning

1. Josephine Van Peursem, "Arab Home Life," *Neglected Arabia*, no. 79 (October–December 1911): 15.

2. Eleanor Taylor Calverley, "Arab Women of the Persian Gulf," *Asia* (May 1938): 307.

3. Azeezah A. al-Manea, "Historical and Contemporary Policies of Women's Education in Saudi Arabia" (Ph.D. diss., University of Michigan, 1984), p. 63.

4. The argument that women deserve to be educated equally with men because as Muslims, women, like men, must know God's laws has been used by Saudi Arabian women to justify initiating public education for women and then expanding

the subject areas women are allowed to study. For example, a Saudi writing in the June 1956 issue of *Al-Yamamah*, a Riyadh weekly, commented,

> No one denies the fact that good and useful actions result from useful and good knowledge on the part of both man and woman. If education is good for the one—man—it is good and useful for the other—woman. If it is harmful, it will harm both equally. Ignorance in all its phases is harmful, and the woman who knows her duties and rights is better than the ignorant woman. . . . Islam calls for the education of women, and the Prophet used to teach Muslim woman. In the Islamic Age, there were woman jurists, writers, and poets. Education for both men and women Muslims is among the principles of Islam.

(quoted in anonymous, "Education of Women in Saudi Arabia," "Notes of the Quarter," *Muslim World* 46, no. 4 [October 1956]: 367)

The argument is still used. The director of the Department of Religious Guidance, Abdullah bin Abd al-Aziz bin Baz, stated in a lecture on the qualities of good women that it is the obligation of all believers, men and women, to know the Qur'an and Hadith in order to conform to the practices ordained by God. It is the duty of all men and women, he says, " to have godly manners and to avoid at all times what God forbade and to read the Koran because of its benefit and because it is a sign of noble ethics. . . . The woman who can't read out of laziness has available the Koran broadcasting station which transmits day and night. . . . Furthermore, men and women must heed the Sunna of the Prophet, peace and blessings be upon him, to benefit from it and memorize part of it. . . . The woman who can't read can seek help from an educated woman whether she be her sister or daughter or neighbor" (*al-Riyadh*, December 12, 1981).

5. Muhammad ibn Abd al-Wahhab, *The Three Basic Principles and Their Proofs*, trans. Abdul Munem Salamat (Riyadh: Dar Alhuda, 1996), p. 6.

6. According to Saudi scholar Abd al-Rahman bin Hamid Al Umar,

> Islam classifies knowledge into two categories. . . . [The first is] obligatory knowledge, which is a duty on every Muslim whether he be male or female. The Muslim must know Allah, His Messenger, the prophet Mohammed, peace and blessings of Allah be upon him, and acquire the knowledge concerning the fundamentals of Islam by evidences. . . .
> The second category of knowledge is optional. This refers to a collective duty of individuals in the community to acquire knowledge necessary to the welfare of the community, such as Islamic Law, basic sciences, industry and the professions.

('Abd al-Rahman bin Hamad Al Umar, *Islam: The Religion of Truth* [Riyadh: al-Farazdak, 1974], pp. 42–43)

7. Ibn Abd al-Wahhab, *The Three Basic Principles*, p. 7.

8. John Lewis Burckhardt, "The Catechism (or Creed) of the Wahabys," in *Notes on the Bedouins and Wahabys Collected During His Travels in the East* (London: Henry Colburn and Richard Bently, 1831), 2:363–369.

9. Ahmad Abd al-Ghafour Attar, *Muhammad ibn Abd al-Wahhab*, trans. Rashid al-Barrawi (Mecca: Mecca Printing and Information, 1979), pp. 55–56.

10. John Lewis Burckhardt, *Notes on the Bedouins and Wahabys Collected During His Travels in the East* (London: Henry Colburn and Richard Bently, 1830), 1:99–100.

11. Lady Anne Blunt, *Bedouin Tribes of the Euphrates* (New York: Harper and Brothers, 1879), p. 400.

12. Lady Anne Blunt, *Pilgrimage to Nejd: The Cradle of the Arab Race* (London: Murray, 1881; reprint, London: Century, 1985), p. 125.

13. Georg August Wallin, *Travels in Arabia (1845 and 1848)* (Cambridge: Oleander; Naples: Falcon, 1979), p. 69.

14. Charles M. Doughty, *Travels in Arabia Deserta*, 3d ed. (London, 1936; reprint. New York: Dover, 1979), 2:454–455.

15. Wallin, *Travels*, p. 113.

16. Alois Musil, *In the Arabian Desert* (New York: Liveright, 1930), p. 147.

17. Burckhardt, *Notes*, 1:249.

18. Wallin, *Travels*, p. 71.

19. Doughty, *Travels*, 2:56.

20. Wallin, *Travels*, p. 33.

21. W. G. Palgrave, *Personal Narrative of a Year's Journey through Central and Eastern Arabia (1862–1863)* (London: Macmillan, 1868), p. 313.

22. Wallin, *Travels*, p. 71.

23. Sulayman al-Dakhil, "Nejd," *Lughat al-'Arab* (Baghdad) 1 (1911): 483.

24. Doughty, *Travels*, 2:58–59.

25. Paul Harrison, "The Capital City of the Empire of Muhammed," *Neglected Arabia*, no. 106 (April–June 1918): 23.

26. Paul Harrison, "The Tour to Riadh," *Neglected Arabia*, no. 104 (January–March 1918): 4.

27. H. St. John Philby, Exploration (London: Constable, 1922), 1:297.

28. Hafiz Wahba, *Arabian Days* (London: Baker, 1964), p. 52.

29. Wahba, *Arabian Days*, p. 25.

30. Wells Thoms, "A Missionary Doctor in Arabia," *Church Herald* (October 22, 1937).

31. Wahba, *Arabian Days*, p. 47.

32. Samuel Zwemer, "The Eastern Threshold of Arabia," in *Arabia: The Cradle of Islam* (New York: Revell, 1900), p. 117.

33. Wahba, *Arabian Days*, p. 48.

34. Edwin Calverley, "Evangelistic Activities at Kuweit," *Neglected Arabia*, no. 92 (January–March 1915): 8–10.

35. *Kuweit Evangelical Report* (1912), doc. 69830; (1913) doc. 69819; and ~~(1914), doc. 69826, Calverley Papers, Hartford Theological Seminary.~~

36. Edwin Calverley, "Mission Work at Kuweit, Arabia" (pamphlet) (Bombay: Guardian, 1924), box 139, folder 2458, doc. #6761, Hartford Theological Seminary.

37. Wahba, *Arabian Days*, p. 173.

38. Ameen Rihani, *Maker of Modern Arabia* (Boston: Houghton Mifflin, 1928), p. 207.

39. Violet Dickson, in Harold Dickson, *Kuwait and Her Neighbors* (London: Allen and Unwin, 1956), p. 408.

40. Soraya Altorki and Donald Cole, *Arabian Oasis City: The Transformation of 'Unayzah* (Austin: University of Texas Press, 1989), p. 95. This passage draws on interviews carried out in 1986–87 in Unaiza with women then over the age of sixty.

41. H. St. John Philby, *Arabia of the Wahhabis* (London: Cass, 1977), p. 244.

42. Dorothy Van Ess, "Under the Star and Crescent," *Neglected Arabia* 234 (winter 1953–54): 3.

43. Dorothy Van Ess, "A School of Hopelessness," *Neglected Arabia*, no. 89 (April–June 1914): 16.

44. "Annual Report of the Arabian Mission for 1925," *Neglected Arabia*, no. 137 (April–June 1926): 3–11.

45. G. D. Van Peursem, "Public Schools in Bahrein," *Neglected Arabia*, no. 90 (July–September 1914): 11–13.

46. Mrs. G. Pennings, "From the Cradle to the Grave," *Neglected Arabia*, no. 126 (July–September 1923): 6–7.

47. Paul Harrison, "Signs of the Times in Arabia," *Neglected Arabia*, no. 113 (April–June 1920): 11.

48. Fu'ad I. Khuri, *Tribe and State in Bahrain: The Transformation of Social and Political Authority in an Arab State* (Chicago: University of Chicago Press, 1980) p. 116.

49. Annual Report of the Arabian Mission, "The Ministry of Teaching," *Neglected Arabia*, no. 152 (January–March 1930): 14.

50. Munira A. Fakhro, *Women at Work in the Gulf: A Case Study of Bahrain* (London: Kegan Paul International, 1990) p. 115.

51. Ruth Jackson, "Of Girls in Bahrein," *Arabia Calling*, no. 229 (autumn 1952): 10–11.

52. Fakhro, *Women at Work in the Gulf*, p. 115.

53. "Annual Report of the Arabian Mission for 1925," p. 1.

54. "Annual Report of the Arabian Mission, 1932." *Neglected Arabia*, no. 164 (January–June 1933), p. 11.

55. Cornelia Dalenberg, "Unforgettable Patients," *Arabia Calling*, no. 217 (summer 1949): 14.

56. Sarah Hosmon, "The Girls and Women of Arabia as I Have Seen Them," *Neglected Arabia* 98 (July–September 1916): 5.

57. Minnie Dykstra, "Our Muscat School, 1892–1952," *Arabia Calling*, no. 229 (autumn 1952): 3–7.

58. Haya al-Mughni, *Women in Kuwait: The Politics of Gender* (London: Saqi, 1993).

59. Edwin Calverley, "Education in Kuwait," *Neglected Arabia*, no. 142 (July–September 1927): 14.

60. Al-Mughni, *Women in Kuwait*, pp. 46–47.

61. Calverley, "Education in Kuwait," pp. 13–14.

62. "Evangelistic Work for Women, Kuweit, 1945," Calverley papers, Hartford Theological Seminary.

63. Madeline A. Holmes, "Kuwait, Ancient and Modern," *Arabia Calling*, no. 237 (autumn 1954): 9–12.

64. Literacy reports for women were included in the following, for example: "Kuweit women's Medical Report for 1913," Calverley papers doc. #69822; Josephine van Peursem, "Arab Home Life," *Neglected Arabia*, no. 79 (October–December 1911): p. 15.

65. Mrs. James Cantine, "Mullayas—Mohammedan and Christian," *Neglected Arabia*, no. 112 (January–March 1920): 13.

66. Mrs. Minnie W. Dykstra, "A Trip to the Mainland," *Neglected Arabia*, no. 104 (January–March 1918): p. 15.

67. Eleanor Calverley, "Beauty for Ashes," *Neglected Arabia*, no. 110 (July–September 1919): 1–6.

68. Edwin Calverley to Duncan Macdonald, Kuwait, August 1, 1917, doc. #57365, Calverley Papers, Hartford Theological Seminary.

69. Wahba, *Arabian Days*, p. 25.

70. Philby, *Arabian Jubilee*, p. 109.

71. Calverley, "Arab Women of the Persian Gulf," p. 307.

72. Pennings, "From the Cradle to the Grave," pp. 6–7.

73. Hosmon, "The Girls and Women of Arabia," p. 5.

74. Wahba, *Arabian Days*, p. 173.

75. Anna Harrison, "Desert Diary," *Neglected Arabia*, no. 168 (October–December 1942): 14.

76. When asked in an interview about his father's attitude concerning the education of women, Prince Tallal bin Abd al-Aziz answered that education was not considered appropriate for women in his father's time:

> The opinion of Abd al-Aziz concerning women was the opinion of society at that time, and that is compatible with the opinion of Islam. But . . . during the month before [my father] died . . . I set up a school for my full sister in a house in the Murabba' palace to teach her the English language and some other subjects, and [my father] raised no objection . . . except to ask whether it was to be a school for my sister and those with her in the palace [only], or a school for

the purpose of educating women. . . . Some years after his death I founded such a school and named it "King Abd al-Aziz Charitable Institution for Girls."

("Tallal bin 'Abd al-Aziz Tadhakkir," *al-Riyadh*, September 23, 1981)

2. Prayer, the Mosque, and the Ways Women Worship

1. Paul Harrison, *The Arab at Home* (New York: Crowell, 1924), p. 236.

2. John Bowen, "Salat in Indonesia: The Social Meanings of an Islamic Ritual," *Man*, n.s., 5, no. 1 (1966): p. 610.

3. Muhammad Mahmud Al Sawwaf, *The Muslim Book of Prayer* (Mecca: Dr. Mujahid Muhammad Al Sawwaf, 1977), p. 1. This manual was translated from *Ta'lim al-salah* (Mecca: Dar an-nasr lil taba'at al-Islamiya, 1977) and distributed by the General Presidency of Scientific Research, If'ta, Islamic Propagation and Guidance, Kingdom of Saudi Arabia. To judge by the author's credentials, this manual represents a mainstream view: Al Sawwaf is a member of the Shari'ah College in Mecca; he was educated in Mosul and al-Azhar and taught Shari'ah law in Baghdad before moving to Saudi Arabia in 1959.

4. The contemporary importance of praying in a group may be gauged by commentary in a weekly column of advice on correct Muslim practice that appeared in the Saudi newspaper *Arab News*. A questioner asked, "What is the minimum number of worshipers who can form a proper congregation for Friday prayers?" The answer: "Schools of thought differ as to the minimum number which forms a proper Friday congregation. Some say forty. The Hanafi school requires twelve only. The Maliki school does not specify a number. It requires 'a number that may be described as a *jam'a'a* or a group.' Scholars have indeed ruled that as few as three worshipers may form a proper congregation" ("Islam in Perspective," *Arab News*, April 16, 1982). Another opinion offered in the same column came in answer to a question concerning the importance of attending the sermon on Friday before the midday prayers. "The khutbah, or sermon, on Friday is obligatory, which means that without it prayers are not correct. To attend the khutbah in full is of great advantage to everyone and could be greatly beneficial to the community as a whole" (*Arab News*, March 11, 1983).

5. Harrison, *Arab at Home*, pp. 233–234.

6. Georg August Wallin, *Travels in Arabia (1845 and 1848)* (Cambridge: Oleander; Naples: Falcon, 1979), p. 184. Shammar is the name of the dominant tribal group in the Ha'il region of northern Najd, as well as the name of the ruling family.

7. W. G. Palgrave, *Personal Narrative of a Year's Journey through Central and Eastern Arabia (1862–1863)* (London: Macmillan, 1868), pp. 119–120.

8. Harrison, *Arab at Home*, p. 235.

9. Maulana Muhammad Ali, *A Manual of Hadith* (London: Curzon, 1977), pp. 107, 160.

10. Al Sawwaf, *Muslim Book of Prayer*, p. 53.

11. Omar A. Farrukh, trans., *Ibn Taimiyya on Public and Private Law in Islam; or, Public Policy in Islamic Jurisprudence* (Beirut: Khayats, 1966), pp. 84–85.

12. Paul Harrison, "The Capital City of the Empire of Muhammed," *Neglected Arabia*, no. 106 (April–June 1918): 23.

13. Harrison, *Arab at Home*, pp. 234–235.

14. Ameen Rihani, *Maker of Modern Arabia* (Boston: Houghton Mifflin, 1928), p. 204.

15. Captain G. E. Leachman, "A Journey in North-Eastern Arabia," *Geographical Journal* 37, no. 3 (March 1911): 271; Wallin, *Travels*, p. 70. Abd Allah, of the Al Rashid family, was then the ruler of Ha'il.

16. Paul Harrison, *Arab at Home*, p. 236.

17. Eleanor Calverley, "Beauty for Ashes," *Neglected Arabia*, no. 110 (July–September 1919): 7.

18. H. St. John Philby, *Heart of Arabia: A Record of Travel and Exploration* (London: Constable, 1922), 1:79. Philby, after he had converted to Islam and went on the Pilgrimage, wrote that women always prayed in the open in the Grand Mosque in Mecca, and this he contrasts with the Prophet's mosque in Medina, where women were assigned a separate section behind a screen (*A Pilgrim in Arabia* [London: Robert Hale, 1946], p. 61).

19. H. St. John Philby, *Arabia of the Wahhabis* (London: Cass, 1977), p. 13.

20. Philby, *Arabia of the Wahhabis*, pp. 263–264. In the Qur'an it is Ishmael, not Isaac, whom Abraham is commanded to sacrifice.

21. Wallin, *Travels*, p. 184.

22. Captain Sir Richard Burton, *Personal Narrative of a Pilgrimage to al-Madinah and Mecca* (1893; reprint, New York: Dover, 1964), 2:197.

23. There are Hadith supporting women's right to touch the Qur'an as well as to pray while menstruating, but these have been submerged under the weight of interpretation. For example, Aisha said, "The Prophet said to me, 'Hand me over the mat from the mosque.' I said, 'I am menstruating.' He said, 'Thy menses are not in thy hand' " (Ali, *Manual*, p. 85). See Muhammad ibn Abd al-Wahhab, "Bab al-Haidh," in *Mu'alafat Al Shaikh al-Imam Muhammad ibn 'Abd al-Wahhab*, ed. Abd al-Aziz Zaid al-Rumi, Dr. Muhammad Beltaji, Dr. Sayyid Hijab (Riyadh: Imam Muhammad ibn Sa'ud Islamic University, 1981), pp. 82–88.

24. Calverley, "Beauty for Ashes," p. 6.

25. Dr. Sarah Hosmon, "In the Date Gardens at Sibe," *Neglected Arabia*, no. 116 (January–March 1921): 9.

26. Philby, *Arabia of the Wahhabis*, p. 48. Italics mine.

27. Lady Anne Blunt, *A Pilgrimage to Nejd: The Cradle of the Arab Race* (London: Murray, 1881; reprint, London: Century, 1985), p. 234.

28. H. R. P. Dickson, *The Arab of the Desert: Bedouin Life in Kuwait and Saudi Arabia* (London: Allen and Unwin, 1949), p. 183–184.

29. Donald Cole, *Nomads of the Nomads: The Al Murrah Bedouin of the Empty Quarter*. Arlington Heights, Ill.: Harlan Davidson, 1975), p. 129.

30. Muhammad Mughairabi Fatih al-Madani, *Firqat al-Ikhwan al-Islam bi Najd au Wahhabiya al-Yaum* (1923), p. 41, quoted in Christine Moss Helms, *The Cohesion of Saudi Arabia: Evolution of Political Identity* (Baltimore: Johns Hopkins University Press, 1981), p. 140.

31. John S. Habib, *Ibn Sa'ud's Warriors of Islam* (Leiden: Brill, 1978), pp. 54–55.

32. Muhammad ibn Abd al-Wahhab, "Bab sitru al-'awrah," in *Mu'alafat Al Shaikh al-Imam Muhammad ibn 'Abd al-Wahhab*, ed. Abd al-Aziz Zaid al-Rumi, Dr. Muhammad Beltaji, and Dr. Sayyid Hijab (Riyadh: Imam Muhammad ibn Sa'ud Islamic University, 1981), pp. 105–108.

33. Wallin, *Travels*, p. 184. Wallin's comment on the regularity of women's prayer is puzzling. As a man, he would likely have seen only Bedouin women at prayer, unless he meant that he saw women praying in the mosque. His basis for comparison is unclear as well, although it can be assumed he means Egypt and Hejaz as he traveled to those places before his research in Najd, but, again, where he might have expected to have seen women at prayer in those places is unclear.

34. Charles M. Doughty, *Travels in Arabia Deserta*, 3d ed. (London, 1936; reprint, New York: Dover, 1979), 2: 25.

35. Fanny Lutton, "Moslem Women's Meetings in Bahrein," *Neglected Arabia*, no. 84 (January–March 1913): 14–15.

36. Fanny Lutton, "A Day's Picnic with Arab Ladies of Muscat," *Neglected Arabia*, no. 78 (July–September 1911): 5–6.

37. Fu'ad Khuri, *Tribe and State in Bahrein: The Transformation of Social and Political Authority in an Arab State* (Chicago: University of Chicago Press, 1980), p. 79.

38. Violet Dickson, *Forty Years in Kuweit* (London: Allen and Unwin, 1971), p. 322.

39. C. Snouck Hurgronje, *Mekka in the Latter Part of the Nineteenth Century* (Leiden: Brill and Luzac, 1931; reprint, Leiden: Brill, 1970), pp. 46–48.

40. John Lewis Burckhardt, *Travels in Arabia* (London: Henry Colburn, 1829), 2:269–270.

41. Burton, *Personal Narrative*, 1:328.

42. Holy spots and saints' tombs are exceedingly numerous in both Mecca and Medina, according to Burton's narrative, documented especially in chapter 22, "A Visit to the Saint's Cemetary," and chapter 33, "Places of Pious Visitation at Meccah."

43. Philby, *Pilgrim in Arabia*, p. 61.

44. John Lewis Burckhardt, *Notes on the Bedouins and Wahabys Collected During His Travels in the East* (London: Henry Colburn and Richard Bently, 1831), 1:259–260.

45. Lutton, "Moslem Women's Meetings," p. 14.

46. Khuri, *Tribe and State*, p. 78.

47. Lutton, "Moslem Women's Meetings," p. 16. "Ma'tam" can also refer to the congregation that participates in the mourning ritual.

48. Khuri, *Tribe and State*, p. 154.

49. F. S. Vidal, *The Oasis of al-Hasa* (New York: Arabian American Oil Company, 1955).

50. Lutton, "Moslem Women's Meetings," pp. 17–18. Dr. S. J. Thoms noted these women's meetings years earlier, in 1908: "For ten days before Ashura people are reading in groups; the Sunnis in Bahrein turn Muharrem into a time of feasting and rejoicing. . . . Women have gone to a reading where they were beating their chests and weeping over the death of Hussain. On the tenth day, the burial of Hussein was acted out in vivid and gruesome detail, many of them cutting themselves with swords and daggers, and then, with blood-besmeared bodies and clothing, . . . danc[ing] through the streets beating their chests and heads" ("The Passion Play at Bahrein," *Neglected Arabia*, no. 65 [April–June 1908]: 5).

51. Mrs. James Cantine, "Mullayas—Mohammedan and Christian," *Neglected Arabia*, no. 112 (January–March 1920): 14.

52. Mrs. Rene Harrison, "The Feast of Moharram," *Neglected Arabia*, no. 107 (October–December 1918): 13. Italics mine.

53. Mrs. Harrison's description of the Ashura parade continues on to describe the presentation of a number of horsemen who were Hussein's assassins, accompanied by sword-wielding footmen, a horseman representing Hussein's son with a sword sticking through his skull, a bier with the body of Hussein's son-in-law, and two smaller biers for the son and nephew of Hussein; following was the bier of Hussein himself, draped in white and bearing a pure white dove. "To make the beheading of the beloved hero more realistic, a man lay on the bier with his head out of sight. In the place where the head should have been there protruded the neck of a freshly slaughtered animal which at the beginning of the performance spurted blood in a most gruesome manner" (pp. 13–14).

54. Thoms, "Passion Play at Bahrein," p. 5.

55. Harrison, *The Arab at Home*, p. 226.

56. Thoms, "Passion Play at Bahrein," pp. 4–5. Thoms says he was quoting from Lewis Pelly's translation.

57. Lutton, "Moslem Women's Meeting," p. 18.

58. Samuel M. Zwemer, *Arabia: Cradle of Islam* (New York: Revell, 1900), p. 193.

59. G. E. von Grunebaum, *Muhammadan Festivals* (New York: Schuman, 1951), p. 76.

60. Harrison, *Arab at Home*, p. 227.

61. Muhammad ibn Abd al-Wahhab, *Kitab at-Tawhid: Essay on the Unicity of Allah; or, What Is Due to Allah from His Creatures*, trans. Ismail Raji al-Faruqi (Damascus: International Islamic Federation of Student Organizations, 1979), p. 91.

62. Ahmad Abd al-Ghafour Attar, *Muhammad ibn Abd al-Wahhab*, trans. Dr. Rashid al-Barrawi (Mecca: Mecca Printing and Information, 1979), pp. 150–151.

63. Muhammad Ibn Abd al-Wahhab, *Kitab at-Tawhid*, p. 68, quoted in Attar, *Muhammad Ibn Abd al-Wahhab*, p. 151

64. Ibn Abd al-Wahhab, *Kitab at-Tawhid*, p. 91.

65. Attar, *Muhammad Ibn Abd al-Wahhab*, p. 149.

66. Philby, *Pilgrim in Arabia*, p. 61.

67. Lutton, "Moslem Women's Meetings," pp. 14–15.

68. Attar, *Muhammad Ibn Abd al-Wahhab*, pp. 12–13.

69. Quoted in R. Bayly Winder, *Saudi Arabia in the Nineteenth Century* (London: Macmillan, 1965), p. 12.

70. Ibrahaim al-Rashid, ed., *Documents on the History of Saudi Arabia*, vol. 2 (Salisbury: Document Publications, 1976), pp. 80–81.

71. Attar, *Muhammad Ibn Abd al-Wahhab*, pp. 144–145.

72. Rihani, *Maker of Modern Arabia*, p. 258.

3. The Healing Power of Words

1. Paul Harrison, *The Arab at Home* (New York: Crowell, 1924), pp. 306–307). Thirty years before Harrison arrived in the Gulf, Doughty wrote that "a man of medicine is not found in Nejd" (*Travels in Arabia Deserta*, 3d ed. [London, 1936; reprint, New York: Dover, 1979], 1:300). Doughty had qualified himself to travel as a physician in Najd by equipping himself with a small portable pharmacopoeia, mostly herbal.

2. H. R. P. Dickson, *The Arab of the Desert: Bedouin Life in Kuwait and Saudi Arabia* (London: Allen and Unwin, 1949), p. 505; Hafiz Wahba, "al-Tib fi bilad al-'arab" in *Jazirat al-'arab fi al-qarn al-'ishrin* (1935; reprint, Cairo: Maktaba al-Nahda al-Misriyya, 1961), pp. 121–127; Mrs. Stanley Mylrea, "Arab Superstitions about Diseases and Quackery in Medicine," *Neglected Arabia*, no. 125 (April–June 1925): 12.

3. Ida Patterson Storm, "Touring Troubles," *Arabia Calling*, no. 218 (autumn/ winter 1949): 6.

4. "Kuweit Women's Medical Report for 1913," doc. #69822, Hartford Theological Seminary.

5. Muhammad ibn Abd al-Wahhab, *Kitab at-Tawhid: Essay on the Unicity of Allah; or, What Is Due to His Creatures*, trans. Ismail Raji al-Faruqi (Damascus: International Islamic Federation of Student Organizations, 1979), pp. 103–104.

6. C. Stanley G. Mylrea, "The Thin Edge of the Wedge," *Neglected Arabia*, no. 92 (January–March 1915): 17–22.

7. M. H. Shakir, trans., *The Quran*, 5th ed. (Elmhurst, N.Y.: Tahrike Tarsile Qur'an, 1988), sura 17, verse 82.

8. Ibn Qayyam Al Jawziyya, *Prophetic Medicine*, trans. S. Abi Azar, corr. F. Amira Zrein Matraji (Riyadh: Dar el-Fikr, 1995), p. 16.

9. Also in 'Abd al-Rahman bin Hamad Al Umar, *Islam, The Religion of Truth* (Riyadh: al-Farazdak Press, 1974), p. 53. Calverley noted that this Hadith was everyday knowledge in Kuwait.

10. Ibn Abd al-Wahhab, *Kitab at-Tawhid*, p. 85.

11. Mylrea, "The Thin Edge," 17–22.

12. Mrs. E. E. Calverley, "The Arab Woman and the Lady Physician," *Neglected Arabia*, no. 126 (July–September 1923): 5.

13. Edwin Calverley, "Evangelistic Activities at Kuweit," *Neglected Arabia*, no. 92 (January–March 1915): 8–10.

14. Paul Starr, *The Social Transformation of American Medicine* (New York: Basic, 1982), p. 341.

15. Mary Bruins Allison, *Doctor Mary in Arabia*, ed. Sandra Shaw (Austin: University of Texas Press, 1994), p. 76.

16. Al Jawziyya, *Prophetic Medicine*, p. 212.

17. Wahba, *Arabian Days*, p. 37. Here is an example of a healing verbal formula given by Al Jawziyya: "The Holy Prophet said: 'Put your hand in the painful place of your body and say: "In the name of Allah" three times and "I seek refuge with Allah's might and power from the mischief of the harm that afflicted me and that I am aware of, seven times" ' " (*Prophetic Medicine*, p. 228).

18. Qur'an, sura 14, verse 60: "And as for women advanced in years who do not hope for a marriage, it is no sin for them if they put off their clothes without displaying their ornaments; and if they restrain themselves it is better of them; and Allah is Hearing, Knowing" (Shakir, *The Quran*).

19. Elizabeth Dame, "A King's Favorite," *Neglected Arabia* (Inland Arabia Number), no. 208 (January–March 1946): 11. This article is a retrospective look at Najd. The visit described must have occurred around 1933. The Dames left the mission in 1936.

20. Hamad Al-Baadi, "Social Change, Education, and the Roles of Women in Arabia" (Ph.D. diss., Stanford University, 1982), p. 55. *Qira'a* is also the word used to denote women's group prayer meetings.

21. Cornelia Dalenberg, "Unforgettable Patients," *Arabia Calling*, no. 217 (summer 1949): 14.

22. Donald P. Cole, *Nomads of the Nomads: The Al Murrah Bedouin of the Empty Quarter* (Arlington Heights, Ill.: Harlan Davidson, 1975), p. 111.

23. Doughty, *Travels in Arabia Deserta*, 1:301.

24. Eleanor Calverley, "Beauty for Ashes," *Neglected Arabia*, no. 110 (July–September 1919): 3–11.

25. Edwin Calverley, "Where Mullas Are Doctors," *Neglected Arabia*, no. 105 (April/May 1918): 14.

26. Calverley, "Beauty for Ashes," p. 7.

27. Mylrea, "Arab Superstitions," p. 13.

28. Wahba, *Arabian Days*, p. 37.

29. H. R. P. Dickson, *Kuwait and her Neighbors* (London: Allen and Unwin, 1956), p. 440.

30. Wahba, *Arabian Days*, p. 37. The incident is also discussed in Samuel M. Zwemer, "The Use of Amulets Among Moslems," *Neglected Arabia*, no. 72 (January–March 1910): 8–10.

31. Calverley, "Where Mullas are Doctors," pp. 12–13.

32. Doughty, Arabia Deserta, 1:576–577.

33. Hassan Massoudi, *La Calligraphie arabe vivante* (Paris: Flammarion, 1981).

34. See Edwin Calverley, "Where Mullas are Doctors," p. 15; Wahba, *Arabian Days*, p. 37; and Eleanor Calverley, *My Arabian Days and Nights* (New York: Crowell, 1953), p. 89. Sympathetic magic was commonplace among Arab Christians as well. In the town of Qamishli in the Syrian Jezirah, one Christian who could read and write supplemented his income by preparing spells for his fellow townsfolk up until his death in 1975. His skill in writing spells was in demand by both Christians and Muslims, as he would write passages from either holy book. The writings were buried in the ground, tucked under pillows, or hidden in amulets in hope that some desire might be fulfilled. The custom of concealing holy words in amulets also continues in the use of the mezuzah, a small case containing a piece of parchment with verses from Deuteronomy, which is traditionally attached to the doorpost of a Jewish home.

35. Calverley, *Arabian Days and Nights*, p. 89.

36. Wahba, *Arabian Days*, p. 37.

37. John Lewis Burckhardt, *Notes on the Bedouins and Wahabys Collected During His Travels in the East* (London: Henry Colburn and Richard Bentley, 1831), 1:96.

38. Violet Dickson, *Forty Years in Kuwait* (London: Allen and Unwin, 1971), pp. 282–283.

39. For a discussion of filth as a cultural construct, see Mary Douglas *Purity and Danger: An Analysis of the Concepts of Pollution and Taboo* (New York: Ark, 1966).

40. Mark 8:23; John 9:1–7. An Irish folk remedy was "St. Anthony's spit," spit from a fasting mother delivered right into the afflicted area. See Frank McCourt, *Angela's Ashes: A Memoir* (New York: Scribner, 1996), p. 225.

41. Calverley, "Where Mullas are Doctors," p. 16. Calverley was citing al-Bukhari, sahih 7, p. 150 (n.p., n.d.).

42. Al Jawziyya, *Prophetic Medicine*, p. 211.

43. Doughty, *Arabia Deserta*, 1:359.

44. In *Arab of the Desert*, Dickson reported that a woman might bear up to fifteen children, with only three or four surviving (p. 506), and further noted that Bedouin people rarely lived to be fifty years old (p. 354).

45. Paul Harrison to Dr. Stanley Mylrea, Riyadh, January 18, 1919, doc. #57555, Arabian Mission archives, New Brunswick Theological Seminary, New Brunswick, New Jersey.

46. Starr, *Social Transformation of American Medicine*, p. 82.

4. Engaging Spirits

1. Eleanor Calverley, "Beauty for Ashes," *Neglected Arabia*, no. 110 (July–September 1919): 5.

2. Jacob Neusner, "Science and Magic, Miracle and Magic in Formative Judaism: The System and the Difference," in *Religion, Science and Magic in Concert and in Conflict*, ed. Jacob Neusner, Ernest S. Frerichs, and Paul Virgil McCracken Flesher (Oxford: Oxford University Press, 1989), p. 61.

3. Human Rights Watch, "Saudi Arabia: Flawed Justice, the Execution of 'Abd al-karim Mara'i al-Naqshabandi," *Human Rights Watch / Middle East* 9, no. 9 (October 1997). Another execution for witchcraft occurred in 1995, according to "Media Atmospherics: The Debate Over Witchcraft," an unclassified, unpublished U.S. Information Service document dated April 8, 1995.

4. Samuel M. Zwemer, "The Use of Amulets Among Moslems," *Neglected Arabia*, no. 72 (January–March 1910): 7.

5. H. R. P. Dickson, *The Arab of the Desert: Bedouin Life in Kuwait and Saudi Arabia* (London: Allen and Unwin, 1949), p. 505.

6. Cornelia Dalenberg, *Sharifa* (Grand Rapids, Mich.: Eerdmans, 1983), p. 118.

7. Hafiz Wahba, *Arabian Days* (London: Baker, 1964), p. 44.

8. Zwemer, "The Use of Amulets Among Moslems," p. 7.

9. Wahba, *Arabian Days*, p. 44.

10. Ibn Qayyam Al Jawziyya, *Prophetic Medicine*, trans. S. Abi Azar, corr. F. Amira Zrein Matraji (Riyadh: Dar el-Fikr, 1995), pp. 219–221.

11. Dalenberg, *Sharifa*, p. 119. After telling this story, Dalenberg writes that she told the mother that no fish or amulet designed to protect against the evil eye could save a child from sickness or death: "It was Christ in whom she needed to put her trust" (pp. 119–120).

12. This passage is taken from a letter from a missionary of the Arabian Mission, missing the salutation and signature pages, located in the file "Arabian Mission, 1945–46," in the archives of the Arabian Mission at the New Brunswick Theological Seminary.

13. Eleanor Calverley, *My Arabian Days and Nights* (New York: Crowell, 1953), p. 63.

14. Dorothy Van Ess, "Arab Customs," *Arabia Calling*, no. 243 (spring/summer 1956): 16.

15. Zwemer, "The Use of Amulets Among Moslems," p. 7.

16. Wahba, *Arabian Days*, p. 44.

17. Charles M. Doughty, *Travels in Arabia Deserta*, 3d ed. (London, 1936; reprint, New York: Dover, 1979), 1:300. This is still the case in contemporary Saudi Arabia.

18. Wahba, *Arabian Days*, p. 41. Italics mine.

19. In his doctoral dissertation, "The History of Najd Prior to the Wahhabis: A Study of Social, Political, and Religious Conditions in Najd During Three Centuries Preceding the Wahhabi Reform Movement" (University of Washington, 1983), Uwaidah al-Juhany says that itinerant holy men and saints were numerous in Najd, especially in the region of al-Kharj, near Riyadh. Most of them claimed descent from the Prophet Muhammad and went from one town to another pretending to perform miracles, claiming special religious status, helping people with a variety of problems, and accepting their gifts and offerings (pp. 282–283).

20. Quoted in R. Bayly Winder, *Saudi Arabia in the Nineteenth Century* (London: Macmillan, 1965), pp. 12–13.

21. Muhammad ibn Abd al-Wahhab, *Kitab at-Tawhid: Essay on the Unicity of Allah; or, What Is Due to His Creatures*, trans. Ismail Raji al-Faruqi (Damascus: International Islamic Federation of Student Organizations, 1979), ch. 8, p. 29. The complete Hadith reads: "Oh, Ruwayfi'! May you live a long life! Do spread the word that whoever puts a knot in his beard, wears an amulet, or washes himself with the urine of an animal, has nothing to do with me or my religion."

22. Other examples of Hadith cited by Ibn Abd al-Wahhab to condemn the wearing of amulets include the following: "The Prophet saw a man carrying a garment which he claimed protected him against fever; . . . he tore it to pieces recalling the verse '. . . most of them believe in Allah and still practice shirk' " (ch. 7, p. 26).

23. The exception he cites is doing so to cure jealously and insect stings, because these are special cases prescribed by the Prophet. See Ibn Abd al-Wahhab, *Kitab at-Tawhid*, ch. 8, p. 29.

24. Al Umar, a contemporary Saudi religious scholar, has this to say about fortune tellers: "As for those who pretend to know that which is invisible, or foresee what is hidden in the future, they are unbelievers and flagrant liars. Even if what they foretell happens, it only happens by chance. Both Imam Ahmad and al-Hakim related that the Prophet said, 'Whoever goes to a diviner or a fortune teller and believes in what he says, disbelieves in what had been revealed to Muhammad, peace and blessings of Allah be upon him'" ('Abd al-Rahman bin Hamad Al Umar, *Islam: The Religion of Truth* [Riyadh: al-Farazdak, 1974], p. 21). The parallel attitudes toward medicine, healers, and fortune-tellers in Jewish and Muslim scripture are striking. The skills of physicians are portrayed as ineffective in contrast to God's power to heal. In the Old Testament, augury and witchcraft are forbidden in Leviticus 19:26–28, Deuteronomy 18:10–14, and Jeremiah 27:9, and God is presented as the One who knows the future and predetermines it. See Howard Clarke Kee, "Magic and Messiah," in *Religion, Science and Magic in Concert and in Conflict*, ed. Jacob

Neusner, Ernest S. Frerichs, and Paul Virgil McCracken Flesher (Oxford: Oxford University Press, 1989), p. 126.

25. This translation is taken from M. H. Shakir, trans., *The Quran*, 5th ed. (Elmhurst, N.Y.: Tahrike Tarsile Qur'an, 1988).

26. Hans Wehr, *Dictionary of Modern Written Arabic*, ed. Milton Cowan (Ithaca: Cornell University Press, 1966), p. 982. Mohammed Marmaduke Pickthall translates "those who blow on knots" as "the evil of malignant witchcraft" (*The Meaning of the Glorious Koran* [New York: New American Library, 1958], pp. 454–455). The tyer of knots was also interpreted to be a woman by the eighteenth-century Danish traveler Carsten Niebuhr. As Niebuhr wrote after his 1763 journey to Jeddah and towns along the Red Sea and Gulf coasts: "The Arabs still believe in the virtue of enchantments, and in the art of tying and untying the knots of fate. The miserable victim of the diabolical art addresses some physician or some old woman, for the old women are always skilled in sorcery" (*Travels through Arabia and Other Countries in the East*, trans. Robert Heron [Edinburgh, 1792], 2:216.

27. Ibn abd al-Wahhab, *Kitab at-Tawhid*, ch. 24, p. 78. The definition of sorcery as opposed to witchcraft is as blurred in the Hadith as it is in the *Kitab at-Tawhid*. In a later chapter, Ibn Abd al-Wahhab cites the Hadith "Whoever makes a knot and blows on it has committed sorcery, and thereby, shirk" (ch. 25, p. 79).

28. Historically, Wahba explains, such passages were the subject of debate. Some scholars chose to follow the interpretation of the *salaf*, early Muslims who accepted these passages without seeking explanation or philosophical argument. The *khalaf*, or later generations, who were influenced by Greek, Persian, and Indian philosophy, believed that the anthropomorphic passages could not be taken literally and instead had to be considered allegorical and given a rational interpretation that conformed to the total philosophy of the religion. See Wahba, *Arabian Days*, pp. 55–56.

29. Many passages in the Qur'an and Hadith affirm the existence of a host of invisible beings who inhabit the visible world, such as jinn, Satan, and angels. For example, sura 4, verse 136, reads, "O you who believe! Believe in Allah and His Apostle and the Book which He has revealed to His Apostle, and the Book which He revealed before. And whoever disbelieves in Allah and His angels and His apostles and the last day, he indeed strays off into a remote error" (Shakir, *The Quran*). And in sura 82, verses 10–12 say that men's deeds in life are cataloged by spiritual beings that attend the earthly affairs of men: "And most surely there are keepers over you, honorable recorders. They know what you do" (Shakir, *The Quran*). Al Umar cites these passages to show why belief in angels and spirits is a required part of faith (*Islam*, pp. 12–13). In another verse, amorphous beings are present on Judgment Day: "The merciful sat on the throne; wait they until God comes to them, shaded by clouds and attended by angels. On that day the throne of the Lord shall be carried by eight" (Wahba, *Arabian Days*, p. 55).

30. Shakir, *The Quran*; Al Umar, *Islam*, p. 9.

31. Shakir, *The Quran*, sura 20, verse 55; sura 36, verses 78–79.

32. For example, "Ibn 'Umar says: 'I heard 'Umar ibn al-Khattab curse whoever asked questions about things that did not exist" (Ahmad Abd al-Ghafour Attar, *Muhammad ibn Abd al-Wahhab*, trans. Rashid al-Barrawi [Mecca: Mecca Printing and Information, 1979], p. 114). Attar's book received the stamp of approval of the General Presidency for Religious Guidance.

33. Wahba, *Arabian Days*, p. 62.

34. Mrs. L. P. Dame, "A Trip to Central Arabia," *Neglected Arabia*, no. 167 (January–March 1934): 14. In 1979 the continuing insistence on the literal truth of the Qur'an and Hadith was manifest in the conclusion to the attempt to seize the Grand Mosque at Mecca by one who claimed to be the expected Mahdi. The head of the affairs of the Haramain (the two holy places, Mecca and Medina), Shaikh Nassar ibn Rashid, sought to assuage any lingering doubts that the captured perpetrator was not the true Mahdi. The shaikh stated that a large number of ulama hold prophetic tradition concerning the return of the Mahdi to be genuine, and therefore it was necessary to explain publicly the manner in which the real Mahdi would appear according to correct prophetic tradition. He also wanted to explain how these correct traditions were at variance with the traditions employed by those who followed the leaders of the insurrection. The time for the appearance of the expected Mahdi had not yet come, explained Shaikh Nassar, because, according to correct prophetic tradition, "firstly, if he comes, the expected Mahdi will live seven or eight years after six years during which he will be fought by the False Messiah in Damascus. He will be besieged there with his Muslim companions until Jesus, the son of Mary, comes down on the White Dome, carried by two angels." This was explained in both the Arabic and English press in Saudi Arabia, in the December 20, 1979, issue of *Iqraa'*, a weekly newspaper, and in "Sheikh Describes How Mahdi Will Appear," *Arab News*, December 25, 1979, p. 2.

35. For a discussion of supernatural beings in classical literature, see A. S. Tritton, "Spirits and Demons in Arabia," *Journal of the Royal Asiatic Society of Great Britain and Ireland* (October 1934): 715–726. Bedouin near Kuwait and Hasa, Dickson writes, considered burial places dangerous ground because of jinn, and particular trees, such as the boxthorn, were believed to be under the special protection of jinn and thus were never to be cut (*Arab of the Desert*, pp. 537–538). In northeast Saudi Arabia, a four-acre-wide depression caused by a meteorite was believed by the 'Awazim and 'Ujman to be the haunt of jinn (p. 538).

36. Ibn Abd al-Wahhab, *Kitab at-Tawhid*, p. 85.

37. Al Jawziyya, *Prophetic Medicine*, p. 152. Al Jawziyya also quotes a sahih on the authority of Aisha that links witchcraft with women: " 'The Holy Prophet [*saaws*] has been conjured, so that he imagined that he had sexual intercourse with his wives while he hadn't in reality.' This is the paroxysm of witchcraft, comments Al Jawziyya" (p. 151).

38. Ibn Abd al-Wahhab, *Kitab at-Tawhid*, ch. 8, p. 29.

39. Dickson, *Arab of the Desert*, p. 535. Making a love spell with something from the body of the person seeking another's affection was standard throughout the region. An elderly Christian woman in Homs, Syria, told me that she and her girl-friends went to see a Muslim woman spell maker in the 1920s who prescribed adding a few drops of urine to the teapot before serving a loved one.

40. Samuel M. Zwemer, *Studies in Popular Islam: A Collection of Papers Dealing with the Superstitions and Beliefs of the Common People* (New York: Macmillan, 1936), p. 70.

41. Samuel M. Zwemer, *The Influence of Animism on Islam: An Account of Popular Superstitions* (New York: Macmillan, 1920), p. 71. Minnie Dykstra gave this translation, "Take your due, O devil, and the compassionate one will testify against you." As to the nail trimmings and hair clippings, Mrs. Dykstra adds, "Then on resurrection day God will require all these nail-trimmings, and woe to him who has not carefully preserved them" ("Moslem Funeral Customs," *Neglected Arabia*, no. 109 [April–June 1919]: 12–13. According to Zwemer, superstitions connected with trimming the nails are common to Zoroastrianism and Judaism, as in the Haggadah: "Every pious Jew must purify himself and honour the coming holy day by trimming and cleaning the nails beforehand" (*Studies in Popular Islam*, p. 74).

42. John 9:1–7

43. Dickson, *Arab of the Desert*, pp. 513–514.

44. Mrs. Dirk Dykstra, "Life, Language and Religion," *Neglected Arabia*, no. 110 (July–September 1919): p. 18.

45. Dickson, *Arab of the Desert*, pp. 515, 517.

46. Ibid., pp. 535–56.

47. Wahba, *Arabian Days*, pp. 38–39.

48. Doughty, vol. 1, p. 297.

49. Wahba, *Arabian Days*, p. 62; H. St. John Philby, *Heart of Arabia: A Record of Travel and Exploration* (London: Constable, 1922), 2:335.

50. Wahba, *Arabian Days*, p. 62.

51. Dickson, *Arab of the Desert*, p. 329.

52. H. R. P. Dickson, *Kuwait and Her Neighbors* (London: Allen and Unwin, 1956), p. 368.

53. Dickson, *Arab of the Desert*, p. 534.

54. Wahba, *Arabian Days*, pp. 43–44.

55. Al Umar, the modern interpreter of Wahhabi doctrine, also writes that sorcery is still considered to be "a form of unbelief, especially when it includes grave idolatrous deviations. Therefore, whoever practices sorcery, or gives his consent to such an action after knowing that it is atheism is an unbeliever" (*Islam*, p. 49).

56. I. M. Lewis, introduction to *Religion in Context: Cults and Charisma* (Cambridge: Cambridge University Press, 1989), p. ix.

57. At the time of the execution, Riyadh newspapers were full of articles explaining what witchcraft is. The execution was followed by a fatwa from Bin Baz: "Due to the increasing number of magicians in recent days," he began, "I thought it would

be better to clarify their great danger to Islam and Muslims" (*al-Jazirah*, March 12, 1996, as quoted in United States Information Service, "Media Atmospherics: The Debate over Witchcraft," Riyadh, unclassified document dated April 8, 1995). The fatwa was published along with interviews with other prominent religious scholars who agreed that witchcraft is a crime against Islam. The interior minister and brother of the king, Prince Naif, called for a "joint effort by state organs, Islamic scholars, and citizens to combat witch doctors, an important issue as it is related to our faith and health." The prince warned "everybody, including citizens, residents and visitors, against practicing witchcraft" and added that "the recent execution of a witch-doctor in the Kingdom proves the government's determination to fight this wicked act" ("Prince Naif Warns Against Witchcraft," *Arab News*, April 3, 1995, p. 1).

58. Dickson, *Kuwait and Her Neighbors*, p. 438.

59. Mrs. H. G. Van Vlack, "Arab Babies," *Neglected Arabia*, no. 90 (July–September 1914): 8–11.

60. Ruth Jackson, "Glimpses Behind the Veil," *Neglected Arabia*, no. 138 (July–September 1926): 13. In rural areas of Syria it was common for Muslim women to presume the efficacy of Christian holy relics, shrines, and places. I am told by a priest of the Syrian Orthodox Cathedral in Homs that in the 1940s, when he was a seminary student, Muslim women came to the cathedral asking for water from a well in front of the church that they believed to be holy; drinking the water was supposed to have some efficacious quality even though it was unpotable.

61. Storm, "The Mission Doctor Versus Arab Medical Practice," p. 10.

62. Edwin Calverley, "The Trial by Ordeal in Arabia," *Neglected Arabia*, no. 107 (October–December 1918): 2.

63. John Habib, *Ibn Sa'ud's Warriors of Islam* (Leiden: Brill, 1978), p. 30.

64. John Lewis Burckhardt, *Notes on the Bedouins and Wahabys Collected During His Travels in the East* (London: Henry Colburn and Richard Bently, 1831), 1:12.

65. Lady Anne Blunt, *A Pilgrimage to Nejd: The Cradle of the Arab Race* (London: Murray, 1881; reprint, London: Century, 1985), p. 10.

66. Doughty, *Travels*, 2:209.

67. Niebuhr, *Travels through Arabia*, 1:231.

68. Mrs. Dirk Dykstra, "Zeeraan," *Neglected Arabia*, no. 107 (October–December 1918): 23.

69. C. Snouck Hurgronje, *Mekka in the Latter Part of the Nineteenth Century* (Leiden: Brill and Luzac, 1931; reprint, Leiden: Brill, 1970), p. 100.

70. Elisabet Franke, "The Zar in Egypt." *Moslem World* 3, no. 3 (July 1913): 285. Descriptions of the Zar in Cairo specify that chickens were sacrificed.

71. Musk, according to Mrs. Dykstra, was "very definitely and necessarily part of a woman's toilet" in Bahrain ("Zeeraan," p. 17).

72. All the quotations concerning the Zar performance are taken from Dykstra, "Zeeraan," pp. 17–23.

73. According to Fu'ad Khuri, because the Shi'a peasants claim to be the origi-

nal inhabitants of the island, they call themselves Bahrani as opposed to Bahraini, a word they use to refer to the Sunni. Khuri writes that there are theories regarding the historical origins of the Shi'a of Bahrain but that these in fact remain unknown. "The Shia," he says, "are so varied physically and have such a wide range of linguistic peculiarities that they could not possibly be as historically homogeneous as they think they are. More likely they are the original Bahraini 'pot' into which the human relics of invasions and conquests have melted" (Fu'ad Khuri, *Tribe and State in Bahrain: The Transformation of Social and Political Authority in an Arab State* [Chicago: University of Chicago Press, 1980], p. 265 n. 2.

74. Dykstra, "Zeeraan," p. 18.

75. Edwin Calverley to Duncan Black MacDonald, Kuwait, July 1, 1918, Calverley Papers, Hartford Theological Seminary.

76. Edwin Calverley to Duncan Black Macdonald, August 1, 1917, Calverley papers, Hartford Theological Seminary, box 120, #57365, folder #2224.

77. Eleanor Calverley, unpublished manuscript, "Shaytaan," doc. #6666, Calverley papers, Hartford Theological Seminary, pp. 28–29.

78. Calverley to Macdonald, July 1, 1918. Calverley mailed Macdonald photographs of the Zar dancers, which sadly have not survived.

79. In Cairo in 1913 Christian missionaries thought that belief in the Zar was pervasive throughout society, both Christian and Muslim, and one exorcism attended by a missionary in 1913 was in a Coptic home. "Not only women, but also men, may be 'possessed,' and some need exorcisms at intervals of only three weeks. Of course the common people cannot always have such an expensive performance in their own home. They usually go to certain sanctuaries, where these rituals take place on fixed days" (Elisabet Franke, "The Zar in Egypt," *Moslem World* 3, no. 3 [July 1913]: 285). In Cairo, wrote missionary Anna Thompson, "all the best shaikhas were negroes" ("The Woman Question in Egypt," *Moslem World* 4 [1914]: 266–267). Social gatherings for purposes of exorcism existed in other places as well. In Kairouan, Tunisia, for example, women met for what one observer called "a djinn party" (Dahris Martin, *I Know Tunisia* [New York: Ives Washburn, 1943], pp. 55–73). A documentary film of the Zar ceremony in Morocco was made by Elizabeth Warnock Fernea: "Saints and Spirits" (Granada TV, 1977). See also I. M. Lewis, *Ecstatic Religion* (Baltimore: Penguin, 1971), pp. 30–31, p. 85–92.

80. Thompson, "The Woman Question in Egypt," p. 266.

81. Bertram Thomas, *Alarms and Excursions in Arabia* (Indianapolis: Bobbs-Merrill, 1931), pp. 260–61.

82. Snouck Hurgronje, *Mekka*, pp. 100–103.

83. In Ethiopia the cult is known among its members as *wuqabi*, though outsiders call it *zar*, and Zar spirits are considered to be the creation of the Christian God. See Alice Morton, "Dawit: Competition and Integration In an Ethiopian Wuqabi Cult Group," in *Case Studies in Spirit Possession*, ed. Vincent Crapanzano and Vivian Garrison (New York: Wiley, 1977), p. 194.

84. Contemporary scholars recognize the particular rhythms of Zar music in the performances of professional black musicians in Najd, especially at weddings, but this music is performed without the corresponding Zar spirit-possession ceremonies.

85. Lewis, *Ecstatic Religion*, pp. 30–31, p. 85–92. See also Lucie Wood Saunders, "Variants in Zar Experience in an Egyptian Village," *Case Studies in Spirit Possession*, ed. Vincent Crapanzano and Vivian Garrison (New York: Wiley, 1977).

86. One study of the Zar in Ethiopia also shows that the Zar is personally empowering to women. Alice Morton explains the relationship between the Zar and the possessed individual as follows: The initial illness that alerts the possessed person to the presence of the Zar is only the Zar's means of getting that person's attention. Once the spirit has been honored by ceremonial offerings, the individual recovers, and the Zar will come to protect him or her from a variety of evil spirits. "Ultimately, if the accommodation relationship is successful and maintained by both parties, it is believed that the individual will profit insofar as the spirit helps him or her to vanquish enemies, to make the right choices in a wide range of situations, and to predict the behavior of others." (Alice Morton, "Dawit: Competition and Integration in an Ethiopian Wuqabi Cult Group," in *Case Studies in Spirit Possession*, ed. Vincent Crapanzano and Vivian Garrison [New York: Wiley, 1977], pp. 195–196).

A 1961–62 study of the Zar cult in a village in the central Egyptian delta shows that in this village, belief in Zar spirits is general among people, even among those who deny the reality of spirit possession, and that belief in Zar spirits is more widely associated with women than men.

> All the leading men and most others disavow the possibility of possession publicly, yet reveal some degree of concealed belief in that they fear to disobey the spirits' commands to their wives. . . . Women who go regularly or occasionally or have never gone to the Zar express belief that possession occurs. Thus most women do not publicly deny the possibility of possession, while most men do, and the behavior of both suggests an underlying reservoir of belief which may be maintained more easily because of the general understanding that other kinds of spirits exist, affecting people's welfare, and that any illness or misfortune may have spirit causes.
>
> ──────
> (Saunders, "Variants in Zar Experience," p. 179)

Minnie Dykstra also commented on the ambiguous attitude exhibited by men toward the Zar, as in Bahrain she knew men who wore Zar membership rings but at the same time would never admit to actually attending a ritual performance.

87. Dykstra, "Zeeraan," p. 20.

88. Lewis, *Ecstatic Religion*, pp. 43, 41–42.

89. Lucie Saunders, in "Variants in Zar Experience," showed how attendance at Zar ceremonies in an Egyptian delta village was related to social status, as most of the

wealthy women of the village were associated with the Zar societies while poor women joined less consistently and with less enthusiasm. The reasons for this are that wealthy women are limited by a variety of constraints on their behavior, including the frequency and choice of their interpersonal contacts. For them, participation in the Zar cult is one of the few outlets open to them. The Zar gives such women an additional interest and enlarges their sphere of interpersonal activity but also offers a means of manipulating their husbands' behavior through conveying the desires of the Zar to them and getting them to pay for the fulfillment of those desires. Poor women, on the other hand, have more freedom of movement to begin with and less need of a society to bring about social contacts; poor women also tend to have control over expendable household income so that obtaining money is not an appropriate vehicle.

90. In that year Violet Dickson attended a Zar performance in which all the participants were of African extraction.

> Every Thursday night, and some other nights on special occasions, they
> come together in Al Nuban, which is the name given to their meeting-
> place. There are two of these in Kuwait town: the main one in the
> Murqab quarter to the south-west of the town; the lesser one in the
> small eastern quarter known as the Maidan, which, inhabited mostly
> by Persians and Baharinah, is not far from our house.
>
> The house and small courtyard are on a main road, and a striped
> flagpole in one corner of the yard is all that distinguishes the place
> from any ordinary house. As we neared the door the sounds of drums
> and music, accompanied by a peculiar swishing noise, indicated that
> the dances had begun. . . . Many women were on one side of the
> court, and a few men spectators sat against the wall on the opposite
> side. . . . A tall negress beautifully dressed stood beside me and fanned
> me with a palm-leaf fan. The whole air was heavy with incense that
> burnt in a small earthen mould in front of the stringed instrument
> known as a *tamburah*, before which, as if in deep thought, stood an
> old gray-bearded man. Then he turned towards one of the slaves and
> nodded his head several times. The slave got up and came across to the
> tamburah, but then said he did not know how to play it, so a young
> negro took his place. The tamburah has a very sweet sound, like the
> few centre strings of a harp. Three or four drums placed on the
> ground to one side of it were now beaten and the singing began. It
> was a song quite unlike anything I had heard among the Arabs, or
> even among the slaves on the pearling boats.
>
> As the singing went on, men and women got up and danced with
> a curious bowing, jerky movement. . . . One of the men wore a sort
> of skirt made of many dry lambs' hooves hanging from a broad belt
> round his waist. His swaying to the music caused the hooves to strike

each other and give out the swishing noise we had heard before we entered.

On either side of the courtyard were two rooms. In one the men made coffee, the other being reserved for women who wanted to go in and rest and smoke. No woman may attend this ceremony if she is unclean; should she attempt to do so a string of the tamburah would snap at once, it is said.

———

(Dickson, *Kuwait and Her Neighbors*, pp. 557–559)

This was clearly a Zar ceremony: the instruments being played and the skirt of hooves Dickson described are the same mentioned by Edwin Calverley in 1918 in his discussion of the Zar in Kuwait. Yet Violet Dickson appears not to have understood the significance of the ceremony she was attending, and she referred to it as "an old African voodoo custom" (p. 557). As she described it, there were no Arab participants, and, as before, the majority of people in attendance were women. The musicians, however, appear to have been men. This marginality of the Zar is also in contrast to the Zar in Bahrain of the teens and twenties, when the Zar was so well integrated into indigenous Arab women's society that the Bahrain missionaries did not distinguish it as a ceremony imported by or particular to Ethiopians or Sudanese.

91. Abd al-Mahmud Al-Zubayr, *Kitab irshad al-badw lil-din an-nabawi* (Book of guidance for the Bedouins in the prophetic religion), pamphlet (Mecca, 1976), quoted in *Women's Medicine: The Zar-Bori Cult in Africa and Beyond*, ed. I. M. Lewis, Ahmed al-Safi, and Sayyid Hurreiz (Edinburgh: Edinburgh University Press, 1991), p. 236.

92. Zubaydah Ashkanani, "Zar in a Changing World: Kuwait," in *Women's Medicine: The Zar-Bori Cult in Africa and Beyond*, ed. I. M. Lewis, Ahmed al-Safi, and Sayyid Hurreiz (Edinburgh: Edinburgh University Press, 1991), p. 223.

93. Khuri, *Tribe and State in Bahrain*.

94. This occurred as recently as 1892, well after the bacillus that causes tuberculosis was isolated. See *Vampires of New England* (Connecticut Public Television, 1966).

95. Lewis, *Cults and Charisma*.

96. Mary Douglas, *Purity and Danger: An Analysis of the Concepts of Pollution and Taboo* (New York: Ark, 1966), p. 94.

97. Cynthia Nelson, "Self, Spirit Possession and World View: An Illustration from Egypt," *International Journal of Social Psychiatry* 17 (1971): 194–209.

98. Susan Slyomovics shows how a Zar ceremony in Egypt parodies the wedding experience, reversing the positions of power held by men and women, such that women who are normally absent during contract signing initiate the Zar trance, choose the shaikha, and plan the event ("Ritual Grievance: The Language of Women?" *Women and Performance: A Journal of Feminist Theory* 5, no. 1 (1990): 56.

99. This is a conclusion of I. M. Lewis, but the use of the Zar as a means of manipulating a man in order to experience power was also observed earlier by C. Snouck Hurgronje, Minnie Dykstra, and other later anthropologists.

100. Judith Hoch-Smith and Anita Spring, eds., *Women in Ritual and Symbolic Roles* (New York: Plenum, 1978), p. 15.

5. When Words Fail

1. Mrs. Dirk Dykstra, "Life, Language, Religion," *Neglected Arabia*, no. 110 (July–September 1919): 17–18.

2. In a letter written by Harrison to his colleague Dr. Mylrea back in Kuwait, Harrison wrote, "The whole town was sick, so much so that the bodies were carried out on donkeys and camels two to a donkey and [illegible] to a camel" (Paul Harrison to Dr. Stanley Mylrea, Riyadh, January 18, 1919, doc. #57555, Arabian Mission archives, New Brunswick Theological Seminary, New Brunswick, New Jersey).

3. Dr. Eleanor Calverley's medical reports from Kuwait are in the collection of her correspondence and papers located at the Hartford Theological Seminary.

4. Paul Starr, *The Social Transformation of American Medicine* (New York: Basic, 1982), pp. 49–50.

5. Eleanor Calverley, *My Arabian Days and Nights* (New York: Crowell, 1953), pp. 28–29.

6. "Report of Kuwait Women's Medical Work, 1913–1914," doc. #69825, Hartford Theological Seminary.

7. Mary Bruins Allison, "Hospital Experience in Kuwait," *Church Herald*, February 11, 1944.

8. Calverley, *Arabian Days*, pp. 88–89.

9. Cornelia Dalenberg, *Sharifa* (Grand Rapids, Mich.: Eerdmans, 1983), p. 36.

10. Since the problem of salt packing was noted by new generations of missionary doctors in Kuwait and Bahrain right up to about 1950, I asked a few Bahraini women of my acquaintance, as well as a few Saudi women, if they knew of the procedure. None did. I was told, however, that midwives prepare a salt bath for the postpartum woman to soak in.

11. Howard Haggard, *Devils, Drugs, and Doctors: The Story of the Science of Healing from Medicine Man to Doctor* (New York: Blue Ribbon, 1929), p. 88.

12. Ida Patterson Storm, "Touring Troubles," *Arabia Calling*, no. 218 (autumn/winter 1949): 7.

13. Anna M. Harrison, "Women of the Interior," *Neglected Arabia*, no. 208 (January–March 1946): 7.

14. Anna M. Harrison, "Desert Diary," *Neglected Arabia*, no. 198 (October–December 1942): 14. I asked a number of Syrian woman who gave birth in Syria in the 1940s and 1950s if they were aware of the salt-packing technique, and none had ever heard of it. They did report, however, that Syrian midwives use salt to

cleanse the folds in the baby's skin after birth and lemon juice to clean the baby's eyes; the midwife in Homs, Syria, they said, was always an old woman.

15. Amy E. Zwemer, "Among the Sick in the Hospital Wards," *Neglected Arabia*, no. 77 (April–June 1911): 17.

16. Harrison, "Women of the Interior," p. 7.

17. H. R. P. Dickson, *The Arab of the Desert: Bedouin Life in Kuwait and Saudi Arabia* (London: Allen and Unwin, 1949), pp. 177–178. Carsten Niebuhr wrote that in Cairo the women who perform female circumcision were also midwives and the custom was prevalent in Egypt among both Copts and "Arabs," as well as in Oman and Ethiopia among the Christians. In Cairo, at the home of a "nobleman," Niebuhr records that he asked how the operation was performed, and his host brought in a young girl, showed him the girl's circumcision in front of the servants, and allowed him to sketch a picture of it (*Travels through Arabia and Other Countries in the East*, trans. Robert Heron [Edinburgh, 1792], 2:250–251.

18. Dickson, *Arab of the Desert*, p. 177.

19. H. St. John Philby, *Heart of Arabia: A Record of Travel and Exploration* (London: Constable, 1922), 2:220.

20. H. St. John Philby, *The Empty Quarter, Being a Description of the Great South Desert of Arabia Known as Rub' al Khali* (New York: Henry Holt, 1933), pp. 81–82.

21. Aisha Mohamed Almana, "Economic Development and Its Impact on the Status of Women in Saudi Arabia"(Ph.D. diss., University of Colorado at Boulder, 1981), p. 209.

22. Dickson, *Arab of the Desert*, p. 176.

23. Charles M. Doughty, *Travels in Arabia Deserta*, 3d ed. (London, 1936; reprint, New York: Dover, 1979), 1:437.

24. Dickson, *Arab of the Desert*, pp. 176–177.

25. Almana, "Economic Development," p. 209.

26. Doughty, *Travels*, 1:387.

27. See Jonathan Berkey, "Female Excision and Cultural Accommodation," *International Journal of Middle East Studies* 28, no. 1 (February 1996): 19–38, for a discussion of the historical connections between religion and female circumcision.

28. Quoted in Nahid Toubia, *Female Genital Mutilation* (New York: Women, Ink., 1993), p. 31.

29. Doughty, *Travels*, 1:437.

30. Edwin Calverley, "Where Mullas Are Doctors," *Neglected Arabia*, no. 105 (April–June 1918): 17.

31. Paul Harrison, *The Arab at Home* (New York: Crowell, 1924), p. 308

32. Dickson, *Arab of the Desert*, p. 511.

33. Elizabeth Dame, "A King's Favorite," *Neglected Arabia* (Inland Arabia Number), no. 208 (January–March 1946): 10–12.

34. Hafiz Wahba, *Arabian Days* (London: Baker, 1964), p. 43.

35. Dr. Stanley Mylrea, "The Enemy at the Gates," *Neglected Arabia*, no. 117 (April–June 1921): 6.

36. Wahba, *Arabian Days*, p. 38.

37. Calverley, "Where Mullas Are Doctors," p. 17.

38. Dickson, *Arab of the Desert*, p. 511.

39. Calverley, "Where Mullas are Doctors," p. 17.

40. Violet Dickson, *Forty Years in Kuwait* (London: Allen and Unwin, 1971), p. 105.

41. Doughty, *Travels*, 1:485.

42. Starr, *Social Transformation of American Medicine*, p. 190.

43. Doughty, *Travels*, 1:255.

44. Samuel M. Zwemer, *Arabia: The Cradle of Islam* (New York: Revell, 1900), p. 283.

45. Mrs. H. G. Van Vlack, "Arab Babies," *Neglected Arabia*, no. 90 (July–September 1914).

46. Wahba, *Arabian Days*, p. 40–41.

47. C. Snouck Hurgronje, *Mekka in the Latter Part of the Nineteenth Century* (Leiden: Brill and Luzac, 1931; reprint, Leiden: Brill, 1970), p. 100.

48. Calverley, *Arabian Days*, pp. 97–98;

49. Wahba, *Arabian Days*, p. 39.

50. Dickson, *Arab of the Desert*, p. 51.

51. For the same reason, at least one contemporary Saudi jurist considers that "if a husband sucks breast milk from his wife then their marriage is nullified," for they become as mother and child. "Our Dialogue," a weekly advice column in the Riyadh *Arab News*, April 22, 1983.

52. Dickson, *Arab of the Desert*, p. 160.

53. Philby, *Empty Quarter*, p. 75.

54. John Lewis Burckhardt, *Notes on the Bedouins and Wahabys Collected During His Travels in the East* (London: Henry Colburn and Richard Bently, 1831), 1:262.

55. Harrison, *Arab at Home*, p. 308.

56. Doughty, *Travels*, 1:173–174.

57. Harrison, *Arab at Home*, p. 311.

58. Dickson, *Arab of the Desert*, p. 160.

59. I observed the same technique in Riyadh in 1982.

60. Wahba, *Arabian Days*, p. 41.

61. Dickson, *Arab of the Desert*, p. 504.

62. Harrison, *Arab at Home*, p. 68.

63. Wahba, *Arabian Days*, pp. 38, 121–127.

64. Doughty, *Travels*, 2:229.

65. Carlo Guarmani, *Northern Nejd: A Journey from Jerusalem to Anaiza in Qasim* (London: Argonaut, 1938), pp. 36–37.

66. *Providence Journal*, November 1, 1987.

67. Harrison, *Arab at Home*, p. 312.

68. W. H. Storm, "The Mission Doctor Versus Arab Medical Practice," *Church Herald*, February 6, 1942.

69. A vivid description of the amputation of a hand is contained in Cornelia Dalenberg, *Sharifa* (Grand Rapids, Mich.: Eerdmans, 1983), pp. 176–178.

70. Harrison, *Arab at Home*, p. 311.

71. Harrison, *Arab at Home*, p. 309–10; Wahba, *Arabian Days*, p. 36.

72. Burckhardt, *Notes*, 1:90–91.

73. Doughty, *Travels*, 1:254.

74. Dickson, *Arab of the Desert*, p. 507.

75. Wahba, *Arabian Days*, p. 45.

76. H. St. John Philby, *Arabia of the Wahhabis* (London: Cass, 1977), pp. 254–255.

77. Calverley, *Arabian Days and Nights*, p. 144.

78. Mrs. Stanley Mylrea, "Arab Superstitions about Diseases and Quackery in Medicine," *Neglected Arabia*, no. 125 (April–June 1923): 13–15.

79. Harrison, *Arab at Home*, pp. 307–308.

80. Starr, *Social Transformation of American Medicine*, p. 47.

81. Wahba, *Arabian Days*, p. 43.

82. Harrison, *Arab at Home*, p. 307.

83. Starr, *Social Transformation of American Medicine*, p. 38.

84. Jalal ad-Din Abd ar-Rahman As-Suyuti, *As-Suyuti's Medicine of the Prophet*, trans. Cyril Elgood (London: Ta-Ha, 1997), p. 147.

85. Cited in W. Norman Leak, "Medicine and the Traditions," *Neglected Arabia*, no. 125 (April–June 1923): 4.

86. Ibn Qayyam Al Jawziyya, *Prophetic Medicine*, trans. S. Abi Azar, corr. F. Amira Zrein Matraji (Riyadh: Dar el-Fikr, 1995), pp. 219–220.

87. The Hadith prescribing salt and water to cure a wound reads: "He asked for a vessel containing salt and water. He poured it on the stung place, reciting, 'Say He is Allah, Alone'; along with the Muawithatain suras [the suras of seeking refuge in God] until the pain was soothed" (Al Jawziyya, *Prophetic Medicine*, p. 217).

88. Wahba, *Arabian Days*, p. 42.

89. Leak, "Medicine and the Traditions," p. 3.

90. Another rendition of this Hadith replaces the "scratch of scarification" with "a scratch for the purpose of cupping" (Al Jawziyya, *Prophetic Medicine*, p. 59).

91. Leak, "Medicine and the Traditions," p. 4. Burckhardt had noted the same medical practice: "The Arabs never bleed by opening a vein; but in cases of violent head-aches they draw a few drams of blood, by making, with a knife, small incisions in the skin of the forehead" (*Notes*, 1:94).

92. Calverley, "Where Mullas are Doctors," pp. 16–17. The same Hadith is incorporated into Al Jawziyya, *Prophetic Medicine*, p. 131.

93. Doughty, *Travels*, 1:358.

94. Harrison, *Arab at Home*, p. 309.

95. Al Jawziyya, *Prophetic Medicine*, p. 60: "I forbid my community to use cautery."

96. Dickson, *Arab of the Desert*, p. 507.

97. Storm, "The Mission Doctor.."

98. Wahba, *Arabian Days*, p. 36.

99. Zwemer, "Among the Sick," p. 20. Doughty saw both men and women perform cautery on themselves, but this may or may not have been related to knowledge of Prophetic medicine: "There is also many a bold spirit among the Aarab, of men and women, that being hurt, snatching a brand from the hearth, will sear his wounded flesh, till the fire be quenched in the suffering fibre: and they can endure pain (necessitous persons, whose livelihood is as a long punishment,) with constant fortitude" (Doughty, *Travels*, 1:359).

99. Storm, "The Mission Doctor," p. 10.

100. Leak, "Medicine and the Traditions," p. 4.

101.

102. Rev. L. J. Shafer, "Dr. Harrison's Visit to Riadh and Its Significance," *Neglected Arabia*, no. 103 (October–December 1917): 15–16.

103. Judith Leavitt, *Childbearing in America, 1750–1950* (New York: Oxford University Press, 1986), pp. 154–55.

104. Judith Barrett Litoff, *American Midwives: 1860 to the Present* (Westport, Conn.: Greenwood, 1978; reprint, Westport, Conn.: Greenwood, 1985), p. 69.

105. Leavitt, *Brought to Bed*, pp. 154–55.

Conclusion:
Community, Gender, and the Spiritual Experience

1. Dale F. Eickelman and James Piscatori, eds., *Muslim Travellers: Pilgrimage, Migration, and the Religious Imagination* (Berkeley: University of California Press, 1990), p. 12.

2. Jacob Neusner, "Science and Magic, Miracle and Magic in Formative Judaism: The System and the Difference," in *Religion, Science and Magic in Concert and Conflict*, ed. Jacob Neusner, Ernest S. Frerichs, and Paul Virgil McCracken Flesher (Oxford: Oxford University Press, 1989), p. 61.

3. Jacob Neusner, "Thematic or Systematic Description: The Case of Mishnah's Division of Women," in *Method and Meaning in Ancient Judaism* (Missoula, Mont.: Scholars, 1979), p. 99, quoted in Denise L. Carmody, "Judaism," in *Women in World Religions*, ed. Arvind Sharma (Albany: State University of New York Press, 1987), p. 195.

4. Michelle Zimbalist Rosaldo, "A Theoretical Overview," in *Woman, Culture and Society*, ed. Michelle Zimbalist Rosaldo and Louise Lamphere (Stanford: Stanford University Press, 1974; reprint, Stanford: Stanford University Press, 1993), p. 32.

5. Keith Thomas, *Religion and the Decline of Magic* (New York: Scribners, 1971).

6. Judith Hoch-Smith and Anita Spring, eds., *Women in Ritual and Symbolic Roles* (New York: Plenum, 1978), p. 15.

Epilogue

1. I am grateful to Dr. Abd-Allah S. Al-Uthaimin, secretary general of the King Faisal International Prize, for reviewing Ibn Abd al-Wahhab's text on veiling with me. See Muhammad ibn Abd al-Wahhab, "Bab sitru al-'awrah," in *Mu'alafat Al Shaikh al-Imam Muhammad ibn 'Abd al-Wahhab* (The collected works of Imam Muhammad ibn Abd al-Wahhab) (Riyadh: Muhammad bin Sa'ud University, 1981), pp. 105–108.

2. Contemporary commentators differ on the question of covering the face, as the following examples illustrate. Bin Baz, head of the Supreme Council of Scholars, addressing a woman's group, discussed how promoting modesty practices is a duty:

> Whoever among the women sees her sister or neighbor or relative or brother or father or uncle commit some wrongful deed should condemn the deed and provide advice. Moreover, if she sees another woman alone with a man, or if she notices laxity in performing prayer or some other wrongful act, she must offer advice for the sake of God, whether the other woman went out brazenly dressed or mixed with strange men . . . or anything else of this kind. It is the duty of a woman not to show men her beauty or charms, and not to be too complaisant of speech. She must guard her modesty [*al-hishma*] and wear the veil [*al-hijab*].

At the same forum, bin Baz is asked whether a woman may ask for a divorce because she wishes to wear the veil (hijab) but her husband refuses to allow it. The shaikh tells the woman that "the husband doesn't have the right to force her to commit such grave disobedience and temptation [fitna] against God, because," the shaikh repeats, "God says 'when ye ask women for anything ye want, ask them from behind a screen [hijab].' Women are not to show their charms to men because that is a great temptation [fitna] for the men. The wife must not obey her husband in this regard and she can ask for divorce on these grounds" ("Shaikh bin Baz fi jami'a an-nahda," *al-Riyadh*, December 12, 1981). Another writer in the Saudi press explains Islamic dress as the Prophet's answer to the clothing that women wore during the *jahiliya* [the age of ignorance before Islam]. Before Islam, he imagines, women used to wear tight dresses that allowed their breasts to protrude and revealed the shape of their bodies. "Therefore the Prophet advised his women to wear a long abbaya when they went out of their house, which they should place on top of the head and let fall over the front [of their bodies] in such a way that the hair, part of the face, neck, and breast are concealed and all the body is wrapped entirely in it without revealing its shape" (Hiyam Mulqi, "Ashya 'an al-milabis al-Islamiyya," *al-Riyadh*, August 29, 1981, p. 9). The verse on which this description of proper Islamic dress is based is Qur'an, sura 33, verse 59: "O Prophet! say to your wives and your daugh-

is careful to preserve it, out of mutual desire to achieve more good
Islam and for those who profess it.

mad Abd al-Ghafour Attar, *Muhammad ibn Abd al-Wahhab*, trans. Rashid al-
rawi [Mecca: Mecca Printing and Information, 1979], pp. 73–82)

Al Rashid rulers in Ha'il also supported a morals police force that served
ministers of the religion" who preach in the Friday mosque (Charles M.
Travels in Arabia Deserta, 2 vols., 3d ed. [London, 1936; reprint, New York:
79], 2:396). Pursuing their duties in Jeddah in 1806, when the Wahhabis
ntrol, the mutawwa'in were observed by a Spaniard from Cadiz named
Badia-y-Leblich to be "constables for the punctuality of prayers, almost
with an enormous staff in their hand, [who] were ordered to shout, to
to drag people by the shoulders to force them to take part in public
ve times a day" (quoted in Peter Brent, *Far Arabia: Explorers of the Myth*
Weidenfeld and Nicolson, 1977], p. 69).

erily he among you who lives [long] will see great controversy, so you
to my sunna and to the sunna of the rightly-guided Rashidite Caliphs.
hem stubbornly. Beware of newly invented matters, for every invented
n innovation and every innovation is a going astray" (An-Nawawi, *Forty*
94).

kir, *The Quran*, sura 3, verse 110. There are Hadith that support the con-
mmunal responsibility as well. The *Forty Hadith* of An-Nawawi, for exam-
ection that has been widely circulated in the Arabian peninsula since at
id-nineteenth century, includes the following: "Whosoever of you sees
ion, let him change it with his hand; and if he is not able to do so, then
ngue; and if he is not able to do so, then with his heart—and that is the
faith" (p. 110). Another Hadith with similar meaning, "Everyone of you
rd and everyone is responsible for his subjects," was included in a Wah-
ar distributed as missionary literature during the Ikhwan movement; see
verley, "The Doctrines of the Arabian 'Brethren,'" *Moslem World* 11, no. 4
921): 364–376.

the height of success of the first Wahhabi empire in the early nineteenth
e treatises of Ibn Abd al-Wahhab were examined by shaikhs of the al-
the reform movement that had sprung from Najd was declared to evi-
compatibility with Islamic orthodoxy as understood by the Sunni ulama
ee Sir Harford Jones Brydges, Bart., *An Account of the Transactions of His*
ission to the Court of Persia in the Years 1807–11, to Which Is Appended a Brief
e Wahauby, 2 vols. (London: James Bohn: 1834), 2:111–112.

wearing of gold and silk is forbidden according to a *sahih* (story from
t confirmed to be true) related on the authority of al-Bara ibn Azib:

---

ters and the women of the believers that they let down upon them their over-garments; this will be more proper, that they may be known, and thus they will not be
given trouble; and Allah is Forgiving, Merciful" (M. H. Shakir, trans., *The Quran*, 5th
ed [Elmhurst, N.Y.: Tahrike Tarsile Qur'an, 1988]). In an advice column in the English-language *Arab News*, written for an audience of foreign Muslims, most of whom
come from places such as the Philippines, Pakistan, Palestine, Syria, Sudan, and
Egypt, where veiling is either unknown or is no longer in general use, an inquirer
is told that there is no religious imperative to cover the face. "In the case of having
unusually blue eyes which attract attention," a woman asks, "the question has aris-
en as to whether I should veil my face to protect my soul as well as the souls of my
Muslim brothers, or whether Islamic dress is all that is required?" The author of the
column answers,

> Islam dictates that women should dress themselves modestly and prop-
> erly in any situation where they may mix with or be seen by men. A
> woman should cover herself allowing no part of her body to be seen
> except her face and hands. Her immediate relatives such as her broth-
> ers, uncles and nephews may see more of her body within the recog-
> nized limits of propriety. If, however, a woman does not observe this
> injunction and lets more than the permitted parts of her body be seen
> she commits a serious sin, for which she is liable to be punished by
> Allah unless He, out of His mercy, forgives her.

As to her particular problem, the author writes,

> Islamic dress is all that is required from women generally, whether
> they are attractive and pretty or not. Only in those few individual
> cases where Islamic dress is known for certain not to prevent what is
> termed *fitna* in Arabic, then the veil is recommended. What is meant
> by *fitna* here is causing men to look persistently or repeatedly at the
> woman concerned. If, however, the cause of such persistent glances
> can be removed or hidden without resorting to the veil then such a
> remedy is perfectly acceptable. . . . I would like to say also that even in
> cases of fitna the veil remains voluntary, although a woman who wears
> it to prevent fitna will, Allah willing, receive ample reward.

What is the shaikh's solution? "It seems to me that in this particular case wearing
tinted spectacles may help the questioner and provide an easy answer" (Adil Salahi,
"Islam in Perspective," *Arab News*, February 26, 1982).

3. Hamad Al-Baadi, "Social Change, Education, and the Roles of Women in Arabia" (Ph.D. diss, Stanford University, 1982), pp. 31–32.

4. Muhammad bin Abdul-Aziz al-Musnad, comp., *Islamic Fatawa Regarding Women*
(Riyadh: Darussalam, 1996), pp. 28, 45.

5. Fu'ad Khuri, *Tribe and State in Bahrain: The Transformation of Social and Political Authority in an Arab State* (Chicago: University of Chicago Press, 1980), p. 147.

6. An article revealing striking similarities in gender ideologies between Burma and Saudi Arabia discusses this point about the disparity between ideologies and practice with reference to women in Burmese society and to Buddhism. See Melford E. Spiro, "Gender Hierarchy in Burma: Cultural, Social and Psychological Dimensions," in *Sex and Gender Hierarchies*, ed. Barbara Diane Miller (Cambridge: Cambridge University Press, 1993), pp. 316–333.

7. Dr. Thurayya al-Urayyid, "Limited Opportunities," *al-Jazirah* (Riyadh), June 9, 1997, p. 5.

8. Firdaws Abu al-Qasim, "Work Is No Luxury," *al-Riyadh*, December 17, 1996, p. 4.

9. Hasin al-Bunyan, "Interview with Muhammad Bin Ibrahim Bin Jubayr, Speaker of the Shura Council in Saudi Arabia," *al-Sharq al-Awsat*, July 6, 1997, p. 4. "Out of the question" was the response given by Muhammad Bin Ibrahim Bin Jubayr to a question about women being invited to join the council.

10. Hasan Bin As'd Bin 'Abd-Aziz Bin Sa'id, "The Desired Role of Saudi Women in Development," *al-Jazirah*, December 18, 1996, p. 32; and al-Bunyan, "Interview with Muhammad Bin Ibrahim Bin Jubayr," p. 4.

11. Mai Yamani, "Women in Saudi Arabia," in *Feminism and Islam: Legal and Literary Perspectives*, ed. Mai Yamani (New York: New York University Press, 1996), p. 279.

12. *Al-Nadwa*, September 1, 1994, pp. 1, 5.

13. Abubaker A. Bagader, professor of sociology, Abd al-Aziz University, Jeddah, Saudi Arabia, "Saudi Women's New Public Roles: Can Society Adjust?" a talk given on November 20, 1997, at the Watson Institute, Brown University, Providence, Rhode Island.

14. For a discussion of the effects of economic restructuring on women, see Val Moghadam, *Women, Work, and Economic Reform in the Middle East and North Africa* (Boulder, Colo.: Rienner, 1998).

Appendix

1. R. Bayly Winder, *Saudi Arabia in the Nineteenth Century* (London: Macmillan, 1965), pp. 23–24.

3. The best discussion of the geography of Najd and the relationship among ecology, settled society, and pastoral nomadism is Christine Moss Helms, *The Cohesion of Saudi Arabi: Evolution of Political Identity* (Baltimore: Johns Hopkins University Press, 1981), pp. 29–60.

4. Barclay Raunkiaer, *Through Wahabiland on Camelback* (New York: Praeger, 1969), p. 26.

5. H. St. John Philby, *Heart of Arabia: A Reco* Constable, 1922), 2:112.

6. Charles M. Doughty, *Travels in Arabia Dese* New York: Dover, 1979), 2:319, also glossary,

7. Hamad Al-Baadi, "Social Change, Educati bia" (Ph.D. diss., Stanford University, 1982), p.

8. Obedience to the Muslim ruler as a religio the Prophet Muhammad's farewell sermon, and al-Wahhab from the work of his fourteenth Taimiyya. An-Nawawi's Hadith collection underg the ruled: "The Messenger of Allah (may the bless gave us a sermon by which our hearts were filled We said, 'O Messenger of Allah, it is as though us.' He said, 'I counsel you to fear Allah (may H obedience even if a slave becomes your leader.' trans. Ibrahim Ezzedin and Denys Johnson-Davie 1976], p. 94). Obedience to the ruler as a religio produced by contemporary Saudi scholars empl example, in one book published by the state-fun ance, the author says, "Allah commanded the Mu selves an Imam to be their ruler. Muslims should of authority. They should also unite in one nation lowed to disobey their rulers or leaders except them to commit a sin or an action contrary to th Rahman bin Hamad Al Umar, *Islam: The Religion* yadh: Department of Religious Guidance], p. 4 Muhammad ibn Abd al-Wahhab and the family temporary literature distributed by the Ministry Saudi Arabia, which emphasizes the unique capa correct Islamic practice in Arabia:

> The Wahhabi movement rested on the S
> They were one mind and one hand in g
> peace and war. . . . Wahhabi governmen
> one and the same designation. Ibn Abd
> one hand, one heart, and one mind. The
> practice. . . . This union between the tw
> ing their lifetime, and it survived. The u
> strength to Islam and a source of power
> tween the two families has remained int
> strong as it was between Ibn Abd al-Wal

The Messenger of God, peace be upon him, enjoined on us seven rules and forbade us seven actions: he enjoined on us to visit the sick, to attend the funeral of the dead, to wish health to one when he sneezes, to keep one's oath, to help others keep their paths, to accept an invitation (to a meal), and to defend the oppressed. And he forbade our wearing gold rings, drinking from silver vessels, using carpets and saddles of beasts' skins, wearing dresses of silk, or with alternate stripes of silk and linen as well as dresses of pure silk and brocades.

(Omar A. Farrukh, trans., *Ibn Taimiyya on On Public and Private Law; or, Public Policy in Islamic Jurisprudence* [Beirut: Khayats, 1966], p. 106)

14. Muhammad Ali al-Khuli, *The Light of Islam* (Riyadh: al-Farazdak, 1981), p. 96. "A man cannot wear silk or gold according to Islam," Attar writes. "Wahhabis equally forbid wearing silk and gold. . . . In this they introduce nothing of their own, the prohibition belongs to Allah alone" (*Muhammad ibn Abd al-Wahhab*, p. 155).

15. Al Umar, *Islam*, p. 50. Male circumcision is held to be Sunna, but there is no reference to circumcision in either the Qur'an or the Hadith. "There is no authentic account of the circumcision of Muhammad, but it is asserted by some writers that he was born circumcised. In the sahih of al Bukhari, there are three traditions relating to circumcision: 'Abu Hurairah relates that the Prophet said one of the observances of Fitrah is circumcision'; 'Abu Hurairah relates that the Prophet said that Abraham was circumcised when he was eighty years old'; and ibn Jubair relates that it was asked of ibn Abbas, 'How old were you when the Prophet died?' He said, 'I was circumcised in the days when it occurred' " (Thomas Patrick Hughes, *A Dictionary of Islam, Being a Cyclopedia of the Doctrines, Rites, Ceremonies, and Customs, Together with the Technical and Theological Terms, of the Muhammadan Religion* [1885; reprint, Delhi: Oriental, 1973], p. 57). The earliest known reference to circumcision among Muslims is contained in a late Umayyad Christian text that records a dispute between a monk and a follower of Emir Maslama. In this dispute, the Arab identifies circumcision and sacrifice as the commandments of Abraham to be observed in the new religion. See Patricia Crone and Michael Cook, *Hagarism: The Making of the Islamic World* (Cambridge: Cambridge University Press, 1977), pp. 12–13.

16. These are questions taken up by Ibn Abd al-Wahhab in his fatwas. They are also issues addressed by contemporary religious authorities in Saudi Arabia in the media.

17. Ameen Rihani, *Maker of Modern Arabia* (Boston: Houghton Mifflin, 1928), p. 225.

18. Raunkaier, *Through Wahabiland*, p. 44.

19. See Ahmad Mustafa Abu Hakima, *History of Eastern Arabia, 1750–1800: The Rise and Development of Bahrain and Kuwait* (Beirut: Khayats, 1965), pp. 39, 42. Bar-

clay Raunkiaer, the Danish traveler who journeyed to Najd in 1912, also observed that Zubair was a Najdi town. Of the approach from Basra to Zubair, he wrote, "The distance of 18 kilometres dividing the towns takes you abruptly out of Irak, in cultural respects akin to Persia, to a definitely Arabian and Wahhabi desert town, Zober. . . . The most part of the inhabitants of the town is made up of Najdi Arab and especially of men engaged in caravan trade. In consequence the name of Zober is better known in Nejd than that of Basrah" (*Through Wahabiland*, p. 25).

20. Gerrit J. Pennings, "Kuweit: 'The Little Walled Town,' " *Neglected Arabia*, no. 92 (January–March 1915): 4–6.

21. H. R. P. Dickson, *Kuwait and Her Neighbors* (London: Allen and Unwin, 1956), p. 40.

22. Gerrit Pennings of the Kuwait mission wrote, "The mixture of many different races which is so characteristic of the other Gulf cities is far less prominent here. . . . Life here therefore most nearly resembles that which exists in the towns of the interior" (Pennings, "Kuweit," pp. 4–6).

23. Emile Nakhleh, *Bahrain: Political Development in a Modernizing Society* (Lexington, Mass.: Heath, Lexington Books, 1976), pp. 8–9.

24. See n. 77 of ch. 5.

25. Fu'ad Khuri, *Tribe and State in Bahrain: The Transformation of Social and Political Authority in an Arab State* (Chicago: University of Chicago Press, 1980), p. 4.

26. Bahrain's location brought it into the rivalry among European and Gulf powers over control of shipping in the Gulf waters. During most of the sixteenth century, Bahrain, along with Hormuz and Musqat, was under the control of the Portuguese, and in 1602 it was captured from the Portuguese by the Persians under Shah Abbas. During the first half of the seventeenth century, the Portuguese lost Basra to the Turks and Musqat to the sultan of Oman, and as the Portuguese hegemony in the Gulf faded, it was replaced by the Dutch, who until around 1765 became almost as powerful in the Gulf as the Portuguese had been. In spite of the long history of European intervention in the Gulf, neither the Portuguese or Dutch presence left traceable effects on the society of Bahrain. See John Marlowe, *The Persian Gulf in the Twentieth Century* (London: Cresset, 1962), pp. 7–8.

27. British control in the Gulf began with a firman (decree or command) issued by the Persian ruler to the British East India Company in about the year 1763 that permitted Bushire to become a company station, gave the British company a monopoly of the import of woolens into Persia, freedom from all taxes, and promised that no other European nation would be allowed to establish a trading station at Bushire as long as the British remained there. Harassment of shipping in the Gulf had led the British in 1820 to negotiate a treaty with shaikhs of the "Pirate Coast" that obligated the shaikhs to refrain from piracy. At the same time, a British naval force was stationed in the Gulf and a series of other treaties followed, culminating in 1853 with the Treaty of Peace in Perpetuity, by which the shaikhs of Dubai, Abu

Dhabi, Sharja, Ras al-Khaima, Ajman, Umm al-Qaiwan, and Fujaira recognized the existence of a British protectorate over their territory and the Pirate Coast became the Trucial Coast (Marlowe, *The Persian Gulf*, pp. 9–19, esp. p. 13).

28. J. G. Lorimer, *Gazetteer of the Persian Gulf, Oman, and Central Arabia* (Calcutta: Superintendent Government Printing, India, 1915; reprint, London: Gregg International, 1970), p. 922.

29. Samuel M. Zwemer, "Field Reports of the Arabian Mission," *The Arabian Mission Field Report*, no. 12 (October–December 1894): 6.

30. Lorimer, *Gazetteer*, p. 937.

Archival Sources

Archives of the Dutch Reformed Church in America. Records of the Board of
    Foreign Missions, Record Group 3. Arabian Mission: General Records of
    the Mission. Correspondence and Papers (1890–1946). New Brunswick
    Theological Seminary. New Brunswick, New Jersey.

Hartford Theological Seminary, Hartford, Connecticut. Calverley, Edwin.
    Correspondence and Papers. This collection contains Edwin Calverley's
    correspondence and personal papers from 1908, when he entered
    mission service as a language student in Bahrain. Annual Kuwait
    Evangelical Reports cited in the text, letters from Paul Harrison to
    Calverley, and the Duncan Black Macdonald correspondence are
    contained in this collection.

Hartford Theological Seminary, Hartford, Connecticut. Calverley, Eleanor Taylor.
    Correspondence and Papers. This collection contains Eleanor Calverley's
    correspondence and personal papers from 1908, when she entered mis-
    sion service. Dr. Calverley's fictionalized accounts of her experiences with
    Kuwaiti women and annual medical reports from Kuwait cited in the text
    are contained in this collection.

Private Collection. Gosselink, George. Correspondence. This collection contains
    the letters sent by Mr. Gosselink to the United States from 1922–1925
    and from 1929 until 1962, when he was a missionary with the Arabian
    Mission in Basra.

The Arabian Mission: Published Material
Field Reports, nos. 1–26 (1892–1898).
Quarterly Letters, nos. 27–40 (1898–1901)
Neglected Arabia, nos. 41–215 (1902–1949)
Arabia Calling, nos. 216–250 (1949–1962).

General Bibliography: Books and Articles
Abdalati, Hammudah. *Islam in Focus*. Riyadh: World Assembly of Muslim Youth, 1980.
Abu al-Qasim, Firdaws. "Work Is No Luxury." *Ar-Riyadh*, December 17, 1996, p. 4.
Abu Hakima, Ahmad Mustafa. *History of Eastern Arabia, 1750–1800: The Rise and Development of Bahrain and Kuwait*. Beirut: Khayats, 1965.
Abu Saud, Abeer. *Qatari Women, Past and Present*. London: Longman, 1978.
Abu-Lughod, Lila. "A Community of Secrets." *Signs: Journal of Women in Culture and Society* 10, no. 4 (1985): 637–657.
Abu-Lughod, Lila. "Fieldwork of a Dutiful Daughter." In *Arab Women in the Field: Studying Our Own Society*, ed. Soraya Altorki and Camilia Fawzi El-Solh. Syracuse: Syracuse University Press, 1988.
Abu-Lughod, Lila. "Honor and Sentiments of Loss in a Bedouin Society." *American Ethnologist* 12, no. 2 (May 1985): 245–261.
Abu-Lughod, Lila. *Veiled Sentiments: Honor and Poetry in a Bedouin Society*. Berkeley: University of California Press, 1988.
Afshar, Haleh. *Women, Work and Ideology in the Third World*. London: Tavistock, 1985.
Ali, Maulana Muhammad. *A Manual of Hadith*. London: Curzon, 1977.
Alireza, Marianne. *At the Drop of a Veil*. Boston: Houghton Mifflin, 1971.
Alkhuli, Muhammad Ali. *The Light of Islam*. Riyadh: al-Farazdak, 1981.
Allen, Mea. *Palgrave of Arabia*. London: Macmillan, 1972.
Allison, Mary Bruins. *Doctor Mary in Arabia*, ed. Sandra Shaw. Austin: University of Texas Press, 1994.
Allison, Mary Bruins. "Hospital Experience in Kuwait." *Church Herald*, February 11, 1944.
Almana, Aisha Mohamed. "Economic Development and Its Impact on the Status of Women in Saudi Arabia." Ph.D. diss., University of Colorado at Boulder, 1981.
Altorki, Soraya. "Family Organization and Women's Power in Urban Saudi Arabian Society." *Journal of Anthropological Research* 33 (fall 1977): 277–287.
Altorki, Soraya. *Women in Saudi Arabia: Ideology and Behavior Among the Elite*. New York: Columbia University Press, 1986
Altorki, Soraya, and Donald Cole, *Arabian Oasis City: The Transformation of 'Unayzah*. Austin: University of Texas Press, 1989.
Alusi, M. *Ta'rikh Najd*, ed. M. B. Athari. Cairo: al-Matba'a al-Salafiyya, 1924.

Anderson, Sherry Ruth, and Patricia Hopkins. *The Feminine Face of God: The Unfolding of the Sacred in Women*. New York: Bantam, 1993.

Annual Report of the Arabian Mission, "The Ministry of Teaching," *Neglected Arabia*, no. 152 (January–March 1930).

"Annual Report of the Arabian Mission for 1925." *Neglected Arabia*, no. 137 (April–June 1926).

"Annual Report of the Arabian Mission, 1932." *Neglected Arabia*, no. 164 (January–June 1933).

Anonymous. "Education of Women in Saudi Arabia." "Notes of the Quarter." *Muslim World* 46, no. 4 (October 1956): 366–367.

Anonymous. "Morality and Law in Saudi Arabia." "Notes of the Quarter." *Muslim World* 44, no. 1 (January 1954): 68–69.

Anonymous. "Wise Marriage: Divorce, 'The Most Hated Legitimate Deed Before God.' " "Notes of the Quarter." *Muslim World* 44, no. 1 (January 1954): 69–70.

Antoun, Richard. "On the Modesty of Women in Arab Muslim Villages: A Study in the Accommodation of Traditions." *American Anthropologist* 70, no. 4 (August 1968): 671–697.

Arabian Mission. *Quarterly Letters from the Field* (January–March 1900).

Ashkanani, Zubaydah. "Zar in a Changing World: Kuwait." In *Women's Medicine: The Zar-Bori Cult in Africa and Beyond*, ed. I. M. Lewis, Ahmed al-Safi, and Sayyid Hurreiz, pp. 219–229. Edinburgh: Edinburgh University Press, 1991.

Attar, Ahmad Abd al-Ghafour. *Muhammad ibn Abd al-Wahhab*, trans. Rashid al-Barrawi. Mecca: Mecca Printing and Information, 1979.

Arebi, Saddeka. *Women and Words in Saudi Arabia: The Politics of Literary Discourse*. New York: Columbia University Press, 1994.

Al-Baadi, Hamad. "Social Change, Education, and the Roles of Women in Arabia." Ph.D. diss., Stanford University, 1982.

Badran, Margot. *Feminists, Islam, and Nation: Gender and the Making of Modern Egypt*. Princeton: Princeton University Press, 1995.

Bahry, Louay. "The New Saudi Woman: Modernizing in an Islamic Framework." *Middle East Journal* 36 (1982): 502–515.

Bagader, Abubaker A. "Saudi Women's New Public Roles: Can Society Adjust?" Talk given on November 20, 1997, at the Watson Institute, Brown University, Providence, Rhode Island.

Bagader, Abubaker, Ava M. Heinrichsdorff, and Deborah S. Akers. *Voices of Change: Short Stories by Saudi Arabian Women Writers*. Boulder: Rienner, 1998.

Beck, Lois, and Nikki Keddie. *Women in the Muslim World*. Cambridge: Harvard University Press, 1978.

Beling, Willard A., ed. *King Faisal and the Modernization of Saudi Arabia*. London, 1980.

Bell, Gertrude. *The Letters of Gertrude Bell*. New York: Boni and Liveright, 1927.

Berkey, Jonathan. "Female Excision and Cultural Accommodation." *International Journal of Middle East Studies* 28, no. 1 (February 1996): 19–38.

Bickers, Robert A., and Rosemary Seton, eds. *Missionary Encounters: Sources and Issues.* Richmond, U.K.: Curzon, 1996.

Bidwell, Robin. *Travellers in Arabia.* London: Hamlyn, 1976.

Bin As'd Bin 'Abd-Aziz Bin Sa'id, Hasan. "The Desired Role of Saudi Women in Development." *Al-Jazirah*, December 18, 1996, p. 32.

Blunt, Lady Anne. *A Pilgrimage to Nejd: The Cradle of the Arab Race.* London: Murray, 1881. Reprint. London: Century, 1985.

Blunt, Lady Anne. *Bedouin Tribes of the Euphrates.* New York: Harper and Brothers, 1879.

Bowen, John. "Salat in Indonesia: The Social Meanings of an Islamic Ritual." *Man*, n.s., 5, no. 1 (1966): 600–619.

Braude, Benjamin. "Palgrave and His Critics: The Origins and Implications of a Controversy. Part One: The Nineteenth Century—The Abyssinian Imbroglio." *Arabian Studies*, vol. 7, ed. R. B. Serjeant and R. I. Bidwell, pp. 97–138. London: Scorpion, for the Middle East Centre, University of Cambridge, 1985.

Brent, Peter. *Far Arabia: Explorers of the Myth.* London: Weidenfeld and Nicolson, 1977.

Brock, Sebastian, and Susan Harvey, trans. and eds. Introduction to *Holy Women of the Syrian Orient.* Berkeley: University. of California Press, 1987.

Brydges, Sir Harford Jones, Bart. *An Account of the Transactions of His Majesty's Mission to the Court of Persia in the Years 1807–11, to Which Is Appended a Brief History of the Wahauby.* 2 vols. London: James Bohn, 1834.

al-Bunyan, Hasin. "Interview with Muhammad Bin Ibrahim Bin Jubayr, Speaker of the Shura Council in Saudi Arabia." *Al-Sharq al-Awsat*, July 6, 1997, p. 4.

Burckhardt, John Lewis. *Notes on the Bedouins and Wahabys Collected During His Travels in the East.* London: Henry Colburn and Richard Bently, 1831. Reprint. New York: Johnson Reprint, 1967.

Burckhardt, John Lewis. "The Catechism (or Creed) of the Wahabys." In *Notes on the Bedouins and Wahabys*, 2:363–369. London: Henry Colburn and Richard Bently, 1831.

Burckhardt, John Lewis. *Travels in Arabia.* 2 vols. London: Henry Colburn, 1829.

Burton, Captain Sir Richard. *Personal Narrative of a Pilgrimage to al-Madinah and Mecca.* 2 vols. 1893. Reprint. New York: Dover, 1964.

Butler, Captain S. S. "Baghdad to Damascus via el Jauf, Northern Arabia." *Geographical Journal* 33, no. 5 (May 1909): 517–535.

Calverley, Mrs. E. E. "The Arab Woman and the Lady Physician." *Neglected Arabia*, no. 126 (July–September 1923).

Calverley, Edwin. "The Doctrines of the Arabian 'Brethren.' " *Moslem World* 11, no. 4 (October 1921): 364–376.

Calverley, Edwin. "Education in Kuwait." *Neglected Arabia*, no. 142 (July–September 1927).

Calverley, Edwin. "Evangelistic Activities at Kuwait." *Neglected Arabia*, no. 92 (January–March 1915).

Calverley, Edwin. "The Trial by Ordeal in Arabia." *Neglected Arabia*, no. 107 (October–December 1918).

Calverley, Edwin. "Where Mullas Are Doctors." *Neglected Arabia*, no. 105 (April/May 1918).

Calverley, Eleanor T. "Arab Women of the Persian Gulf." *Asia*, May 1938, 304–308.

Calverley, Eleanor. "The Arabian Secret Service." *Neglected Arabia*, no. 11 (January–March 1913).

Calverley, Eleanor. "Beauty for Ashes." *Neglected Arabia*, no. 110 (July–September 1919).

Calverley, Eleanor T. *My Arabian Days and Nights*. New York: Crowell, 1953.

Calverley, Eleanor. "One of the Least of These—His Sisters." *Neglected Arabia*, no. 96 (January–March 1916).

Calverley, Eleanor T. "Pioneer Women of Arabia, 1889–1939." Pamphlet. New York: Woman's Board of Foreign Missions, 1939.

Cantine, James. "Sharon J. Thoms, M.D.: An Appreciation." *Neglected Arabia*, no. 85 (April–June 1913).

Cantine, Mrs. James. "Arab Women and the War." *Neglected Arabia*, no. 108 (January–March 1919).

Cantine, Mrs. James. "Mullayas—Mohammedan and Christian." *Neglected Arabia*, no. 112 (January–March 1920).

Carmody, Denise L. "Judaism." In *Women in World Religions*, ed. Arvind Sharma. Albany: State University of New York Press, 1987.

Carruthers, Douglas. "Captain Shakespear's Last Journey." *Geographical Journal* 59, no. 6 (June 1922): 401–418.

Chamberlayne, John. "The Family in Islam." *Numen: International Review for the History of Religions* 15 (1968): 119–141.

Cheesman, Major R. E. *In Unknown Arabia*. London: Macmillan, 1926.

Cole, D. P. "Bedouin Life and Social Change in Saudi Arabia." In *Change and Development in Nomadic and Pastoral Societies*, ed. John B. Galaty and Philip C. Salzman. Leiden: Brill, 1981.

Cole, Donald P. "The Enmeshment of Nomads in Sa'udi Arabian Society: The Case of Al Murrah." In *The Desert and the Sown: Nomads in the Wider Society*, ed. Cynthia Nelson, pp. 113–127. Berkeley: University of California Institute for International Studies, 1973.

Cole, Donald P. *Nomads of the Nomads: The Al Murrah Bedouin of the Empty Quarter*. Arlington Heights, Ill.: Harlan Davidson, 1975.

Cole, Donald P. "Pastoral Nomads in a Rapidly Changing Economy: The Case of

Saudi Arabia." In *Social and Economic Development in the Arab Gulf,* ed. Tim
Niblock, pp. 106–120. Kent: Croom Helm, 1980.

Coleman, John A. "Catholic Integralism as a Fundamentalism." In *Fundamentalism
in Comparative Perspective,* ed. Lawrence Kaplan. Amherst: University of
Massachusetts Press, 1992.

Combs-Schilling, M. E. *Sacred Performances: Islam, Sexuality, and Sacrifice.* New York:
Columbia University Press, 1989.

Crapanzano, Vincent, and Vivian Garrison. *Case Studies in Spirit Possession.* New York:
Wiley, 1977.

Crone, Patricia, and Michael Cook, *Hagarism: The Making of the Islamic World.* Cambridge: Cambridge University Press, 1977.

al-Dakhil, Sulayman. "Al-Artawiya au Bilada Jadida fi Diyar Najd." *Lughat al-'Arab*
(Baghdad) 2 (1912): 481–488.

Dalenberg, Cornelia. *Sharifa.* Grand Rapids, Mich.: Eerdmans, 1983.

Dalenberg, Cornelia. "Unforgettable Patients." *Arabia Calling,* no. 217 (summer
1949).

Dame, Elizabeth. "A King's Favorite." *Neglected Arabia* (Inland Arabia Number),
no. 208 (January–March 1946).

Dame, Mrs. L. P. "A Trip to Central Arabia." *Neglected Arabia,* no. 167 (January–
March 1934).

Davis, Susan Schaefer. *Patience and Power: Women's Lives in a Moroccan Village.* Cambridge, Mass.: Schenkman, 1983.

De Gaury, Gerald. *Arabia Phoenix: An Account of a Visit to Ibn Saud, Chieftain of the
Austere Wahhabis and Powerful Arabian King.* London: Harrap, 1946.

di Varthema, Ludovico. *The Itinerary of Ludovico di Varthema of Bologna from 1502 to
1508.* London: Argonaut, 1928.

Dickson, H. R. P. *The Arab of the Desert: Bedouin Life in Kuwait and Saudi Arabia.*
London: Allen and Unwin, 1949.

Dickson, H. R. P. *Kuwait and Her Neighbors.* London: Allen and Unwin, 1956.

Dickson, Violet. *Forty Years in Kuwait.* London: Allen and Unwin, 1971.

"Discussion and Debate." *American Anthropologist* 72, no. 5 (October 1970): 1070–
1092.

Doughty, Charles M. *Travels in Arabia Deserta.* 2 vols. 3d ed. London, 1936. Reprint. New York: Dover, 1979.

Douglas, Mary. *Purity and Danger: An Analysis of the Concepts of Pollution and Taboo.*
New York: Ark, 1966.

Doumato, Eleanor Abdella. "The Ambiguity of Shariah and the Politics of Rights."
In *Faith and Freedom,* ed. Mahnaz Afkhami. London: IB Taurus, 1995.

Doumato, Eleanor Abdella. "Gender, Monarchy and National Identity in Saudi
Arabia." *British Journal of Middle Eastern Studies* 19, no. 1 (1992): 31–47.

Doumato, Eleanor Abdella. "Hearing Other Voices: Christian Women and the

Coming of Islam." *International Journal of Middle East Studies* 23, no. 2 (May 1991): 177–199.

Doumato, Eleanor Abdella. "The Society and Its Environment." In *Saudi Arabia: A Country Study*, ed. Helen Metz. Washington, D.C.: Library of Congress, 1994.

Doumato, Eleanor Abdella. "Women and Political Stability in Saudi Arabia." *Middle East Report*, July 1991, 34–37.

Dykstra, Mrs. Dirk. "Life, Language and Religion." *Neglected Arabia*, no. 110 (July–September 1919).

Dykstra, Mrs. Dirk. "A Tour to Quriyat." *Neglected Arabia*, no. 171 (April–June 1935).

Dykstra, Mrs. Dirk. "Zeeraan." *Neglected Arabia*, no. 107 (October–December 1918).

Dykstra, Minnie. "Moslem Funeral Customs." *Neglected Arabia*, no. 109 (April–June 1919).

Dykstra, Minnie. "Our Muscat School, 1892–1952." *Arabia Calling*, no. 229 (autumn 1952).

Dykstra, Minnie W. "A Trip to the Mainland." *Neglected Arabia*, no. 104 (January–March 1918).

Ebrahim, Mohammed Hossein Saleh. "Problems of Nomad Settlement in the Middle East with Special Reference to Saudi Arabia." Ph.D. diss., Cornell University, 1981.

Eickelman, Dale F. *The Middle East: An Anthropological Approach*. New York: Prentice-Hall, 1981.

Eickelman, Dale F. "The Study of Islam in Local Contexts." In *Contributions to Asian Studies*, 17:1–16. Leiden: Brill, 1982.

Eickelman, Dale F., and James Piscatori, eds. *Muslim Travellers: Pilgrimage, Migration, and the Religious Imagination*. Berkeley: University of California Press, 1990.

Eilberg-Schwartz, Howard, and Wendy Doniger. *Off with Her Head! The Denial of Women's Identity in Myth, Religion, and Culture*. Berkeley, University of California Press, 1995.

Fabietti, Ugo. "Sedentarisation as a Means of Detribalisation: Some Policies of the Saudi Arabian Government Towards the Nomads." In *State, Society, and Economy in Saudi Arabia*, ed. Tim Niblock, pp. 186–197. New York: St. Martin's, 1982.

Fakhro, Munira A. *Women at Work in the Gulf: A Case Study of Bahrain*. London: Kegan Paul International, 1990.

Falk, Nancy, and Rita Gross, eds. *Unspoken Worlds: Women's Religious Lives in Non-Western Cultures*. San Francisco: Harper and Row, 1980.

Farrukh, Dr. Omar A., trans. *Ibn Taimiyya on Public and Private Law in Islam; or, Public Policy in Islamic Jurisprudence*. Beirut: Khayats, 1966.

Fernea, Elizabeth. *Guests of the Sheikh.* Garden City, N.Y.: Anchor, 1969.

Fernea, Elizabeth. "Saints and Spirits." Granada TV, 1977.

Fernea, Elizabeth. "Some Women of Marrakech." Granada TV, 1976.

Fernea, Elizabeth Warnock, ed. *Women and the Family in the Middle East: New Voices of Change.* Austin: University of Texas Press, 1985.

Fernea, Elizabeth, and Basima Qattan Bezirgan, eds. *Middle Eastern Women Speak.* Austin: University of Texas Press, 1976.

Fernea, Elizabeth, and Robert Fernea. "Variation in Religious Observance Among Islamic Women." In *Scholars, Saints, and Sufis: Muslim Religious Institutions since 1500,* ed. Nikki Keddie. Berkeley: University of California Press, 1972.

Fernea, Robert A. "Arabia Deserta: The Ethnographic Text." In *Explorations in Doughty's Arabia Deserta,* ed. Stephen E. Tabachnick, pp. 201–219. Athens: University of Georgia Press, 1987.

Franke, Elisabet. "The Zar in Egypt." *Moslem World* 3, no. 3 (July 1913): 275–289.

Freeth, Zahra, and H. V. F. Winston. *Explorers of Arabia: From the Renaissance to the End of the Victorian Era.* New York: Africana, 1978.

Freeth, Zahra. *A New Look at Kuwait.* London: Allen and Unwin, 1972.

Freeth, Zahra. *Kuwait Was My Home.* New York: Macmillan, 1956.

Geertz, Clifford. *Islam Observed.* Chicago: University of Chicago Press, 1981.

Geertz, Clifford. "Religion as a Cultural System." In *The Interpretation of Cultures.* New York: Basic, 1973.

Gellner, Ernest. "Doctor and Saint." In *Scholars, Saints, and Sufis: Muslim Religious Institutions in the Middle East since 1500,* ed. Nikki Keddie, pp. 307–326. Berkeley: University of California Press, 1972.

Ginat, Joseph. *Women in Muslim Rural Society.* New Brunswick, N.J.: Transaction, 1982.

Goldrup, Lawrence. "Saudi Arabia, 1902–1932: The Development of a Wahhabi Society." Ph.D. diss., University of California, Los Angeles, 1971.

Graham, William. "Islam in the Mirror of Ritual." In *Islam in Tribal Societies from the Atlas to the Indus,* ed. Akbar S. Ahmed and David M. Hart, pp. 53–71. London: Routledge and Kegan Paul, 1984.

Great Britain, Geographical Section of the Naval Intelligence Division, Naval Staff, Admiralty. *A Handbook of Arabia.* 2 vols. London: His Majesty's Stationery Office, 1920.

Guarmani, Carlo. *Northern Nejd: A Journey from Jerusalem to Anaiza in Kasim.* Foreword by Douglas Carruthers. London: Argonaut, 1938.

Habib, John S. *Ibn Sa'ud's Warriors of Islam.* Leiden: Brill, 1978.

Haggard, Howard. *Devils, Drugs, and Doctors: The Story of the Science of Healing from Medicine Man to Doctor.* New York: Blue Ribbon, 1929.

Harrison, Anna M. "Desert Diary." *Neglected Arabia,* no. 198 (October–December 1942).

Harrison, Anna M. "Women of the Interior." *Neglected Arabia*, no. 208 (January–March 1946).

Harrison, Paul. *The Arab at Home*. New York: Crowell, 1924.

Harrison, Paul. "The Capital City of the Empire of Muhammed." *Neglected Arabia*, no. 106 (April–June 1918).

Harrison, Paul. "Signs of the Times in Arabia." *Neglected Arabia*, no. 113 (April–June 1920).

Harrison, Paul. "The Tour to Riadh." *Neglected Arabia*, no. 104 (January–March 1918).

Harrison, Mrs. Rene. "The Feast of Moharram." *Neglected Arabia*, no. 107 (October–December 1918).

Harvey, Susan. "Women in Early Byzantine Hagiography: Reversing the Story." In *That Gentle Strength: Historical Perspectives on Women in Christianity*, ed. Lynda L. Coon, Katherine Haldane, and Elisabeth Sommer. Charlottesville: University Press of Virginia, 1990.

Hassan, Javid. "Saudi Women Given Green Light in Hotel Industry." *Internet Arab View in English* (February 28, 1997), quoted in FBIS-NES-97-070, March 11, 1997.

Helms, Christine Moss. *The Cohesion of Saudi Arabia: Evolution of Political Identity*. Baltimore: Johns Hopkins University Press, 1981.

Hill, Patricia. *The World Their Household: The American Woman's Foreign Mission Movement and Cultural Transformation, 1870–1920*. Ann Arbor: University of Michigan Press, 1985.

Hoch-Smith, Judith, and Anita Spring, eds. *Women in Ritual and Symbolic Roles*. New York: Plenum, 1978.

Hogarth, D. G. "Gertrude Bell's Journey to Hayil." *Geographical Journal* 70, no. 1 (July 1927): 1–17.

Holden, P., ed. *Women's Religious Experience*. Totowa: Barnes and Noble, 1983.

Holmes, Madeline A. "Kuwait, Ancient and Modern." *Arabia Calling*, no. 237 (autumn 1954).

Holt, Major Al. "The Future of the North Arabian Desert." *Geographical Journal* 62, no. 4 (October 1923): 259–271.

Hosmon, Sarah. "The Girls and Women of Arabia as I Have Seen Them." *Neglected Arabia* 98 (July–September 1916).

Hosmon, Dr. Sarah. "In the Date Gardens at Sibe." *Neglected Arabia*, no. 116 (January–March 1921).

Hughes, Thomas Patrick. *A Dictionary of Islam: Being a Cyclopedia of the Doctrines, Rites, Ceremonies, and Customs, Together with the Technical and Theological Terms, of the Muhammadan Religion*. 1885. Reprint. Delhi: Oriental, 1973.

Hunter, Jane. *The Gospel of Gentility: American Women Missionaries in Turn-of-the-Century China*. New Haven: Yale University Press, 1984.

ibn Abd al-Wahhab, Muhammad. "Bab al-haidh." In *Mu'alafat Al Shaikh al-Imam*

Muhammad ibn 'Abd al-Wahhab, ed. Abd al-Aziz Zaid al-Rumi, Dr. Muhammad Beltaji, and Dr. Sayyid Hijab, pp. 82–88. Riyadh: Imam Muhammad ibn Sa'ud Islamic University, 1981.

ibn Abd al-Wahhab, Muhammad. "Bab sitru al-'awrah." In Mu'alafat Al Shaikh al-Imam Muhammad ibn 'Abd al-Wahhab, ed. Abd al-Aziz Zaid al-Rumi, Dr. Muhammad Beltaji, and Dr. Sayyid Hijab, pp. 105–108. Riyadh: Imam Muhammad ibn Sa'ud Islamic University, 1981.

ibn Abd al-Wahhab, Muhammad. *The Excellent Qualities of the Holy Qur'an*, trans. Muhammad Iqbal Siddiqi. Lahore: Qazi, 1981.

ibn Abd al-Wahhab, Muhammad. *Kitab at-Tawhid: Essay on the Unicity of Allah; or, What Is Due to His Creatures*, trans. Ismail Raji al-Faruqi. Damascus: International Islamic Federation of Student Organizations, 1979.

ibn Abd al-Wahhab, Muhammad. *Mu'alafat Al Shaikh al-Imam Muhammad ibn 'Abd al-Wahhab* (The collected works of Imam al-Shaikh Muhammad ibn Abd al-Wahhab), ed. Abd al-Aziz Zaid al-Rumi, Dr. Muhammad Beltaji, and Dr. Sayyid Hijab. Riyadh: Imam Muhammad ibn Sa'ud Islamic University, 1981.

ibn Abd al-Wahhab, Muhammad. *The Three Basic Principles and Their Proofs*, trans. Abdul Munem Salamat. Riyadh: Dar Alhuda, 1996.

ibn Abd al-Wahhab, Muhammad. *Three Essays on Tawhid*, trans. Ismail Raji al Faruqi. Riyadh: International Islamic Publishing House, 1979.

ibn Mutrafi, Saad. Haiat al-'Amr bil Ma'ruf circular no. 1039, issued January 9, 1979, Jeddah.

ibn Muhammad al-Dubaikhi, Abdullah. Haiat al-'Amr bil Ma'ruf, Eastern Province Branch, circular no. 178/6/T/129/1, issued September 13, 1982.

Indarqiri, Yassin Sallah. "Development of Human Resources by Applying Sociology to Education in the Capital of the Kingdom of Saudi Arabia, Riyadh." Ph.D. diss. (in Arabic), Cairo University, 1975.

"Islam in Perspective." *Arab News*, April 16, 1982.

Jackson, Ruth. "Of Girls in Bahrein," *Arabia Calling*, no. 229 (autumn 1952).

Jackson, Ruth. "Glimpses Behind the Veil." *Neglected Arabia*, no. 138 (July–September 1926).

al-Jasir, Ahmad. "Al-mar'a fi hayat Imam al-Da'wat Al Shaikh Muhammad ibn 'Abd al-Wahhab." In *Bahuth usbu Al Shaikh Muhammad bin 'Abd al-Wahhab*, 1:159–188. Riyadh: Muhammad bin Sa'ud University, 1983.

Al Jawziyya, ibn Qayyam. *Prophetic Medicine*, trans. S. Abi Azar, corr. F. Amira Zrein Matraji. Riyadh: Dar el-Fikr, 1995.

al-Juhany, U. M. "The History of Najd Prior to the Wahhabis: A Study of the Social, Political, and Religious Conditions in Najd During the Three Centuries Preceding the Wahhabi Reform Movement." Ph.D. diss., University of Washington, 1983.

al-Juwayer, Ibrahim ibn Mubarak. "Development and Family in Saudi Arabia: An

Exploratory Study of the Views of University Students in Riyadh." Ph.D. diss., University of Florida, 1984.

Katakura, Motoko. *Bedouin Village.* Tokyo: University of Tokyo Press, 1977.

Keating, Karl. *Catholics and Fundamentalism.* San Francisco: Ignatius, 1988.

Keddie, Nikki. "Problems in the Study of Middle Eastern Women." *International Journal of Middle East Studies* 10 (1979): 225–240.

Kee, Howard Clarke. "Magic and Messiah." In *Religion, Science and Magic in Concert and in Conflict*, ed. Jacob Neusner, Ernest S. Frerichs, and Paul Virgil McCracken Flesher, pp. 121–141. Oxford: Oxford University Press, 1989.

al-Khuli, Muhammad Ali. *The Light of Islam.* Riyadh: al-Farazdak, 1981.

Khuri, Fu'ad I. *Tribe and State in Bahrain: The Transformation of Social and Political Authority in an Arab State.* Chicago: University of Chicago Press, 1980.

Konczacki, Z. A. *Economics of Pastoralism.* London: Cass, 1978.

Lancaster, William. *The Rwalla Bedouin Today.* Cambridge: Cambridge University Press, 1981.

Leachman, Captain G. E. "A Journey in North-Eastern Arabia." *Geographical Journal* 37, no. 3 (March 1911): 265–274.

Leachman, Captain G. E. "A Journey through Central Arabia." *Geographical Journal* 43, no. 5 (May 1914):. 501–520.

Leak, W. Norman. "Medicine and the Traditions." *Neglected Arabia*, no. 125 (April–June 1923).

Leavitt, Judith. *Brought to Bed: Childbearing in America, 1750–1950.* New York: Oxford University Press, 1986.

Leeds, A., and A. P. Vayda, eds. *Man, Culture, and Animals.* Washington, D.C.: American Association for the Advancement of Science, 1965.

Lemu, B. Aisha, and Fatima Heeren. *Woman in Islam.* London: Islamic Foundation, 1978.

Lewis, I. M. *Ecstatic Religion.* Baltimore: Penguin, 1971.

Lewis, I. M. *Religion in Context: Cults and Charisma.* Cambridge: Cambridge University Press, 1989.

Litoff, Judith Barrett. *American Midwives: 1860 to the Present.* Westport, Conn.: Greenwood, 1978; reprint, Westport, Conn.: Greenwood, 1985.

Lorimer, J. G. *Gazetteer of the Persian Gulf, Oman, and Central Arabia.* 5 vols. Calcutta: Superintendent Government Printing, India, 1915. Reprint. London: Gregg International, 1970.

Lutton, Fanny. "A Day's Picnic with Arab Ladies of Muscat." *Neglected Arabia*, no. 78 (July–September 1911).

Lutton, Fanny. "Moslem Women's Meetings in Bahrein." *Neglected Arabia*, no. 84 (January–March 1913).

McCourt, Frank. *Angela's Ashes: A Memoir.* New York: Scribner, 1996.

Makhlouf, Carla. *Changing Veils.* London: Croom Helm, 1979.

Malik, Saleh Abdullah. "Rural Migration and Urban Growth in Riyadh, Saudi Arabia." Ph.D. diss., University of Michigan, 1973.

al-Manea, Azeezah A. "Historical and Contemporary Policies of Women's Education in Saudi Arabia." Ph.D. diss., University of Michigan, 1984.

Markis, G., and Ahmad al-Safi. "The Tumbura Spirit Possession Cult of the Sudan, Past and Present." In *Women's Medicine: The Zar-Bori Cult in Africa and Beyond*, ed. I. M. Lewis, Ahmed al-Safi, and Sayyid Hurreiz, pp. 118–135. Edinburgh: Edinburgh University Press, 1991.

Marlowe, John. *The Persian Gulf in the Twentieth Century*. London: Cresset, 1962.

Martin, Dahris. *I Know Tunisia*. New York: Ives Washburn, 1943.

Mason, Rev. Alfred Dewitt, and Rev. Frederick J. Barny. *History of the Arabian Mission*. New York: Board of Foreign Missions, Reformed Church in America, 1926.

Mernissi, Fatima. *Beyond the Veil: Male Female Dynamics in a Modern Muslim Society*. Bloomington: Indiana University Press, 1987.

Mernissi, Fatima. "Women, Saints, and Sanctuaries." *Signs: Journal of Women in Culture and Society* 3, no. 1 (autumn 1975): 101–112.

Moghadam, Val. *Women, Work, and Economic Reform in the Middle East and North Africa*. Boulder, Colo.: Rienner, 1998.

Moghadam, Val. "Women, Work and Ideology in the Islamic Republic." *International Journal of Middle East Studies* 20, no. 2 (May 1988): 221–243.

Monroe, Elizabeth. *Philby of Arabia*. London: Luzac, 1974.

Morton, Alice. "Dawit: Competition and Integration in an Ethiopian Wuqabi Cult Group." In *Case Studies in Spirit Possession*, ed. Vincent Crapanzano and Vivian Garrison, p. 194. New York: Wiley, 1977.

al-Mughni, Haya. *Women in Kuwait: The Politics of Gender*. London: Saqi, 1993.

Mulqi, Hiyam. "Ashya 'an al-milabis al-Islamiyya." *Ar-Riyadh*, August 29, 1981, p. 9.

Murphy, Dervla. Introduction to Lady Anne Blunt, *Pilgrimage to Nejd: The Cradle of the Arab Race*. London: Murray, 1881. Reprint. London: Century, 1985.

Musallam, B. F. *Sex and Society in Islam: Birth Control Before the Nineteenth Century*. Cambridge: Cambridge University Press, 1983.

Musil, Alois. *Arabia Deserta*. Oriental Explorations and Studies No. 2. New York: American Geographical Society, 1927.

Musil, Alois. *In the Arabian Desert*. New York: Liveright, 1930.

Musil, Alois. *Northern Negd: A Topographical Itinerary*. New York: Czech Academy of Sciences and Arts, 1928.

al-Musnad, Muhammad bin Abdul-Aziz, comp. *Islamic Fatawa Regarding Women*. Riyadh: Darussalam, 1996.

Mylrea, C. S. G. "Medievalism in Arabia." *Moslem World* 22 (July 1932): 247–255.

Mylrea, C. Stanley G. "A Council of War." *Neglected Arabia*, no. 88 (January–March 1914).

Mylrea, C. Stanley G. "The Thin Edge of the Wedge." *Neglected Arabia*, no. 92 (January–March 1915).

Mylrea, Dr. Stanley. "The Enemy at the Gates." *Neglected Arabia*, no. 117 (April–June 1921).

Mylrea, Mrs. Stanley. "Arab Superstitions about Diseases and Quackery in Medicine." *Neglected Arabia*, no. 125 (April–June 1925).

Nakhleh, Emile. *Bahrain: Political Development in a Modernizing Society*. Lexington, Mass.: Heath, Lexington Books, 1976.

Nath, Kamla. "Education and Employment Among Kuwaiti Women." In *Women in the Muslim World*, ed. Lois Beck and Nikki Keddie, pp. 172–188. Cambridge: Harvard University Press, 1978.

An-Nawawi, Imam. *Forty Hadith*, trans. Ibrahim Ezzeddin and Denys Johnson-Davies. Damascus: Holy Koran Publishing House, 1976.

Nelson, Cynthia. "Public and Private Politics: Women in the Middle Eastern World." *American Ethnologist* 1, no. 3 (August 1974): 551–563.

Nelson, Cynthia. "Self, Spirit Possession and World View: An Illustration from Egypt." *International Journal of Social Psychiatry* 17 (1971): 194–209.

Nelson, Cynthia. "Women and Power in Nomadic Societies of the Middle East." In *The Desert and the Town: Nomads in the Wider Society*, ed. Cynthia Nelson, pp. 43–57. Berkeley: University of California Institute for International Studies, 1973.

Neusner, Jacob. "Science and Magic, Miracle and Magic in Formative Judaism: The System and the Difference." In *Religion, Science and Magic in Concert and in Conflict*, ed. Jacob Neusner, Ernest S. Frerichs, and Paul Virgil McCracken Flesher, pp. 61–81. Oxford: Oxford University Press, 1989.

Neusner, Jacob. "Thematic or Systematic Description: The Case of Mishnah's Division of Women." In *Method and Meaning in Ancient Judaism*. Missoula, Mont.: Scholars, 1979.

Newman, Lucille F., ed. *Women's Medicine: A Cross-Cultural Study of Indigenous Fertility Regulation*. New Brunswick, N.J.: Rutgers University Press, 1985.

Niebuhr, Carsten. *Travels through Arabia and Other Countries in the East*, trans. Robert Heron. 2 vols. Edinburgh, 1792.

"Notes of the Quarter." *Muslim World* 46, no. 4 (October 1956): 367.

Ochsenwald, William. *Religion, Society, and the State in Arabia: The Hijaz Under Ottoman Control, 1840–1908*. Columbus: Ohio State University Press, 1984.

Palgrave, W. G. *Personal Narrative of a Year's Journey through Central and Eastern Arabia (1862–1863)*. London: Macmillan, 1868.

Parssinen, Catherine. "The Changing Role of Women." In *King Faisal and the Modernization of Saudi Arabia*, ed. Willard Beling. London: Croom-Helm; Boulder, Colo.: Westview, 1980.

Pelly, Lewis. *Report on a Journey to Riyadh in Central Arabia (1865)*. Cambridge:

Oleander, n.d. Reprint of *Report on a Journey to the Wahhabee Capital of Riyadh in Central Arabia*. Bombay, 1866.

Pennings, Gerritt. "The Bedouin and the Motor Car." *Church Herald*, February 23, 1940.

Pennings, Gerrit J. "Kuweit: 'The Little Walled Town.' " *Neglected Arabia*, no. 92 (January–March 1915).

Pennings, Mrs. G. "From the Cradle to the Grave." *Neglected Arabia*, no. 126 (July–September 1923).

Peters, Emrys. "The Paucity of Ritual Among Middle Eastern Pastoralists." In *Islam in Tribal Societies from the Atlas to the Indus*, ed. Akbar S. Ahmed and David M. Hart, pp. 187–219. London: Routledge and Kegan Paul, 1984.

Philby, H. St. John. "Across Arabia: From the Persian Gulf to the Red Sea." *Geographical Journal* 56, no. 6 (December 1920): 446–468.

Philby, H. St. John. *Arabia of the Wahhabis*. London: Cass, 1977.

Philby, H. St. John, *Arabian Days: An Autobiography*. London: Hale, 1948.

Philby, H. St. John. *Arabian Jubilee*. New York: Day, 1953.

Philby, H. St. John. *The Empty Quarter, Being a Description of the Great South Desert of Arabia Known as Rub' al Khali*. New York: Henry Holt, 1933.

Philby, H. St. John. *Heart of Arabia: A Record of Travel and Exploration*. 2 vols. London: Constable, 1922.

Philby, H. St. John. *A Pilgrim in Arabia*. London: Hale, 1946.

Philby, H. St. John. "Riyadh: Ancient and Modern." *Middle East Journal* 13 (spring 1959): 129–141.

Philby, H. St. John. *Saudi Arabia*. 1955. Reprint. Beirut: Librairie du Liban, 1968.

Philby, H. St. John. "Southern Najd." *Geographical Journal* 55, no. 3 (March 1920): 161–191.

Pickthall, Mohammed Marmaduke, trans. *The Meaning of the Glorious Koran*. New York: New American Library, 1958.

Post, Eunice. "Girls' Education of the Future." *Arabia Calling*, no. 232 (summer 1953).

"Prince Naif Warns Against Witchcraft." *Arab News*, April 3, 1995.

al-Rashid, Ibrahaim, ed. *Documents on the History of Saudi Arabia*. 3 vols. Salisbury: Document Publications, 1976.

Raunkiaer, Barclay. *Through Wahhabiland on Camelback*. New York: Praeger, 1969.

"Report of the Arabian Mission for 1914." *Neglected Arabia*, no. 93 (April–June 1915).

Reuther, Rosemary, ed. *Religion and Sexism: Images of Women in Jewish and Christian Traditions*. New York: Simon and Schuster, 1974.

Rihani, Ameen. *Maker of Modern Arabia*. Boston: Houghton Mifflin, 1928.

Rihani, Ameen. *Ta'rikh Najd al-Hadith. Al-a'mal al-'arabiyya al-Kamila*, vol. 5. Beirut: al-Mu'asisa al-'Arabiyya al-Dirasat wa al-Nashr, 1970.

Rosaldo, Michelle Zimbalist. "A Theoretical Overview." In *Woman, Culture, and Society*, ed. Michelle Zimbalist Rosaldo and Louise Lamphere. Stanford: Stanford University Press, 1974; reprint, Stanford: Stanford University Press, 1993.

Rosaldo, Michelle Zimbalist, and Louise Lamphere, eds. *Woman, Culture, and Society*. Stanford: Stanford University Press, 1974; reprint, Stanford: Stanford University Press, 1993.

Reuther, Rosemary, ed. *Religion and Sexism: Images of Women in Jewish and Christian Traditions*. New York: Simon and Schuster, 1974.

Reuther, Rosemary, and Eleanor McLaughlin, eds. *Women of the Spirit: Female Leadership in the Jewish and Christian Tradition*. New York: Simon and Schuster, 1979.

Rutter, Eldon. "Damascus to Hail." *Journal of the Royal Central Asian Society* 18 (1931): 61–73.

Rutter, Eldon. "A Journey to Hail." *Geographical Journal* 80 (July–December 1932): 322–331.

al-Ruwaithia, Muhammad A. *Sukkan al-mamlaka al-'arabiya al-sa'udiya*. Cairo: n.p., 1978.

Said, Edward. *Orientalism*. New York: Vintage, 1979.

Salahi, Adil. "Islam in Perspective." *Arab News*, February 26, 1982.

al-Salloom, Hamad I. *Education in Saudi Arabia*. 2d ed. Beltsville, Md.: Amana, 1995.

Sanad, Jamal, and Mark Tessler. "The Economic Orientations of Kuwaiti Women: Their Nature, Determinants and Consequences." *International Journal of Middle Eastern Studies* 20, no. 4 (November 1988): 443–486.

Saudi Arabia, Ministry of Planning. *Third Development Plan (1980–1985)*. Riyadh, 1980.

Saunders, Lucie Wood. "Variants in Zar Experience in an Egyptian Village." In *Case Studies in Spirit Possession*, ed. Vincent Crapanzano and Vivian Garrison. New York: Wiley, 1977.

Al Sawwaf, Muhammad Mahmud. *The Muslim Book of Prayer*. Mecca: Dr. Mujahid Muhammad Al Sawwaf, 1977.

Al Sawwaf, Muhammad Mahmud. *Ta'lim al-salah*. Mecca: Dar an-nasr lil taba'at al-Islamiya, 1977.

Sayigh, Rosemary. "Roles and Functions of Arab Women: A Reappraisal." *Arab Studies Quarterly* 3 (1981): 258–274.

As-Suyuti, Jalal ad-Din Abd ar-Rahman. *As-Suyuti's Medicine of the Prophet*, trans. Cyril Elgood. London: Ta-Ha, 1997.

Seaman, Bryant. "Islamic Law and Modern Government: Saudi Arabia Supplements the Sharia to Regulate Development." *Columbia Journal of Transnational Law* 18 (1980): 143–481.

Searle, Rev. J. P. "After Twenty Years: As to Beginnings." *Neglected Arabia*, no. 68 (January–March 1909).

Senbel, A. Aziz Abdullah. "The Goals of Women's Literacy Education in Saudi Arabia as Perceived by Saudi Arabian University Professors, Female Literacy Teachers, and Female Adult Learners." Ph.D. diss., University of Nebraska–Lincoln, 1984.

Sered, Susan. *Women as Ritual Experts: The Religious Lives of Elderly Jewish Women in Jerusalem*. Oxford: Oxford University Press, 1992.

Shafer, Rev. L. J. "Dr. Harrison's Visit to Riadh and Its Significance." *Neglected Arabia*, no. 103 (October–December 1917).

"Shaikh bin Baz fi jami'a an-nahda." *Ar-Riyadh*, December 12, 1981.

"Sheikh Describes How Mahdi Will Appear." *Arab News*, December 25, 1979, p. 2.

Shaker, Fatina Amin. "Modernization of the Developing Nations: A Case of Saudi Arabia." Ph.D. diss., Purdue University, 1972.

Shakir, M. H., trans. *The Quran*. 5th ed. Elmhurst, N.Y.: Tahrike Tarsile Qur'an, 1988.

Shamekh, Ahmed A. "Spatial Patterns of Bedouin Settlement in Al-Qasim Region of Saudi Arabia." Ph.D. diss., University of Kentucky, 1975.

Sim, Katherine. *Jean Louis Burckhardt: A Biography*. London: Quartet, 1981.

Slyomovics, Susan. "Ritual Grievance: The Language of Woman?" *Women and Performance: A Journal of Feminist Theory* 5, no. 1 (1990/1992): 53–60.

Smith, Jane, ed. *Women in Contemporary Muslim Societies*. Cranbury, N.J.: Associated University Presses, 1980.

Smith, Wilfred Cantwell. *Islam in Modern History*. Princeton: 1957.

Snouck Hurgronje, C. *Mekka in the Latter Part of the Nineteenth Century*. Leiden: Brill and Luzac, 1931. Reprint. Leiden: Brill, 1970.

Soffan, Linda. *The Women of the United Arab Emirates*. London: Croom Helm, 1980.

Spiro, Melford E. "Gender Hierarchy in Burma: Cultural, Social and Psychological Dimensions." In *Sex and Gender Hierarchies*, ed. Barbara Diane Miller, pp. 316–333. Cambridge: Cambridge University Press, 1993.

Starr, Paul. *The Social Transformation of American Medicine*. New York: Basic, 1982.

Storm, Harold. *Whither Arabia? A Survey of Missionary Opportunity*. London: World Dominion, 1938.

Storm, Ida Patterson. "Touring Troubles." *Arabia Calling*, no. 218 (autumn/winter 1949).

Storm, W. H. "The Mission Doctor Versus Arab Medical Practice." *Church Herald*, February 6, 1942.

Stowasser, Barbara Fryer. *Women in the Qur'an, Traditions, and Interpretation*. Oxford: Oxford University Press, 1994.

Tabachnick, Stephen E., ed. *Explorations in Doughty's Arabia Deserta*. Athens: University of Georgia Press, 1987.

"Tallal bin Abd al-Aziz Tadhakkir." *Ar-Riyadh*, September 23, 1981.

al-Tameemi, Dr. Abd el-Malik. "The Political Activity of Missionaries in the Persian Gulf Region." *Journal of the Gulf and Arabian Peninsula* (in Arabic) 17, no. 20 (1979): 103–114.

al-Tamimi, al-Shaikh al-'Alim al-Rubani Muhammad bin Sulaiman. *Mabadi' al-Islam* (Fundamentals of Islam). Riyadh: Department of Religious Guidance, Kingdom of Saudi Arabia (Ri'asat adarat al-ba'uth al-'alamiya wa al-'ifta wa al-da'wa wa al-arshad), n.d.

al-Tayash, Fahad. "The Jinni Is Out of the Bottle: An Ethnography of Samiri Tradition and Zar Dances in Saudi Arabia." *Al-ma'thurat al-sha'biyyah* (Folk heritage) 3, no. 9 (January 1988): 23–38.

Thesiger, Wilfred. *Arabian Sands*. London: Longmans, Green, 1959.

Thomas, Bertram. *Alarms and Excursions in Arabia*. Indianapolis: Bobbs-Merrill, 1931.

Thomas, Keith. *Religion and the Decline of Magic*. New York: Scribner, 1971.

Thomas, R. Hughes, comp. and ed. *Arabian Gulf Intelligence: Selections from the Records of the Bombay Government, Concerning Arabia, Bahrain, Kuwait, Muscat and Oman, Qatar, United Arab Emirates and the Islands of the Gulf*. New series, no. 24 (1856). Reprint. Cambridge: Oleander, 1985.

Thompson, Anna Y. "The Woman Question in Egypt." *Moslem World* 4 (1914): 266–272.

Thoms, Dr. S. J. "The Passion Play at Bahrein." *Neglected Arabia*, no. 65 (April–June 1908).

Thoms, Wells. "A Missionary Doctor in Arabia." *Church Herald*, October 22, 1937.

Tidrick, Margaret. *Heart-beguiling Araby: Englishmen in Arabia*. Cambridge: Cambridge University Press, 1981.

Toubia, Nahid. *Female Genital Mutilation*. New York: Women, Ink, 1993.

Tritton, A. S. "Spirits and Demons in Arabia." *Journal of the Royal Asiatic Society of Great Britain and Ireland* (October 1934): 715–726.

Tuchman, Barbara. *A Distant Mirror: The Calamitous Fourteenth Century*. New York: Scribner, 1978.

Tucker, Judith. *Women in Nineteenth Century Egypt*. Cambridge: Cambridge University Press, 1985.

Al Umar, 'Abd al-Rahman bin Hamad. *Islam: The Religion of Truth (Al-Islam Din al-Haqq)*. Riyadh: al-Farazdak, 1974.

United States Information Service. "Media Atmospherics: The Debate over Witchcraft." Riyadh, unclassified typescript dated April 8, 1995.

al-Urayyid, Dr. Thurayya. "Limited Opportunities." *Al-Jazirah* (Riyadh), June 9, 1997, p. 5.

Utas, Bo, ed. *Women in Islamic Societies: Social Attitudes as Historical Perspectives*. London: Curzon, 1983.

Vampires of New England. Connecticut Public Television, 1966.

Van Ess, Dorothy. "Arab Customs." *Arabia Calling*, no. 243 (spring/summer 1956).

Van Ess, Dorothy. *Fatima and Her Sisters*. New York: Day, 1961.

Van Ess, Dorothy. *Pioneers in the Arab World*. Grand Rapids, Mich.: Eerdmans, 1974.

Van Ess, Dorothy. "A School of Hopelessness." *Neglected Arabia*, no. 89 (April–June 1914).

Van Ess, Dorothy. "Under the Star and Crescent." *Neglected Arabia* 234 (winter 1953–54).

Van Peursem, G. D. "From the Palace of Ibn Saud." *Church Herald*, June 18, 1943.

Van Peursem, G. D. "Guests of King ibn Sa'ud." *Moslem World* 26, no. 1 (July 1936): 113–118.

Van Peursem, G. D. "Public Schools in Bahrein." *Neglected Arabia*, no. 90 (July–September 1914).

Van Peursem, Gerrit. "How Can the Medical Work Best Help the Evangelistic?" *Neglected Arabia*, no. 97 (April–June 1916).

Van Peursem, Josephine. "Arab Home Life." *Neglected Arabia*, no. 79 (October–December 1911).

Van Peursem, Josephine. "A Christian and a Moslem Deathbed." *Neglected Arabia*, no. 101 (April–June 1917).

Van Peursem, Josephine. "Christians in a Moslem Stronghold." *Church Herald*, September 17, 1943.

Van Sommer, Annie, and Samuel M. Zwemer, *Our Moslem Sisters: A Cry of Need from Lands of Darkness Interpreted by Those Who Heard It*. New York: Revell, 1907.

Van Vlack, Mrs. H. G. "Arab Babies." *Neglected Arabia*, no. 90 (July–September 1914).

Vidal, F. S. *The Oasis of al-Hasa*. New York: Arabian American Oil Company, 1955.

von Grunebaum, G. E. *Muhammadan Festivals*. New York: Schuman, 1951.

Wahba, Hafiz. *Arabian Days*. London: Baker, 1964.

Wahba, Hafiz. *Jazirat al-'arab fi al-qarn al-'ishrin*. 1935. Reprint. Cairo: Maktaba al-Nahda al-Misriyya, 1961.

Wallin, Georg August. *Travels in Arabia (1845 and 1848)*. Cambridge: Oleander; Naples: Falcon, 1979.

Wehr, Hans. *Dictionary of Modern Written Arabic*, ed. Milton Cowan. Ithaca: Cornell University Press, 1966.

Wikan, Uni. *Behind the Veil in Arabia: Women in Oman*. Baltimore: Johns Hopkins University Press, 1982.

Winder, R. Bayly. *Saudi Arabia in the Nineteenth Century*. London: Macmillan, 1965.

Yagil, Reuven. *Desert Camel: Comparative Physiological Adaptation*. Basel, Switzerland: Karger, 1985.

Yamani, Mai. "Women in Saudi Arabia." In *Feminism and Islam: Legal and Literary Perspectives*, ed. Mai Yamani. New York: New York University Press, 1996.

al-Yassini, Ayman. *Religion and State in the Kingdom of Saudi Arabia*. Boulder, Colo.: Westview, 1985.

al-Zaid, Dr. Abdulla Mohamed. *Education in Saudi Arabia: A Model with a Difference*, trans. Omar Ali Afifi. Jeddah: Tihama, 1981.

Al-Zubayr, Abd al-Mahmud. *Kitab irshad al-badw lil-din an-nabawi* (Book of guidance for the Bedouins in the prophetic religion). Pamphlet. Mecca, 1976.

Zwemer, Amy E. "Among the Sick in the Hospital Wards." *Neglected Arabia*, no. 77 (April–June 1911).

Zwemer, Samuel M. *Arabia: The Cradle of Islam*. New York: Revell, 1900.

Zwemer, Samuel M. "The Arabian Mission Field Report." *Neglected Arabia*, no. 3 (July–October 1892): 6.

Zwemer, Samuel M. "The Clock and the Calendar." *Moslem World* 3, no. 3 (July 1913): 262–274.

Zwemer, Samuel M. "Field Reports of the Arabian Mission." *The Arabian Mission Field Report*, no. 12 (October–December 1894).

Zwemer, Samuel M. *The Influence of Animism on Islam: An Account of Popular Superstitions*. New York: Macmillan, 1920.

Zwemer, Samuel M. *Studies in Popular Islam: A Collection of Papers Dealing with the Superstitions and Beliefs of the Common People*. New York: Macmillan, 1936.

Zwemer, Samuel M. "The Use of Amulets Among Moslems." *Neglected Arabia*, no. 72 (January–March 1910)

Zwemer, Dr. and Mrs. Samuel M. Zwemer. *Moslem Women*. West Medford, Mass.: Central Committee of the United Study of Foreign Missions, 1926.

ters and the women of the believers that they let down upon them their over-garments; this will be more proper, that they may be known, and thus they will not be given trouble; and Allah is Forgiving, Merciful" (M. H. Shakir, trans., *The Quran*, 5th ed [Elmhurst, N.Y.: Tahrike Tarsile Qur'an, 1988]). In an advice column in the English-language *Arab News*, written for an audience of foreign Muslims, most of whom come from places such as the Philippines, Pakistan, Palestine, Syria, Sudan, and Egypt, where veiling is either unknown or is no longer in general use, an inquirer is told that there is no religious imperative to cover the face. "In the case of having unusually blue eyes which attract attention," a woman asks, "the question has arisen as to whether I should veil my face to protect my soul as well as the souls of my Muslim brothers, or whether Islamic dress is all that is required?" The author of the column answers,

> Islam dictates that women should dress themselves modestly and properly in any situation where they may mix with or be seen by men. A woman should cover herself allowing no part of her body to be seen except her face and hands. Her immediate relatives such as her brothers, uncles and nephews may see more of her body within the recognized limits of propriety. If, however, a woman does not observe this injunction and lets more than the permitted parts of her body be seen she commits a serious sin, for which she is liable to be punished by Allah unless He, out of His mercy, forgives her.

As to her particular problem, the author writes,

> Islamic dress is all that is required from women generally, whether they are attractive and pretty or not. Only in those few individual cases where Islamic dress is known for certain not to prevent what is termed *fitna* in Arabic, then the veil is recommended. What is meant by *fitna* here is causing men to look persistently or repeatedly at the woman concerned. If, however, the cause of such persistent glances can be removed or hidden without resorting to the veil then such a remedy is perfectly acceptable. . . . I would like to say also that even in cases of fitna the veil remains voluntary, although a woman who wears it to prevent fitna will, Allah willing, receive ample reward.

What is the shaikh's solution? "It seems to me that in this particular case wearing tinted spectacles may help the questioner and provide an easy answer" (Adil Salahi, "Islam in Perspective," *Arab News*, February 26, 1982).

3. Hamad Al-Baadi, "Social Change, Education, and the Roles of Women in Arabia" (Ph.D. diss, Stanford University, 1982), pp. 31–32.

4. Muhammad bin Abdul-Aziz al-Musnad, comp., *Islamic Fatawa Regarding Women* (Riyadh: Darussalam, 1996), pp. 28, 45.

5. Fu'ad Khuri, *Tribe and State in Bahrain: The Transformation of Social and Political Authority in an Arab State* (Chicago: University of Chicago Press, 1980), p. 147.

6. An article revealing striking similarities in gender ideologies between Burma and Saudi Arabia discusses this point about the disparity between ideologies and practice with reference to women in Burmese society and to Buddhism. See Melford E. Spiro, "Gender Hierarchy in Burma: Cultural, Social and Psychological Dimensions," in *Sex and Gender Hierarchies*, ed. Barbara Diane Miller (Cambridge: Cambridge University Press, 1993), pp. 316–333.

7. Dr. Thurayya al-Urayyid, "Limited Opportunities," *al-Jazirah* (Riyadh), June 9, 1997, p. 5.

8. Firdaws Abu al-Qasim, "Work Is No Luxury," *al-Riyadh*, December 17, 1996, p. 4.

9. Hasin al-Bunyan, "Interview with Muhammad Bin Ibrahim Bin Jubayr, Speaker of the Shura Council in Saudi Arabia," *al-Sharq al-Awsat*, July 6, 1997, p. 4. "Out of the question" was the response given by Muhammad Bin Ibrahim Bin Jubayr to a question about women being invited to join the council.

10. Hasan Bin As'd Bin 'Abd-Aziz Bin Sa'id, "The Desired Role of Saudi Women in Development," *al-Jazirah*, December 18, 1996, p. 32; and al-Bunyan, "Interview with Muhammad Bin Ibrahim Bin Jubayr," p. 4.

11. Mai Yamani, "Women in Saudi Arabia," in *Feminism and Islam: Legal and Literary Perspectives*, ed. Mai Yamani (New York: New York University Press, 1996), p. 279.

12. *Al-Nadwa*, September 1, 1994, pp. 1, 5.

13. Abubaker A. Bagader, professor of sociology, Abd al-Aziz University, Jeddah, Saudi Arabia, "Saudi Women's New Public Roles: Can Society Adjust?" a talk given on November 20, 1997, at the Watson Institute, Brown University, Providence, Rhode Island.

14. For a discussion of the effects of economic restructuring on women, see Val Moghadam, *Women, Work, and Economic Reform in the Middle East and North Africa* (Boulder, Colo.: Rienner, 1998).

Appendix

1. R. Bayly Winder, *Saudi Arabia in the Nineteenth Century* (London: Macmillan, 1965), pp. 23–24.

3. The best discussion of the geography of Najd and the relationship among ecology, settled society, and pastoral nomadism is Christine Moss Helms, *The Cohesion of Saudi Arabi: Evolution of Political Identity* (Baltimore: Johns Hopkins University Press, 1981), pp. 29–60.

4. Barclay Raunkiaer, *Through Wahabiland on Camelback* (New York: Praeger, 1969), p. 26.

5. H. St. John Philby, *Heart of Arabia: A Record of Travel and Exploration* (London: Constable, 1922), 2:112.

6. Charles M. Doughty, *Travels in Arabia Deserta*, 3d ed. (London, 1936; reprint, New York: Dover, 1979), 2:319, also glossary, p. 671.

7. Hamad Al-Baadi, "Social Change, Education, and the Roles of Women in Arabia" (Ph.D. diss., Stanford University, 1982), p. 30.

8. Obedience to the Muslim ruler as a religious obligation comes originally out of the Prophet Muhammad's farewell sermon, and the idea was extrapolated by Ibn Abd al-Wahhab from the work of his fourteenth-century intellectual ancestor, Ibn Taimiyya. An-Nawawi's Hadith collection undergirds the bond between the ruler and the ruled: "The Messenger of Allah (may the blessings and peace of Allah be upon him) gave us a sermon by which our hearts were filled with fear and tears came to our eyes. We said, 'O Messenger of Allah, it is as though this is a farewell sermon, so counsel us.' He said, 'I counsel you to fear Allah (may He be glorified) and to give absolute obedience even if a slave becomes your leader.' " (Imam An-Nawawi, *Forty Hadith*, trans. Ibrahim Ezzedin and Denys Johnson-Davies [Damascus: Holy Koran Publishing, 1976], p. 94). Obedience to the ruler as a religious obligation is reiterated in writings produced by contemporary Saudi scholars employed by the Saudi government. For example, in one book published by the state-funded Department of Religious Guidance, the author says, "Allah commanded the Muslims to appoint from among themselves an Imam to be their ruler. Muslims should acknowledge to their ruler the rights of authority. They should also unite in one nation and never disperse. They are not allowed to disobey their rulers or leaders except in one case, when the ruler orders them to commit a sin or an action contrary to the commandments of Allah" (Abd al-Rahman bin Hamad Al Umar, *Islam: The Religion of Truth* [al-Islam Din al-Haqq] [Riyadh: Department of Religious Guidance], p. 45). The special relationship between Muhammad ibn Abd al-Wahhab and the family of Al Sa'ud is also promoted in contemporary literature distributed by the Ministry of Information of the Kingdom of Saudi Arabia, which emphasizes the unique capacity of the Al Sa'ud family to ensure correct Islamic practice in Arabia:

> The Wahhabi movement rested on the Shaikh and the family of Sa'ud.
> They were one mind and one hand in government and politics, in
> peace and war. . . . Wahhabi government is Saudi government, both are
> one and the same designation. Ibn Abd al-Wahhab and Ibn Sa'ud were
> one hand, one heart, and one mind. They were united in dogma and
> practice. . . . This union between the two men was never severed dur-
> ing their lifetime, and it survived. The union of the two families is
> strength to Islam and a source of power for Muslims. This union be-
> tween the two families has remained intact to the present day and is as
> strong as it was between Ibn Abd al-Wahhab and Ibn Sa'ud. Each fami-

ly is careful to preserve it, out of mutual desire to achieve more good
for Islam and for those who profess it.

———

(Ahmad Abd al-Ghafour Attar, *Muhammad ibn Abd al-Wahhab*, trans. Rashid al-
Barrawi [Mecca: Mecca Printing and Information, 1979], pp. 73–82)

9. The Al Rashid rulers in Ha'il also supported a morals police force that served
as "public ministers of the religion" who preach in the Friday mosque (Charles M.
Doughty, *Travels in Arabia Deserta*, 2 vols., 3d ed. [London, 1936; reprint, New York:
Dover, 1979], 2:396). Pursuing their duties in Jeddah in 1806, when the Wahhabis
were in control, the mutawwa'in were observed by a Spaniard from Cadiz named
Domingo Badia-y-Leblich to be "constables for the punctuality of prayers, almost
naked and with an enormous staff in their hand, [who] were ordered to shout, to
scold and to drag people by the shoulders to force them to take part in public
prayers, five times a day" (quoted in Peter Brent, *Far Arabia: Explorers of the Myth*
[London: Weidenfeld and Nicolson, 1977], p. 69).

10. "Verily he among you who lives [long] will see great controversy, so you
must keep to my sunna and to the sunna of the rightly-guided Rashidite Caliphs.
Cling to them stubbornly. Beware of newly invented matters, for every invented
matter is an innovation and every innovation is a going astray" (An-Nawawi, *Forty
Hadith*, p. 94).

11. Shakir, *The Quran*, sura 3, verse 110. There are Hadith that support the concept of communal responsibility as well. The *Forty Hadith* of An-Nawawi, for example, a collection that has been widely circulated in the Arabian peninsula since at
least the mid-nineteenth century, includes the following: "Whosoever of you sees
an evil action, let him change it with his hand; and if he is not able to do so, then
with his tongue; and if he is not able to do so, then with his heart—and that is the
weakest of faith" (p. 110). Another Hadith with similar meaning, "Everyone of you
is a shepherd and everyone is responsible for his subjects," was included in a Wahhabi circular distributed as missionary literature during the Ikhwan movement; see
Edwin Calverley, "The Doctrines of the Arabian 'Brethren,' " *Moslem World* 11, no. 4
(October 1921): 364–376.

12. At the height of success of the first Wahhabi empire in the early nineteenth
century, the treatises of Ibn Abd al-Wahhab were examined by shaikhs of the al-
Azhar, and the reform movement that had sprung from Najd was declared to evidence no incompatibility with Islamic orthodoxy as understood by the Sunni ulama
of Egypt. See Sir Harford Jones Brydges, Bart., *An Account of the Transactions of His
Majesty's Mission to the Court of Persia in the Years 1807–11, to Which Is Appended a Brief
History of the Wahauby*, 2 vols. (London: James Bohn: 1834), 2:111–112.

13. The wearing of gold and silk is forbidden according to a *sahih* (story from
the Prophet confirmed to be true) related on the authority of al-Bara ibn Azib: